THEORISING MEDIA AND CONFLICT

Anthropology of Media
Series Editors: Mark Peterson and Sahana Udupa

The ubiquity of media across the globe has led to an explosion of interest in the ways people around the world use media as part of their everyday lives. This series addresses the need for works that describe and theorize multiple, emerging, and sometimes interconnected, media practices in the contemporary world. Interdisciplinary and inclusive, this series offers a forum for ethnographic methodologies, descriptions of non-Western media practices, explorations of transnational connectivity, and studies that link culture and practices across fields of media production and consumption.

Volume 10
Theorising Media and Conflict
Edited by Philipp Budka and Birgit Bräuchler

Volume 9
Media Practices and Changing African Socialities: Non-media-centric Perspectives
Edited by Jo Helle-Valle and Ardis Storm-Mathisen

Volume 8
Monetising the Dividual Self: The Emergence of the Lifestyle Blog and Influencers in Malaysia
Julian Hopkins

Volume 7
Transborder Media Spaces: Ayuujk Videomaking Between Mexico and the US
Ingrid Kummels

Volume 6
The Making of the Pentecostal Melodrama: Religion, Media and Gender in Kinshasa
Katrien Pype

Volume 5
Localizing the Internet: An Anthropological Account
John Postill

Volume 4
Theorising Media and Practice
Edited by Birgit Bräuchler and John Postill

Volume 3
News as Culture: Journalistic Practices and the Remaking of Indian Leadership Traditions
Ursula Rao

Volume 2
The New Media Nation: Indigenous Peoples and Global Communication
Valerie Alia

Volume 1
Alarming Reports: Communicating Conflict in the Daily News
Andrew Arno

Theorising Media and Conflict

Edited by
Philipp Budka and Birgit Bräuchler

berghahn
NEW YORK • OXFORD
www.berghahnbooks.com

First published in 2020 by
Berghahn Books
www.berghahnbooks.com

© 2020, 2023 Philipp Budka and Birgit Bräuchler
First paperback edition published in 2023

All rights reserved. Except for the quotation of short passages for the purposes of criticism and review, no part of this book may be reproduced in any form or by any means, electronic or mechanical, including photocopying, recording, or any information storage and retrieval system now known or to be invented, without written permission of the publisher.

Library of Congress Cataloging-in-Publication Data
Names: Budka, Philipp, editor. | Bräuchler, Birgit, editor.
Title: Theorising media and conflict / [edited by] Philipp Budka and Birgit Bräuchler.
Description: New York : Berghahn Books, 2020. | Series: Anthropology of media ; volume 10 | Includes bibliographical references and index.
Identifiers: LCCN 2019057670 (print) | LCCN 2019057671 (ebook) | ISBN 9781789206821 (hardback) | ISBN 9781789206838 (ebook)
Subjects: LCSH: Mass media and war–Case studies. | Violence in mass media–Case studies. | Mass media–Political aspects–Case studies. | Social media–Political aspects–Case studies.
Classification: LCC P96.W35 T47 2020 (print) | LCC P96.W35 (ebook) | DDC 302.23–dc23
LC record available at https://lccn.loc.gov/2019057670
LC ebook record available at https://lccn.loc.gov/2019057671

British Library Cataloguing in Publication Data
A catalogue record for this book is available from the British Library

ISBN 978-1-78920-682-1 hardback
ISBN 978-1-80073-648-1 paperback
ISBN 978-1-78920-683-8 ebook

https://doi.org/10.3167/9781789206821

Contents

Preface   viii
     Philipp Budka

PART I. KEY DEBATES

Introduction. Anthropological Perspectives on Theorising
     Media and Conflict   3
     Birgit Bräuchler and Philipp Budka

1.   Transforming Media and Conflict Research   33
     Nicole Stremlau

PART II. WITNESSING CONFLICT

2.   Just a 'Stupid Reflex'? Digital Witnessing of the *Charlie Hebdo*
     Attacks and the Mediation of Conflict   57
     Johanna Sumiala, Minttu Tikka and Katja Valaskivi

3.   The Ambivalent Aesthetics and Perception of Mobile Phone
     Videos: A (De-)Escalating Factor for the Syrian Conflict   76
     Mareike Meis

PART III. EXPERIENCING CONFLICT

4.   Banal Phenomenologies of Conflict: Professional Media
     Cultures and Audiences of Distant Suffering   99
     Tim Markham

5. Learning to Listen: Theorising the Sounds of Contemporary
Media and Conflict 116
Matthew Sumera

PART IV. MEDIATED CONFLICT LANGUAGE

6. Trolling and the Orders and Disorders of Communication
in '(Dis)Information Society' 137
Jonathan Paul Marshall

7. 'Your Rockets Are Late. Do We Get a Free Pizza?':
Israeli-Palestinian Twitter Dialogues and Boundary
Maintenance in the 2014 Gaza War 158
Oren Livio

PART V. SITES OF CONFLICT

8. What Violent Conflict Tells Us about Media and
Place-Making (and Vice Versa): Ethnographic Observations
from a Revolutionary Uprising 181
Nina Grønlykke Mollerup

9. An Ayuujk 'Media War' over Water and Land: Mediatised
Senses of Belonging between Mexico and the United States 196
Ingrid Kummels

PART VI. CONFLICT ACROSS BORDERS

10. Transnationalising the Nagorno-Karabakh Conflict:
Media Rituals and Diaspora Activism between California
and the South Caucasus 217
Rik Adriaans

11. Stones Thrown Online: The Politics of Insults, Distance
and Impunity in Congolese *Polémique* 237
Katrien Pype

PART VII. AFTER CONFLICT

12. Mending the Wounds of War: A Framework for the
Analysis of the Representation of Conflict-Related
Trauma and Reconciliation in Cinema 257
Lennart Soberon, Kevin Smets and Daniel Biltereyst

13. Going off the Record? On the Relationship between
Media and the Formation of National Identity in
Post-Genocide Rwanda   277
Silke Oldenburg

14. From War to Peace in Indonesia: Transforming Media
and Society   295
Birgit Bräuchler

Afterword   319
John Postill

Index   327

Preface

Philipp Budka

The idea of compiling an edited volume on media and conflict was first brought up at a meeting of the European Association of Social Anthropologists (EASA) Media Anthropology Network, which was held on 23–24 October 2015 at the Department of Social and Cultural Anthropology of the University of Vienna, Austria. This was initiated by John Postill, convenor of the EASA Media Anthropology Network at the time, together with the local organisers Philipp Budka and Elke Mader. Supported by the EASA, the Austrian Research Association (ÖFG) and the University of Vienna's Department of Social and Cultural Anthropology, the meeting brought together anthropologists and media scholars to collectively discuss the elusive relationship between media and conflict from different theoretical perspectives. Drawing on their own research and field experience, participants addressed key questions, such as: what is the present state of anthropological and interdisciplinary knowledge on media and conflict? What are the main questions in need of urgent research? How can the subfield of media anthropology contribute to the interdisciplinary effort of theorising media and conflict? The event closed with discussions about a joint publication, ideally a volume on *Theorising Media and Conflict*, to be published within the 'Anthropology of Media' series of Berghahn Books.

To continue, broaden and conceptually advance the discourse on theorising media and conflict, the organisers set up a well-attended e-seminar via the EASA Media Anthropology Network's mailing list. From 10 to 24 November 2015 and after an opening statement by Birgit Bräuchler, a wider community of media anthropologists as well as media and communication scholars shared their manifold ideas and experiences in researching the relationship between media and conflict. This demonstrated that the scholarly interest in media and conflict was not only growing but also quite diverse, covering a number of different theoretical perspectives, methodological approaches and research sites. Anthropologists and media scholars alike have been studying media in conflict and post-conflict contexts, working on topics such as news reporting, cyberwar, internet and social media activism, social protest, radio propaganda and conflict transformation, but so far they had done so in relative isolation from one another. The planned book therefore needed to live up to the diversity of this research field while, at the same time, overcoming its fragmentation and a dissipation of efforts.

Thankfully, Birgit Bräuchler agreed to join John Postill and Philipp Budka on the editorial team. Together, they prepared a call for chapters, managed the selection process, and started the first rounds of reviewing. This resulted in a mix of contributions by participants of the meetings and by authors who had no opportunity to participate in them. John Postill, who launched and led this book project, then had to leave the team of editors to return later in the process as author of the volume's afterword. Without him, *Theorising Media and Conflict* would not have come into being. This book, of course, would not have been possible without the chapter authors and their continuing efforts and commitment to this project. Not only did they share, discuss and reflect upon their original work, they also contributed to an internal review process, which was initiated to complement the anonymous review procedure organised by Berghahn Books. Such close engagement with each other's work and the collegial and highly constructive feedback provided within this process further improved the quality of the individual chapters and contributed decisively to the overall coherence of the edited collection.

Theorising Media and Conflict is the result of a joint and interdisciplinary effort to set the theoretical and empirical agenda in theorising upon the complex relationship between media and conflict. By considering the theorisation work accomplished by the 'Anthropology of Media' series forerunner *Theorising Media and Practice* (edited by Bräuchler and Postill), it takes the notion of media (as) practice to new terrain. It thus counters studies that display Western biases, normative assumptions and unsubstantiated claims about 'media effects' in conflict situations. Through ground-up theorising, careful contextualisation, comparative perspectives, ethnographic and other qualitative methods, it provides evidence for the co-constitutiveness of media and conflict, and contributes to the consolidation of media and conflict as a distinct area of scholarship. While the contributions to this book deal with different kinds of media and conflict situations in distinct world regions and examine various aspects of media use, they all engage with media and conflict dynamics from a participant's perspective as well as from an analytical perspective. Such an approach allows for the theorisation of media and conflict beyond a particular type of media, conflict or region. This edited collection is of interest to students and scholars working across the humanities and social sciences, as well as policy-makers, activists and practitioners interested in the sociocultural, political and physical consequences of media, and the lived realities and dynamics of contemporary conflicts.

PART I
Key Debates

Introduction

Anthropological Perspectives on Theorising Media and Conflict

Birgit Bräuchler and Philipp Budka

The relationship between media and conflict is highly elusive and complex. Conflict dynamics in one of the largest island states, where media have been contributing decisively to a feeling of national belonging (Anderson 1983), illustrate this. In 1999, the outbreak of the Moluccan conflict in Eastern Indonesia destroyed the existing media landscape, in which journalists and media workers collaborated irrespective of their religious affiliation. The conflict was mainly fought along religious lines and triggered the re-emergence of a totally different media landscape: a broad range of media – from newspapers, to the internet, to radio and graffiti – was now divided along religious lines, fuelling religious hatred and propelling the conflict to new levels. Such escalation and years of violence in turn made Moluccan people wake up and promote the transformation of society to peace through, among other things, social media, newspapers, theatre performances and poetry. Thus, media became a tool to provoke peace and to resist social injustices underlying the physical violence in Maluku. It was only through long-term ethnographic research that this intimate relationship between media, conflict and societal transformation revealed itself (see also Bräuchler, this volume). This example reminds us that asking about the impact or effect of media on conflict and violence – a question that continues to preoccupy media scholars, psychologists, sociologists and political scientists – is in fact a 'methodological error' that tries to build 'discussion about human values around a mathematical metaphor' (Smith 1978: 129–30).

Instead of looking at media and conflict as two separate spheres or at unidirectional causality, this edited volume brings together anthropologists as well as media and communication scholars to collectively look at the interpenetration and the co-constitutiveness of media and conflict. In doing so, it cannot possibly cover all variations of conflict and media. Instead, it puts forward the notion of mediation to focus upon wider media-related processes and practices in everyday contexts and of conflicts as social processes and culturally constructed. While the analyses in this book are embedded in a broader discourse on conflict as an inherent part and a central organising principle of social life, they mainly focus on conflicts involving extraordinary forms of violence that have become part of the everyday. In seven parts, the authors theorise on central aspects of the relationship between media and conflict: (I) key debates and anthropological approaches, (II) witnessing and (III) experiencing conflict, (IV) language and (V) sites of conflict, as well as (VI) cross-border conflict and (VII) conflict transformation. Through epistemological and methodological reflections and the analyses of various case studies from around the globe, this volume contributes to the consolidation of media and conflict as a distinct area of scholarship.

No matter whether through war propaganda, news media and embedded journalists, pictures and videos of drones and gun cameras, media activism and citizen journalism, social media use or video games, we are all becoming increasingly entangled in violent conflicts worldwide (e.g. Karmasin et al. 2013: xi; Mortensen 2015: 2; Seib 2013: 7). Scholars are grappling with the variety and increasing mediation of conflict experiences and the extents of conflict immersion in people's everyday mediated life. In a recent literature survey on media and conflict, for instance, Schoemaker and Stremlau (2014) found that a majority of studies display Western biases, normative assumptions and unsubstantiated claims about the so-called 'impact of media' in conflict situations. This is characteristic of research that aims to identify the effect or the impact of media, rather than looking into the complex relationship between media and, in our case, conflict. Moreover, there are only limited efforts in media and conflict studies to correlate, for instance, media framing results with on-the-ground research findings (Vladisavljević 2015: 1). In her chapter in this volume, Nicole Stremlau criticises how technology companies, such as Facebook and Google, attempt to connect the unconnected in developing regions and in conflict situations. These internet giants, she notes, focus on what international, industry-led interventions can do to regulate inflammatory (dis)information and media communication rather than looking into local agency and the lived reality of conflicts.

With its cross-cultural and context-sensitive approach, its ethnographic methods and ground-up theorising, anthropologically informed media research is well placed to make a strong contribution to the advancement of research into media and conflict (see Sumera, Marshall, Mollerup, Kummels, Pype, Oldenburg, and Bräuchler, this volume). The same goes for qualitative media and communication studies that emphasise contextualisation and critical theorising (see Sumiala, Tikka and Valaskivi, Meis, Markham, Livio, Adriaans, and Soberon, Smets and Biltereyst, this volume). This book thus goes beyond the search for media effects and also sets a counterpoint to the predominance of quantitative studies that frequently fail to take into account people's lived experiences in the understanding of conflict dynamics (Bräuchler 2015: 209).

To explore these lived experiences of people in relation to media practices in a range of contexts requires knowledge of and training in relevant methods and methodologies, such as ethnographic fieldwork, participant observation and qualitative interviewing (Bräuchler 2018b; Carayannis 2018). However, this is something some disciplines in this field of research are lacking. They tend to look into violence, conflict and media by building on media content and quantitative data sets, generated through statistics, modelling or geographic information systems, to pin down the effects of media on conflict occurrence and dynamics (see e.g. a special issue of the *Journal of Peace Research*, a flagship journal of peace and conflict studies, on 'Communication, Technology, and Political Conflict'; Weidmann 2015). While some projects dedicated to the study of conflict in an increasingly mediated world, such as the journal *Media, War & Conflict* (Hoskins, Richards and Seib 2008), do promote a diversity of theoretical and methodological approaches in exploring the relationship between media and conflict, anthropologically informed and ethnographically grounded research is still under-represented.

Nevertheless, a growing number of anthropologists have begun to study media in conflict and post-conflict contexts – working on topics such as news reporting (e.g. Arno 2009; Pedelty 1995), war (e.g. Bräuchler 2013; Stroeken 2012), digital activism (e.g. Barassi 2015), social protest and political change (e.g. Juris and Khasnabish 2013; Postill 2018), media use in diasporic networks (e.g. Bernal 2014), video-making (e.g. Kummels 2017), radio propaganda (e.g. Li 2007), conflict transformation (e.g. Bräuchler 2011) or spiritual and religious struggles (e.g. Pype 2012) – but so far they have done so in relative isolation from one another. This volume helps to overcome this fragmentation of the field by bringing together, in a synergetic effort, media anthropologists and media and communication scholars researching the multiple ways in which different kinds of media and conflict interpenetrate in a number of regional settings. In doing so, this book sets the field's theoretical and empirical agenda for students, scholars, activists and civil society groups alike.

In this introductory chapter, we continue outlining the specifics of our approach to theorise on media and conflict. To do so, it is necessary to reconsider two established anthropological fields of research: the anthropology of media and the anthropology of conflict. We argue that considerable societal and media-related transformation processes and changes have brought these research fields closer together, even suggesting an inevitable and synergetic merging on a conceptual level. Thus, we outline in a first section how to approach media and conflict from an anthropological perspective. In a second section, we develop the various aspects of how the volume's chapters and an anthropological approach contribute to the theorising of media and conflict. Whereas references to the individual contributions are included throughout, a brief outline of the book's structure concludes the chapter.

Approaching Media and Conflict from an Anthropological Perspective

We promote an anthropologically informed, non-media-centric and contextualised approach to conflict and media that accentuates: (a) the deconstruction of deterministic notions of media effects and of simplistic categorisations of media-conflict relations; (b) a focus on the lived realities of conflicts through cross-cultural comparison and ethnographic methodology; and (c) the co-constitution of media and conflict and therefore the necessary linking of conceptual approaches that have been shaping the anthropology of conflict and media.

Beyond Media Effects

In the late 1970s and the 1980s, media studies experienced an ethnographic turn. Inspired by anthropology and particularly cultural studies, scholars started to research media as embedded in everyday contexts, not as something set apart from it. They began to challenge and deconstruct prevailing communication models and 'the power of the media texts that shape attitudes and ideas' of a passive, homogeneous audience (Askew 2002: 5). This new wave of media scholars promoted ideas of an active audience or audiences who interpret, attribute and produce heterogeneous meanings (e.g. Morley 1980, 1992) in relation to wider social, cultural and political settings, fields and practices, including power hierarchies or gender relations (Dracklé 2005: 189–90). Longstanding perceptions of boundaries between media production and media reception started to dissolve (Ginsburg, Abu-Lughod and Larkin 2002b: 1). Such developments have been pushed further by interactive digital media technologies, internet platforms and particularly social media, where media users are – or can be – audience and producer at the same time (e.g. Bruns 2008; Sumiala and Tikka 2011). Despite this turn, questions about media effects and the impact of media use and coverage still seem to preoccupy scholars who are looking, for instance, at the role of media in conflict and post-conflict scenarios (Schoemaker and Stremlau 2014: 185; Zeitzoff 2017: 1971), the effects that media coverage has on terrorist attacks (Asal and Hoffmann 2016) or the impact of information wars (Allagui and Akdenizli 2019).

However, as, for instance, Igreja's (2015) ethnography on violence glorifying films in conflict zones in Mozambique, and Straus' (2007) study on the relationship between hate radio and violence during the Rwandan Civil War illustrate, one has to be very careful in identifying a causal relationship between media content and violent actions (see also Oldenburg, this volume). Both authors challenge linear media approaches and argue for a more nuanced understanding of the complexity of violence, and the culturally and historically situated experiences and interpretations of people exposed to it. Igreja questions simplifying notions of the negative effects film violence has on young viewers in post-war and conflict settings by analysing the ambivalent responses of local residents. He argues that film violence can 'enhance ongoing processes of self-assertion among young people in unpredictable ways', leading to either the incitement or containment of violence, 'while stimulating the consciousness of existing … languages and mechanisms of mediation' (Igreja 2015: 678, 679). Straus, in turn, counters the prevailing scholarly opinions that radio broadcasts 'were a primary determinant of genocide' (2007: 609) by sparking extreme violence, thus invoking the image of passive listeners with little or no agency (2007: 615). Rather, he found that Rwandan radio did not trigger the violence, but 'emboldened hard-liners [and not the general audience] and reinforced face-to-face mobilization, which helped those who advocated violence [in particular elites] assert dominance and carry out the genocide' (Straus 2007: 631). Both studies emphasize the need to go beyond simplistic frameworks and look into the 'less obvious and more tense and negotiated process of social change' (Igreja 2015: 689) and the 'complex issues of agency, context, institutions, and history' (Straus 2007: 632) – something contributions to this volume do. Stremlau, for example, puts forward the importance of considering regional and national political ideologies as well as their historical and sociocultural contextualisation for understanding the complex relationship of media and conflict at the Horn of Africa. Such complexities render it futile, or at least limiting the research perspective, to ask about the effects or impact of media on conflict or war (see also Couldry and Hepp 2013).

We aim for a non-media-centric, non-media-deterministic approach – a constitutive quality of media anthropology (e.g. Peterson 2003) – that focuses on the contexts of both conflict and media. The challenge here is to avoid media-centrism (e.g. Moores 2018) – even when most contributions to this book take media as a window to look at certain conflict and peace dynamics – in order to ensure a proper contextualisation of our media perspectives on conflicts. We counter, for example, views that reduce digital media platforms to 'archives of [decontextualised] online behavior' that 'have opened up unrivaled amounts of data that are now available for analysis' (Gohdes 2018: 100), neglecting the lived experience of people involved in producing, communicating, receiving, digesting, interpreting or manipulating those 'data'. A non-media-centric approach to mediated conflict makes it possible to deconstruct normative views of technology that either celebrate media as a democratising and liberating force (Schoemaker and Stremlau 2014: 187) or promote overly technical notions of media and conflict alliances such as media war, cyber-war, hacktivism, cyberattacks, cybersecurity or cybercrime (e.g. Ghosh and Turrini 2010; Jordan and Taylor 2004) (for a critique, see also Stremlau, this volume). What has become known as the 'first war in cyberspace' in April–May 2007 in Estonia feeds into this (Landler and Markoff 2007).[1] Waves of denial-of-service attacks that 'brought down the Websites of the Estonian President, Parliament, a series of government agencies, the news media, [and] the two largest banks' (Hansen and Nissenbaum 2009: 1168) triggered a response by the Estonian government that blocked all international web traffic, 'effectively shutting off the "most wired country in Europe" from the rest of the world' (Richards 2009). Incidents like this and publicly mediated concerns over the use of the internet by terrorist and extremist groups feed well into security policies of well-armed states, such as the United States and Singapore, as well as into global risks models developed by international organisations (e.g. Conway 2006; World Economic Forum 2019). As various case studies in this volume show, it is not easy to categorise online conflicts due to the ambivalent nature of the internet (see also Bräuchler 2007).

A non-media-centric approach helps to avoid and deconstruct overly reifying and constraining conflict categories and, instead, look at conflict realities as embedded social practices and actions (see also Arno 2009; Smets 2017). The expansion of contemporary warfare into cyberspace and onto digital platforms does get scholarly attention, but ethnographic research that follows a particular conflict for an extended period of time is still the exception (e.g. Bräuchler 2013). The field is still dominated by political scientists, international relations and communication scholars who tend to focus on state security and so-called 'cyber security' (e.g. Karatzogianni 2009; Latham 2003). Given current technological developments, anthropologists working on conflict issues need to join hands with media anthropologists even more in order to grasp the complexity of how media technologies, sensory perceptions and social life are interrelated (e.g. Robben 2016). It is obvious that people engage with media in different ways and under changing conditions. Some people access and use specific media technologies; some do not, for various reasons. Media involve people as objects of and content for media coverage or in other 'arenas of circulation' (Slevin 2000: 81). But media also connect people; they provide new, sometimes alternative, ways to communicate and interact. To explore this diversity of media engagements, it is necessary to look into people's lived realities, in our case the realities of conflict.

The Lived Realities of Conflict

Most books on the subject of media and conflict look at one type of media (e.g. news media or the internet – see Arno 2009; Karatzogianni 2009), at a specific aspect of media (e.g. media power or media rituals – see Couldry and Curran 2003a; Grimes et al. 2011), at a certain kind of conflict (e.g. religious conflicts or terror – see Marsden and Savigny 2009a; Veer and Munshi 2004) or at a particular region or country (e.g. Indonesia or Rwanda – see Bräuchler 2013; Thompson 2007). Others limit their research focus to specific aspects of the interlinkage of media and conflict by discussing, for instance, war and conflict coverage (e.g. Pedelty 1995; Vladisavljević 2015) or religion and news media (Marsden and Savigny 2009b). The contributions to this book deal with different kinds and forms of media technologies and conflicts in various world regions, and examine multiple aspects of media engagements and practices in relation to conflictual situations and events. This allows for the theorisation of the relationship between media and conflict beyond the particular type of media, conflict and locality. Moreover, the volume considers media's role in transitional phases from conflict to peace.

Beyond simply juxtaposing media and conflict, this book examines the lived sociocultural realities of conflict and conflict transformation, of which media have become integral parts. We are therefore sceptical of the notion of 'mediatisation of conflicts' in the sense of looking at '*how the media do things with conflicts*' (Cottle 2006: 9, emphasis in original). Such unidirectional, causal relations are only part of the story and do not sufficiently capture the complex relationship between media and conflicts. We would instead like to put more emphasis on how media *are co-constitutive of conflicts* (see also Cottle 2006: 187). Referring to the interlinkage of media communication and conflict as a social and cultural process, Karmasin et al. highlight that 'war has been an important factor in the evolution of new forms of social communication, and at the same time new means of communication have altered the relationship between war and the mass media' (2013: ix). New media technologies, formats and practices change the lived realities of conflicts, conflict participants and conflict observers. But conflicts also *do things to media* as they change the way in which media are defined, used, adopted, adapted, manipulated, integrated or excluded. Conflicts can emerge on and through media, for example, through the construction or enforcement of group boundaries along ethnic or religious lines (e.g. Nakamura and Chow-White 2012). But as media have become integral parts of our (conflictual) lives, this renders any neat analytical distinction between media and conflict-related activities impossible and rather counterproductive.

Looking into the lived realities of conflicts requires careful contextualisation, anthropologically informed theorising and ethnographic methods. While ethnography investigates everyday sociocultural processes and practices through participant observation and other qualitative methods, anthropology connects ethnographic material through comparison and contextualisation to a wider set of questions on the human condition (Howell 2018; Sanjek 2010). While this volume is predominantly grounded in empirical ethnographic and anthropological research, it is also interdisciplinary, including and applying theoretical approaches from media, communication and audiovisual studies, such as the phenomenology of conflict reporting and the aesthetics of media (discourses). It approaches the relationships between media and conflict from a participant's perspective – experiencing and witnessing conflict – as well as from a more removed, analytical perspective (key debates as well as sites and scales of conflict). Thus, it provides a situated, multiscalar perspective to the empirical study of media and conflict.

In addition, this volume takes the notion of media practices (Bräuchler and Postill 2010; Couldry 2010) to new terrain, namely to theorise the elusive relationship between media and conflict by decentring media. These practices must be tracked in both their continuities and changes over time in specific sites and scales of conflict. Therefore, the study of contemporary conflict and media landscapes requires a multi-sited (Marcus 1995) and a multi-temporal (Bräuchler 2015), or diachronic (Postill 2017), dimension. Nevertheless, as Werbner (2010: 193) emphasises in her reflections on the possible contributions of anthropologists to understanding the dynamics of global terror, 'our ethnographic mediations still start from the bottom – from the small places where we do our ordinary, quotidian research'. This can turn out to be very challenging – for instance, given the difficulties in terms of access to interlocutors or conflict sites or safety concerns when collecting data – for both research subjects and researchers.

Theorising Media and Conflict

With legal anthropology being one of the oldest sub-branches of the discipline, anthropologists have identified various means by which local societies cope with conflict in the absence of formal courts beyond the state, from avoidance and arbitration to violence and war (e.g. Bohannan 1967; Elwert, Feuchtwang and Neubert 1999; Moore 1978, 2005). Anthropologists such as Gluckman (1963), Comaroff (1981, together with Roberts) and Elwert (2004) counter the notion of conflict as extraordinary, chaotic and structureless. They conceptualise conflicts as processes that are partly embedded in broader 'ensembles of moral values, norms and institutional arrangements' and follow culturally coded patterns (including symbolism, ritual and communication culture; notions of reciprocity, scarcity and identity), but also contain 'elements of surprise' (*Element von Überraschung*) (Elwert 2004: 29). More than two decades ago, Robben and Nordstrom (1995: 10) already emphasised that the 'everydayness of violence' does not preclude the uncertainty of violence that is always related to 'a summoning of fear, terror, and confusion as well as resistance, survival, hope and creativity'. Violence and conflict thus need to be conceptualised in broader ways, including their destructive and their reconstructive potential (1995: 6).

Anthropologists have found that conflict is part of everyday life, but the majority agrees that aggression is not innate to human nature –

a view that is linked to the so-called 'nature versus nurture debate' about whether human behaviour is genetically or socioculturally determined. In our case, it is about whether human nature is intrinsically violent and malicious, and therefore in need of civilisation (nurture) to be pacified, or whether humanity is nonviolent and good by nature (Kemp 2004: 2–3). Montagu (1994: xii) argues in line with other anthropologists that aggressive behaviour is culturally determined (e.g. Orywal 1996: 15, Scheper-Hughes and Bourgois 2004: 3). Mead (2000: 20) understands conflict and war as societal inventions and cultural constructs just as writing or marriage. It is 'the social and cultural dimensions of violence … [that give] violence its power and meaning' (Scheper-Hughes and Bourgois 2004: 1). This constructedness of war, as Mead (2000: 22) continues, implies that it can be deconstructed and, as Bräuchler (2015: 28) points out, that peace also needs to be interpreted as a construction. Moreover, both 'peace and war result from complex social dynamics' (Rubinstein and Foster 1988: 1) and are 'made sense of discursively and culturally' (Cottle 2006: 4–5). Anthropological research has thus built 'a powerful literature of the everyday experiences and suffering of victims of civil wars and state terror and the embedded myths-cum-ideologies used by perpetrators of violence' (Werbner 2010: 195).

In this volume, authors are interested in the ways in which media are part of such social dynamics and get involved in such cultural construction and deconstruction processes – symbolically loaded processes shaped by practices that can be grasped and analysed through ethnographic in-depth research. We understand media as technologies that mediate and modify human communication, interaction and culture. Consequently, the anthropology of media 'should be seen not simply as an inquiry into communication technologies and their contents but as the study of the broader processes of mediation. Mediation refers to the material frameworks (including human bodies) humans use to enable and constrain communicative action within and across multiple social orders' (Postill and Peterson in press).[2] A focus on mediation facilitates the conceptual merging of (research on) media with (research on) conflict because it decentres media technologies by concentrating on mediation processes and practices rather than on a specific communication medium and its effects, for instance (e.g. Boyer 2012; Bräuchler and Postill 2010). As a conceptual tool, mediation supports attempts to theorise upon wider sociocultural transformation processes that unfold in nonlinear manners (Couldry 2008: 379–81; Mazzarella 2004: 360–61), such as the (continuously modified) co-constitutiveness of conflict and media.[3]

Theorising media as practice makes it possible to focus on: (a) mediation practices in an everyday context; (b) the relationship between media (technologies) and the human body; and (c) the diversity of fields of media production (Postill 2010: 12–16; see also Moores 2018). Such a conceptualisation of media is intrinsically interrelated with ethnographically grounded fieldwork. For Postill, 'a practice theory approach to media suggests that people use a range of media partly to try to maintain – not always with success – a sense of ontological security in a modern world' (2010: 18). Media practices should thus also be understood in relation to rituals and other performative practices of social life (e.g. Hughes-Freeland 1998; Luger, Graf and Budka 2019). Given the multitude of sociocultural practices, it seems helpful to identify and investigate the 'range of practices [that] are oriented to media' and the 'role of media-oriented practices in ordering other practices' (Couldry 2010: 50). Hobart (2010) contends that it is particularly important here to consider the relations between different practices (of social life). Consequently, he argues for the conceptualisation of media practices as 'media-related practices' to 'provide an initial circumscription out of the whole range of identifiable practices in a society at any moment' (2010: 67). As contributions to this collection indicate, a practice approach and the conduct of ethnographic research are particularly conducive to grasp the subtleties and the intricacies of media-conflict entanglements. They can help to unmask and deconstruct notions of an alleged 'media logic' (Altheide 2013), internationally popular patterns of conflict interpretation that are imposed on local settings (Straus 2007; Stremlau, this volume) and an international peace industry that aims to solve local conflicts according to a global blueprint (Bräuchler 2015).

In this volume, our focus is on conflict related to violence, one way or the other, thus diverging from the rich literature that has evolved over the last decade on resistance and activist movements, such as the global Occupy movement or the Indignados movement in Spain, and their skilful use of a broad variety of media, most prominently digital and social media, and their rich 'nonviolent' protest aesthetics in the sense of the predominant abstinence from physical violence (e.g. Postill 2018; Werbner, Webb and Spellman-Poots 2014). As indicated above and as was obvious in the 2009 postpresidential election protests in Iran, it is important here to bear in mind that 'social media tools can simultaneously support grass-roots political mobilizations as well as government surveillance and human rights violations' (Coleman 2010: 493). Digital culture is essentially ambiguous (Miller and Horst 2012:

4); it opens and closes possibilities (for political activism, for instance) at the same time (see also Tufekci 2017).

Like Robben and Nordstrom (1995: 2, 6), we want to focus on 'the experiential dimension of conflict' and violence's expression in the everyday, but with a specific focus on their interlinkage with media. Due to their cultural and social embeddedness, conflicts and violence can be attributed multiple meanings by participants, witnesses, observers or interveners (1995: 5), and critical research needs to be explicit about the layers and contexts it is looking at (e.g. Vladisavljević 2015: 1). Tim Markham, for instance, theorises in his chapter about distant witnessing of conflict by deploying a phenomenological approach in reframing journalistic practices – in his case of media practitioners in Beirut – and audience experiences. Such an approach, he argues, demonstrates that objectification (of subjectivities and suffering) is a matter of everyday life rather than a reduction of conflict to a mediated spectacle and that it does not prevent an apprehension of conflict by media producers or audiences. As all the contributions to this volume vividly illustrate, conflict and its resolution can take on very different shapes and scales, depending on the actors involved.

Structural Violence, Power and Ritual

Many anthropologists have adopted Galtung's (1969) notion of structural violence – the idea that violence is more than mere physical violence and is ingrained in societal structures, producing and perpetuating inequalities of power and agency (e.g. Farmer 2004; Scheper-Hughes 2004). Analogously, 'positive peace' is more than the absence of violence (as 'negative peace'); it is the extinction of structural violence (Galtung 1969). Anthropologists engage with both the structures underlying conflicts and the roles and practices of local actors, since agency and creativity are as essential for the construction of conflict and violence as they are for rebuilding peace (e.g. Bräuchler 2015; Nordstrom 1997a, 1997b). Media technologies can be used to both exert or mediate physical violence, through attacks on computer systems or the visualisation of violence, and to contribute to structural violence in terms of media access, literacy and skills or the way in which people are represented – be it conflict parties or others.

What has been true for the internet (Bräuchler 2013) is even more so for social media (Zeitzoff 2017): costs of communication are reduced (which does not imply that everybody has access); the speed of dissemination increases tremendously with news and images going viral; they are participative, which is effective for mobilisation; they are creatively adopted and adapted; they provide data on conflict, but also for conflict actors; and they are (strategically) used by a broad range of people. Even though social media can give a voice to increasing numbers of people, the challenge remains how to make it heard (Couldry 2015) and be listened to (Dreher, McCallum and Waller 2016). It is a matter of power, perception management and representation, about whose voices are heard on what media – questions that are as relevant today as they were a decade ago (Bräuchler 2005, 2013), despite changes in media and technology infrastructure (Budka 2015). In his chapter, Jonathan Paul Marshall conceptualises trolling as a practice that marks orders and disorders of group allegiance, meaning-making and conflictual communication in what he calls 'disinformation society'. As he shows through the case study of an Australian media celebrity, trolling has become part of today's social media experience to frame selected communicative interactions as dismissible, thus contributing decisively to the (dis)ordering of digital communication.

Media as such are the results of 'battles over who has the power to represent the reality of others' (Couldry and Curran 2003b: 6; see also Doudaki and Carpentier 2017). Media participation alone is not only a matter of mobilisation (Atton 2015: 7), but of skills and resources, including infrastructure, time, prior experience, social and cultural capital and networks (Bräuchler 2018a; Budka 2019). Not everybody has such skills, be it media skills or mediation and negotiation skills. Nordstrom (1997a: 191) therefore suggests that the creative members of a society such as healers, visionaries and performers – or Postill's (2018: 1) 'techno-political nerds' – need to act as multipliers and mobilise the rest. Processes of conflict and peace are often heavily loaded by cultural and religious symbols and rituals, in particular when identity issues are involved. Usually, they are emotionally charged and thus can easily be instrumentalised and manipulated to mobilise people (for war and peace), but also to enable social control. Symbols are often multivocal and can invoke diverse, context-depending associations (Turner 1975). This allows for the instrumentalisation and manipulation of symbols (for war and conflict) and the mobilisation of integrative effects of symbols (for reconciliation and peace).

Looking at both ritualised forms of conflict and violence and the role of symbols and rituals in mediated conflict (Grimes 2011: 22–24), the volume's contributors also address the ritual dimension of media, conflict and conflict resolution. Rik Adriaans analyses in his chapter the ritualisation and deritualisation of conflict-related diasporic media events. He investigates how competing telethon broadcasts of the Armenian diaspora in the United States alter the politics, framing and scale of the Nagorno-Karabakh conflict, thus enlisting diasporic Armenians in this conflict through a transnational, humanitarian sphere of media rituals. Katrien Pype discusses in her chapter ritualised speech acts; Ingrid Kummels investigates ritualised, mediated conflicts over diverging land claims; Oren Livio explores communication rituals in a conflict setting; and Lennart Soberon, Kevin Smets and Daniel Biltereyst analyse ritualised, visual remembering. Other contributions address newly emerging ritualised practices in the media, such as hate speech and trolling (Marshall) and 'off-the-record' practices in a post-genocide media environment (Oldenburg).

Changing Fields

As notions of culture and locality were increasingly de-essentialised from the 1980s onwards, anthropologists increasingly turned towards phenomena, processes and dimensions of violence and/or conflict that transcend the local through multi-sited ethnography (e.g. Nordstrom 1997a, 2004). This brings us back to our methodological reflections. As Appadurai has argued, 'globalization, as a specific way in which states, markets, and ideas about trade and governance have come to be organized, exacerbates the conditions of large-scale violence because it produces a potential collision course between the logics of uncertainty and incompleteness, each of which has its own form and force' (2006: 8–9). While being aware of the translocal, transnational and global embeddedness of certain conflicts (e.g. Juris and Khasnabish 2013), anthropologists still conduct research from the ground up, adding local perspectives to national and international interventionist approaches to conflict that often ignore the messiness and cultural specificity of conflict dynamics and the existence of local means to resolve conflicts.

As the volume's chapters show (see in particular those by Oldenburg, Kummels, Pype and Livio), neither conflict dynamics nor the turn towards peace can be understood without taking local culture, local conflict and conflict resolution traditions, and local conceptualisation of conflict, violence, peace, trauma, justice and truth into account (see also Bräuchler 2018c; Bräuchler and Naucke 2017). Kummels, for example, investigates in her chapter the role of digital media and communication in an agrarian conflict between villages in the Mexican state of Oaxaca and how 'ethnic influencers' – some of them in the U.S. diaspora – shape this conflict with the support of social media platforms. She reminds us that even though digital media technologies contribute to the transnationalisation of conflicts, these new, mediated conflicts, or 'media wars', are also deeply embedded in local (conflict) culture and cannot be disconnected from earlier conflict phases when nondigital media were utilised, in her case historical maps to which people still refer today.

At first glance, and in particular given the emergence of social media, one might be tempted to suggest that media allow for a 'safer' approach to conflict and violence than previous 'fieldwork under fire' (Nordstrom and Robben 1995). Theoretically, we could research violence from afar, via media, and thus avoid the chaos, the 'bewilderment', the 'disorientation', the 'existential shock' that hits us, when we physically emerge in conflict zones and warscapes, where the boundaries between life and death have become erratic (1995: 13). However, the 'powerful roles of mediated visual imagery during wartime' (Parry 2010: 417), the virality and the participatory character of social media, and the immediacy with which we can experience conflict and violence via a broad range of media challenge such simplistic assumptions, as various contributions to this volume illustrate.

Given the media saturation of conflict and peacescapes, boundaries between a safe home for the conduct of research (or witnessing) and the places where violence takes place dissolve (see e.g. Markham, Meis, Mollerup, and Sumiala, Tikka and Valaskivi, this volume). Witnessing acquires yet another significance, with fieldworkers not only observing or witnessing conflict and violence on the ground, but also observing or witnessing what people on the ground do with media. In her chapter, Nina Grønlykke Mollerup conceptualises media as place-making in the context of the Egyptian uprising (2011–13). As communicative processes across space, media open up places to other places by enabling 'a presence' of elements of one place in others. And this, she argues, happens when people sensorily experience mediated conflict and violence, in her case through online videos. Media and conflict are thus also co-constitutive of places.

Image, Sound and Peace

De Franco (2012: 2) argues that the element of visibility and visuality alters everything; it modifies perceptions and behaviours, from sport to war. But visual media technologies do not only bring conflicts into people's home via the news; social media – particularly in connection with mobile digital devices such as smartphones – make users increasingly vulnerable to tracking, monitoring and surveillance by state governments or corporations (e.g. Fuchs 2014). Embedded photojournalists give the viewer the impression that they are directly following what happens on the ground, often not taking into account how these journalists have staged, selected or maybe even reworked the pictures (Alper 2013: 1237). And social media can absorb users into conflict dynamics, through the sharing and circulation of journalistic and amateur content, as some chapters illustrate. Johanna Sumiala, Minttu Tikka and Katja Valaskivi, for instance, analyse the dynamics of digital witnessing in the context of the *Charlie Hebdo* attacks in 2015 in Paris. They identify several media-oriented practices that are co-constitutive of digital witnessing, such as taking videos and pictures as well as sharing, remediating and engaging with these visual materials. These digital practices contributed decisively to the shaping of the attacks as a violent media event by anchoring people, for example, as (amateur) witnesses (see also Meis on mobile phone videos in the Syrian conflict, and Mollerup on digital videos in the Egyptian uprising). Moreover, conflict imageries are circulated to raise international awareness about conflicts, but they are also strategically selected and manipulated in order to make a stronger case and further mobilise for a specific cause, up to a point where the reality of conflict becomes, in fact, invisible. Taking such critique to the extreme, Baudrillard argued in 1995 that the Gulf War did not really take place and only existed as 'the simulacra of modern mediated warfare' (Alper 2013: 1239).

The growing importance of digital videos and live streaming reminds us that it is not only the visualisation of violence on people's mobile devices but also sounds that impact the witnessing experience. Seib, for instance, mentions Edward R. Murrow, an American journalist who was reporting from the rooftops of London during air raids in the Second World War, thus bringing 'the sounds of war' into people's homes and affecting how they looked at the war and government policies (Seib 2013: 8). Sound, much less than imagery, cannot be escaped, as Matthew Sumera vividly shows in his chapter on the relationship between sounds and conflict. He not only explores the meanings and purposes of different types of sounds in contexts of war, but also their materiality and impact on people and their bodily experiences in conflict situations and in engaging with war films and video games. In doing so, he builds on Bakhtin's notion of 'chronotopes' to theorise on the processual nature of sound by combining the temporal and spatial qualities of media sounds.

Despite clear indications of the power of media for peacebuilding (e.g. Acayo and Mnjama 2004; Howard et al. 2005; Kahl and Puig Larrauri 2013; and Bräuchler, this volume), media research has so far clearly focused more on conflict with some of the major recent handbooks on peacebuilding having no section or entry on media (e.g. Mac Ginty 2013; Richmond, Pogodda and Ramović 2016; Webel and

Galtung 2007). Also, broadcasting companies and journalists seem to find it more rewarding to cover conflict than peace. As pointed out by Grimes, 'most of the pictures chosen for World Press Photo awards, for example, are embroiled in conflict, not nestled in the warm bed of peace' (2011: 21). Aiming towards a change in focus or at least a more balanced look at media's role in both conflict and peacebuilding, this volume also includes a section on transitions to peace in the aftermath of conflict. Soberon, Smets and Biltereyst explore in their chapter the contribution of films to transnational discourses of remembrance. In doing so, they conceptualise film as a locus of storing and communicating traumatic histories that is part of broader, collective practices of remembering trauma. Filmic representations and narratives, particularly those that counter dominant Western accounts of war and conflict, thus enable conversations on how to interact with (post)conflict reconciliation. Silke Oldenburg discusses in her chapter the relationship between media and collective identity formation in post-genocide Rwanda by looking into journalists' everyday practices. She concludes that Rwanda's historical legacy, the authoritarian political situation and the lack of a debating culture resulted in an 'off-the-record' media culture that is shaped by, and at the same time shapes, practices of avoidance. Birgit Bräuchler examines in her chapter how media in Maluku, Eastern Indonesia, facilitated the transition from conflict to peace. Through a context-oriented, integrative and agency-oriented approach, she illustrates how society and media are interdependent and how media and conflict are co-constitutive. These are first steps into a field slowly gaining in prominence and in need of future research.

Media Convergence and Changing Power Constellations

Media allow for another kind of immersion into conflict and other ways to participate, follow and observe different types of conflict. Moreover, the requirements of conflict and peace change the way in which media are used, as, for example, war photography, hate radio, trauma healing performances and the utilisation of drones or digital networks show (e.g. Moeller 1989; Steel 2015; Thompson 2007; Waterson 2010). In the Israel–Palestine conflict, for instance, state, military and grassroots activists have been using various media and communication channels provided by the internet to construct and disseminate their own narratives about current and past events, thus altering 'the nature of the Arab-Israeli conflict and the Israeli occupation of Palestinian lands' (Kuntsman and Stein 2010). Livio investigates in his chapter the use of

Twitter for cross-national dialogue between left-wing Israeli activists and representatives of Hamas during the Gaza War in 2014. As he shows, such interactions follow distinct cultural and linguistic patterns and contribute to the (re)construction of group boundaries and internal sociality rather than to reconciliatory dialogue. Such ambivalence of media use in conflict prevents easy categorisations, as outlined above.

Due to the broad range of (often highly interlinked) media that are deeply ingrained in contemporary war and peacescapes, we are invited to change our notions of conflict and peace and what their lived realities look like. As Kaempf puts it, 'a new heteropolar mediascape has emerged as a result of the multiplication and simultaneous diversification of structurally different media actors' (2013: 602). In our understanding, there is no hierarchy of media technologies – they are all part of a broader, multifaceted communication culture. The convergence and hybridisation of media technologies and media forms (Chadwick 2013; Jenkins 2008) have become an inherent part of our media environments and practices, and thus of the way we communicate and interact with each other in an increasingly digital world (Madianou and Miller 2012). In contemporary protest movements and recent prominent uprisings, such as the Arab Spring, different media forms, formats and channels have been strategically complementing and reinforcing each other (Aday et al. 2012: 14). This is equally true for the conflictual environments analysed in this volume, such as by Kummels on agrarian conflicts in Mexico, Sumera on the role of sound in conflicts and Pype on digital protest culture in the Congolese diaspora. Pype explores the politics of insults, the culture of violent text and the discursive practices of conflict genres in the Congolese online sphere. By discussing digital protest practices of the political opposition movement in the Congolese diaspora, she emphasises the importance of cultural and historical contextualisation of communicative phenomena as well as the spatial work of media in generating conflict (see also Mollerup, this volume).

Going beyond notions of hierarchised media (structures) also implies the need to deconstruct existing power hierarchies. In particular digital and social media, where boundaries between producer and audience are frequently dissolving, challenge existing power structures as various chapters illustrate. The Syrian conflict, for example, has been described as 'the most socially mediated civil conflict in history', alluding to the fact that most of what 'the outside world knows – or thinks it knows – about [the war] … has come from videos, analysis, and commentary circulated through social networks' (Lynch, Freelon and Aday 2014: 5). According to Lynch et al., activists were hoping that it would trigger 'international outrage, delegitimize the regime, bear witness and document the atrocities for future crimes justice' (2014: 6), hopes that were hardly fulfilled. They also highlight that the extensive use of social media led to polarisation and extremism, further fuelling the violence and undermining the efforts of nonviolent activists (2014: 6). In her contribution, Mareike Meis underlines this ambivalence of media practices. She analyses mobile phone videos and their escalating and de-escalating effect in the Syrian conflict as perceived by Syrian refugees in Germany by discussing the strategic selection of video material, aesthetics and discourse practices – practices that contribute to the blurring of boundaries between allegedly authentic first-hand videos and fabricated material. The Syrian case thus prominently challenges the 'illusion of unmediated information flows' (Lynch, Freelon and Aday 2014: 5), but also of the egalitarian and empowering nature of social media.

As outlined earlier, access, skills and networking are of the utmost importance for strategic media use. In Meis' case, those being part of key video production and circulation circles were at the forefront of shaping outside perceptions of the war. What Lynch et al. have called 'key curation hubs' are those influential networks of activists who generate particular narratives about the conflict through their media usage; it is important to note that these hubs may now play 'a gatekeeping role as powerful as that of television producers and newspaper editors' (2014: 3), thus challenging existing and establishing new power structures and dependencies. This is very much in line with critical voices in the growing body of literature on contemporary protest movements that challenge the alleged leaderlessness of movements, such as the Occupy movement, and their claim to give voice to 99 per cent of society, that address issues of representation and discuss the role of gatekeepers, choreographers and leaders in such movements (e.g. Bräuchler 2018a; Gerbaudo 2012; Juris et al. 2012).

An anthropology of media and conflict has much to say about everyday situations in which diverse modes of (mediated) communication are entangled with conflicts of various kinds. Through careful theorisation, which considers cross-cultural comparison and contextualisation as well as ethnographic methodology, it contributes to the deconstruction of deterministic notions of media effects on conflicts and thus provides answers to how humans in different times and places use media to create, escalate, de-escalate, manage and end conflicts. It also addresses questions about how the lived sociocultural realities of conflicts shape mediation processes and practices on individual, collective, local and global scales, thus emphasising a contextualised and non-media-centric approach. In doing so, an anthropologically informed approach to media and conflict pays particular attention to how media and conflict are co-constituted in a variety of ways.

Outline of the Book

This volume is divided into seven parts to indicate the multifacetedness of the elusive relationship between media and conflict and to visualise similarities between individual contributions. The first part includes this introduction and Stremlau's discussion of the changing role of new media technologies in conflict societies, in which she highlights the challenges media technology projects pose for 'developing' regions by looking into international communication infrastructure initiatives, national media policies and community media strategies at the Horn of Africa. The chapters in Part II provide examples of mediated witnessing of conflict: Sumiala, Tikka and Valaskivi analyse the practice of digital witnessing in context of the *Charlie Hebdo* attacks, and Meis looks into the de-/escalation effect of mobile phone videos for the Syrian conflict. The chapters in Part III theorise the experiencing of conflict: Markham reassesses, through a phenomenological approach to mediated conflict, how subjective recognition operates in the everyday lives of conflict journalists and audiences, and Sumera discusses the complex relationship between music, sound, conflict and bodily experience. Part IV looks at the phenomenon of mediated conflict language: Marshall examines how the experience of trolling is embedded within the (dis)orders of digital communication and Livio's chapter investigates social media as alternative means for dialogue between Israeli activists and Hamas during the 2014 Gaza War. Part V investigates sites of conflict: Mollerup develops an understanding of media as place-making to allow for an analysis of the entanglements of people and things related to media in the context of conflict, in her case the Egyptian uprising, and Kummels explores the interplay of media and conflict relating to longstanding agrarian disputes in Mexico. The chapters in Part VI focus on conflict across borders: Adriaans analyses media rituals in the Armenian diaspora and their relation to eruptions of violence in the homeland, and Pype discusses the politics of insults in the Congolese digital diaspora. The seventh and final part looks at what happens after conflict: Soberon, Smets and Biltereyst develop a theoretical framework to understand the multifaceted relationship between cinema and conflict-related trauma and how visual narratives create a hegemonic remembering of events, Oldenburg explores how media practitioners in post-genocide Rwanda engage in media freedom while preventing hate speech, and Bräuchler illustrates the interdependent post-conflict transformation of Moluccan society and media landscape. The book closes with an afterword by John Postill and his critical reflections upon the elusive and complex relationship between media and conflict.

Birgit Bräuchler is Senior Lecturer in Anthropology at the School of Social Sciences, Monash University, Melbourne. Her research interests include media anthropology, conflict and peace studies, protest movements, human and cultural rights, anthropology of law and religion; Southeast Asia, especially Indonesia. Among others, she is author of *Cyberidentities at War* (transcript, 2005/Berghahn, 2013), *The Cultural Dimension of Peace* (Palgrave Macmillan, 2015), editor of *Reconciling Indonesia* (Routledge, 2009) and coeditor of *Theorising Media and Practice* (Berghahn, 2010, with John Postill) and has published widely in peer-reviewed journals.

Philipp Budka is Lecturer in the Department of Social and Cultural Anthropology, University of Vienna, and the Visual and Media Anthropology MA programme at the Free University Berlin. His research areas include digital anthropology and ethnography, the anthropology of media and technology as well as visual culture and communication. He is the coeditor of *Ritualisierung – Mediatisierung – Performance* (Vienna University Press, 2019) and his research has been published in journals and books such as *Journal des Anthropologues*, the *Canadian Journal of Communication* and *Ethnic Media in the Digital Age* (Routledge, 2019).

Notes

1. For efforts to categorise and classify conflicts on and around the internet, see e.g. Arquilla and Ronfeldt (1993); Karatzogianni (2006, 2009).
2. For detailed introductions to the anthropology of media as well as other definitions of this research field, see e.g. Ginsburg (2005); Ginsburg, Abu-Lughod and Larkin (2002a); Peterson (2003). For critical discussions on media anthropology's relevance, see e.g. Boyer (2012); Pertierra (2017); Postill and Peterson (2009).
3. In contrast to mediation, the concept of 'mediatisation' tends to ascribe a 'single media-logic' – mostly determined by Euroamerican stakeholders – to media-related transformation processes, thus neglecting the heterogeneity of these processes (Couldry 2008: 378). For a discussion of the utilisation of these two concepts (in combination with the notion of 'media practices') in theorising about social movements, see Mattoni and Treré (2014). For different conceptualisations of media in general, see e.g. Boyer (2012); and Mazzarella (2004).

References

Acayo, C., and N. Mnjama. 2004. 'The Print Media and Conflict Resolution in Northern Uganda', *African Journal on Conflict Resolution* 4(1): 27–43.

Aday, S. et al. 2012. *New Media and Conflict after the Arab Spring*. Washington, DC: United States Institute of Peace.

Allagui, I., and B. Akdenizli. 2019. 'The Gulf Information War and the Role of Media and Communication Technologies: Editorial Introduction', *International Journal of Communication* 13: 1287–300.

Alper, M. 2013. 'War on Instagram: Framing Conflict Photojournalism with Mobile Photography Apps', *New Media & Society* 16(8): 1233–48.

Altheide, D. 2013. 'Media Logic, Social Control, and Fear', *Communication Theory* 23: 223–38.

Anderson, B. 1983. *Imagined Communities: Reflections on the Origin and Spread of Nationalism*. London: Verso.

Appadurai, A. 2006. *Fear of Small Numbers: An Essay on the Geography of Anger*. Durham, NC: Duke University Press.

Arno, A. 2009. *Alarming Reports: Communicating Conflict in the Daily News*. New York: Berghahn Books.

Arquilla, J., and D. Ronfeldt. 1993. 'Cyberwar is Coming!', *Comparative Strategy* 12(2): 141–65.

Asal, V., and A.M. Hoffmann. 2016. 'Media Effects: Do Terrorist Organizations Launch Foreign Attacks in Response to Levels of Press Freedom or Press Attention?', *Conflict Management and Peace Science* 33(4): 381–99.

Askew, K. 2002. 'Introduction', in K. Askew and R.R. Wilk (eds), *The Anthropology of Media: A Reader*. Malden, MA: Blackwell, pp. 1–13.

Atton, C. 2015. 'Introduction: Problems and Positions in Alternative and Community Media', in C. Atton (ed.), *The Routledge Companion to Alternative and Community Media*. New York: Routledge, pp. 1–18.

Barassi, V. 2015. *Activism on the Web: Everyday Struggles against Digital Capitalism*. New York: Routledge.

Bernal, V. 2014. *Nation as Network: Diaspora, Cyberspace, and Citizenship*. Chicago: University of Chicago Press.

Bohannan, P. (ed.). 1967. *Law and Warfare: Studies in the Anthropology of Conflict*. New York: Natural History Press.

Boyer, D. 2012. 'From Media Anthropology to the Anthropology of Mediation', in R. Fardon et al. (eds), *The SAGE Handbook of Social Anthropology*. Los Angeles: Sage, pp. 383–92.

Bräuchler, B. 2005. *Cyberidentities at War: Der Molukkenkonflikt im Internet*. Bielefeld: transcript.

———. 2007. 'Religious Conflicts in Cyberage', *Citizenship Studies* 11(4): 329–47.

———. 2011. 'The Transformation of the Media Scene: From War to Peace in the Moluccas, Eastern Indonesia', in K. Sen and D.T. Hill (eds), *Politics and the Media in 21st Century Indonesia*. London: Routledge, pp. 119–40.

———. 2013. *Cyberidentities at War: The Moluccan Conflict on the Internet*. New York: Berghahn Books.

———. 2015. *The Cultural Dimension of Peace. Decentralization and Reconciliation in Indonesia*. London: Palgrave Macmillan.

———. 2018a. 'Bali Tolak Reklamasi: The Local Adoption of Global Protest', *Convergence*. Retrieved 7 October 2019 from doi.org/10.1177/1354856518806695.

———. 2018b. 'Contextualizing Ethnographic Peace Research', in G. Millar (ed.), *Ethnographic Peace Research: Approaches and Tensions*. London: Palgrave Macmillan, pp. 21–42.

———. 2018c. 'The Cultural Turn in Peace Research: Prospects and Challenges', *Peacebuilding* 6(1): 17–33.

Bräuchler, B., and P. Naucke. 2017. 'Peacebuilding and Conceptualisations of the Local', *Social Anthropology* 25(4): 422–36.

Bräuchler, B., and J. Postill (eds). 2010. *Theorising Media and Practice*. New York: Berghahn Books.

Bruns, A. 2008. *Blogs, Wikipedia, Second Life, and Beyond: From Production to Produsage*. New York: Peter Lang.

Budka, P. 2015. 'From Marginalization to Self-Determined Participation: Indigenous Digital Infrastructures and Technology Appropriation in Northwestern Ontario's Remote Communities', *Journal des Anthropologues* 142–43(3): 127–53.

———. 2019. 'Indigenous Media Technologies in "The Digital Age": Cultural Articulation, Digital Practices, and Sociopolitical Concepts', in S.S. Yu and M.D. Matsaganis (eds), *Ethnic Media in the Digital Age*. New York: Routledge, pp. 162–72.

Carayannis, T. 2018. 'Rethinking the Politics of Violent Conflict', *Items*, 23 January 2018. Retrieved 7 October 2019 from https://items.ssrc.org/from-our-programs/rethinking-the-politics-of-violent-conflict.

Chadwick, A. 2013. *The Hybrid Media System: Politics and Power*. Oxford: Oxford University Press.

Coleman, E.G. 2010. 'Ethnographic Approaches to Digital Media', *Annual Review of Anthropology* 30: 487–505.

Comaroff, J.L., and S. Roberts. 1981. *Rules and Processes: The Cultural Logic of Dispute in an African Context*. Chicago: University of Chicago Press.

Conway, M. 2006. 'Terrorist "Use" of the Internet and Fighting Back', *Information & Security* 19: 9–30.

Cottle, S. 2006. *Mediatized Conflict: Developments in Media and Conflict Studies*. Maidenhead: Open University Press.

Couldry, N. 2008. 'Mediatization or Mediation? Alternative Understandings of the Emergent Space of Digital Storytelling', *New Media Society* 11: 373–91.

———. 2010. 'Theorising Media as Practice', in B. Bräuchler and J. Postill (eds), *Theorising Media and Practice*. New York: Berghahn Books, pp. 35–54.

———. 2015. 'Alternative Media and Voice', in C. Atton (ed.), *The Routledge Companion to Alternative and Community Media*. New York: Routledge, pp. 43–53.

Couldry, N., and J. Curran (eds). 2003a. *Contesting Media Power: Alternative Media in a Networked World*. Lanham, MD: Rowman & Littlefield.

———. 2003b. 'The Paradox of Media Power', in N. Couldry and J. Curran (eds), *Contesting Media Power: Alternative Media in a Networked World*. Lanham, MD: Rowman & Littlefield, pp. 3–16.

Couldry, N., and A. Hepp. 2013. 'Conceptualizing Mediatization: Contexts, Traditions, Arguments', *Communication Theory* 23: 191–202.

Dracklé, D. 2005. 'Vergleichende Medienethnografie', in A. Hepp, F. Krotz and C. Winter (eds), *Globalisierung der Medien: Eine Einführung*. Wiesbaden: VS Verlag für Sozialwissenschaften, pp. 187–205.

Dreher, T., K. McCallum and L. Waller. 2016. 'Indigenous Voices and Mediatized Policy-Making in the Digital Age', *Information, Communication & Society* 19(1): 23–39.

Doudaki, V., and N. Carpentier (eds). 2017. *Cyprus and its Conflicts: Representations, Materialities, and Cultures*. New York: Berghahn Books.

Elwert, G. 2004. 'Anthropologische Perspektiven auf Konflikt', in J. Eckert (ed.), *Anthropologie der Konflikte: Georg Elwerts konflikttheoretische Thesen in der Diskussion*. Bielefeld: transcript, pp. 26–38.

Elwert, G., S. Feuchtwang and D. Neubert (eds). 1999. *Dynamics of Violence: Processes of Escalation and De-escalation in Violent Group Conflicts*. Berlin: Duncker & Humblot.

Farmer, P. 2004. 'An Anthropology of Structural Violence', *Current Anthropology* 45(3): 305–25.

Franco, C. de. 2012. *Media Power and the Transformation of War*. Basingstoke: Palgrave Macmillan.

Fuchs, C. 2014. *Social Media: A Critical Introduction*. London: Sage.

Galtung, J. 1969. 'Violence, Peace, and Peace Research', *Journal of Peace Research* 6(1): 167–91.

Gerbaudo, P. 2012. *Tweets and the Streets: Social Media and Contemporary Activism*. London: Pluto Press.

Ghosh, S., and E. Turrini (eds). 2010. *Cybercrimes: A Multidisciplinary Analysis*. Berlin: Springer.

Ginsburg, F.D. 2005. 'Media Anthropology: An Introduction', in E.W. Rothenbuhler and M. Coman (eds), *Media Anthropology*. Thousand Oaks, CA: Sage, pp. 17–25.

Ginsburg, F.D., L. Abu-Lughod and B. Larkin (eds). 2002a. *Media Worlds: Anthropology on New Terrain*. Berkeley: University of California Press.

———. 2002b. 'Introduction', in F.D. Ginsburg, L. Abu-Lughod and B. Larkin (eds), *Media Worlds: Anthropology on New Terrain*. Berkeley: University of California Press, pp. 1–36.

Gluckman, M. 1963. *Order and Rebellion in Tribal Africa*. London: Cohen & West.

Gohdes, A.R. 2018. 'Studying the Internet and Violent Conflict', *Conflict Management and Peace Science* 35(1): 89–106.
Grimes, R.L. 2011. 'Ritual, Media, and Conflict: An Introduction', in R.L. Grimes et al. (eds), *Ritual, Media, and Conflict: An Introduction*. Oxford: Oxford University Press, pp. 1–44.
Grimes, R.L. et al. (eds). 2011. *Ritual, Media, and Conflict*. Oxford: Oxford University Press.
Hansen, L., and H. Nissenbaum. 2009. 'Digital Disaster, Cyber Security, and the Copenhagen School', *International Studies Quarterly* 53: 1155–75.
Hobart, M. 2010. 'What Do We Mean by Media Practices?', in B. Bräuchler and J. Postill (eds), *Theorising Media and Practice*. New York: Berghahn Books, pp. 55–75.
Hoskins, A., B. Richards and P. Seib. 2008. 'Editorial', *Media, War & Conflict* 1(1): 5–7.
Howard, R. et al. (eds). 2005. *The Power of the Media: A Handbook for Peacebuilders*. Utrecht: European Centre for Conflict Prevention.
Howell, S. 2018. 'Ethnography', in F. Stein et al. (eds), *The Cambridge Encyclopedia of Anthropology*. Retrieved 7 October 2019 from http://doi.org/10.29164/18ethno.
Hughes-Freeland, F. (ed.). 1998. *Ritual, Performance, Media*. London: Routledge.
Igreja, V.M.F. 2015. 'Media and Legacies of War: Responses to Global Film Violence in Conflict Zones', *Current Anthropology* 56(5): 678–700.
Jenkins, H. 2008. *Convergence Culture: Where Old and New Media Collide*. New York: New York University Press.
Jordan, T., and P.A. Taylor. 2004. *Hacktivism and Cyberwars: Rebels with a Cause?* London: Routledge.
Juris, J.S., and A. Khasnabish (eds). 2013. *Insurgent Encounters: Transnational Activism, Ethnography and the Political*. Durham, NC: Duke University Press.
Juris, J.S. et al. 2012. 'Negotiating Power and Difference within the 99%', *Social Movement Studies* 11(3–4): 434–40.
Kaempf, S. 2013. 'The Mediatisation of War in a Transforming Global Media Landscape', *Australian Journal of International Affairs* 67(5): 586–604.
Kahl, A., and H. Puig Larrauri. 2013. 'Technology for Peacebuilding', *Stability: International Journal of Security & Development* 2–3(61): 1–15.
Karatzogianni, A. 2006. *The Politics of Cyberconflict*. London: Routledge.
———. (ed.) 2009. *Cyber Conflict and Global Politics*. New York: Routledge.
Karmasin, M. et al. 2013. 'Preface: Perspectives on the Changing Role of the Mass Media in Hostile Conflicts', in J. Seethaler et al. (eds), *Selling War: The Role of the Mass Media in Hostile Conflicts from World War I to the 'War on Terror'*. Bristol: Intellect, pp. ix–xv.
Kemp, G. 2004. 'The Concept of Peaceful Societies', in G. Kemp and D.P. Fry (eds), *Keeping the Peace: Conflict Resolution and Peaceful Societies around the World*. New York: Routledge, pp. 1–10.
Kummels, I. 2017. *Transborder Media Spaces: Ayuujk Videomaking between Mexico and the US*. New York: Berghahn Books.

Kuntsman, A., and R.L. Stein. 2010. 'Another War Zone: Social Media in the Israeli-Palestinian Conflict', *Middle East Report Online*. Retrieved 7 October 2019 from http://reliefweb.int/sites/reliefweb.int/files/resources/849D4BB7DAD95F6549257798000F9F16-Full_Report.pdf.

Landler, M., and J. Markoff. 2007. 'In Estonia, What May Be the First War in Cyberspace', *New York Times*, 28 May 2007. Retrieved 7 October 2019 from http://www.nytimes.com/2007/05/28/business/worldbusiness/28iht-cyberwar.4.5901141.html?pagewanted=2.

Latham, R. (ed.) 2003. *Bombs and Bandwidth: The Emerging Relationship between Information Technology and Security*. New York: The New Press.

Li, D. 2007. 'Echoes of Violence: Considerations on Radio and Genocide in Rwanda', in A. Thompson (ed.), *The Media and the Rwanda Genocide*. London: Pluto Press, pp. 90–109.

Luger, M., F. Graf and P. Budka (eds). 2019. *Ritualisierung – Mediatisierung – Performance*. Göttingen: V&R Unipress/Vienna University Press.

Lynch, M., D. Freelon and S. Aday. 2014. 'Syria's Socially Mediated Civil War', January. *The United States Institute of Peace*. Retrieved 7 October 2019 from https://www.usip.org/publications/2014/01/syrias-socially-mediated-civil-war.

Mac Ginty, R. (ed.). 2013. *Routledge Handbook of Peacebuilding*. London: Routledge.

Madianou, M., and D. Miller 2012. 'Polymedia: Towards a New Theory of Digital Media in Interpersonal Communication', *International Journal of Cultural Studies* 16(2): 169–87.

Marcus, G.E. 1995. 'Ethnography in/of the World System: The Emergence of Multi-sited Ethnography', *Annual Review of Anthropology* 24: 95–117.

Marsden, L., and H. Savigny (eds). 2009a. *Media, Religion and Conflict*. Aldershot: Ashgate.

———. 2009b. 'Towards a Theorisation of the Link between Media, Religion and Conflict', in L. Marsden and H. Savigny (eds), *Media, Religion and Conflict*. Aldershot: Ashgate, pp. 145–62.

Mattoni, A., and E. Treré. 2014. 'Media Practices, Mediation Processes, and Mediatization in the Study of Social Movements', *Communication Theory* 24: 252–71.

Mazzarella, W. 2004. 'Culture, Globalization, Mediation', *Annual Review of Anthropology* 33: 345–67.

Mead, M. 2000. 'Warfare is Only an Invention – Not a Biological Necessity', in D.P. Barash (ed.), *Approaches to Peace: A Reader in Peace Studies*. Oxford: Oxford University Press, pp. 19–22.

Miller, D., and H. Horst. 2012. 'The Digital and the Human: A Prospectus for Digital Anthropology', in H. Horst and D. Miller (eds), *Digital Anthropology*. London: Berg, pp. 3–35.

Moeller, S.D. 1989. *Shooting War: Photography and the American Experience of Combat*. New York: Basic Books.

Montagu, A. 1994. 'Foreword', in L.E. Sponsel and T. Gregor (eds), *The Anthropology of Peace and Nonviolence*. Boulder: Lynne Rienner, pp. ix–xiv.

Moore, S.F. 1978. *Law as Process: An Anthropological Approach*. London: Routledge & Kegan Paul.

———. 2005. 'Certainties Undone: Fifty Turbulent Years of Legal Anthropology', in S.F. Moore (ed.), *Law and Anthropology: A Reader*. Malden, MA: Blackwell, pp. 343–67.

Moores, S. 2018. *Digital Orientations: Non-media-centric Media Studies and Non-representational Theories of Practices*. New York: Peter Lang.

Morley, D. 1980. *The Nationwide Audience: Structure and Decoding*. London: BFI.

———. 1992. *Television Audiences & Cultural Studies*. London: Routledge.

Mortensen, M. 2015. *Journalism and Eyewitness Images: Digital Media, Participation, and Conflict*. New York: Routledge.

Nakamura, L., and P.A. Chow-White (eds). 2012. *Race after the Internet*. New York: Routledge.

Nordstrom, C. 1997a. *A Different Kind of War Story*. Philadelphia: University of Pennsylvania Press.

———. 1997b. 'The Eye of the Storm: From War to Peace – Examples from Sri Lanka and Mozambique', in D.P. Fry and K. Björkqvist (eds), *Cultural Variation in Conflict Resolution: Alternatives to Violence*. Mahwah, NJ: Lawrence Erlbaum Associates, pp. 91–103.

———. 2004. *Shadows of War: Violence, Power, and International Profiteering in the Twenty-First Century*. Berkeley: University of California Press.

Nordstrom, C., and A.C.G.M. Robben (eds). 1995. *Fieldwork under Fire: Contemporary Studies of Violence and Culture*. Berkeley: University of California Press.

Orywal, E. 1996. 'Krieg und Frieden in den Wissenschaften', in E. Orywal, A. Rao and M. Bollig (eds), *Krieg und Kampf: Die Gewalt in unseren Köpfen*. Berlin: Dietrich Reimer Verlag, pp. 13–43.

Parry, K. 2010. 'Media Visualisation of Conflict: Studying News Imagery in 21st Century Wars', *Sociology Compass* 4(7): 417–29.

Pedelty, M. 1995. *War Stories: The Culture of Foreign Correspondents*. New York: Routledge.

Pertierra, A.C. 2017. *Media Anthropology for the Digital Age*. Cambridge: Polity.

Peterson, M.A. 2003. *Anthropology and Mass Communication: Media and Myth in the New Millennium*. New York: Berghahn Books.

Postill, J. 2010. 'Introduction: Theorising Media and Practice', in B. Bräuchler and J. Postill (eds), *Theorising Media and Practice*. New York: Berghahn Books, pp. 1–32.

———. 2017. 'The Diachronic Ethnography of Media: From Social Changing to Actual Social Changes', *Moment. Journal of Cultural Studies* 4(1): 19–43.

———. 2018. *The Rise of Nerd Politics: Digital Activism and Political Change*. London: Pluto Press.

Postill, J., and M.A. Peterson. 2009. 'What is the Point of Media Anthropology?', *Social Anthropology* 17(3): 334–44.

———. in press. 'Anthropology of Media', in P. Barbaro (ed.), *Ethnology, Ethnography and Cultural Anthropology: UNESCO Encyclopedia of Life Supporting Systems (EOLSS)*. Paris: UNESCO.

Pype, K. 2012. *The Making of the Pentecostal Melodrama: Religion, Media and Gender in Kinshasa*. New York: Berghahn Books.

Richards, J. 2009. 'Denial-of-Service: The Estonian Cyberwar and Its Implications for U.S. National Security', *International Affairs Review*. Retrieved 21 June 2011 from http://www.iar-gwu.org/node/65.

Richmond, O.P., S. Pogodda and J. Ramović (eds). 2016. *The Palgrave Handbook of Disciplinary and Regional Approaches to Peace*. London: Palgrave Macmillan.

Robben, A.C.G.M. 2016. 'Rethinking the Anthropology of Violence for the Twenty-First Century: From Practice to Mediation', *Conflict and Society: Advances in Research* 2: 1–3.

Robben, A.C.G.M., and C. Nordstrom. 1995. 'Introduction: The Anthropology and Ethnography of Violence and Sociopolitical Conflict', in C. Nordstrom and A.C.G.M. Robben (eds), *Fieldwork under Fire: Contemporary Studies of Violence and Culture*. Berkeley: University of California Press, pp. 1–23.

Rubinstein, R.A., and M. LeCron Foster. 1988. 'Introduction – Revitalizing International Security Analysis: Contributions from Culture and Symbolic Process', in R.A. Rubinstein and M.L. Foster (eds), *The Social Dynamics of Peace and Conflict: Culture in International Security*. Boulder: Westview Press, pp. 1–14.

Sanjek, R. 2010. 'Ethnography', in A. Barnard and J. Spencer (eds), *The Routledge Encyclopedia of Social and Cultural Anthropology*. London: Routledge, pp. 243–49.

Scheper-Hughes, N. 2004. 'Dangerous and Endangered Youth: Social Structures and Determinants of Violence', *Annals of the New York Academy of Sciences* 1036(1): 13–46.

Scheper-Hughes, N., and P. Bourgois. 2004. 'Introduction: Making Sense of Violence', in N. Scheper-Hughes and P. Bourgois (eds), *Violence in War and Peace: An Anthology*. Malden, MA: Blackwell, pp. 1–31.

Schoemaker, E., and N. Stremlau. 2014. 'Media and Conflict: An Assessment of the Evidence', *Progress in Development Studies* 14(2): 181–95.

Seib, P. 2013. 'Introduction: Delivering War to the Public: Shaping the Public Sphere', in J. Seethaler et al. (eds), *Selling War: The Role of the Mass Media in Hostile Conflicts from World War I to the 'War on Terror'*. Bristol: Intellect, pp. 1–14.

Slevin, J. 2000. *The Internet and Society*. Cambridge: Polity.

Smets, K. 2017. 'The Way Syrian Refugees in Turkey Use Media: Understanding "Connected Refugees" Through a Non-media-centric and Local Approach', *Communications* 43(1): 113–23.

Smith, A. 1978. *The Politics of Information: Problems of Policy in Modern Media*. London: Macmillan Press.

Steel, H. 2015. 'Streets to Screens: Mediating Conflict through Digital Networks', *Information, Communication & Society* 18(11): 1269–74.

Straus, S. 2007. 'What Is the Relationship between Hate Radio and Violence? Rethinking Rwanda's "Radio Machete"', *Politics & Society* 35(4): 609–37.

Stroeken, K. (ed.). 2012. *War, Technology, Anthropology.* New York: Berghahn Books.

Sumiala, J., and M. Tikka. 2011. 'Imagining Globalised Fears: School Shooting Videos and Circulation of Violence on YouTube', *Social Anthropology* 19(3): 254–67.

Thompson, A. (ed.). 2007. *The Media and the Rwanda Genocide.* London: Pluto Press.

Tufekci, Z. 2017. *Twitter and Tear Gas: The Power and Fragility of Networked Protest.* New Haven: Yale University Press.

Turner, V. 1975. *Dramas, Fields, and Metaphors: Symbolic Action in Human Society.* Ithaca, NY: Cornell University Press.

Veer, P. van der, and S. Munshi (eds). 2004. *Media, War, and Terrorism: Responses from the Middle East and Asia.* London: Routledge.

Vladisavljević, N. 2015. 'Media Framing of Political Conflict: A Review of the Literature', *Media, Conflict and Democratisation*, May. Retrieved 7 October 2019 from http://www.mecodem.eu/wp-content/uploads/2015/05/Vladisavljevi%C4%87-2015_Media-framing-of-political-conflict_-a-review-of-the-literature.pdf.

Waterson, R. 2010. 'Testimony, Trauma and Performance: Some Examples from Southeast Asian Theatre', *Journal of Southeast Asian Studies* 41(3): 509–28.

Webel, C., and J. Galtung (eds). 2007. *Handbook of Peace and Conflict Studies.* London: Routledge.

Weidmann, N.B. 2015. 'Communication, Technology, and Political Conflict: Introduction to the Special Issue', *Journal of Peace Research* 52(3): 263–68.

Werbner, P. 2010. 'Notes from a Small Place: Anthropological Blues in the Face of Global Terror', *Current Anthropology* 51(2): 193–221.

Werbner, P., M. Webb and K. Spellman-Poots (eds). 2014. *The Political Aesthetics of Global Protest: The Arab Spring and Beyond.* Edinburgh: Edinburgh University Press.

World Economic Forum. 2019. *Risks Report 2019.* Geneva: World Economic Forum. Retrieved 7 October 2019 from http://www3.weforum.org/docs/WEF_Global_Risks_Report_2019.pdf.

Zeitzoff, T. 2017. 'How Social Media Is Changing Conflict', *Journal of Conflict Resolution* 61(9): 1970–91.

CHAPTER 1

Transforming Media and Conflict Research

Nicole Stremlau

There are unprecedented efforts underway to connect the unconnected, many of whom live in conflict-affected rural environments. The UN's Agenda for Sustainable Development outlines the goals that all countries should adopt for addressing global poverty and peace over the next fifteen years, including a commitment to provide internet connectivity to all by 2020 (United Nations n.d.). While it seems clear that this goal will not be met, ambitious experiments are underway. Western corporations are attempting to lead the efforts – Google is experimenting with drones and hot air balloons, what it has termed 'project loon'. The balloons are currently in a first commercial trial in rural, mountainous communities in Kenya, where it would be expensive to build infrastructure on the ground. Elon Musk's SpaceX has deployed the first batch of what is expected to include tens of thousands of satellites he hopes will provide global internet coverage from space by flying in a low orbit above earth. Facebook has recently announced a plan to build underwater sea cables – a project dubbed 'Simba' after the Disney film *The Lion King* – around the continent (such a title is unlikely to dispel concerns that these efforts are part of a new form of colonisation). Access is expected to be offered on an open-access basis and is partly motivated by an effort to extend the reach of Free Basics (a Facebook service that links with local telecoms carriers and provides people with free access to Facebook and certain websites) and associated products. With markets in North America and Europe nearly saturated, the developing world, and Africa in particular, offers the growth market for the next billion users. But there has been little discussion about what kind of impact these technologies will have on conflict-affected societies. Comments by Facebook founder Mark Zuckerberg, when he was in Colombia for the launch of internet.org (the predecessor to Free Basics), reflect this gap when he suggested that the internet will open new spaces for dialogue, including between the government and the Fuerzas Armadas Revolucionarias de Colombia (FARC rebels) who were leading a guerrilla war from 1964 to 2017 in Colombia: 'I think a lot of conflicts are caused by misunderstandings. The internet as a whole and social media will bring reconciliation and peace' ('Facebook Founder in Colombia to Promote Affordable Internet' 2015). Similar to many of Africa's protracted violent conflicts, violence in Colombia has been driven by a complex network of interests (economic, ideological, political, etc.) rather than simply a lack of dialogue. While there is growing attention to the role of fake news and the manipulation of media content around elections (particularly in rich democracies), there is an urgent need for a deeper understanding of the interaction between social media and violent conflict, or peace-making efforts, as the contributions to this volume show.

In the United States and across much of Europe, citizens are becoming more vocal in their criticism of large technology companies, asking, for example, whether Facebook is 'breaking democracy' or whether it is actually undermining informed political participation ('Do Social Media Threaten Democracy?' 2017; Lovink 2011; Morozov 2012, 2013). There is a growing acceptability that in certain circumstances, it might be useful, if not necessary, to shut down social media as part of a broader effort to disrupt protests or interrupt terrorist attacks. While the U.K. government has been an outspoken critic of internet shutdowns as are often employed in much of Asia and Latin America, there was little criticism around the British Transport Police's recent effort to interrupt climate change protests by shutting off internet access on the London Tube in April 2019. This was a far more isolated incident than a nationwide shutdown, but it reflects an increased willingness to see social media disruption as a tool for managing both present and potential conflicts.

International focus on the potentially destabilising effects of social media has been far more muted in poorer countries and places that are deeply affected by violent conflict. Only recently, for example, has debate broadened on the role of social media in violence in Myanmar, and pressure has been increased on companies such as Facebook that are providing the platforms on which such speech occurs to address it. The Chairman of the UN Independent International Fact-Finding Mission on Myanmar noted that Facebook has played a 'determining role' in the violence against the Rohingya ('U.N. Investigators

Cite Facebook Role in Myanmar Crisis' 2018). This is despite many earlier and repeated warnings by academics and nongovernmental organisations (NGOs) about the growing role of dangerous speech (Gagliardone et al. 2015; 'Myanmar Activists Launch Anti-"Hate Speech" Campaign' 2014). However, it has really only been in the wake of the 'fake news' scandal in the United States that pressure on U.S. companies has increased to address this issue (albeit very slowly). Social media companies such as Facebook have invested significant funding in human moderators and artificial intelligence (AI) as part of an effort to remove false information that could lead to physical violence. But success has been elusive and, given the scale, the varying political and cultural contexts, and evolving technology, it is unclear whether such speech can be curbed on social media platforms. How exactly this will be implemented is unclear.

Many of the world's most significantly conflict-affected regions are in Africa and are a priority area for these companies' planned expansions. This chapter explores a few of the potential challenges and implications of these largescale technology projects to connect more rural communities in the developing world, drawing on extensive research I have conducted in the Horn of Africa to illustrate these challenges.[1] The Horn of Africa is a unique research site due to its variable communications environment – from the restrictive internet and media in Ethiopia to the far more liberal and innovative information and communications technology (ICT) environment in neighbouring Somalia. The region as a whole has suffered from continued violence raising important issues about the complex relationship between media and conflict.

This chapter is by no means a comprehensive analysis, but rather highlights a few key areas at the transnational, national and local levels.[2] Rather than pursuing a deterministic approach focusing on the potentially liberating (Diamond and Plattner 2012; Shirky 2011) or peacemaking (Loewenberg 2006; Paluck 2009; Paluck and Green 2009; Stauffacher et al. 2005) effects of social media, the chapter focuses on what types of questions might lead to alternative ways of understanding, how these experiments with internet expansion can be understood and the particular challenges conflict-affected markets pose. Within each of these three broad areas – the international (or transnational), the national and the local – one specific issue or angle is raised to offer a view to elevate issues that are often overlooked.

The strategies and role of transnational actors, and particularly companies such as Facebook and Google, to extend the internet is considered first. The current efforts to 'connect the unconnected' differ from earlier efforts to extend connectivity to Africa. Initiatives such as the African Marine System, an ongoing effort to connect the continent through submarine fibre optics, is indicative; cables usually go to the densest and richest markets first, where providers are most likely to recover their costs, whereas current strategies are focusing on rural communities. Many of the current efforts focus on rural regions that are also some of the most conflict-affected areas of the continent where infrastructure has been difficult to put in place and the margins of profit are slim for telecommunications companies. But these initiatives are usually driven with little consideration of the context in which they are operating, or how their platform might be interpreted or used in ways that were not intended.

The chapter then proceeds to examine the national, including national debates about information systems in conflict and post-conflict situations. It focuses on the challenge of how to move beyond normative debates around national media policy that typically focus on legal processes and associated political reforms. At present, there is an overwhelming focus on what the state should be doing and how it falls short of international standards. An alternative approach emphasises the importance of ideas, ideology and the national vision of the type of society governments and political leaders are attempting to craft.

And, finally, community-level strategies of innovation and regulating speech are considered. The importance of this analysis is often clearest in spaces, frequently rural, where the state might not be present or might have limited reach. This is particularly relevant as many of the current initiatives by large multinational companies to connect the unconnected focus on such regions. It also highlights just how challenging it is to marry global policies and 'community standards' (as often termed by social media companies) with very particular local realities, whether it is about what is hate speech or whether certain speech constitutes incitement to violence.

International Interventions and the Provision of Communications Infrastructure in Conflict-Affected Regions

There is a substantial history of international organisations and various aid agencies providing communications infrastructure, supporting media outlets and developing programming for conflict-affected regions (Price and Thompson 2002). The beginnings of this approach can be seen in a range of interventions, from supporting the media apparatuses of guerrilla insurgencies in Africa, to providing equipment and training of journalists, to developing language programming and broadcasting by stations such as the BBC World Service or Voice of America to advance foreign affairs priorities and support certain values (and consequently parties) in conflict situations (Allen and Seaton 1999; Lewis 2002: 301–2). More recently, the UN has established an active communications sector that often partners peacekeeping operations with media, typically radios, that support the funders' objectives. UN peacekeeping missions all have a Public Information Office that often comprises a media relations unit, a photography unit and a radio unit, among others, with the objective of both providing information about the operation and engaging with 'influencers', including local journalists, the military and policy-makers. Radio Okapi, for example, which started in the Democratic Republic of Congo, is often cited as one of the more successful 'peace radios' (Betz 2004), although there have been others with varying impact, including Radio Miraya in South Sudan, UNMIL (United Nations Mission in Liberia) Radio in Liberia and Radio Barkulan in Somalia, broadcasting in collaboration with the African Union (Orme 2010). The World Bank has also been deeply involved in the provision of communications infrastructure in conflict-affected regions. In Somalia, for example, it has invested tens of millions of dollars in projects that include building infrastructure to support government ministries and education resource networking that are all part of trying to build a viable state and empower the government to provide security and services (and, as a consequence, increase its legitimacy). A priority has been on developing legal and regulatory frameworks for the flourishing telecommunications sector that has, so far, largely been operating entirely beyond state regulation ('Legal ICT Framework is Pivotal Moment for Somalia' 2017). A subsequent phase will focus on expanding connectivity and access from coastal areas to the interior (ICT Sector Support in Somalia Phase II 2018).

While there are certainly limits to these types of interventions by international organisations, and the effectiveness of such media development interventions can also be questioned, particularly in conflict situations (Schoemaker and Stremlau 2014), there is even less understanding or research on the growing role of companies such as Facebook and Google in conflict-affected regions, particularly in Africa.[3] However, what does seem evident is that while tech companies have become increasingly responsive (although still surprisingly slow) to respond to complaints and inquiries by Western governments into the use and abuse of their platform, whether around hate speech in Germany or fake news and manipulation by the Russian government in the United States, they have been even slower to respond to cases outside of rich countries (Roose 2017). And the response, or preventative measures have often been erratic or splotchy, lacking a coherent strategy.

For example, Facebook appears to have been comparatively engaged and aggressive in addressing the potential of hate speech and fake news on its platform during the Kenyan elections in 2017. These elections were tense and widely watched across the world as previous elections been associated with significant violence and media had a role in inflaming tensions (Stremlau and Price 2009). Facebook attempted different strategies to raise awareness in Kenya, including taking out full-page ads in local newspapers informing readers about how to identify false news online and enabling mechanisms for users to report, and counter, such news, along with existing measures to identify hate speech or incitement to violence (Hume 2017). But this type of pre-emptive approach has not been adopted across the continent where there has been a real threat of violence or where the platform has been associated with hate speech and violence. The last elections in Ethiopia (2015), for example, as well as ongoing violence in the Oromia region, did not elicit engagement from Facebook, despite the fact that the Ethiopian government has long cited the use of incitement on the platforms as a reason for widespread internet shutdowns and monitoring of social media (Gagliardone et al. 2016; Karanja, Xynou and Filastò 2016). Facebook Live has exploded in popularity within the Somali territories, building on Somalis' strong tradition of orality, but at the same time it has rapidly become a platform for hateful political rhetoric that is difficult to monitor, flag and take down.

The challenge is that as social media companies increasingly focus on rural communities, they are reaching out to individuals that are often first-time internet users, with limited media literacy. How this technology will be used, and interpreted, in very different contexts cannot be assumed. Technology companies have often been quick to argue that their platforms are 'neutral' or that they are not media companies (with the associated responsibilities of being a publisher) (Segreti 2016), but there can be significant differences in how users assess, understand and critically analyse the type of misinformation, and even what might be accurate information on social media (Stremlau, Gagliardone and Price 2018; see also Marshall, this volume). While there is a lack of bottom-up research from rural and conflict-affected communities in Sub-Saharan Africa on how people are understanding information on social media, some of the research on more traditional media, including radio and television, particularly by anthropologists, offers some insight into the complexity of interpreting information through different mediums, particularly around elections. The use of radio in Ethiopia's last competitive elections illustrates this challenge.

In the run-up to the 2005 elections in Ethiopia, the Ethiopian People's Revolutionary Democratic Front (EPRDF) opened the media space and allowed an unprecedented level of debate in what has been one of the most restrictive countries on the continent. Political parties were allocated airtime in a relatively balanced and transparent process, and coverage of opposition rallies, interviews and manifestos was even included on government media (Stremlau 2011). In a country that was long dominated by media sympathetic to the government, the inclusion of opposition voices on government media was highly unusual. The impact of providing these opposing political parties with increased access to the mainstream media was more significant than the ruling party anticipated, particularly in rural areas. With the handful of private radio stations restricted to music and entertainment, and unable to air news or debates, the freedoms the private press enjoyed had a limited impact among the literate and those wealthy enough to buy newspapers in urban areas. The reach of government radio and the unprecedented airing of opposition views and political debates challenged expectations in rural communities and perceptions of Ethiopia's long-established hierarchical political culture (Stremlau 2011). It was not so much the content or substance of the debates that affected how people voted, but the fact that, as Lefort (2007: 265) argued, people now perceived the government to be 'so weak that it must sit with its enemies'. For rural audiences that had not been exposed to similar political debates, hearing the government openly criticised and mocked on national radio, with little response or crackdown from the government as was the case in the past, suggested that the government was too weak to respond. Within some communities, this was seen as a signal that the government was soon to fall and that a new leadership would take over. From the farmers' perspectives, they did not want be on the wrong side of a collapsing government, so they gave their allegiance and support to those that they perceived were stronger (Lefort 2007). Furthermore, in a highly polarised political space, the ruling party believed not only that it had total control of security and politics, but that the opposition was too fragmented and weak to offer an alternative to 'revolutionary democracy' in such a diverse and complex state. Given this assessment, the ruling party did not develop a serious campaign agenda, but (even more counterproductively) it followed its usual approach of refusing to respond to or engage with the criticism and debates that were emerging from the increasingly vibrant media. After the results became public and it became clear that the opposition had made significant gains in Parliament, the government contested the results, leading to widespread protests that soon turned violent. The government partially attributed this violence to the inflammatory role of the media, and the use of social media and SMS to mobilise protesters (Stremlau 2011), but the most significant aspect was likely, as Lefort described, a clash of expectations and misperceptions about the political process that was enhanced by the unprecedented use of radio in the country. There was a speedy reversal of political and media freedoms, with SMS messaging closed down for more than a year and journalists and politicians arrested, and tens of thousands of citizens were imprisoned throughout the post-election period.

The intersection between media and politics in Ethiopia's elections highlights the often unexpected or unanticipated effects of media, particularly in communities that have not had previous exposure to a particular media or forum. This is not to be deterministic, but rather suggests the challenges in understanding how technologies and messages might be understood in very different contexts with communities that may have varying interpretations and expectations of these technologies (this has also been explored through some of the literature on technopolitics; see e.g. Gagliardone 2016). This potential for unintended consequences is often overlooked. Just as the Ethiopian government did not anticipate that allowing the opposition time on the radio would lead some listeners to believe that the government was falling, the discourse from tech companies planning these large expansions of their platforms and products is uniformly optimistic and, in this case, based on an assumption that these products and their broader efforts to 'connect the unconnected' will offer neutral platforms that will in turn be constructive in fostering 'meaningful communities' that will engage in positive change (Zuckerberg 2018).

National Politics and Ideologies

Particularly when it comes to the national level and national debates, a challenge for those working in the international development or conflict resolution field, and engaging with media policy issues, is how to move beyond the normative free expression agenda that tends to place an overwhelming focus on what the state should be doing, how it should be performing and where it is falling short of international standards, particularly in relation to democratisation or freedom of expression (see also Oldenburg, this volume). It is in this context that the deep ethnographic work on media and conflict illuminated in this book can offer alternative perspectives.

This bias towards the state is rooted in media policy debates, which tend to follow democracy promotion efforts focusing on the legal environment, support for civil society, and political reforms such as elections (Bridoux and Kurki 2014). This focus on the state is also the grounding for most large-scale comparative analyses, whether in comparative media studies (Blumler and Gurevitch 1995; Eribo and Jong-Ebot 1997; Hallin and Mancini 2011) or media freedom indexes (Freedom House, 2017), or the World Bank Governance Indicators, which also has a key strand on media and information. But this emphasis can also obscure understandings, for example, of why governments or political leaders adopt particular policies in relation to media and what the motivations and political ideas that inform such approaches are.

Much of the public debate on media and conflict issues in Africa is centred on the growing 'internet shutdowns' debate. There has been a dramatic increase in governments completely shutting down the internet, often in the name of conflict prevention or in response to violent (or even nonviolent) protests. Election periods are a particularly sensitive time and preserving the integrity of the electoral process, or maintaining national security, is often used as a justification. The brazenness to close the internet at a national level contrasts with many other countries in Asia and the Middle East, where the shutdown of the internet tends to be limited to particular regions or cities.[4]

At the time of writing, public debates around internet shutdowns in Africa are driven by activists and advocacy groups such as Access Now and the #KeepItOn campaign promoted on Twitter, which, as their names suggest, campaign against internet shutdowns and on related freedom of expression and digital rights issues such as improving access. These activists (including NGOs in the Global North, along with their partner local NGOs and technology advocates) are raising awareness of the issue, but their narrative is largely limited to suggesting that 'autocratic' governments are shutting down the internet and they should keep it on because it is a 'right' (UN General Assembly 2016) and it has economic consequences (West 2016). This approach has proved highly limiting. While galvanising activists, it has the alternative effect of closing down dialogue and efforts to engage with, or evaluate, the concerns or claims from policy-makers justifying the closures, particularly in the context of growing frustration with the seeming inability of large tech companies to effectively address issues of extreme speech on their platforms. While in most cases governments cite little evidence to support such drastic measures, there is also an absence of evidence about the effects of closures in limiting the phenomenon that they are attempting to control, such as stopping the spread of rumours, false news or incitement of violence (Freyburg and Garbe 2018).

An alternative approach to understanding national media policy in conflict situations also requires a greater focus on political ideology. This is an area that much of the research on media in conflict situations has often overlooked, but the conflict or political science literature has engaged with more fully (e.g. Clapham 1998; Sikkink 1991). While much of this research on Africa has tended to remain on the peripheries, some research programmes have sought to emphasise the importance of engaging with the nuances of contexts, including understanding of the role of political ideology and various political authorities (Africa Power and Politics (APPP) 2018; Pettit 2013). This perspective is less focused on extremist ideology (as is often commonly assumed), but rather on political ideology about how leaders, governments and local authorities are thinking about the role of information and security. Understanding this requires a highly contextual and historical approach, and one that is often provided by anthropologists.

Again, returning to the case of contemporary Ethiopia, it is almost impossible to understand the government's reaction, as well as proactive measures, to the use of social media during current conflicts without examining how information and media was used during the guerrilla struggle between the 1970s and the early 1990s. Accounting for these historical roots and, if one wishes to go even further, the ways in which ideology was crafted during the student movement in the 1960s is an essential part of interpreting how contemporary media policy has been shaped in Ethiopia. The central and distinctive role of ideology in governance in Ethiopia led to increasing political polarisation during the first twenty years of EPRDF leadership. Heavily influenced by leaders such as Mao, Lenin and Marx, the Tigreyan People's Liberation Front, the core of guerrilla fighters that fought against the Soviet-backed government and later formed the current ruling party (the EPRDF), was deeply committed to the political education of their cadres and peasantry. While this evolved over the decades, the unique approach was reinforced during the leadership of the first Prime Minister, Meles Zenawi, in what became known as 'Revolutionary Democracy' and, subsequently, the 'Developmental Democratic State' (Stremlau 2018b). According to Donald Kaberuka, the former President of the African Development Bank, this approach has served as 'another form of governance model for leaders in Africa to emulate' (as quoted in Kwibuka

2015) and it has been given prominence by influential leaders such as Paul Kagame of Rwanda.

The approach of the developmental democratic state is evident in media policies ranging from the reluctance of the EPRDF to extend the state's monopoly of telecommunications to private companies to ambitious projects like WoredaNet and SchoolNet. These large-scale projects, the first which establishes a link between the central government and local regional governments (*woredas*) via satellite video conferencing to enable one-way political education (from the central government to the *woredas*) and the latter that relies on a similar satellite video system while focusing on the political education of high school students, both attempt to extend the power of the central government to the peripheries (Gagliardone 2016). These projects have been in response to the challenges of governing a highly fragmented and diverse society, and one that has embedded into the constitution some of the most ambitious laws on federalism, enabling any region to vote for secession in theory but not in practice (as evidenced by the continuing regional and secessionist struggles in the Ogaden and Oromo regions; see Turton 2006).

The point is that, like the internet shutdown campaigns, the role of political thought and ideology when it comes to how media is used during conflict is often neglected. And similarly overlooked are the politics that are so often embedded in the technologies and policies. If there is a desire by international actors, as there often is, to intervene or develop ways of mitigating violence, or to challenge a government response, towards media and information during conflict, understanding it through the specific experiences and the lens of those in power is crucial. This includes taking role of ideas and ideology seriously, and engaging with the arguments that governments might be making justifying policies or approaches.

Customary Mechanisms for Regulating Speech During Conflict

As this volume argues, and other chapters empirically demonstrate, there needs to be a more grounded approach to understanding media and conflict. This is particularly complex because in many conflict-affected regions, it likely means understanding spaces where the state might not be present or might have limited reach. This is especially important as the current efforts to improve access to the internet focus on rural areas. Research on hybrid governance (Booth 2011; Meagher 2012) and on public authorities, particularly in regions where the state may just be one authority among many (Hagmann and Hoehne 2009; Lund 2006), provides some insight into how such an approach might be structured. The experience and role of customary law in regulating voice and resolving media disputes is instructive in illuminating the importance of an alternative strategy of analysis. Perhaps nowhere is the role of customary law more central than in conflict regions such as Somalia, which has been without a functioning central state for more than two decades. Similar arguments could likely be made for other war-affected regions with strong traditional authorities, such as Yemen and Afghanistan.

One of the most extraordinary aspects of the Somali conflict is the extent to which telecommunications and media have managed to grow and innovate despite the instability and absence of a capable national government. Media have been entwined with the ongoing violence; over the years, there have been dozens of radios that have been advocating for particular warlords, diaspora satellite television stations are highly popular and political, and the UN/African Union established an ambitious radio station, Radio Bar Kulan, to support their troops and push their organisations' political agenda in the country (and it is one that is not without its critics and dissenters). One of the world's most advanced experiments in mobile money has also emerged in Somalia, and the country enjoys relatively fast and inexpensive access to the internet as a result of a highly competitive telecoms market. This poses the important question of how media has developed in such a context that in many ways is the antithesis of the generally accepted 'enabling environment' for supporting the development of 'free' media (Price and Krug 2000). What has facilitated, and even encouraged, investment in infrastructure and local businesses, despite weak security, a lack of government protections and regulations? The prevailing approach by international development actors is to look at what is *not* working and suggest reforms – new media laws, training of journalists in international standards, and new associations to support media organisations.[5] Looking at what *is* actually working, and asking why, is seldom considered. In the case of Somalia, while the state may have limited reach, there is a strong historical precedent of *xeer* law regulating speech, addressing concerns of slander or incitement to violence, and protecting property (van Notten 2005). As the introduction to this volume indicates, legal anthropologists have long argued that there is a certain logic or pattern to conflict; it is not structureless or simply chaos. And a similar argument can be made about how disputes regarding the role of media, or voice, during conflict where the state has limited reach might be regulated.

The continued relevance and role of *xeer* law and shari'a in Somalia is debated, with some arguing that, particularly with *xeer* law, there has been a tendency to romanticise or overstate its role in peacebuilding or maintaining justice and order (especially in the Western sense of the term) (Schlee 2013). *Xeer* law is comprised of bilateral agreements between clans (family groupings); it is not codified, but based on precedent and, as a consequence, works in varying ways across the Somali territories and diaspora, with greater relevancy in some communities than others. In Somaliland (the self-declared independent region in the north), for example, *xeer* law is more influential and widely used than in the south, partly because the British, who colonised the north, did not dismantle local structures of governance to the same extent as the Italian colonisers in the south. And the north has also had far less of the relentless violence that has plagued the south, including the associated international interventions and various attempts at establishing a government. These processes of peace-making have often sought to co-opt local elders who are central to adjudicating disputes. Furthermore, as a form of a pact between clans, *xeer* law inevitably empowers certain clans (including those that are larger, wealthier and more politically influential), while marginalising others. Despite these imbalances and however variable it is, *xeer* law has had a continued role in regulating the media sector and different principles are drawn upon depending on the nature of the dispute (Stremlau and Osman 2015).

When it comes to regulating libel and slander in Somalia with *xeer* law, poetry offers a precedent and provides some case law for disputes involving mass media and new communications technologies. Such offences are taken very seriously; reputation is extremely important, almost a currency, and is regarded as an essential component of trust and order. Both sides of a dispute are typically eager to resolve conflict to maintain the reputation of a clan member and of the clan as a whole. There are limits to this approach. In some cases, the person who committed an offence is known as a wayward family member and others are reluctant to weigh in on their behalf, and similarly elders may be reluctant to judge a repeat offender. It may also be that an individual or a clan will not recognise the legitimacy or authority of the traditional elders. Some of the most popular media outlets are diverse and transnational, with journalists in the diaspora, and are not always constituted along clan lines. In previous cases involving the mass media, outlets have tried to argue that they represent a larger community and have pressed for the dispute to be heard in the court system (which is also seen as far more corruptible; see e.g. the case of Yusuf Gabobe, editor of *Haatuf* newspaper, and former President Riyaale in Stremlau 2012).

When it comes to enabling investment in the telecommunications sector and infrastructure in particular, *xeer* has provided a foundation for protecting and resolving property disputes, an essential enabler for international (almost exclusively diaspora) investment. Given the newness of ICTs and many media platforms, there is not necessarily precedent within *xeer* for adjudicating such disputes, but it can provide direction by considering how other property disputes have been resolved, particularly around livestock (Little 2003). The experience of regulating other, more traditional, sectors can be applied to telecommunications infrastructure and demonstrates its continued relevance. Clans are traditionally responsible for providing security and support for pastoralists. In the context of telecoms infrastructure, companies are often careful to employ people on the basis of clan affiliation in order to ensure that their property and interests will be protected in the same way that they would be if the owner was from the local clan; this also ensures that a company will have sufficient access to local recourse in the case of disputes (Stremlau 2018a: 302).

As media policy and media law-making efforts intensify in Somalia, as part of the efforts to extend the influence and capacity of the weak Federal Government, there have been several large-scale initiatives, including an ambitious World Bank-sponsored Communications Act (2018), a new Media Law (2017) and intensive training efforts by the UN and other international organisations to promote freedom of expression. With the emphasis on encouraging the development of a Western-style media system, these initiatives almost entirely ignore the role of *xeer* law and the present practice of how disputes are resolved. The continued relevancy and applicability of *xeer* law in Somalia's media environment challenges the focus on the state, and its associated laws and policies, that prevailing indicators and frameworks relating to freedom of expression tend to adopt. This leads to overlooking more nuanced contexts for voice. Accounting for this highly varied legal and policy landscape, particularly in countries affected by conflict, is a crucial consideration in relation to how greater access to social media might intersect with conflicts.

Conclusion

This volume has called for more bottom-up approaches to understanding media and conflict, but developing and implementing such approaches, particularly when it comes to large-scale or comparative research, is difficult. Furthermore, capturing the significant divides, or variance, of media and the experience of conflict across a state, or even a community, makes generalisations about the role of media in conflict (and conflict on media) challenging.

At the same time, there is a clear pushback in some universities in the Global South, as well as segments of academia further afield in the United States and the United Kingdom, to 'decolonise' or 'transform' curricula in order to make them more reflective of diverse viewpoints, including research from, and about, societies that have been marginalised (Mano 2009; Wa Thiong'o 1992). These debates, particularly in Africa, are longstanding and have gone through periods where they flourished and waned. The 1960s, as decolonisation movements swept across the continent, accompanied by vibrant media and literature, was arguably one such period. And there is a similar urgency to the present debates and movements as populism rises and many are questioning whether globalisation has been working in their favour or simply aiding the wealthy and powerful. The most recent wave has been spurred on by protests in 2015 at the University of Cape Town, South Africa, which became known as #Rhodesmustfall for the Twitter hashtag that mobilised students. Originally centred around calls for taking down a statue of Cecil Rhodes at the university, the protest spread to other campuses and broadened to include calls for debate on racial transformation (and white privilege in particular), curriculum transformation (with a focus on de-Westernisation) and free access to university. This movement spread abroad, sparking debates at the University of Oxford (which had its own Cecil Rhodes statue) and the United States, where buildings at rich universities have often been named after their benefactors, despite their controversial history and source of the wealth, for example, as slave owners.

These calls to decolonise or 'internationalise' (Thussu 2009) media studies, and academia more generally, highlight a critical gap relevant to the media and conflict field of research. The current discourse by Western companies around efforts to connect the unconnected in conflict situations follows the trend in much of the literature on media and conflict to focus on questions about what 'outsiders' or international interventions may be able to do to stop the inflammatory role of media; what can be done to rebuild or reconstruct media systems after violence (media development), again typically with international support; or analysing the way in which media have contributed to fuelling violence or how certain programmes (often on radio or television) can be used to bridge societal divides.[6]

As this chapter has suggested, there are several areas where more interdisciplinary and particularly ethnographic research can offer critical insights into the very significant anticipated changes, and possibly complex impact, that rapid expansion of the internet will have in conflict-affected regions. A greater and more nuanced sensitivity on the part of both the technology companies and local public authorities to how technology will interact, including being reshaped or reinterpreted, is one aspect. As multinational companies take on unprecedented roles in providing the platforms for media and information, their involvement with critical issues relating to conflict, such as elections, remains underexamined, particularly in Africa. Greater attention to the variance of authorities in conflict situations, including the political ideologies and ways in which speech might be regulated beyond the state, will also support the development of more bottom-up approaches.

Nicole Stremlau is Head of the Programme in Comparative Media Law and Policy at the Centre for Socio-Legal Studies, University of Oxford. She is also Research Professor at the University of Johannesburg. Her research focuses on Africa and the Horn of Africa in particular. Her recent publications include *Media, Conflict and the State in Africa* (Cambridge University Press, 2018) and *Speech and Society in Turbulent Times* (coedited with Monroe Price) (Cambridge University Press, 2018).

Notes

1. This chapter draws on research that has been conducted by the author as part of the European Research Council ConflictNet project (grant agreement no. 716686). The author has undertaken extensive field research in Ethiopia, Kenya and the Somali territories. This chapter also takes forward findings from her field research that have been explored in *Media, Conflict and the State in Africa* (Stremlau 2018b), as well as various articles on Somalia that have been cited here.
2. The concept of 'the local', and what it means in research on peace and conflict, is contested. While the term has gained in prominence over the past decade, and organisations such as the World Bank and the UN often issue calls for greater local participation and input, it is often employed in a way that results in 'selective glorification', where certain aspects of what might be considered 'local' are decontextualised and idealised (Bräuchler and Naucke 2017: 432).
3. Facebook itself has acknowledged this and in April 2018 established an independent commission to study the effects of social media on democracy. This initiative is intended to be a new approach to partnerships between industry and academia (Schrage and Ginsberg 2018).
4. See e.g. the database on internet shutdowns around the world kept by Access Now (2018).
5. See e.g. the type of analysis produced by the National Union of Somali Journalists (2018).

6. The work by NGOs, such as Search for Common Ground (2018), is indicative of this type of approach.

References

Access Now. 2018. '#KeepItOn'. Retrieved 8 October 2019 from https://www.accessnow.org/keepiton.
Africa Power and Politics (APPP). 2018. 'About'. Retrieved 8 October 2019 from http://www.institutions-africa.org/page/about%2Bappp.html.
Allen, T., and J. Seaton (eds). 1999. *The Media of Conflict: War Reporting and Representations of Ethnic Violence*. London: Zed Books.
Betz, M., 2004. 'Radio as Peacebuilder: A Case Study of Radio Okapi in the Democratic Republic of Congo', *Great Lakes Research Journal* 1: 38–50.
Blumler, J.G., and M. Gurevitch. 1995. *The Crisis of Public Communication*. London: Psychology Press.
Booth, D. 2011. 'Introduction: Working with the Grain? The Africa Power and Politics Programme', *IDS Bulletin* 42(2): 1–10.
Bräuchler, B., and P. Naucke. 2017. 'Peacebuilding and Conceptualisations of the Local', *Social Anthropology* 25(4): 422–36.
Bridoux, J., and M. Kurki 2014. *Democracy Promotion: A Critical Introduction*. Oxford: Routledge.
Clapham, C.S. (ed.). 1998. *African Guerrillas*. Oxford: James Currey Publishers.
Diamond, L., and M.F. Plattner. 2012. *Liberation Technology: Social Media and the Struggle for Democracy*. Baltimore: Johns Hopkins University Press.
'Do Social Media Threaten Democracy?'. 2017. *The Economist*, 4 November. Retrieved 8 October 2019 from https://www.economist.com/news/leaders/21730871-facebook-google-and-twitter-were-supposed-save-politics-good-information-drove-out.
Eribo, F., and W. Jong-Ebot. 1997. *Press Freedom and Communication in Africa*. Trenton, NJ: Africa World Press.
'Facebook Founder in Colombia to Promote Affordable Internet'. 2015. *Business Times*, 15 January. Retrieved 8 October 2019 from http://www.businesstimes.com.sg/technology/facebook-founder-in-colombia-to-promote-affordable-internet.
Frenkle, S. 2018. 'Facebook to Pull Posts that Incite Violent Acts', *New York Times*, 19 July, B5.
Freedom House. 2017. 'Freedom of the Press 2017 Methodology'. Retrieved 8 October 2019 from https://freedomhouse.org/report/freedom-press-2017-methodology.
Freyburg, T., and L. Garbe. 2018. 'Blocking the Bottleneck: Internet Shutdowns and Ownership at Election Times in Sub-Saharan Africa', *International Journal of Communication* 12(2018): 1–12.

Gagliardone, I. 2016. *The Politics of Technology in Africa: Communication, Development, and Nation-Building in Ethiopia*. Cambridge: Cambridge University Press.

Gagliardone, I. et al. 2015. *Countering Online Hate Speech*. Paris: UNESCO.

———. 2016. *Mechachal: Online Debates and Elections in Ethiopia: From Hatespeech to Engagement in Social Media*. Oxford: PCMLP.

Hagmann, T., and M.V. Hoehne. 2009. 'Failures of the State Failure Debate: Evidence from the Somali Territories', *Journal of International Development* 21(1): 42–57.

Hallin, D.C., and P. Mancini. 2011. *Comparing Media Systems beyond the Western World*. Cambridge: Cambridge University Press.

Hume, T. 2017. 'Facebook is Worried about Fake News in Kenya's Election', *Vice News*, 4 August. Retrieved 9 October 2019 from https://news.vice.com/en_ca/article/zmy8ee/facebook-is-worried-about-fake-news-in-kenyas-election.

'ICT Sector Support in Somalia Phase II'. 2018. World Bank. Retrieved 9 October 2019 from http://projects.worldbank.org/P152358/?lang=en&tab=overview.

Irwin, C. 2002. *The People's Peace Process in Northern Ireland*. Basingstoke: Palgrave Macmillan.

Karanja, M., M. Xynou and A. Filastò. 2016. How the Ethiopia Protests Were Stifled by a Coordinated Internet Shutdown', *Quartz Africa*, 14 August. Retrieved 9 October 2019 from https://qz.com/757824/how-the-ethiopia-protests-were-stifled-by-a-coordinated-internet-shutdown.

Kwibuka, E. 2015. 'Democracy and Development Are Inseperable – Kagame', *New York Times*, 22 August. Retrieved 9 October 2019 from http://www.newtimes.co.rw/section/article/2015-08-22/191795.

Lefort, R. 2007. 'Powers – Mengist – and Peasants in Rural Ethiopia: The May 2005 Elections', *Journal of Modern African Studies* 45(2): 253–73.

'Legal ICT Framework Is Pivotal Moment for Somalia'. 2017. World Bank, 2 October. Retrieved 9 October 2019 from http://www.worldbank.org/en/news/feature/2017/10/02/legal-ict-framework-is-pivotal-moment-for-somalia.

Lewis, I.M., 1999. *A Pastoral Democracy: A Study of Pastoralism and Politics among the Northern Somali of the Horn of Africa*. Oxford: James Currey Publishers.

———. 2002. *A Modern History of the Somali: Nation and State in the Horn of Africa*. Athens: Ohio University Press.

Little, P.D. 2003. *Somalia: Economy without State*. Bloomington: Indiana University Press.

Loewenberg, S. 2006. 'United Nations Media Strategy: Recommendations for Improvement in Peacekeeping Operations'. *United Nations Department of Peacekeeping Operations Best Practices Unit*, 4.

Lovink, G. 2011. *Networks without a Cause: A Critique of Social Media*. Cambridge: Polity Press.

Lund, C. 2006. 'Twilight Institutions: Public Authority and Local Politics in Africa', *Development and Change* 37(4): 685–705.

Mano, W. 2009. 'Re-conceptualizing Media Studies in Africa', in D. Thussu (ed.), *Internationalizing Media Studies*. Oxford: Routledge, pp. 277–93.

Meagher, K. 2012. 'The Strength of Weak States? Non-state Security Forces and Hybrid Governance in Africa', *Development and Change* 43(5): 1073–101.

'Myanmar Activists Launch Anti-"Hate Speech" Campaign'. 2014. Thompson Reuters Foundation, 3 April. Retrieved 8 October 2019 from http://news.trust.org//item/20140403131148-4mqvg.

Morozov, E. 2012. *The Net Delusion: The Dark Side of Internet Freedom*. New York: Public Affairs.

———. 2013. *To Save Everything, Click Here: The Folly of Technological Solutionism*. New York: Public Affairs.

National Union of Somali Journalists. 2018. Retrieved 9 October 2019 from http://www.nusoj.org.

Orme, B. 2010. 'Broadcasting in UN Blue: The Unexamined Past and Uncertain Future of Peacekeeping Radio'. *Center for International Media Assistance*, 8 February. Retrieved 9 October 2019 from https://www.cima.ned.org/publication/broadcasting-in-un-blue-the-unexamined-past-and-uncertain-future-of-peacekeeping-radio.

Paluck, E.L. 2009. 'Reducing Intergroup Prejudice and Conflict Using the Media: A Field Experiment in Rwanda', *Journal of Personality and Social Psychology* 96(3): 574–87.

Paluck, E.L., and D.P. Green. 2009. 'Deference, Dissent, and Dispute Resolution: An Experimental Intervention Using Mass Media to Change Norms and Behavior in Rwanda', *American Political Science Review* 103(4): 622–44.

Pettit, J. 2013. *Power Analysis: A Practical Guide*. Stockholm: Swedish International Development Cooperation Agency. Retrieved 9 October 2019 from https://www.sida.se/contentassets/83f0232c5404440082c9762ba3107d55/power-analysis-a-practical-guide_3704.pdf.

Price, M., B. Rozumilowicz and S. Verhulst. 2003. *Media Reform: Democratizing the Media, Democratizing the State*. London: Routledge.

Price, M.E., and P. Krug. 2000. 'The Enabling Environment for Free and Independent Media', *Cardozo Law School Public Law Research Paper No. 27*. Retrieved 9 October 2019 from https://papers.ssrn.com/sol3/papers.cfm?abstract_id=245494.

Price, M. and M. Thompson (eds). 2002. *Forging Peace: Intervention, Human Rights, and the Management of Media Space*. Bloomington: Indiana University Press.

Roose, K. 2017. 'Forget Washington: Facebook's Problems Abroad Are Far More Disturbing', *New York Times*, 29 October. Retrieved 8 October 2019 from https://www.nytimes.com/2017/10/29/business/facebook-misinformation-abroad.html.

Schlee, G. 2013. 'Customary Law and the Joys of Statelessness: Idealised Traditions versus Somali Realities', *Journal of Eastern African Studies* 7(2): 258–71.

Schoemaker, E., and N. Stremlau. 2014. 'Media and Conflict: An Assessment of the Evidence', *Progress in Development Studies* 14(2): 181–95.

Schrage, E., and D. Ginsberg. 2018. 'Facebook Launches New Initiative to Help Scholars Assess Social Media's Impact on Elections'. Retrieved 9 October 2019 from https://newsroom.fb.com/news/2018/04/new-elections-initiative.

Search for Common Ground. 2018. Retrieved 9 October 2019 from https://www.sfcg.org.

Segreti, G. 2016. 'Facebook CEO Says Group Will Not Become a Media Company', *Reuters*, 29 August. Retrieved 8 October 2019 from https://www.reuters.com/article/us-facebook-zuckerberg-idUSKCN1141WN.

Shirky, C. 2011. 'The Political Power of Social Media', *Foreign Affairs* 90(1): 28–41.

Sikkink, K. 1991. *Ideas and institutions: Developmentalism in Brazil and Argentina*. Ithaca: Cornell University Press.

Stauffacher, D. et al. 2005. *Information and Communication Technology for Peace: The Role of ICT in Preventing, Responding to and Recovering from Conflict*, vol. 11. New York: United Nations Publications.

Stremlau, N. 2011. 'The Press and the Political Restructuring of Ethiopia', *Journal of Eastern African Studies* 5(4): 716–32.

———. 2012. 'Media Law in the Absence of a State'. *International Journal of Media and Cultural Politics* 8(2–3): 159–74.

———. 2018a. 'Law and Innovation in the Somali Territories', in B. Mutsvairo (ed.), *The Palgrave Handbook of Media and Communication Research in Africa*. London: Palgrave Macmillan, pp. 297–310.

———. 2018b. *Media, Conflict and the State in Africa*. Cambridge: Cambridge University Press.

Stremlau, N., and R. Osman. 2015. 'Courts, Clans and Companies: Mobile Money and Dispute Resolution in Somaliland', *Stability: International Journal of Security and Development* 4(1). Retrieved 9 October 2019 from http://doi.org/10.5334/sta.gh.

Stremlau, N., and M.E. Price. 2009. 'Media, Elections and Political Violence in Eastern Africa', *An Annenberg-Oxford Occasional Paper in Communications Policy Research*. Retrieved 9 October 2019 from http://global.asc.upenn.edu/fileLibrary/PDFs/PostelectionViolencereport.pdf.

Stremlau, N., I. Gagliardone and M.E. Price. 2018. *World Trends in Freedom of Expression and Media Development*. Paris: UNESCO.

Thussu, D. (ed.) 2009. *Internationalizing Media Studies*. Abingdon: Routledge.

Turton, D. 2006. *Ethnic Federalism: The Ethiopian Experience in Comparative Perspective*. Oxford: James Currey Publishers.

United Nations. n.d. 'Goal 9: Build Resilient Infrastructure, Promote Sustainable Industrialization and Foster Innovation'. Retrieved 9 October 2019 from https://www.un.org/sustainabledevelopment/infrastructure-industrialization.

UN General Assembly, Human Rights Council. 2016. Thirty-Second Session, Agenda Item 3, 'The Promotion, Protection and Enjoyment of Human Rights on the Internet', 27 June, oral revisions of 30 June. Retrieved 8 October 2019 from https://www.article19.org/data/files/Internet_Statement_Adopted.pdf.

'U.N. Investigators Cite Facebook Role in Myanmar Crisis'. 2018. *Reuters*, 12 March. Retrieved 8 October 2019 from https://www.reuters.com/article/us-myanmar-rohingya-facebook/u-n-investigators-cite-facebook-role-in-myanmar-crisis-idUSKCN1GO2PN.

Van Notten, M. 2005. *The Law of the Somalis: A Stable Foundation for Economic Development in the Horn of Africa*. Trenton: Red Sea Press.

Wa Thiong'o, N. 1992. *Decolonising the Mind: The Politics of Language in African Literature*. Nairobi: East African Publishers.

West, D.M. 2016. 'Internet Shutdowns Cost Countries $2.4 Billion Last Year', *Center for Technology Innovation at Brookings*, October. Retrieved 8 October 2019 from https://www.brookings.edu/wp-content/uploads/2016/10/intenet-shutdowns-v-3.pdf.

Zuckerberg, M. 2018. 'Bringing the World Closer Together'. Retrieved 8 October 2019 from https://www.facebook.com/notes/mark-zuckerberg/bringing-the-world-closer-together/10154944663901634.

PART II

Witnessing Conflict

CHAPTER 2

Just a 'Stupid Reflex'?

Digital Witnessing of the Charlie Hebdo *Attacks and the Mediation of Conflict*

Johanna Sumiala, Minttu Tikka and Katja Valaskivi

Witnessing with a Mobile Camera

A particularly significant and symbolic moment in the 2015 *Charlie Hebdo* attacks[1] was the killing of police officer Ahmed Merabet, a Muslim of Algerian origin. Merabet was in his forties when he was shot on 7 January 2015 by the Kouachi brothers, the two perpetrators of the attacks, while patrolling the neighbourhood near the *Charlie Hebdo* newspaper office. This shooting soon became the most visible testimony to the violence of these attacks. First gunned down to the ground, Merabet was then killed by a gunshot to the head.

A key witness to Merabet's killing was an accidental bystander, Jordi Mir, who was at home sending emails when the sound of gunshots interrupted him and drew him to the window. As an accidental eyewitness, Mir captured the shooting on his mobile phone and uploaded the video to Facebook. He later testified in an exclusive interview with the *Associated Press* (Satter 2015) that, at first, he had no idea what he was documenting on his phone; the thought of a bank robbery crossed his mind. When the police arrived on the scene, he handed over his amateur video as a piece of recorded eyewitness material. In the interview, Mir expressed regret about his decision to post the video online. He removed it from his Facebook page, on which he had 2,500 friends, only fifteen minutes later, but he could not prevent its circulation in the digital media environment. According to the *Associated Press*, someone picked up the video and uploaded it to YouTube. Less than an hour after he had taken down the video, Mir saw it broadcast on television (for a full account of the *Associated Press* interview, see Satter (2015)). This was the first step and prerequisite of the complex dynamics of digital witnessing in the global media in the case of Merabet's killing in the *Charlie Hebdo* attacks.

In this chapter, we analyse digital witnessing as a media-oriented practice (Couldry 2004) and examine how Jordi Mir's amateur piece of digital witnessing and related responses in digital media shaped the *Charlie Hebdo* attacks as a violent media event triggered by religiously inspired terrorist fury (see Sumiala et al. 2018). By media-oriented practices, we refer to Nick Couldry's (2004) work on media as practice and offer a practice-centred reading of the *Charlie Hebdo* attacks as a violent media event (Sumiala et al. 2018). In his approach, Couldry (2004: 117) focuses specifically on 'the open set of practices relating to, or oriented around, media'. Instead of looking at media as a text or a process of production, he theorises on how people orient their lives towards media. Although media-oriented, this type of adaptation towards media, Couldry maintains (2012), does not happen without human agency. Hence, it should not be perceived as a deterministic process that is simply defined by the latest developments in media technology. This said, he advances a media-oriented practice theory to better grasp its non-media-centric character. According to this line of thought, human agency, as something that is socially formed, is credited for its individual and collective abilities to create and modify social lives lived in relation to practices that are relevant for media. However, these practices are not created in a vacuum; they should be viewed in connection to the categorisation and ordering in which media are deeply involved (see e.g. Couldry 2012: 33–58; on further discussions of media-oriented and media-related practices, see also Bräuchler and Budka, this volume; Bräuchler and Postill 2010; Couldry and Hobart 2010: 77–82; Hobart 2010).

In this chapter, we elaborate Couldry's (2004) argument and maintain that media-oriented practices play, not a deterministic but a nonetheless privileged, role in anchoring people in violent media events and shape their social construction as events of conflict (Sumiala et al. 2018). This is how media-oriented practices also contribute to people's lived experiences in the context of the *Charlie Hebdo* attacks (see also Bräuchler and Budka, this volume). Furthermore, media-oriented practices impose media event power (Rojek 2013) – that is, the idea of media (event) as the centre of society in mediating conflicts and, consequently, as creating mediated communities around such violent incidents of global appeal (see Couldry 2003). In the age of digital media, this myth of media centrality can also be discussed as 'a myth of us' (Couldry 2015). In this myth, digital media – namely, social media – is established as a 'natural' access point for social participation in such violent conflicts.

Daniel Dayan and Elihu Katz, who developed media event theory in 1992, argue that a media event is a special genre that is powerful enough to interrupt the everyday media flow, bring the viewer in touch with society's central values and invite the audience to participate in the event (Dayan and Katz 1992: 5–9). In their lexicon, media events have (a) their own grammar, (b) their own meaning structure (story form or script) and (c) their own practices characterised by live broadcasting: the interruption of daily media rhythms and routines, the scripting and advance preparation of the event, a huge audience (the 'whole world' is watching; see e.g. Gitlin 2003), social and normative expectations attached to viewing ('must see'), the ceremonial tone of media narration and the intention to connect people through this experience of shared viewing (see also Scannell 1996). Dayan and Katz (1992) indicate that the significance of media events lies in their ability to reach a larger audience than any event that requires physical presence. In so doing, they take the question of a media event pointing beyond itself to a new media saturation level. From their perspective, the audience is well aware of this as they follow the unfolding media event in different locations, which may be private, semi-public or public, local, national or transnational, and even global.

Today, the debate on media events is very much alive, and new theoretical angles are being introduced into the discussion around those spectacular moments of history in which something exceptional and unique breaks the flow of ordinary and mundane life and calls for mediated participation (see e.g. Sonnevend 2016). Today, many scholars of media events agree that while the media environment has changed radically since the time of Dayan and Katz's original work, the interest in making and shaping media events, whether ceremonial and/or disruptive in nature, remains undiminished. The phenomenon of the media event still exists in the contemporary social reality and can be studied as a category that has been reformed in the context of digital media.

Currently, the research on media events is placing more emphasis on the growing role of new global communication technology in enabling today's media events and on the complex relationships between the actors and media platforms involved in making and participating in those events on a global scale (Vaccari, Chadwick and O'Loughlin

2015). These changing conditions also pose a major challenge for rethinking not only what today's media events are, but what they do in telling the story of 'us' and 'them' in these global high moments of ceremony and/or disruption (for a more detailed discussion of contemporary media events, see e.g. Sonnevend 2016; Sumiala et al. 2018).

Thus, we investigated digital witnessing as a practice oriented towards a media event and examined how, by whom and with what kinds of implications for digital media witnessing was undertaken in the case of the *Charlie Hebdo* attacks. We assert that the practices of digital witnessing in this case are profoundly embedded in implementations of visuality and related visibility in conflict (see also Bräuchler and Budka, Kummels, and Meis, this volume). These practices of digital witnessing include: (a) taking videos and pictures on mobile phone cameras; (b) sharing these testimonies online via a range of different media platforms; (c) remediating such testimonies from social media to online news media and vice versa; and (d) morally engaging with such witnessing by commenting, negotiating and critiquing testimonies (Bruns and Hanusch 2017; Chouliaraki 2015; Mortensen 2015a). Furthermore, these practices are most frequently adopted by ordinary media users, such as Jordi Mir; hence, we discuss digital witnessing in this chapter primarily within the framework of amateur digital witnessing (see e.g. Chouliaraki 2010, 2015; Mortensen 2015a; see also the chapters by Meis and Mollerup, this volume).

In our analysis, we applied a digital media ethnographic approach to study the practices related to the digital witnessing of the *Charlie Hebdo* attacks as a violent media event. We carried out fieldwork on several online media platforms, including such online news media as the *New York Times*, *Le Monde*, *The Guardian*, the BBC and CNN and such social media sites as Twitter, YouTube and Facebook. The internet fieldwork was conducted between 2015 and 2017.[2]

This chapter is divided into four sections. First, we provide a theoretical outline of the idea of media witnessing as a media-oriented practice in a violent media event. Second, we briefly discuss our methodological approach (i.e. digital media ethnography) and its implications for analysing the digital witnessing of this media event. Third, we present an empirical examination of the practices related to the digital witnessing of this media event in the case of the killing of police officer Ahmed Merabet. Fourth, we conclude by reflecting on how digital witnessing as a media-oriented practice contributed to the mediation of conflict in the *Charlie Hebdo* attacks as a violent media event.

On Witnessing Violent Media Events

Recent theories of media witnessing of violent media events connected to conflict, war and disaster centre on three key debates. The first and most conventional debate addresses the issue of eyewitnessing versus media witnessing (see e.g. Frosh and Pinchevski 2009a, 2009b; Ong 2014; Peters 2001, 2009). The key aspect concerns the distinction between eyewitnessing – that is, physical presence or 'being there' in both time and space at a violent event (Mortensen 2015a: 14–17) – and witnessing violent events 'vicariously' (Ashuri and Pinchevski 2009: 133–35) in and via the media. Following the insight of communication philosopher John Durham Peters (2001: 720), compared to eyewitnessing, media witnessing can be organised into three subcategories: (a) witnessing of live transmissions of violent events (present in time, but removed in space); (b) media witnessing related to mediated historical events associated with violent events (present in space, but removed in time); and (c) media witnessing that contributes to the witnessing of recorded violent events (removed in time and space) (see Mortensen 2015a: 16; for a divergent discussion on media and place-making, see also Mollerup, this volume). Another question related to eyewitnessing versus media witnessing violent events concerns the issue of who counts as a legitimate witness of such events. Given journalists' traditional task of witnessing the world's violent events through conventional news reporting, much of the research on media witnessing and violent events has focused on journalism (e.g. Zelizer 2002, 2007, 2010). However, in recent years, more research has been conducted on ordinary people's media witnessing (see e.g. Chouliaraki 2006, 2015; Gregory 2015; see also the chapters by Markham and Meis, this volume).

The second debate on media witnessing concerns the meaning of media representations as witnessing evidence during violent events. Tamar Ashuri and Amit Pinchevski (2009) introduce the concept of 'vicarious witnessing' as 'indirect' witnessing. They expand the idea of witnessing and argue that, in addition to human testimonies, media representations can provide testimonies about violent events (see also Frosh and Pinchevski 2009b). In this interpretation, visual media, such as film, TV news clips, YouTube videos and mobile videos, play an important role in providing pictorial testimonies of such events (see also Mortensen 2015a).

Finally, the third, most recent, thread in theorising media witnessing of violent events is linked to the role and place of the audience in such events. John Ellis' (2000) work on 'mundane witnessing' is particularly relevant here. Ellis (2000) underlines witnessing as an everyday practice carried out on our TV screens. The role of the audience in mundane witnessing is to passively consume news of violent events including conflicts, war and terror. As mentioned previously, more recently, ordinary citizens' use of visual mobile technologies, such as mobile cameras, to record videos and images has gained increasing interest among scholars theorising about witnessing in the digital condition (e.g. Allan 2013; Andén-Papadopoulos 2013; Chouliaraki 2015). The idea of amateur digital witnessing (e.g. Andén-Papdopoulos 2013; Chouliaraki 2015; Mortensen 2015a, 2015b) has been developed to better address these new aspects in the present-day mediated witnessing of violent events. This new condition has shifted the categories of media witnessing production, representation and reception in new ways. It has also challenged the idea of a passive audience and has invited scholars (see Peters 2001, 2009) to view audience members as potentially active participants (and witnesses) in today's violent events. As Mette Mortensen (2015a: 16) describes, while television and journalism have the capacity to turn media viewers into witnesses, digital media has turned witnesses into producers of witnesses.

Lilie Chouliaraki (2015: 1364–65) argues that this rise in ordinary media users as witnesses in digital media has had at least two implications for the issue of truth value in violent events. First, the development of ordinary media users as witnessing agents has broken the professional monopoly of news and journalism as the only legitimate producers of media witnessing. This has democratised media witnessing and has made it a more explicitly bottom-up activity (i.e. from ordinary people to professional media institutions). It can be considered a fragile practice that gives suffering a human face through the voice of an ordinary media witness. Second, questions of doubt emerge. This disbelief associated with ordinary media users' truthfulness as witnesses relates both to their motivations and to the doubt associated with digital technologies as tools that ordinary people apply for witnessing. The use of such technologies (e.g. mobile cameras) and digital media practices (e.g. the instant circulation of visual evidence in digital media) have also been criticised for dehumanising the process of witnessing and the victims to whose suffering they provide witness. From this perspective, the digital contents of witnessing have been critiqued for concealing more truth than they reveal (Chouliaraki 2015: 1365; see also Meis, this volume).

In the following, we demonstrate how we applied these theoretical ideas regarding digital witnessing in our empirical analysis. In particular, we explore: (a) how amateur digital witnessing worked as a media-oriented practice in the *Charlie Hebdo* attacks as a violent media event; (b) the role of visual representations as vicarious pieces of witnessing the violent event; (c) how amateur practices of digital witnessing are connected to professional news media; and (d) the implications of digital witnessing for mediating the *Charlie Hebdo* attacks as a violent media event and the social construction of victimhood in this event.

Digital Media Ethnography

In this chapter, we discuss the application of digital media ethnography as an interdisciplinary research approach to studying digital witnessing as a media-oriented practice surrounding a violent media event. Digital media ethnography typically draws on digitally oriented media anthropology and internet studies inspired by digital sociology (see e.g. Boyer 2012; Hine 2015; Postill and Pink 2012). As a research site, we considered the digital media dispersed across the internet, which is best characterised as a fluid research environment for conducting fieldwork (Postill and Pink 2012: 125). We tracked and traced practices of digital witnessing on several digital media platforms and gave special attention to those practices that travelled across these platforms. Our objective in following this flow of practices was to grasp circulations between different actors (witnessing agents and their audiences) and media representations (witnessing pieces). Our research approach thus owes much to Latour's (2005) work emphasising the complex interplay between human and nonhuman agency and the practices created in those encounters. We argue that this research orientation enabled us to better explore the 'messy web' (Hine 2015: 13; Postill and Pink 2012: 125), the ways in which media-oriented practices – and specifically digital witnessing – are carried out in the present digital environment, and how the actors, actions and messages of witnessing circulate and are made meaningful in the digital context (see also Hine 2015: 1–6). We took field notes, provided documentation (e.g. on newspaper articles and tweets) and recorded data (e.g. YouTube videos addressing Mir's video) using the various digital technological means available. In our empirical work, we saved links and took screenshots and printouts. We followed and traced various digital platforms, including the websites of *The Guardian*, the *New York Times* and *Le Monde*, as well as Twitter, Facebook and YouTube. In addition, we followed Mir's video and such actors as Mir himself, Merabet's family members (namely, his brother, mother and spouse) and politicians (e.g. François Hollande) via their media representations.[3] The analysed period covered the vivid circulation of the event via digital media from Mir's eyewitness of Merabet's killing on 7 January 2015 until the reporting of Merabet's public funeral on 11 January. However, the timeframe of the digital media ethnography concerning the debates surrounding Merabet's death was much longer, spanning 2015 to 2017. The first phase of the project was during the attacks, but the remaining phases began six months after the attacks took place, when the big data material of more than five million tweets was gathered. As fieldworkers of digital media, we acknowledge the fluid nature of our research sites and recognise that some materials may have disappeared between the first and subsequent phases of the ethnographic fieldwork. By visiting and revisiting our digital sites of research, we aimed to gather the different testimonial layers constructed around the digital witnessing of the given violent media event.

Shooting Merabet's Killing on Video as Digital Witnessing

A key practice of digital witnessing of the *Charlie Hebdo* attacks was Mir's graphic testimony (in the form of a video clip) of Merabet's shooting. For this witnessing act to take place, many ordinary, almost banal, details had to align. For example, had Mir (or someone else) not been at home at the time of the attacks, Merabet's killing would have been left unrecorded. What oriented this act of witnessing (i.e. shooting a video on a mobile camera) towards the media was that it resonated with other practices typical of social media use. It has become common practice to record events and incidents on mobile cameras and then share them on social media (see e.g. Meikle 2016). In this sense, Mir's actions perfectly fit the logic of social media and its related search for attention and the spectacular. Mir himself later described in news media interviews that his actions had been motivated by a 'stupid reflex' (Satter 2015): an almost automatised practice. The spectacular oddity of witnessing a police officer being killed on the street in the middle of the day caught Mir's attention and he immediately began to film it (see also Mortensen 2015a).

A deeper analysis of Mir's action as a media-oriented practice of witnessing raised the question of the motivation behind this act of witnessing. Initially, Mir did not know what he was filming; thus, he was an unintentional witness. However, he did not carry out his subsequent actions by accident. He gave the material to the police and put it into circulation. These actions made his video a precarious piece of witnessing representation (Ashuri and Pinchevski 2009), and although he later removed the video from his Facebook page, his actions could not be undone. The video immediately went viral and began to circulate on social media platforms, including YouTube, Twitter and Facebook, and the websites of various news media, including the *New York Times*, Reuters and *The Guardian*. The following day, a picture of Merabet being shot in the head appeared on the front pages of *The Times*, the *Daily Telegraph*, the *New York Times*, the *Daily Mirror*, *The Sun*, the *Daily Mail* and other newspapers. The Associated Press described the reactions in the global news media as follows: 'The video unleashed a worldwide wave of revulsion.' British tabloids described it as 'shocking' and 'sickening'. France's *Le Figaro* ran a still from the footage on its front page over a caption reading 'War'. CNN's Randi Kaye called it 'an unforgettable image forever associated with this horrible attack' (Satter 2015).

Due to his unique position as a key witness to Merabet's death, Mir also gained considerable publicity in the aftermath of the attacks. This can be interpreted as another example of how digital witnessing is connected with other media-oriented practices in a violent media event. We may call this the celebrification of digital witnessing of today's media events. Mir was interviewed by various news media outlets, but his actions were also criticised in and by the digital public, making his status somewhat ambivalent and challenging his position as a 'morally pure' digital witness to Merabet's suffering and death. We will return to this issue and examine it in more detail when we discuss the fourth media-oriented practice of digital witnessing: moral engagement.

Sharing and Circulating Visual Evidence

The second media-oriented practice in the digital witnessing of Merabet's death was created around the sharing and circulation of Mir's video as a piece of visual evidence of this media event. To function as an object of digital witnessing and have moral meaning for the public, this piece of vicarious witnessing (Ashuri and Pinhevski 2009) had to be given a narrative framework. This task was undertaken primarily by the online news media and professional journalists. Many national and international online news media outlets created storylines around Merabet's life. They stated that he had grown up in Livry-Gargan in the northeastern suburbs of Paris and graduated from the local *lycée* in 1995. *Paris Match* reported that Merabet's father, Kaddour, had migrated from Algeria to France in 1955 and that his mother, Houria, had migrated in 1962 (Lallement 2015). Merabet was said to have fulfilled his responsibility as the family's eldest son to look after his mother and siblings after his father's death. Like many other newspapers, *Le Figaro* (Mareschal 2015) portrayed Merabet and his family as good, hard-working citizens. He was praised as a devoted officer who worked hard to earn promotions in the police force. Malek, Merabet's brother, described him in a 10 January news story in *The Guardian* as follows: 'Through sheer determination he had recently passed the CID [Criminal Investigation Department] entrance exam and was due to come off the beat. His colleagues describe him as a man of action who was passionate about his job' (Graham-Harrison 2015).

The online news stories associated with this witness portrayed Merabet as a good man, a Muslim, a police officer and a French citizen. He was said to have come from a relatively humble Maghreb Muslim background in one of the *banlieues* of Paris. He nonetheless carved out a life for himself as a son, partner, brother and respected colleague, and died defending the very people who offended his religion. His tragic fate was to die only one day before he was due to be promoted to detective, which would have relieved him of his patrolling duties. In short, the online news media portrayed Merabet as a tragic, masculine, Muslim hero – a dramatic contrast to the killers, who were depicted as bad Muslims. In other words, the news media narrativised Merabet's life into a heroic story of a good Muslim who had not only adjusted to French society but had even internalised its (secular) values. As *The Guardian* reported, Malek, who became a prominent witness to his brother's character as a good Muslim and French citizen, described Merabet as follows:

> My brother was Muslim, and he was killed by two terrorists, by two false Muslims, he said. Islam is a religion of peace and love. As far as my brother's death is concerned, it was a waste. He was very proud of the name Ahmed Merabet, proud to represent the police and of defending the values of the Republic: liberty, equality, fraternity. (Graham-Harrison 2015)

Merabet's partner, Morgane Ahmad, also appeared in public to comment on his fate. The family's message called for calm and unity, and their comments, statements and interviews were circulated from one news media platform to another. In Ahmad's words published in *The Guardian*: 'What the family and I want is for everyone to be united. We want everyone to be able to demonstrate in peace. We want to show respect for all the victims and that the demonstration should be peaceful' (Graham-Harrison 2015).

As a media-oriented practice of digital witnessing, the sharing and circulating of vicarious witnessing played an important role not only in telling the truth about what had happened to Merabet but also in providing a broader narrative frame for what Merabet's death meant and how the audience should morally engage with and respond to it in the digital media. Here, the online news media took over social media and, in so doing, began to give the digital witnessing of Merabet's death global attention (e.g. Sumiala et al. 2018). Thus, as a ritualistic and symbolic practice, digital witnessing sustained the social meaning of this mediated conflict and helped participants anchor the moral framework of this globally mediated community momentarily established around digital media.

'#JesuisAhmed': Remediation in Digital Witnessing

The wide circulation and sharing of the video of Merabet's killing is closely connected with the third media-oriented practice of digital witnessing: remediation (Bolter and Grusin 1998) of the digital witnessing of Merabet's death. Here, the initial emphasis was on social media. On Twitter in particular, the public, who had become morally engaged with Merabet's death, began to react to this testimony by expressing sentiments of collective mourning over the conflict. Different versions of the slogan, hashtag and message *Je suis Charlie* ('I am Charlie'), the most-tweeted message in the immediate aftermath after the attacks (Sumiala et al. 2018), were converted into the slogan and hashtag *Je suis Ahmed* ('I am Ahmed') and widely circulated on different platforms.

A particular tweet received significant attention. It stated: 'I am not Charlie. I am Ahmed the dead cop. Charlie ridiculed my faith and culture, and I died defending his right to do so. #JesuisAhmed' (@Aboujahjah, 8 January 2015). This tweet became one of the most retweeted messages after the attacks and signalled explicit solidarity over Merabet and what he represented as a Muslim and a French citizen. The *Daily Mail* offered the following headline: 'He died defending the right to ridicule his faith: France unites behind #JesuisAhmed on Twitter in tribute to Muslim officer slain by fanatics as he begged for his life' (Bentley et al. 2015). The story described how thousands of people paid tribute to the dead Muslim police officer by using the rallying cry 'Je suis Ahmed' in street demonstrations and on Twitter and interpreted these activities as expressions of admiration for Merabet's sacrifice while defending the right to freedom of speech. The story also reproduced several tweets to illustrate these performances of solidarity.

The *New York Times* interpreted the expressions of solidarity around 'Je suis Ahmed' by stating that 'users praised him as a hero and, in some cases, a potent symbol in the debate about free speech and religious tolerance' (Breeden 2015).

The remediation of digital witnessing in this violent media event can be interpreted as a media-oriented practice that determined the value of Merabet's death and made him a symbolically significant victim in this mediated conflict. The remediation of digital witnessing also provided means for the audience to morally engage with Merabet's death and demonstrate solidarity in posting such tweets as 'Je suis Ahmed' and related versions. The practice of remediation in digital witnessing thus resonates with other media-oriented practices, such as ritualised mourning (Sumiala 2013), which also confirms moral norms and what can be called 'appropriate' ways of responding to such violence in real-time violent media events carried out in digital contexts.

Moral Engagement: Controversy over the Digital Witnessing

As discussed earlier in this chapter, Chouliaraki (2015) maintains that digital witnessing paradoxically both humanises and dehumanises death and suffering in violent media events. The fourth media-oriented practice in the digital witnessing of Merabet's death as part of a violent media event involved moral debates triggered by the very act of the witnessing of the shooting. In particular, Mir's position as a key eyewitness became publicly contested. Mir's video clip and related still images of Merabet's killing deeply disturbed and upset Merabet's family. Morgane Ahmad, Merabet's partner, testified on *BBC News* (10 January 2015) that she had first learned of her partner's death on television, although she did not recognise him in the video: 'I was in a restaurant and a television was on … I didn't recognise him. I only saw the picture of a man on the pavement. I tried to call him, sent messages. I went back to work, and then his sister called me.' In interviews, Mir responded to the critique and apologised to the family and the general public for sharing his video on social media. As a *Time* headline printed on 11 January 2015 states: 'Man who filmed terrorists shooting Paris cop says he regrets sharing video' (Linshi 2015). In his first interview with the *Associated Press*, Mir described his actions as a 'stupid reflex':

> 'I was completely panicked', he said in an exclusive interview across from the Parisian boulevard where the officer was shot to death by terrorists

Wednesday morning. ... 'I had to speak to someone', Mir said. 'I was alone in my flat. I put the video on Facebook. That was my error'. Later in the same interview, he reflects on his decision to publish the video as part of the wider social media culture: 'There's no answer', he [Mir] said. (Satter 2015)

The journalist interviewer commented as follows:

> Perhaps a decade of social networking had trained him to share whatever he saw. 'I take a photo – a cat – and I put it on Facebook. It was the same stupid reflex', he said. ... 'On Facebook, there's no confidentiality', he said. 'It's a lesson for me.' (Satter 2015)

In this public disapproval of Mir's actions (concerning his decision to publicly share his video), the main concern was Mir's moral reliability. He was accused not of not telling the truth about Merabet's death, but of seeking questionable attention in doing so. In putting the video of Merabet's killing into digital circulation, Mir also contributed to the public exposure of Merabet's body, thereby robbing him of his dignity as a dying human being. From this perspective, it is worth noting that digital witnessing as a practice (carried out here by Mir) can also become a morally questionable public practice if it is too closely associated with other media-oriented practices (e.g. self-promotion) that enforce the power of media events in social life (Couldry 2003).

Digital Witnessing and the Issue of Mediating Conflict in a Violent Media Event

In this chapter, we endeavoured to demonstrate how media-oriented practices of digital witnessing, such as taking pictures, sharing and circulating visual evidence, remediating digital witnessing and morally engaging with the digital witnessing of Ahmed Merabet's death played a part in shaping people's lived experience of the conflict (Bräuchler and Budka, this volume) and contributed to the mediation of the *Charlie Hebdo* attacks as a violent media event. There are three insights that we wish to discuss in our conclusions. The first concerns the finding that digital witnessing in this violent media event, particularly with respect to Ahmed Merabet's death, was experienced and carried out in a complex web of communicative networks involving amateur digital witnesses, witnessing representations and the dynamics between online professional news media and social media.

The second observation involves the relationship between digital witnessing and the mediation of this violent media event. We argue that the digital witnessing of Ahmed Merabet's killing during the *Charlie Hebdo* attacks played an important role in shaping the social construction of victimhood in this violent media event triggered by religiously inspired terrorist violence. In digital witnessing, these two aspects are strongly related. Without Mir's action, there would be no visual evidence of Merabet's death; however, it was the practice of circulating and sharing this visual evidence that provided the narrative frame necessary for the remediation of the digital witnessing and related solidarity to emerge in the event. Elsewhere (Sumiala et al. 2018), we have argued that Merabet's body became a 'mediating, masculine, Muslim body' in the digital construction of this violent event; thus, it was used to minimise the explicit conflict between the narrative of the 'radical, terrorist Islam' and the 'peaceful, secular, West'. The digital witnessing of Merabet's death was central in this process.

Third, we wish to reflect on our findings concerning digital witnessing as a media-oriented practice and how it impacts the power that a media event wields and the idea of the media as an imagined centre of society (e.g. Couldry 2003) and, hence, its conflicts. The filming of Merabet's killing and subsequently sharing and circulation of the video on various digital media platforms make a case for what Mortensen (2015b) calls 'connective witnessing', in which eyewitnessing and media witnessing as media-oriented practices become closely connected through the actions of a witness — in our analysis, Jordi Mir, an ordinary bystander. While this action can be seen as humanising Merabet's suffering and taking digital witnessing to the level of ordinary people (i.e. not monopolised by professional journalism), it also gives rise to suspicions. Such reservations concern the moral position and motivation of the amateur witness, in the logic of contemporary digitally saturated violent media events, as well as the moral implications of circulating the visual evidence of the killing in question. We may argue that the logic of digital witnessing in the mobile and rapid digital circulation of today's violent media events not only calls for the 'right to look' but also makes it difficult to avoid bearing witness to such events, creating an 'obligation to be seen' (Chouliaraki 2015: 4). Hence, we may acknowledge that such media-oriented practices of digital witnessing of violent media events involve an element of exploitation. Thus, amateur digital witnessing of the killing of victims is never an innocent or singular practice; it is always embedded in broader questions of the power of violent media events to mediate conflicts in the current age of digital saturation.

Johanna Sumiala is Associate Professor of Media and Communication Studies at the University of Helsinki. She is an expert in the fields of media sociology and media anthropology, digital media ethnography and visual culture. She has recently published articles on mediated violence and ritualised online communication, and she coauthored the book *Hybrid Media Events: The Charlie Hebdo Attacks and the Global Circulation of Terrorist Violence* (Emerald, 2018) with Katja Valaskivi, Minttu Tikka and Jukka Huhtamäki.

Minttu Tikka is finalising her doctoral thesis in media and communication studies at the University of Helsinki. Her fields of interest include research on digital witnessing, mediated crises and disasters and social media, online news and digital media ethnography.

Katja Valaskivi is Associate Professor of the Study of Religions at the University of Helsinki. She has published widely on the issues of media and social theory, violent media events and the circulation of emotions in digital media. The title of her most recent book is *Traces of Fukushima: Global Events, Networked Media and Circulating Emotions* (Palgrave Macmillan, 2019), coauthored with Anna Rantasila, Mikihito Tanaka and Risto Kunelius.

Notes

1. The *Charlie Hebdo* attack was initiated on Wednesday 7 January 2015 by French-Algerian brothers Saïd and Chérif Kouachi, who killed twelve people purportedly as an act of jihadist terrorism (e.g. Kepel 2017; Roy 2016; Titley 2017). The police organised a massive manhunt that attracted considerable media attention not only in national and international news media but also on social media, including Twitter, Facebook and YouTube. As events unfolded, another perpetrator, Amedy Coulibaly, surfaced and connected his assault of a kosher supermarket with the Kouachi brothers' terrorist mission. The manhunt ended on 9 January, when French police killed all three perpetrators after two deadly hostage situations.
2. The empirical material of this chapter draws on research carried out in two research projects conducted as part of a collaboration between the University of Helsinki and the University of Tampere. The first (already concluded) project, 'Je Suis Charlie: The Symbolic Battle and Struggle over Attention' (2015–17), was funded by Helsingin Sanomat, and the second (ongoing) project, 'Hybrid Terrorizing: Developing a New Model for the Study of Global Media Events of Terrorist Violence' (2017–21), is funded by the Academy of Finland. The third partner in the 'Hybrid Terrorizing' project is the National Defence University in Finland.
3. We gained access to Twitter data through a third-party social media analytics service called Pulsar. The data were collected using three search and filtering

criteria: search terms, time window and language. All tweets collected were sent between 7 and 16 January 2015. The phrases and hashtags gathered included 'je suis charlie', 'je ne suis pas charlie', 'je suis ahmed', #jesuischarlie, #jenesuispascharlie and #jesuisahmed. All selected tweets were written in English, French or Arabic. The total number of tweets was 5.2 million, of which 1.5 million were original tweets and the rest retweets.

References

Aboujahjah. 2015. Retrieved 11 October 2019 from https://twitter.com/aboujahjah/status/553169081424420864?lang=en.
Alexander, H. 2015. 'Funeral for French Policeman Ahmed Merabet Held in Paris', *The Telegraph*, 11 January. Retrieved 11 October 2019 from http://www.telegraph.co.uk/news/worldnews/europe/france/11338404/Funeral-for-French-policeman-Ahmed-Merabet-held-in-Paris.html.
Allan, S. 2013. *Citizen Witnessing: Revisioning Journalism in Times of Crisis*. Cambridge: Polity Press.
Andén-Papadopoulos, K. 2013. 'Media Witnessing and the "Crowd-Sourced Video Revolution"', *Visual Communication* 12(3): 341–57.
Ashuri, T., and A. Pinchevski. 2009. 'Witnessing as a Field', in P. Frosh and A. Pinchevski (eds), *Media Witnessing: Testimony in the Age of Mass Communication*. Basingstoke: Palgrave Macmillan, pp. 133–57.
Bentley, P. et al. 2015. '"He Died Defending the Right to Ridicule His Faith": France Unites behind #JeSuisAhmed on Twitter in Tribute to Muslim Officer Slain by Fanatics as He Begged for His Life', *Daily Mail*, 8 January. Retrieved 10 October 2019 from http://www.dailymail.co.uk/news/article-2901081/Hero-police-officer-executed-street-married-42-year-old-Muslim-assigned-patrol-Paris-neighbourhood-Charlie-Hebdo-offices-located.html.
Bolter, J., and R. Grusin. 1999. *Remediation: Understanding New Media*. Cambridge, MA: MIT Press.
Boyer, D. 2012. 'From Media Anthropology to the Anthropology of Mediation', in R. Fardon et al. (eds), *The Sage Handbook of Social Anthropology*. London: Sage, pp. 411–22.
Breeden, A. 2015. 'Alongside "Je Suis Charlie", Slain Officer Inspires His Own Social Media Refrain', *New York Times*, 8 January. Retrieved 10 October 2019 from https://www.nytimes.com/2015/01/09/world/europe/charlie-hebdo-terror-attack-je-suis-ahmed-merabet.html.
Bruns, A., and F. Hanusch. 2017. 'Conflict Imagery in a Connective Environment: Audiovisual Content on Twitter Following the 2015/2016 Terror Attacks in Paris and Brussels', *Media, Culture & Society* 39(8): 1122–41.
Bräuchler, B., and J. Postill (eds). 2010. *Theorising Media and Practice*. New York: Berghahn Books.
Chouliaraki, L. 2006. *The Spectatorship of Suffering*. London: Sage.

———. 2010. 'Ordinary Witnessing in Post-television News: Towards a New Moral Imagination', *Critical Discourse Studies* 7(4): 305–19.
———. 2015. 'Digital Witnessing in Conflict Zones: The Politics of Remediation', *Information, Communication & Society* 18(11): 1362–77.
Couldry, N. 2003. *Media Rituals: A Critical Approach*. London: Routledge.
———. 2004. 'Theorising Media as Practice', *Social Semiotics* 14(2): 115–32.
———. 2012. *Media, Society, World: Social Theory and Digital Media Practice*. Cambridge: Polity Press.
———. 2015. 'The Myth of "Us": Digital Networks, Political Change and the Production of Collectivity', *Information, Communication & Society* 18(6): 608–26.
Couldry, N., and M. Hobart. 2010. 'Media as Practice: A Brief Exchange', in B. Bräuchler and J. Postill (eds), *Theorising Media and Practice*. New York: Berghahn Books, pp. 77–82.
Dayan, D., and E. Katz. 1992. *Media Events: The Live History of Broadcasting*. Cambridge, MA: Harvard University Press.
Ellis, J. 2000. *Seeing Things: Television in the Age of Uncertainty*. London: I.B. Tauris.
Frosh, P., and A. Pinchevski. 2009a. 'Crisis-Readiness and Media Witnessing', *Communication Review* 12(3): 295–304.
———. (eds). 2009b. *Media Witnessing: Testimony in the Age of Mass Communication*. Basingstoke: Palgrave Macmillan.
Gitlin, T. 2003. *The Whole World is Watching: Mass Media in the Making and Unmaking of the New Left*. Berkeley: California University Press.
Graham-Harrison, E. 2015. 'Paris Policeman's Brother: "Islam is a Religion of Love. My Brother Was Killed by Terrorists, by False Muslims"', *The Guardian*, 10 January. Retrieved 10 October 2019 from https://www.theguardian.com/world/2015/jan/10/charlie-hebdo-policeman-murder-ahmed-merabet.
Gregory, S. 2015. 'Ubiquitous Witnesses: Who Creates the Evidence and the Live(d) Experience of Human Rights Violations', *Information, Communication & Society* 18(11): 1378–92.
Hine, C. 2015. *Ethnography for the Internet: Embedded, Embodied and Everyday*. London: Bloomsbury.
Hobart, M. 2010. 'What Do We Mean by Media Practices?', in B. Bräuchler and J. Postill (eds), *Theorising Media and Practice*. New York: Berghahn Books, pp. 55–75.
Kepel, G. 2017. *Terror in France: The Rise of Jihad in the West*. Princeton: Princeton University Press.
Lallement, P. 2015. 'L'itinéraire exemplaire d'Ahmed Merabet', *Paris Match*, 23 January. Retrieved 10 October 2019 from http://www.parismatch.com/Actu/Societe/Son-itineraire-exemplaire-Ahmed-Merabet-695190.
Latour, B. 2005. *Reassembling the Social: An Introduction to Actor-Network-Theory*. Oxford: Oxford University Press.

Linshi, J. 2015. 'Man Who Filmed Terrorists Shooting Paris Cop Says He Regrets Sharing Video', *Time*, 11 January. Retrieved 10 October 2019 from http://time.com/3662914/paris-attack-video.

Mareschal, E. 2015. 'Musulmans, juifs et policiers pleurent Ahmed Merabet', *Le Figaro*, 13 January. Retrieved 10 October 2019 from http://www.lefigaro.fr/actualite-france/2015/01/13/01016-20150113ARTFIG00418-musulmans-juifs-et-policiers-pleurent-ahmed-merabet.php.

Meikle, G. 2016. *Social Media: Communication, Sharing and Visibility*. New York: Routledge.

Mortensen, M. 2015a. *Journalism and Eyewitness Images: Digital Media, Participation, and Conflict*. New York: Routledge.

———. 2015b. 'Connective Witnessing: Reconfiguring the Relationship between the Individual and the Collective', *Information, Communication & Society* 18(11): 1363–406.

Ong, J. 2014. '"Witnessing" or "Mediating" Distant Suffering? Ethical Questions across Moments of Text, Production, and Reception', *Television & New Media* 15(3): 179–96.

Peters, J.D. 2001. 'Witnessing', *Media, Culture & Society* 23(6): 707–23.

———. 2009. 'An Afterword: Torchlight Red on Sweaty Faces', in P. Frosh and A. Pinchevski (eds), *Media Witnessing: Testimony in the Age of Mass Communication*. Basingstoke: Palgrave Macmillan, pp. 42–48.

Postill, J. 2010. 'Introduction: Theorising Media and Practice', in B. Bräuchler and J. Postill (eds), *Theorising Media and Practice*. New York: Berghahn Books, pp. 1–22.

Postill, J., and S. Pink 2012. 'Social Media Ethnography: The Digital Researcher in a Messy Web', *Media International Australia* 145(1): 123–34.

Rojek, C. 2013. *Event Power: How Global Events Manage and Manipulate*. London: Sage.

Roy, O. 2016. *Jihad and Death: The Global Appeal of Islamic State*. London: Hurst & Company.

Satter, R. 2015. 'AP Exclusive: Witness to Paris Officer's Death Regrets Video', *Associated Press*, 11 January. Retrieved 10 October 2019 from https://www.apnews.com/5e1ee93021b941629186882f03f1bb79.

Scannell, P. 1996. *Radio, Television and Modern Life*. Oxford: Blackwell.

Sonnevend, J. 2016. *Stories without Borders: The Berlin Wall and the Making of a Global Iconic Event*. New York: Oxford University Press.

Sumiala, J. 2013. *Media and Ritual: Death, Community and Everyday Life*. Abingdon: Routledge.

Sumiala, J. et al. 2018. *Hybrid Media Events: The Charlie Hebdo Attacks and Circulation of Terrorist Violence*. Bingley: Emerald.

Titley, G. 2017. 'Introduction: Becoming Symbolic: From Charlie Hebdo to "Charlie Hebdo"', in G. Titley et al. (eds), *After Charlie Hebdo: Terror, Racism and Free Speech*. London: Zed Books, pp. 1–27.

Vaccari, C., A. Chadwick, and B. O'Loughlin. 2015. 'Dual Screening the Political: Media Events, Social Media, and Citizen Engagement', *Journal of Communication* 65(6): 1041–61.

Zelizer, B. 2002. 'Finding Aids in the Past: Bearing Personal Witness to Traumatic Events', *Media, Culture & Society* 245: 697–714.

——. 2007. 'On "Having Been There": "Eyewitnessing" as a Journalistic Key Word', *Critical Studies in Media Communication* 24(5): 408–28.

——. 2010. *About to Die: How News Images Move the Public.* New York: Oxford University Press.

CHAPTER 3

The Ambivalent Aesthetics and Perception of Mobile Phone Videos

A (De-)Escalating Factor for the Syrian Conflict

Mareike Meis

Syria continues to be the setting of an exceptional conflict experience. On a large scale, people around the globe are becoming witnesses to conflict scenes by watching and sharing amateur videos on the internet (see also Markham, this volume). In its first months, journalists, activists and academic scholars alike saw Syria as the exemplary conflict in which mobile phone videos (MPVs) disseminated via social media sites – in particular YouTube and Facebook – played a major role in the fight of civil society against a brutal regime. However, the peaceful civil protest that started in January 2011 in course of the Arab Spring[1] revolutions soon turned into a violent conflict setting. From mid March onwards, a complex civil war emerged, with diverse and changing actors involved who follow their own agenda (Asseburg 2013: 11; Wimmen 2011). Thus, the initial enthusiasm already gave way to more sobering viewpoints from 2012 onwards, when military, paramilitary and rebel actors began to use online videos for their own ends (Khamis, Gold and Vaughn 2012: 1; Lynch, Freelon and Aday 2014: 8–10).

Still, both positive and negative appraisals of MPVs subsist in public discourse on the Syrian conflict. These videos are not only an integral part of the lived reality of the conflict for many Syrians within Syria; they also play a central role for Syrians abroad, as discussed in this chapter, who left their home country before or during the civil war. Influencing the Syrians' view of the conflict's past, present and future,

MPVs continually co-constitute the Syrian conflict. This insight derives from research for my Ph.D. dissertation on the interconnected relationship of the aesthetics of and discourse(s) on MPVs. This chapter presents and discusses parts of the research I conducted on the internet, in museums, at art exhibitions and by talking to people in different locations in Germany from 2012 to 2018. Focusing on the perceived and experienced reality of the Syrian conflict, I engaged with video material from the Syrian conflict and in conversations with conflict-affected Syrians in Germany about their perception of and experiences with mobile phone videos in the Syrian conflict. My argument links this perceived and experienced reality to an ambivalent (de-)escalation effect for the Syrian conflict that is inscribed in the media apparatus of MPVs itself. On the one hand, MPVs are related to documentary practices and allow for a feeling of closeness and genuineness; on the other hand, they provide the technological means for modification and fabrication that make their authenticity always disputable.

Considering the broad neglect of media aesthetics in current research on the relationship of media and conflict (Meis 2016: 1–2), my research design proceeds from an interrelated understanding of media aesthetics and discourse practices in the co-constitution of media and conflict. It combines a media-cultural-studies approach towards the aesthetics of and discourses on MPVs with the concept of situated knowledge and an open ethnographic perspective. After outlining this research design, the chapter provides a synopsis of media usage in the Syrian conflict and of interrelated aesthetical and discursive aspects of MPVs by differentiating three conflict phases: an early conflict phase from early 2011 to early 2012, an intermediate conflict phase from early 2012 to early 2013 and a later conflict phase from early 2013 onwards. The following paragraphs present central statements from conversations with four conflict-affected Syrians in Germany regarding the perceived role of MPVs in the (de-)escalation of the Syrian conflict. The conclusion summarises the co-constitutive relationship of MPVs and the Syrian conflict and gives an outlook for future research.

Linking Media Aesthetics, Discourse Theory, Situated Knowledge and Ethnographic Thinking

Scholars of media aesthetics have argued that perception is a relational engagement with the world: it is experienced as 'changing contextual relationships' (Zettl 2011: 3), i.e. that the contextual circumstances of perception determine *how* we perceive the world and *what* we perceive as reality. As an analytical approach, media aesthetics address the techniques and means inherent in a media apparatus – the material appearance of a media formation – as such contextual determinants of perception (Schnell 2002: 208). Building on the theoretical premise of media aesthetics, the underlying assumption of my research is that the perception of conflicts is shaped by the interplay of the media aesthetics of images and of discourse practices that are informed by constitutive epistemological rules – so-called 'regulative formations'. These regulative formations determine (or at least constrain) which statements we consider or recognise as meaningful or true within a particular discursive field (Foucault 2002: 177–78; Foucault 2008: 588). How we – the spectators of different kinds of media material who are directly or indirectly affected by the displayed happenings – perceive and interpret images of conflict is closely linked to discourses on conflict *and* to discourses on the medium itself, including its media-historical weight as well as its (ascribed) potentialities and features (Meis 2016: 9–13).[2] Accordingly, I presuppose a co-constitutive relationship of media and conflict as suggested by Bräuchler and Budka in the Introduction to this volume or – more specifically – of media aesthetics and the perceived and experienced reality of conflict.

In addition, I draw on the concept of situated knowledge as introduced by Haraway (1988). Haraway does not consider objects and subjects of knowledge as predetermined entities, but as historical contingent. They emerge from ever changing, never-ending demarcation practices. In her view, being in the world means being in a constant process of becoming. Even the world itself she does not consider as a pregiven entity, but as the undetermined result of an open-ended 'being in relation' (Deuber-Mankowsky and Holzhey 2013: 9; Haraway 1988: 595, 1992: 297–99). Accordingly, practices of knowledge originate in this process of becoming (Barad 2013: 55).

Being a researcher thus implies that one is an integral part of what one endeavours to study. Practices of knowledge are not only a course of action for generating, disseminating and acquiring knowledge, but are complex techniques with a material, literary and social dimension. The reciprocal constitution of objects and subjects thus requires the researcher to situate herself within the process of scientific observation. This includes both to disclose the apparatus of knowledge production underlying those relations that are constitutive for one's own viewpoint, and to comprehend the local and temporal, cultural and social embeddedness of one's viewpoint as constitutive for what becomes visible or invisible within a research process (Haraway 1997: 23–26). Consequently, Haraway calls for an immersive inquiry by adopting an 'ethnographic attitude' as 'a mode of practical and theoretical attention, a way of remaining mindful and accountable' (1997: 191). Ethnography in this regard does not refer to any particular methodology, but to a study perspective of 'being at risk in the face of the practices and discourses into which one inquires' (1997: 190).

With this ethnographic lens, I conducted conversations with four Syrians between the ages of twenty-five and forty-five in Germany in early 2015. I actively engaged in these conversations by bringing my own experiences and viewpoints up for discussion without challenging the other's perspective, but informing the other's and my own perspective. I came into contact with them via my personal networks and the professional network of Flüchtlingsrat Nordrhein-Westfalen e.V.[3] The only rationale behind choosing these interlocutors was their direct or indirect affectedness by the Syrian conflict and their experience with MPVs from the Syrian conflict. Three of them had been exposed directly to the conflict in Syria. The conflict had severe consequences for their daily life and had forced them to leave Syria in 2014 or 2015. None of them had filmed videos themselves, but all of them stated that they know people who did. All of them described that they were mostly exposed to MPVs on social media sites while they were living in Syria. To prevent psychic stress, they had either stopped watching videos completely before coming to Germany or they had kept it at a minimum since they left Syria. My fourth interlocutor had already left Syria to study in Germany before the conflict started, but he has been connected to relatives and friends – some of them filming and distributing MPVs themselves – via social media ever since. For him, MPVs shared via social media are a means of staying in contact and communicating with relatives and friends back in Syria.

I followed an open, ethnographic interview style that recognises the researcher's embeddedness in the research process and allowed for my active role in a dialogic manner as, e.g., Hammersley and Atkinson (1995: 151–55) suggest. In these narrative dialogues, question-and-answer episodes took turns in which both conversation partners were equally involved. Only the overall topic of conversation was set in advance. This helped to deal with the conversation partners' personal – and sometimes dramatic – experiences from the Syrian conflict and to link those to my overall research subjective. After the first contact via email, the conversations took place according to the preferences of my interlocutors either in their working or living areas in two big cities in Germany. When referring to any particular conversation in this text, only initial letters of names will be used to anonymise my data. Depending on the person's language proficiency, the conversations were conducted either in English or German.[4] I analysed the Syrians' individual perceptions of and experiences with MPVs presuming an interconnected relationship of aesthetics and discourse(s) (see also Meis 2016).

Media and the Syrian Civil War

Prior to the protests in early 2011, the media landscape in Syria was already restrictive and repressive.[5] The Syrian government used mainstream media as a propaganda tool and to control the masses. During the government of Bashar al-Assad's father, Hafez al-Assad (1970–2000), no private media was permitted and almost no independent journalism existed. After Bashar took over in July 2000, the ban of private media was lifted, but severe restrictions remained. Only those close to the government's party were granted permission to launch media outlets. Whoever deviated from the preset course of the party ran the risk of being closed down. After the protests in Syria escalated in mid March 2011, censoring measures and restrictive policies for public media became even more severe. Moreover, an extensive disinformation campaign took place: footage was recorded in such a way as to make protests look like minor events, chants were reframed, fatalities among the protestors were negated, protestors were declared terrorists, and snipers from the regime's armed forces were passed off as foreign agents. International journalists became subject to entry bans and expulsions, imprisonment, torture and killings (along with local journalists). Armed government personnel monitored the staff of the national Syrian Arab News Agency (SANA), which resulted in self-censorship (Khamis, Gold and Vaughn 2012: 9; Reporters Without Borders 2013: 3, 5, 8, 24–26).

Faced with this severe repression of press freedom, citizen journalism and media activism emerged. With their mobile phone and handheld cameras, Syrian citizens started to record protests in low-quality video and provided news agencies all over the world with their accounts or uploaded the footage to the internet (Khamis, Gold and Vaughn 2012: 9–10). Making themselves a target for military and political actions by only holding a camera in a ready-to-record modus, Syrian videographers and photographers put themselves in a very vulnerable position, as online videos from the first weeks of the conflict testify (Al Jazeera English 2011; see also Mollerup and Mortensen 2018). Still, videography continued and after a while, the media activists adopted sophisticated divisions of labour and established media offices in almost every Syrian city. Soon, Syria was the most-documented conflict worldwide (Khamis, Gold and Vaughn 2012: 9–10; Reporter Without Borders 2013: 26–27). Mainly by using YouTube and Facebook, citizen journalists and media activists succeeded in producing a counter image and counter narrative in 2011 and early 2012 that challenged the image and narrative produced by the Syrian regime and state-controlled media. For example, one of my Syrian interlocutors described one of his first encounters with online video material as a shocking experience because it ran counter to everything he had seen on Syrian TV outlets before: 'I remember a video in low quality that the public media claimed to have been recorded outside of Syria. But a few days later I saw a similar video in the same place showing the same people who explained what was actually happening and that the regime was lying. That was the first shock. I felt like being brainwashed' (MN, personal communication, 19 January 2015).

In particular, international media took up amateur videos of the brutal crackdowns on unarmed protesters recorded on mobile phones or other handheld digital devices. Thus, such low-quality MPVs became a central weapon in the media activists' fight against the Syrian regime (Gerlach and Metzger 2013: 5; Lynch, Freelon and Aday 2014: 9). During this early phase, the image of the Syrian conflict brought forward by MPVs on social media sites and in international news media presented predominantly the resistance of Syrian citizens – armed only with their mobile phones or handheld digital cameras – against the military and technologically superior forces of the Syrian regime. On a media aesthetical level, those low-quality MPVs played the role of a video antagonist who opposes the high-quality material broadcast on official Syrian news channels (Meis 2013; Mroué 2012: 32).

While the Syrian regime continued to use military force, the opposition took up arms too. In the spring of 2012, when the conflict had already turned into a civil war, videos made available on social media platforms no longer mainly depicted street protests in which Syrian civilians and military forces opposed each other; they displayed a fight between paramilitary groups of the Syrian opposition and military units of the Syrian regime. In this increasingly violent atmosphere, different conflict actors[6] started to use videos and photographs of brutal military attacks, war crimes and human rights violations for their own purposes: for propaganda, to attract financial supporters, or to discredit and intimidate the enemy. One of my Syrian interlocutors even claimed that regime combatants recorded battles in order to sell the video footage to their opponents, who in turn would use it for their own ends (MN, personal communication, 19 January 2015).

Thus, whereas video recording during the initial protest stage until about mid 2011 was chiefly motivated by the desire to capture an extraordinary, revolutionary event, the videos became more and more politically motivated thereafter. They were not only increasingly used in military warfare, but also to express a moral outrage through pictures and sounds. They were the means to document an excessive and disproportionate use of violence, repressions and war atrocities to the world at large (Wessels 2016: 33–34).

In parallel to this development, the more general discourse on MPVs and the usage of mobile phones and social media in conflict and/or war settings in academic literature as well as in popular accounts is ambiguous. On the one hand, mobile phones and social media are hailed as democratising tools in upholding the ideals of press freedom and freedom of speech, and bringing forward new practices of political activism and mobilisation that may overthrow authoritarian regimes. On the other hand, they are discarded for their misuse for, e.g., terroristic intentions and their potential for strengthening authoritarian regimes (Meis 2014; Morozov 2011; Rheingold 2002). Moreover, from the fierce online battle between different warring parties grew the impression among international scholars and stakeholders that the videos themselves were fuelling the Syrian conflict. From this viewpoint, the omnipresence of mobile camera phones and social media facilitates new types of combination of propaganda, intimidation and uninhibited exhibition of horrific conflict scenes and atrocities. However, more moderate voices also point out that such atrocities have always taken place in times of war (Lynch, Freelon and Aday 2014: 10–11).[7]

Thus, reservations among international journalists and mainstream media about the accuracy of amateur accounts grew steadily in this intermediate conflict phase since late 2012 and stirred debates on their authenticity, neutrality and potential for misuse and prolonging the conflict (Lynch, Freelon and Aday 2014: 8). It became apparent that the virality of violent online videos has often unexpected effects. Videos may reappear in very different contexts – often embedded in alien material or in a reprocessed fashion[8] – and take various meanings that influence the perceptions of and views on the videos and of the Syrian conflict. Still, such videos remained of substantial value to the Syrian opposition in that the footage provided evidence of the regime's brutality and legitimated the opposition's accounts and actions. In some cases, huge amounts of online videos were gathered as legal evidence for a later judgment of the regime's crimes (Lynch, Freelon and Aday 2014: 6, 14; Meis 2016: 8–12).

Then, in the later conflict phase from early 2013 onwards, the aesthetics of online videos began to change. During the first two years of the conflict, many of the videos uploaded on YouTube were of a pixelated resolution that is characteristic of low-quality MPVs. Videos made available in the later stages of the conflict were of an increasingly higher resolution, while keeping a low (or amateurish) quality in terms of tilted framing, shaky camera movements, and unedited image and sound. On YouTube, many of such videos are advertised as a close and immediate war experience in high definition and are more akin to first-person-shooter video games, film trailers or pornographic compilations than to witness documents of street fights. Frequently such videos are labelled 'GoPro' in the title – the brand name of the popular producer of action camcorders – to catch the viewers' attention by promising an extraordinary online-adventure war experience. All too often, conflict actors – most prominently Islamic State (IS), who appeared on the conflict scene in mid 2014 – incorporate self-generated or appropriated HD helmet or body camera material in their media and PR strategy (Krautkrämer 2014: 124; Steinberg 2014; Wessels 2016: 44; Winter 2015: 5). Such highly professional and often dramatic staging in HD video quality – in particular the infamous beheading videos by IS – undermines the perception of MPVs of the early and intermediate conflict phase. The immediacy and genuineness of MPVs' account on the Syrian conflict – brought forward precisely because of their 'accidental' low quality – were increasingly called into question (Meis 2013). With the further development of the Syrian conflict and the accompanying advancement of video quality and staging, the awareness of not only an increasing professionalisation of video material but also of the willingness to deliberately fabricate such video material grew. This growing awareness led one of my Syrian interlocutors to comment on mobile phone videos in a quite devaluing way: 'And many videos are fabricated. Many, many, many. 99 per cent are fabricated. 99 of them will show that someone is bombed in a mosque or the capital or something ... after a week or month you discover ... that the people from the same street have done this to blame the other side and you see a full video without cuts. And you see the faces, they are laughing' (B, personal communication, 9 March 2015).

In the next section, I will draw further on my previous research (see Meis 2013, 2014, 2016) and statements from my Syrian interlocutors in Germany to elaborate on the perceptive effects related to this growing awareness.

MPVs and the Syrian Conflict

From a media-aesthetic and discourse perspective, the ambivalence of MPVs with regard to their documentary and objective character is obvious: their blurry and pixelated visual appearance is in stark contrast to the representational function of the photographic and video image. However, it is also this very appearance that becomes a testament to their immediacy, genuineness and closeness to both the moment of recording and what is recorded. According to Hüppauf (2008: 560–63), blurriness is contrary to the idea of documentation because it is the aesthetic means of empathy and imagination. It leaves no room for the affirmative or for political and moral judgements. Perception becomes uncertain and starts to digress. Therefore, it runs counter to the logic of representation and reflection that underlies the principle of unambiguousness and acuity, and that presupposes that the image corresponds with the objects of the physical world. Since the blurred image does not serve only illustrative purposes, it may contribute to the production of what it only seems to mirror.

Blurred images thus break with the idea of the photography's objective representation. For Fiske (2002: 387), this is not only due to the fact that photography is subject to the laws of nature. Every photograph carries 'bits of unnecessary information' that 'substantiate its "truth injunction"' too. But he also points out that this additional information makes a photograph discursive variable because it makes different interpretations possible and traceable (Fiske 2002: 387). However, in the case of low-quality MPVs from the early and intermediate phases of the Syrian conflict, it is not the additional (and supposedly unnecessary) information that makes them particularly adaptable to different perceptions and interpretations; rather, it is the *lack* of information. Many of the videos from the early and intermediate phases of the conflict provide only limited information on what can really be seen – including the footage itself and the metadata generated in the publishing process on social media platforms.[9] The majority of viewers, who are not very familiar with the region, the conflict and local language and culture can only translate such audiovisual impressions into intelligible information because the publishing platforms provide some kind of contextualisation.[10] Even Syrians themselves often rely on additional information provided on social media platforms or by their social networks to get a solid idea of what those videos actually do show (MN, personal communication, 19 January 2015; OC, personal communication, 21 January 2015). Such contextualisation always includes interpretative efforts of different actors who pursue their own interests and try to shape public discourse by making something seen or *not* seen in these videos. Considering the importance of discursive visibility for objects, subjects, issues, orders, relations and so forth to be recognised as existent, low-quality MPVs from the early and intermediate phases of the Syrian conflict are thus themselves a co-constitutive factor for producing discursive significance (Maasen, Mayerhauser and Renggli 2006: 14; Meis 2016: 10).

In this process, the digital nature of MPVs plays a considerable role. Digital technologies allow for unlimited and even undetectable postprocessing and compilation before an image (re)enters discourse (Fiske 2002: 388). This holds true for every digital video material, but the detection of postprocessing gets even harder in the case of low-quality MPVs because of their pixelated resolution and often distorted and choppy sound. Thus, low-quality MPVs are not only especially open to a continuing and recurrent (re)contextualisation and (re)interpretation; they actually require such contextualising and interpretative efforts because of their ambiguous aesthetic appearance and discursive relations. As such, the low-quality MPVs from the Syrian conflict are highly volatile and variable regarding their aesthetic and discursive effects.

At the same time, low-quality MPVs refer to what Fiske (2002: 387) calls 'the videolow': the social domain of low capital, low technology and low power that is associated with 'the people'. Due to its 'lack of resources to intervene in its technology', the videolow and its media output are attributed to high trustworthiness in comparison to 'the videohigh' that is associated with 'the power bloc' (2002: 387). The latter is met with suspicion because of its ability of technological and social intervention that outmatches the capabilities of the common people. In case of the Syrian conflict, MPVs of the early conflict phase recorded by Syrian citizens and activists are associated with the videolow. These low-quality videos oppose the high-quality ones produced by state-controlled media outlets because of their 'poor but closely involved vantage points, their moments of loss of technical control (blurred focus, too-rapid pans, tilted or dropped cameras), and their reduced editing' (2002: 389). They disclose the Syrian regime's high-capital and high-technological production settings and expose the phoniness of its images in its attempt to stay in power and maintain its discursive hegemony (Krautkrämer 2014: 115; Meis 2013; Mroué 2012: 32). Accordingly, one of my Syrian interlocutors described the low quality of MPVs as a verifying factor because it would affirm that common people recorded a particular video rather than any professional state-media representative. At the same time, he regarded high-quality images provided by state-media outlets with suspicion *a priori* because he had witnessed that such images had been produced with military personnel in the background who oversaw the production process (MN, personal communication, 19 January 2015).

Furthermore, the media aesthetics of low-quality MPVs evoke a particular experience of genuineness. According to Dovey (2000: 55), who refers to the incorporation of the low-quality video image in high-quality TV settings, the low-quality video image signifies 'an indexical reproduction of the real world' because it appears to be the result of the absence of professional interference. Techniques such as to-camera close-up and shaky camera as well as an embodied intimacy of the technical process create a feeling of immediacy to the presence and the film making, and have an authenticating effect. This especially holds true when the poor quality appears to be an unintended result of the recording process in the form of a mistake or disturbance. As accidental effect, the low-quality image provides seeming evidence to a non-manipulative technical process and to its origin in an uncontrolled interaction between the object and the technical apparatus (Hüppauf 2008: 563). Accordingly, many of the low-quality MPVs from the early phase of the Syrian conflict were recognised by online spectators, news agencies and international scholars alike as unplanned and random accounts of affected people recording right from the middle of (life-threatening) events (Meis 2016: 10; Mroué 2012: 31).

However, as Beil (2011: 86–87) remarks, a low-quality image may be recognised as interference and defect at first: a distortion of perception that draws attention to the media apparatus and suspends the ideal of media transparency. In any case, it may also function as a stylistic device and operate as an aesthetic strategy. Thus, while the low-quality MPVs from the Syrian conflict might have appeared as an accidental product in the beginning, they became a deliberately applied aesthetic means from early 2012 onwards for different conflict parties. So, even though the low quality of MPVs has a highly authenticating effect, international journalists, mainstream media and scholars alike have considered their authenticity questionable since the intermediate conflict phase because of their strategic applicability for diverse and opposing interests of different actors (Krenzer 2013: 3–5; Lynch, Freelon and Aday 2014: 11). In terms of digital videos' inherent discursive variability and nearly unlimited modifiability, low-quality MPVs were thus considered dubious at least. This dubiousness is also closely linked to the question of authorship. Who recorded a digital video and put it on the internet in the first place and for what purpose is often as difficult to tell as fact-checking the video's content or the information provided on the publishing platform.[11]

Even though it has never been possible to tell for certain whether a particular video was recorded on a mobile phone or a camcorder (Krautkrämer 2014: 116), this differentiation became even more difficult with the constant enhancement of recording quality in the further course of the conflict from 2013 onwards. Footage in high definition may be recorded on smartphones, HD camcorders or even professional video cameras from actors of very different statuses and affiliations. In this cacophony of war and combat video footage in the later conflict phase, it was not only the video images available on digital platforms that became interchangeable; Fiskes' differentiation between the videolow and the videohigh also began to dissolve as low tech, low power and low capital were no longer clear-cut criteria to either distinguish the different conflict parties involved in the Syrian Civil War or their media output. This is also reflected in the views of my Syrian interlocutors in Germany. They did not appraise such media usage in unison, but judged it quite negatively.

Perceptions of the (De-)Escalating Effects of Mobile Phone Videos

In the conversations with my Syrian interlocutors in Germany, appreciations and condemnations of MPVs took turns. On the one hand, they described MPVs as important means to spread the Syrian opposition's accounts of what has been happening in Syria and to counter the regime's perspective that communicates a contained situation in Syria: 'Only with video you can know that and what the regime tries to hide. When you watch public media, you get the impression that the crisis has already ended, the regime is already winning, and everything is fine and nothing is happening. Only bad people, terrorists have died or have been killed' (MN, personal communication, 19 January 2015). This interlocutor ascribed a de-escalating effect to MPVs – not in the sense of bringing the conflict faster to an end, but of lowering the probability of civilian casualties. He considered videos to have the ability to restrain the regime from launching any large-scale military attacks on civilian grounds such as the one in 1982 in Hama.[12] At that time, the regime succeeded in covering up their actions by effectively controlling the media coverage and kept the national and international public in the dark for several years (Lynch, Freelon and Aday 2014: 8). In particular, this interlocutor referred to the so-called 'Hama massacre' as a counter-example of the ongoing conflict situation in Syria in which MPVs are considered to be the means to prevent anything similar from happening again: 'In the past, there has also been a crisis in Syria, maybe in 1982, and more than 40,000 people have been killed and nobody knew what happened, because video has not been available in those days' (MN, personal communication, 19 January 2015).[13]

My interlocutors pointed out different escalating effects of MPVs. For example, one described a cascade effect for shocking videos. To counter the dulling effect of the omnipresence of violent images, an increasing intensity of violence and brutality would become inevitable to maintain a certain state of shock that ensures the visibility of the concerning conflict party and its point of view in public discourse. In this context, he not only mentioned cases of staged scenes or performances of violent acts just for the purpose of video recording from the later conflict phase; he also referred to re-enacted events in the early or intermediate conflict phase – for instance, of snipers positioned on high buildings who target unarmed civilians crossing the street below – that had taken place without any recording devices being present. In the sense of a backlash effect, MPVs were subsequently put under the general suspicion of fabrication so that their authenticity was called into question *a priori*. This would have even led to disagreements among activists fighting for the same cause because some saw their revolutionary goals put in jeopardy by such re-enactments. Others saw them as necessary means to put the regimes ruthlessness on display (OC, personal communication, 21 January 2015).

Moreover, two interlocutors referred to MPVs as exacerbating or even triggering the conflict. One described situations in which videos on social media sites had stirred conflict among relatives and friends and had led to fierce arguments that rendered moderate or neutral positions impossible: 'And some of my friends stopped talking to me because of my opinions. They don't really want me to be neutral ... But both sides, they see me as an enemy for them because I am not biased to them. I should be biased either to right or left. There is no way for a neutral person' (B, personal communication, 9 March 2015). In particular, they indicated the fragmentariness of videos as causes for such arguments in that they would not only present a subjective viewpoint but also a well-chosen section of events taking place, e.g., by showing only the beating up of some person while cutting out the preceding circumstances that led to this situation. As such cut-out, omnipresent presentations of conflict, videos would harden the viewers' stances on the conflict and reinforce the boundaries of conflicting groups (B, personal communication, 9 March 2015; J, personal communication, 9 March 2015). Here, the ambivalent aesthetic and discursive effects of MPVs play a major role. For one thing, it is the videos' conveyed impression of a genuine and authentic account of conflict-affected people that makes the viewer take sides and adopt a firm attitude, and facilitates the formation of conflicting factions. For another thing, it is the videos' inherent openness to different contextualisation and interpretation efforts of various actors and their almost unverifiable authorship and origin that constantly undermines the very same impression of genuineness and authenticity providing the basis for the conflicting factions' attitude.

With the growing awareness that videos may be deliberately fabricated, modified and recontextualised in order to achieve (any) political end, the former positive appraisals of MPVs of these two Syrians thus changed into a condemnation in principle. One even criticised MPVs, social media platforms and the internet for providing an open, public space for speaking one's mind because it would incite people to conflict: 'In the past, there is no way to spit and shout and for a million, a thousand people to hear your voice. But now it's free and cheap. You don't have to ... have (a) TV to talk, just record anything and put it on the internet. That's why the internet is (inciting) the conflicts more and more' (B, personal communication, 9 March 2015). From this viewpoint, MPVs in particular and online videos in general convey the Syrian Civil War from the public sphere to the private sphere in which it is no longer conflict parties who fight against each other, but individuals who may or may not identify themselves with one of the warring actors. In this sense, MPVs are escalating factors to the overall conflict in that they drive the division of civil society and desperation among Syrians forward: 'We can't trust anything. Now we are fed up. We ... (left Syria) to concentrate on our families because we don't see any hope, any future, any horizons' (B, personal communication, 9 March 2015).

Conclusion

The ambivalent perception of MPVs that is observable in the two-sided views of my Syrian interlocutors is in line with more general accounts in academic literature and the news media that present equally opposing views on the usage of mobile phones and social media in conflict and/or war settings. The statements of my four interlocutors reflect the ambivalent aesthetic and discursive aspects of MPVs described in this chapter. In their perception, the multiple features and potentialities of MPVs are related to both de-escalating and escalating effects for conflict depending on their individual conflict experience. For three of them, the unconditional enthusiasm about MPVs during the early phase of the Syrian conflict did not last when, first, MPVs became a warring tool for various conflict actors during the intermediate conflict phase, and then videos of higher resolution entered the scene in the later conflict phase and produced a mix-up of staged and fabricated material on the one hand and candid and authentic material on the other. The aesthetic and discursive variability of MPVs described above makes online videos easily corruptible and highly unpredictable in times of war and conflict. This led to a more general negative view on the possible outcomes of the Syrian Civil War and initial hopes invested in MPVs were abandoned in the further course of the conflict. Still, two of them held on to an overall positive view on MPVs, in particular regarding their evidential function for holding the regime and its supporters accountable for their actions.

As bearers of both hope and despair, MPVs are co-constitutive of the Syrian conflict: on the ground, when different conflict actors incorporate video recording(s) in their military and media strategies, and on the internet, when the same conflict actors fight for the interpretational sovereignty in a highly mediated civil war. MPVs change the lived reality of the conflict for Syrians – not only for those who actively engage in video recording, watching and sharing, but also for those who do not deliberately take part in any video-related activities. The videos pervade their everyday life via social media platforms and become the basis for constant debates on the conflict in the private sphere. Thus, the argument of this chapter underscores the volume's underlying premise that conflicts can emerge on and through media and vice versa.

As the future prospects of the Syrian conflict grew darker, so did the 'paintings' of MPVs in social media. Today, one finds satirical videos dealing with MPVs on different levels, ranging from sarcastic pieces dealing with the usage of video recording in war and conflict in general to more differentiated parodies of action patterns of individual conflict actors (e.g. Deek Jackson 2014; Johnny Cirucci 2015). They all give rise to questions on the (de-)escalating effects of such video works as well as their overall role in the Syrian Civil War. As this chapter indicates, such research requires a comprehensive perspective that interrelates media aesthetics with analytical aspects from the discursive dimensions of conflict in the study of the co-constitutive relationship of media and conflict.

Mareike Meis is Research Associate at the Institute for International Law of Peace and Armed Conflict and Director of the NOHA Master's Programme in International Humanitarian Action at Ruhr University Bochum. She is trained in social psychology, social anthropology and media studies, and did her Ph.D. at the Institute for Media Studies at Ruhr University Bochum. In her Ph.D. thesis, she focused on mobile phone videos from the Syrian conflict and the aestheticisation and politicisation of death. Her latest publications include: *Die Ästhetisierung und Politisierung des Todes – Handyvideos von Gewalt und Tod im Syrienkonflikt* (transcript, 2020/forthcoming); 'When is a Conflict a Crisis?' (*Media, War & Conflict*, 2016); 'Protest per Handycam' (*Tectum*, 2014); and 'Mobile Death Videos in Protest Movements' (*Thanatos Journal*, 2013).

Notes

1. The Arab Spring refers to a major protest wave in the Middle East that was sparked off in mid December 2010 in Tunisia when street vendor Mohamed Bouazizi set himself on fire because he no longer saw any perspective in his life. Thereafter, protests in Egypt, Morocco, Yemen, Oman, Libya, Syria and Jordan took place. However, Arab-Spring-related demonstrations also took place in non-Arabic countries like China and Iran (Asseburg 2011; Rosiny and Richter 2016).
2. One example in this respect is the news coverage of Western media of the Iranian Green Revolution in 2009. Mobile phones were considered to play a major role in driving the movement forward from its outset. They were interpreted as *bringers of freedom and emancipation* to the repressed Iranian civilian population in general and Iranian women in particular. This perception largely derived from a more general perception that is deeply embedded in the technological and discursive apparatus of mobile phones: an unlimited spatial and temporal mobility and flexibility leading its users into social independence, emancipation and political autonomy (Meis 2014: 44–48, 91–94).
3. The Refugee Council of North Rhine-Westphalia is a registered society in the federal state of North Rhine-Westphalia in Germany.
4. English translations will be used in this text when citing from the German conversations.
5. Since the first World Press Freedom Index was published in 2002, Syria has been ranked at the end of this list. But from 2010 onwards, Syria's ranking dropped significantly. In 2010, Syria was listed 173 out of 178 countries in the World Press Freedom Index, showing a loss of eight positions from 2009. Then in 2011, Syria lost another three places ranking on position 176 out of 179. Today, in 2019, it is still at the bottom of the list, ranking 174 out of 180 countries (Reporters Without Borders 2016a, 2016b, 2016c, 2019).
6. Already in its early stages, the conflict situation of the Syrian Civil War was quite complex in regard to the high number and heterogeneity of oppositional actors involved and their changing ideologies and alliances (Zein 2013: 17).
7. For similar dynamics in a presocial media era, see also Bräuchler (2013).
8. For example, on YouTube, various actors adopt videos from different YouTube channels and combine them with self-recorded video material to create their own news programme in a mocking or ironic manner.

9. This metadata can be retrieved with the help of online metadata viewers like the one provided by Amnesty International USA (2017).
10. Such contextualisation on social media platforms takes place in the form of user comments and discussions or, in the case of video platforms such as YouTube, in the form of related videos in the 'next video' section. The suggested videos in the 'next video' section follow complex algorithms that are generated from the user's watching history and many other parameters that are hidden in the platform's engineered structure (Gielen and Rosen 2016). An exemplary video on YouTube of this kind of contextualisation is 'Man Films His Own Death in Syria Protest' (netspanner 2011).
11. Media outlets even provide accounts on their decision-making process regarding the broadcasting of online video material while stressing the limits of their authenticating methods (e.g. Tanneberger 2016).
12. Syrians frequently referred to this past event when the then-Syrian regime carried out a military strike against the Sunni opposition represented by the Muslim brotherhood in Hama that caused thousands of deaths in a short space of time (Lynch, Freelon and Aday 2014: 7–8).
13. However, the real impact of this ascribed effect of MPVs remains arguable, especially regarding the supposed use of toxic gas by the Syrian regime in April 2017 (Reinbold, Reuter and Sydow 2017).

References

Al Jazeera English. 2011. 'Syrian Protesters Capture Own Death on Camera'. *YouTube*. Retrieved 13 October 2019 from http://www.youtube.com/watch?v=QnqiQICRD8w.

Amnesty International USA. 2017. 'YouTube DataViewer'. Retrieved 13 October 2019 from https://citizenevidence.amnestyusa.org.

Asseburg, M. 2011. 'Die historische Zäsur des Arabischen Frühlings', *Bundeszentrale für politische Bildung*, 11 October 2011. Retrieved 13 October 2019 from http://www.bpb.de/internationales/afrika/arabischer-fruehling/52389/einfuehrung?p=all.

———. 2013. 'Syrien: ziviler Protest, Aufstand, Bürgerkrieg und Zukunftsaussichten', *Aus Politik und Zeitgeschichte – Beilage zur Wochenzeitschrift 'Das Parlament'* 63(8): 11–17.

Barad, K. 2013. 'Diffraktionen: Differenzen, Kontingenzen und Verschränkungen von Gewicht', in C. Bath et al. (eds), *Geschlechter Interferenzen. Wissensformen – Subjektivierungen – Materialisierungen*. Berlin: Lit, pp. 27–67.

Beil, B. 2011. '8-Bit-High-Definition: Zu verpixelten Bildern in hochaufgelösten Filmen und Computerspielen', *Navigationen. Zeitschrift für Medien- und Kulturwissenschaft* 11(1): 83–106.

Bräuchler, B. 2013. *Cyberidenties at War: The Moluccan Conflict on the Internet*. New York: Berghahn Books.

Deek Jackson. 2014. 'FILMED TO DEATH IN SYRIA, UKRAINE, EGYPT, IRAQ, AFGHANISTAN, ETC. Bla Bla'. YouTube. Retrieved 13 October 2019 from https://www.youtube.com/watch?v=h5oCm6IFIbw&t=1s.

Deuber-Mankowsky, A., and C.F.E. Holzhey. 2013. 'Einleitung. Denken mit Canguilhem und Haraway', in A. Deuber-Mankowsky and C.F.E. Holzhey (eds), *Situiertes Wissen und regionale Epistemologie: Zur Aktualität Georges Canguilhems und Donna J. Haraways*. Vienna: Turia + Kant, pp. 7–34.

Dovey, J. 2000. *Freakshow: First Person Media and Factual Television*. London: Pluto Press.

Fiske, J. 2002. 'Videotech', in N. Mirzoeff (ed.), *The Visual Cultural Reader*. New York: Routledge, pp. 383–91.

Foucault, M. 2002 [1971]. 'Nietzsche, die Genealogie, die Historie', in *Dits et Ecrits. Schriften. Band II. 1970–1975*. Frankfurt am Main: Suhrkamp, pp. 166–91.

———. 2008 [1969]. 'Archäologie des Wissens', in *Michel Foucault: Die Hauptwerke*. Frankfurt am Main: Suhrkamp, pp. 471–699.

Gerlach, D., and N. Metzger. 2013. 'Wie unser Bild vom Krieg entsteht', *Aus Politik und Zeitgeschichte – Beilage zur Wochenzeitschrift 'Das Parlament'* 63(8): 3–11.

Gielen, M., and J. Rosen. 2016. 'Reverse Engineering: The YouTube Algorithm'. Retrieved 13 October 2019 from http://www.tubefilter.com/2016/06/23/reverse-engineering-youtube-algorithm.

Hammersley, M., and P. Atkinson. 1995. *Ethnography: Principles in Practice*, 2nd ed. London: Routledge.

Haraway, D. 1988. 'Situated Knowledges: The Science Question in Feminism and the Privilege of Partial Perspective', *Feminist Studies* 14(3): 575–99.

———. 1992. 'The Promises of Monsters: A Regenerative Politics for Inappropriate/d Others', in L. Grossberg, C. Nelson and P.A. Treichler (eds), *Cultural Studies*. New York: Routledge, pp. 295–337.

———. 1997. *Modest_Witness@Second_Millenium.FemaleMan©_Meets_OncoMouse™. Feminism and Technoscience*. New York: Routledge.

Hüppauf, B. 2008. 'Unschärfe: Unscharfe Bilder in Geschichte und Erinnerung', in P. Gerhard (ed.), *Das Jahrhundert der Bilder. Band II: 1949 bis heute*. Bonn: bpb, pp. 558–65.

Johnny Cirucci. 2015. 'LATEST IS BEHEADING VIDEO IS CHILLING!' YouTube. Retrieved 30 October 2017 from https://www.youtube.com/watch?v=AF6jDlPCEsU&t=4s.

Khamis, S., P.B. Gold and K. Vaughn. 2012. 'Beyond Egypt's "Facebook Revolution" and Syria's "YouTube Uprising": Comparing Political Contexts, Actors and Communication Strategies', *Arab Media & Society* 15. Retrieved 13 October 2019 from http://www.arabmediasociety.com/?article=791.

Krautkrämer, F. 2014. 'Revolution Uploaded: Un/Sichtbares im Handy-Dokumentarfilm', *Zeitschrift für Medienwissenschaft* 11(2): 113–26.

Krenzer, C. 2013. 'Die Wahrheit, 1000 Kbit/s: Eine Studie zu Handy-Videos aus Krisengebieten', M.A. thesis. Potsdam: Fachhochschule Potsdam.

Lynch, M., D. Freelon, and S. Aday. 2014. 'Syria's Socially Mediated Civil War', *USIP Peaceworks* 91. Retrieved 13 October 2019 from http://www.usip.org/sites/default/files/PW91-Syrias%20Socially%20Mediated%20Civil%20War.pdf.

Maasen, S., T. Mayerhauser and C. Renggli. 2006. 'Bild-Diskurs-Analyse', in S. Maasen et al. (eds), *Bilder als Diskurse – Bilddiskurse*. Weilerswist: Velbrück Wissenschaft, pp. 7–26.

Meis, M. 2013. 'Mobile Death Videos in Protest Movements: Cases from Iran and Syria', *Thanatos* 2(2): 25–42. Retrieved 24 July 2016 from http://thanatos-journal.com/2012/12/11/thanatos-vol-222013.

———. 2014. *Protest per Handycam: Die Grüne Bewegung im Iran*. Marburg: Tectum.

———. 2016. 'When is a Conflict a Crisis? On the Aesthetics of the Syrian Civil War in a Social Media Context', *Media, War & Conflict* 10(1): 69–86.

Mollerup, N.G., and M. Mortensen. 2018. 'Proximity and Distance in the Mediation of Suffering: Local Photographers in War-Torn Aleppo and the International Media Circuit', *Journalism* 1–17.

Morozov, E. 2011. *The Net Delusion: How Not to Liberate the World*. London: Allen Lane/Penguin.

Mroué, R. 2012. 'The Pixelated Revolution', *TDR/The Drama Review* 56(3): 24–35. Retrieved 13 October 2019 from http://www.mitpressjournals.org/toc/dram/56/3.

netspanner. 2011. 'Man Films His Own Death in Syria Protest'. YouTube. Retrieved 13 October 2019 from http://www.youtube.com/watch?v=j5JPFHL5rGk&bpctr=1369676086.

Reinbold, F., C. Reuter and C. Sydow. 2017. 'Giftgasangriff in Syrien – Die Indizien, die Verschwörungstheorien, die Fakten', *SpiegelOnline*, 12 April. Retrieved 13 October 2019 from http://www.spiegel.de/politik/ausland/syrien-die-indizien-die-verschwoerungstheorien-die-fakten-zum-giftgasangriff-a-1143009.html.

Rheingold, H. 2002. *Smart Mobs: The Next Social Revolution*. Cambridge, MA: Basic Books.

Rosiny, S., and T. Richter. 2016. 'Der Arabische Frühling und seine Folgen', *Informationen zur politischen Bildung* 331/2016. Retrieved 13 October 2019 from http://www.bpb.de/izpb/238933/der-arabische-fruehling-und-seine-folgen?p=all.

Reporter Without Borders. 2013. 'Journalism in Syria: Impossible Job?' Retrieved 13 October 2019 from https://rsf.org/en/reports/journalism-syria-impossible-job.

———. 2016a. 'Reporter Without Borders Publishes the First Worldwide Press Freedom Index (October 2002)'. Retrieved 13 October 2019 from https://rsf.org/en/reporters-without-borders-publishes-first-worldwide-press-freedom-index-october-2002.

———. 2016b. 'World Press Freedom Index 2010'. Retrieved 13 October 2019 from https://rsf.org/en/world-press-freedom-index-2010.

———. 2016c. 'World Press Freedom Index 2011/2012'. Retrieved 13 October 2019 from https://rsf.org/en/world-press-freedom-index-20112012.
———. 2019. 'World Press Freedom Index 2019'. Retrieved 13 October 2019 from https://rsf.org/en/ranking.
Schnell, R. 2002. 'Medienästhetik', in U. Schanze (ed.), *Metzler Lexikon: Medientheorie – Medienwissenschaft*. Stuttgart: Verlag J.B. Metzler, pp. 207–11.
Steinberg, G. 2014. 'Der Islamische Staat im Irak und in Syrien (ISIS)', in *Bundeszentrale für politische Bildung (bpb)*, 26 August. Retrieved 11 October 2018 from www.bpb.de/politik/extremismus/islamismus/190499/der-islamische-staat-im-irak-und-syrien-isis.
Tanneberger, C. 2016. 'Abschuss eines russischen Helikopters: Verifikation von YouTube-Videos', *blog.tagesschau.de*, 2 August. Retrieved 13 October 2019 from http://blog.tagesschau.de/2016/08/02/abschuss-eines-russischen-helikopters-verifikation-von-youtube-videos.
Wessels, J.I. 2016. 'YouTube and the Role of Digital Video for Transitional Justice in Syria', *Politik* 19(4): 30–54.
Wimmen, H. 2011. 'Syriens langer Weg an den Rand des Abgrunds', *Bundeszentrale für politische Bildung*, 24 October. Retrieved 13 October 2019 from http://www.bpb.de/internationales/afrika/arabischer-fruehling/52411/syrien.
Winter, C. 2015. 'Documenting the Virtual Caliphate', *Quilliam*. Retrieved 13 October 2019 from http://www.quilliaminternational.com/wp-content/uploads/2015/10/FINAL-documenting-the-virtual-caliphate.pdf.
Zein, H. 2013. 'Identitäten und Interessen der syrischen Opposition', *Aus Politik und Zeitgeschichte – Beilage zur Wochenzeitschrift 'Das Parlament'* 63(8): 17–23.
Zettl, H. 2011. *Sight, Sound, Motion. Applied Media Aesthetics*, 6th edn. Boston: Wadsworth.

PART III
Experiencing Conflict

CHAPTER 4

Banal Phenomenologies of Conflict

Professional Media Cultures and Audiences of Distant Suffering

Tim Markham

Recent research on mediated conflict has often emphasised how it is experienced by audiences (see e.g. Boltanski 1999; Chouliaraki 2006, 2013; Rancière 2009; Silverstone 2006). Instead of reading the ethics of media depictions of conflict into the content of its texts, scholars have tried to develop a better understanding of the relationship between viewer and viewed. The starting assumption is that this relationship is dysfunctional (Carruthers 2008), with audiences not properly recognising the nature and scale of the suffering depicted. Susan Moeller (1999: 17–32) calls this compassion fatigue, a condition attributable to corporate media with an interest in selling violence and suffering, and doing so in spectacular and insensitive ways. Keith Tester (1994: 130) goes one step further, arguing that the proliferation of mediated suffering is perversely counterproductive: the greater the coverage, the less visible the reality of the conflict.

In media scholarship, the pivotal question is whether the dehumanisation of others is a product of the particular media we have, or of mediation itself. Richard Sennett (1977: 116) connects this to a debate that goes back to the eighteenth century, with Jean-Jacques Rousseau (1968 [1758]) positing that any representation of human suffering relying on dramatic performance is liable to undermine the ethical impulse that motivates it (see Chouliaraki 2013). Jean le Rond d'Alembert had argued that only dramatic discourse can do justice to the reality of human experience (Rousseau 1968 [1758]: 4), anticipating Luc

Boltanski's (1999: 169) injunction that there is something distinctly monstrous about mechanically recounting the facts of genocide. Lilie Chouliaraki (2013) shows how Adam Smith's *Theory of Moral Sentiments* (1817) ploughs the same furrow in arguing that, whether one uses fact or fiction or a combination of the two to depict human suffering, audiences need to be invited to imagine what that experience would be like, for example, through open-ended narratives as opposed to definitive accounts of events, rather than told what to think and feel (see also Taylor 2004).

The spectacularisation critique mostly takes aim at the distance media representation creates between viewer and viewed, though others have highlighted the dangers of media annihilating that distance (Heidegger 1971), and Roger Silverstone (2006) instead writes about a proper distance between sufferer and spectator. What constitutes 'proper' is a matter of the recognition of that the other who is the object of your gaze is just as much an autonomous agent as you are (see especially Fraser and Honneth 2003). Responding to this, Chouliaraki (2006) disavows the metaphysical claim that there is just something about mediation that reduces others to spectacle, and instead investigates what kinds of spectacles are produced and with what implications for recognition, empathy and action. It is unarguable that some representations of trauma invite cheap thrills, and also that there are established kinds of reading texts by way of the tropes of drama and tragedy. Chouliaraki (2006) identifies three distinct forms of spectatorship of suffering. One is essentially entertainment, with little scope for subjective recognition. A second encompasses empathic responses to mediatised conflict. It remains debatable whether pity can ever form a basis for subjective recognition, let alone mutual citizenship or cosmopolitanism (see especially Beck 2002): the former hinges on whether pity reduces a suffering other to nothing more than their victimhood, the latter on whether emotional engagement with others is unavoidably depoliticising.

Chouliaraki's third response to a mediated encounter with a suffering other is ecstatic: literally that which takes one out of oneself, disrupts our habitual, comfortable sense of being in the world. In this she echoes Susan Sontag's (2003) wish that the photographs of the tortured prisoners of Abu Ghraib would shock viewers out of their media-induced slumber to finally grasp the reality of war. However, underpinning these discussions is a dubious premise: that media audiences do not care enough about the violence they see on their screens. And from this premise springs a professional mantra that is likewise questionable: what can practitioners do to make people care more? This chapter presents a reframing of audience experiences of mediated suffering characterised by an absence of revelatory moments of recognition, starting from the well-established proposition (Ang 1991) that 'the audience' is itself a contestable term, in light of which a focus on the lived experience of differently situated viewers, listeners, readers and so on is necessary. It does so by way of an examination of the experience of professionals who really do care about others: twenty journalists in Beirut and Cairo whose work focuses on the living conditions of refugees, human rights violations and the war in Syria. The empirical basis of this chapter is participant observation conducted between 2013 and 2014 at two newspapers – *Al-Ahram* in Cairo and *As-Safir* in Beirut – as well as phenomenological interviews (see e.g. Bourdieu 1999) with journalists working there. This approach asks participants to walk the interviewer through an ordinary day, encouraging them to focus on the smaller details of their work lives – everything from transport and emailing to food and office interactions – rather than abstract articulations of professional principle and motivation. Seen at the level of the everyday, this experience can be similarly lacking in revelation and intensity most of the time, but its meaningfulness is not undermined by its mundaneness. Indeed, it appears that the merely felt experiences of everyday life are the very things that sustain meaningful recognition of others. After surveying recent theorisations of the spectatorship of distant conflict and exploring professional media cultures in Cairo and Beirut, the final section of the chapter explores the possibility of reading across from the journalist's experience of conflict in everyday life and that of the media audience. Needless to say, the experiences of conflict by practitioners and audiences are in some ways divergent, but the phenomenological approach taken here posits two fundamental continuities. First, for journalists as for viewers, the experience of encountering conflict is necessarily repetitive and generic; there is no immediate understanding of an instance of violence, for instance, on its own terms – only ways of reading it. Second, each group is in its own way motivated by what Heidegger (1962 [1927]) calls care, the felt knowledge that there are stakes associated with how one responds to a phenomenal class of object – in this case conflict – over time. The chapter ends by asking whether a similar kind of affective, often mundane and fleeting experience might underpin a more substantive political relationship to distant suffering over time.

More broadly, investigating the experience of media practitioners opens up potentially fruitful lines of inquiry regarding the relationship between media and conflict. Sources encountered by these journalists often include those affected by war, revolution and injustice, and yet the routine nature of journalistic work means that as phenomenological objects, they can appear on the face of it to have been rendered banal, mere tasks to be accomplished. Yet, the findings of this fieldwork suggest the opposite: that it is precisely the mundane, often affective rendering of these sources that affords a relationship of principled solidarity over time – more than would be afforded by the kind of apprehension of the experience of the suffering other that disrupts the journalist's everyday rhythms and routines. Similarly, while the audience's experience of the manifold suffering others they encounter in their habitual media use might be little more than affective and transitory, this does not necessarily mean a foreclosure of subjective recognition; as with the journalists, it may be just this kind of affective objectification of conflict that affords engaged, sustainable audience engagement over time. This is in line with Pierre Bourdieu's (1990) generative conception of practice as simultaneously structured and structuring, as well as Anthony Giddens' (1984) model of structuration: practices are determinations of their contexts, but determinations with the potential over time to exceed their origins. In Theodore Schatzki's (2005: 471) words, practices thus conceived are 'open-ended spatial-temporal manifolds of actions'. Similarly, Ulf Hannerz (2004) shows how the professional principles of the 'tribe' of global journalists are sustained by local structurations of media work cultures. The mediation of conflict is criticised as a reduction of conflict to mere spectacle, but a phenomenological approach counters that objectification is simply a fact of everyday experience, and not necessarily a dead end preventing a substantive apprehension of conflict by either media producers or consumers.

Witnessing Conflict from Afar

It is straightforward enough to concede that many of those who witnessed the various uprisings of the early part of this decade framed as the Arab Spring did so from afar, often with a limited understanding of history, politics and language (Blaagaard et al. 2017; Chouliaraki 2015; von Engelhardt 2015). But are naive distant spectators chipping in with their view on events in Tahrir Square on Twitter somehow worse than those who do not engage at all? Like everything else encountered in the world, the people, places and events of the Arab world appear to others as objects – of journalism, international relations, travel and so on. Objectification is a given; the key task is to pull apart how it proceeds and on the basis of what assumptions, always bearing in mind the

Hegelian (Hegel 1979: 105 [1803]) ethical imperative of apprehending the full subjectivity of that objectified other, a subjectivity for which we in turn are other.

Recognition of the subjective other is no small feat, still less embedding recognition in professional practice in relation to violence and institutionalising it in broadcaster mission statements and journalistic codes of practice. Emmanuel Levinas (1989) argues that all intentive awareness of the other inflicts subjective violence on them – this is the necessary consequence of what happens when a subject tries to make its object identical to them, phenomenologically speaking. Judith Butler (1993) puts it politically, arguing that the act of recognising amounts to the incited performance of subjectivity on the part of the recognised: it is not just that we do not see them for who they are, we require them to be the selves that we see – the victim, the refugee, the warmonger. How then can we make people more aware not only of the subjective lives of traumatised others, but of the implicatedness of our own lived presents? And, finally, how can we ensure apprehension by audiences and publics of what is at stake in how things unfold from here, for both those caught up in violence and ourselves? An important starting point is to disentangle what is at stake in the unfolding of history and what is at stake in each encounter – everything in the case of the former, this chapter contends, but not so much in the latter. Rowing back from the idea that particular mediated encounters between distant others matter makes the question of solidarity one of ongoing work, work that does not have to be continuous, intense and focussed. This changes the game for journalists, humanitarian campaigners and academics from one in which the goal is to produce critical encounters that break through habituated experience to something less intense but more protracted, and able to underpin a more dispersed, generalised orientation towards subjective recognition.

Apathy and fatalism are real among publics and audiences in many parts of the world, and yet subjectivity by definition lacks foreclosure; it is an ongoing process in whose unfolding individuals and collectives have an interest. Engagement with the world is not all or nothing, but enacted improvisationally amid the messiness of everyday life. It might not be the case that left to our own devices, we are all equally disposed towards developing an orientation to the world built around solidarity with suffering others, but we are inclined towards developing an orientation that sustains a consistent sense of who we are and how we are seen. In everyday contexts, while in situ we might look disengaged, distracted or self-regarding, over time this can crystallise into something more substantive. This might include an orientation to the world that is not rocked to its existential core in each encounter with actual others, but one through which we are nonetheless able to recognise, over time, the subjective reality of those living through conflict.

Professional Media Cultures in Cairo and Beirut

When they talked in general terms about what motivates them in their work covering regional conflict, human rights abuses and the lives of refugees, participants consistently expressed a keen sense of public duty, a passionate commitment to human rights and social justice, and a steadfast belief in the importance of deliberation. Now, it is always technically possible to reduce all expressions of altruism to self-interest, but this makes little practical sense in the face of interviewees who were able seamlessly to speak to personal principles both in the abstract and in relation to the realities of everyday life. This is where the meaningfulness of principled practice is sustained or not, after all. And homing in on these humdrum realities tells us a lot about what it means to be principled in one's professional practice.[1] When social media was brought up in interviews, for instance, it was usually to explain how much of a drain on time it was rather than something that transformed respondents' political agency; covering demonstrations on the other side of town wiped out the possibility of getting anything else done, while emails piled up mercilessly; interfering editors were criticised not for traducing journalists' professional integrity, but for creating needless extra work. Interviewees consistently observed an explosion of political activism in both Cairo and Lebanon, and while this was usually held to be a good thing, it too was framed in terms of labour: the time taken to report protests, the resources required, being deprived of sleep, being constantly on the phone, not spending enough time with friends or the kids. Yet, the contention here is that these experiences should not be thought of as competing encroachments on one's being in the world but complementary affordances. Subjectivity is sustained through the little things and not in spite of them. It is plausible that the sense of constant busyness that journalistic work affords is at the core of respondents' generalised experience of meaningfulness. It is the regularity and frequency of practices from typing and attending editorial meetings to texting and checking in on social media that sustain professional principle, as much as principle sustaining the meaningfulness of these practices.

The social lives of my interlocutors can be interpreted in a similar fashion. After Bourdieu (1994), this might be characterised as illusio, that the collective suspension of disbelief about meaningfulness that goes on in all working life. But for Bourdieu, this is predicated on the alignment of shared social practices in the unacknowledged service of structural reproduction, though this presumption of complicity is questionable. It is possible that, as with the busyness of work, social routines sustain professional meaningfulness as much as any deeply held conviction about what counts as meaningful sustains cultures of socialising between colleagues. While the demands of work got in the way of many respondents' social lives, it was also clear that being in the office or out on the streets was itself very sociable. Exchanging pleasantries in work contexts is of course one of the unspoken rules of professional interaction, while attending a demonstration in Cairo or London inevitably entails as much catching up with acquaintances, as it does chanting slogans. There were sarcastic jibes in the workplace about colleagues who were boorish or lazy, but plenty of comments too in observations of newsroom life about workmates being like a second family or just enjoyable to be around. During the interviews, largely conducted in a newsroom or office, colleagues routinely stuck their heads around each other's doors, catching up, exchanging gossip and making plans for the evening. Sociologically we would conventionally interpret such conviviality as what happens when individuals who share a pre-existing professional passion and political commitment come together (Cottle 2007). But it works the other way too: affectively enjoyable daily routines sustain that sense of passion and commitment over time. The latter is contingent on the former: principles are not innate, but experienced as integral to one's identity only to the extent that conditions exist in which their habituated enactment is experienced as second nature. Principles are not internally hardwired and externally expressed in spite of external obstacles; they are subjectively meaningful only insofar as there are contexts in which they are just thinkable and just doable.

Interviewees spoke at length about politics, activism and the state of the news industry, but also music, fashion and food. When prompted to say what they thought of colleagues, friends and interlocutors, they focussed more on personalities than their politics, and that observation holds when the relationship was one characterised by political commitments and goals. Instead of expressing approval of someone's dedication to a cause, approbation more commonly took the form of references to their children, sense of humour or integrity – disapproval of their stinginess, elitism or self-importance. A picture emerges of a sprawling network of strong and weak ties, sustained though myriad routine encounters that are sometimes overtly political, but mostly just human. It is this mesh of social interactions, often pleasurable, usually banal and sometimes annoying, that allows for the collective meaningfulness of professional principle to crystallise and sustain – instead of the inherent meaningfulness of abstract principle sparking that mesh into life.

While this sketch of journalistic workplaces paints a rosy scene of easy conviviality and pulling together, it is worth noting that respondents also reported a fair amount of friction, tension, cynicism and mistrust. Older respondents among the Beirut cohort were mostly of the view that the Lebanese Civil War had not really ended, but had been swept under the carpet, and this brought a distinctly bitter tang of incredulity and sullenness to the work they were engaged in on a day-to-day basis. The more experienced professionals in Cairo, too, tended to be the most jaded, with systemic corruption and pervasive cronyism in the Egyptian media industries rendering their own effectiveness a laughable impossibility. Yet, in neither case does this justify casting journalists in the Arab world as noble guardians of truth and accountability, valiantly persevering in their mission despite untold obstacles. There are palpable risks faced by politically active media practitioners in Egypt and Lebanon, and these should not be underestimated. Journalists have been imprisoned in large numbers in Egypt, and for all the talk of the ineffectuality of government censors, intimidation is experienced regularly in both countries. But the interviewees could not reasonably be characterised as intrinsically principled, holding on to their core beliefs about human rights or social justice in spite of everything conspiring against them. Rather, principles are made meaningful by shared cultures of practice that, even in times of crisis, are often mundane and affect-driven. Principle is not predicated on a *happy* workplace or social network. All manner of affective routines can sustain it, from simple familiarity to, counter-intuitively, ambivalence or fatalism. Wearily conceding that things will never improve is an effective means of enacting principled subjectivity in everyday life; it is not about clinging doggedly to inner principle for want of contexts in which it can be put to effective use.

Most participants explicitly rejected the idea that they were passive witnesses to events, there to inform but not unduly influence their audience. Several talked of being careful to avoid indoctrinating their audiences, but there was little doubt that they aimed to cultivate influence. Those who actively organised and participated in demonstrations rather than just covering them were, strikingly, also quick to dispel any notion of a self-organising, collective protest culture. They unequivocally saw themselves as leaders and were not shy about the fact that ego is an important motivating force. They certainly went further than coordinating and collaborating with others, but were not in the business of creating a cult of personality around themselves. Put simply, they most evidently derived satisfaction from their role as authorities, expressed in terms of guiding others while being careful not to dictate to them, generating new ideas and lines of argument, carving out new discursive spaces in which others could participate. This too could be seen as something sustained by personal conviction, and there was certainly a good deal of confidence and passion on display. Importantly, though, occupying a privileged position appears to have been experienced not so much as a burden or solemn duty, but often as plainly enjoyable. There is satisfaction to be had in doing worthy work well, but also, in a visceral sense, from the buzz of getting likes and retweets on Facebook and Twitter. Importantly, this is nothing like as frivolous as it sounds: regular, rhythmic affective pleasures can be just as generative in the sense of nourishing conviction as deeply held principle. Close awareness of audience reach and impact on social media, and obvious affective delight at having a lot of approving followers, might underpin political commitment over time.

In line with other sociologies of professions (Goffman 1959), enduring identity for these journalists was predicated on the mastery of a shared repertoire of practices, some more banal and affective than others. Reflexivity was conspicuous: most displayed a heavily ironic perspective on their own status, fully aware that a good deal of performance and identity management is required to achieve recognition and status. Talk of the absurdity of media activism was frequent, with the requirement for believable sincerity always undercut by the desire to be famous and influential. But it is a game worth playing, not only because of the political stakes but personal ones too. More specifically, confident enjoyment of the game spoke to a shared though implicit feeling that everything was always to play for, for them if not for the country as a whole. This in no way casts their activism as narcissistic; it is precisely what provides the day-to-day momentum of their work. This is significant in itself, but in what follows it will be seen to have real implications for how we think about audiences of conflict as well, the experience of the self seen not as comprising stable, established beliefs and values, but very much as a work in progress. The pleasure this group of professionals derive from their work comes not from simply expressing what they think, but from participating in an environment in which how they are seen and what they can do with that is open-ended and influenceable.

The implications of this research are fourfold. First, affect matters when it comes to engagement with conflict. Yet, this is not the same as the familiar call for emotion to play more of a role in public life (Arendt 1971) – this is affect in the sense that is more often than not meant pejoratively, referring to how things are experienced amid routines of everyday practices, things that are merely felt and not fully apprehended. Second, social capital is potentially just as potent as a commitment to solidarity when it comes to political engagement – and this is not necessarily social capital in the bonding, collaborative sense of Robert Putnam (2000), but the more strategic Bourdieusian social capital (1990), acquired through game-playing as much as merit, and associated with the pursuit of status. However, while for Bourdieu this was about how entrenched power secures its place in a field and how its structures are reproduced, the analysis here suggests that game-playing and principle are not mutually exclusive; indeed, the former can sustain the latter in everyday contexts.

The manner in which participants referred to principle frequently came across as tartly ironic, playful and even self-serving, but their principles were no less genuine for it. This is because, third, principle is experienced not as the expression of some innate core of identity, but as ongoing work to do, necessary to achieve political aims but also self-management. Politics is part of the daily grind, sitting among myriad other routines, regular but also discontinuous. Engagement with suffering others may frequently appear to lack intensity, politicality or even seriousness, but this is precisely the point: it is not the externalisation of a deep-seated, originary political subjectivity, but part of the neverending work of subjectification, work that plays out in the dance of everyday life. The implication is that, fourth, the experience of mediated violence is not about revelation, of grasping the enormity of things going on out there. It is about an orientation to the everyday world experienced by these journalists and audiences alike affectively, habitually, as given. The way we experience conflict in everyday life does not necessarily hinder grasping what is at stake in it for the individual, group and society as a whole; on the contrary, it is (or can be) the routines and felt experiences that sustain such an awareness and active engagement in environments in which one's subjectivity and what that affords are not always and already foreclosed. We get recognition wrong most of the time; after Simone de Beauvoir (1948) and Martin Heidegger (1962 [1927]), recognitive failure is the norm in most encounters in the world. However, subjectivity – not just how we see ourselves, but how we see other objects, human and otherwise, and how we appear to them as objects – is temporally open-ended, something we work at through and not in spite of the way we experience the small stuff.

Reading across to Audience Experiences of Mediated Conflict

Could a similar logic be said to apply to the media audience's experience of conflict? It is against the irreproachable credentials of professionals like these that Western audiences are compared and found lacking. Individuals having their say about political issues on social media are derided as 'slacktivists' – lacking the requisite political engagement to count as activism proper (see Morozov 2009) – but there is a cogent response in asking exactly what would count as caring enough to amount to substantive engagement. Acting politically is generally sufficient for the political scientist and, while there is disagreement about thresholds of politicality, templates exist for recording political behaviour. But acting politically is categorically different from being political (Isin 2002): subjectivity demands not just certain behaviour, but a particular experience of engagement. The analogy here is that the ordinary viewer of mediated violence does not attain the status of a witness who really recognises what is going on unless they also suffer (Peters 2001) – whether emotionally, or through time given to paying attention, or by acting on what they have seen. Just how much pain and cost must accrue to constitute proper witnessing of distant conflict? How much of a jolt does someone has to have experienced in order to have really registered the magnitude of a popular revolution? If, on the other hand, it can be demonstrated that ethically principled practices of media production and activism can also be experienced as ambivalent, mundane or even enjoyable, then it should be possible to imagine different criteria for assessing mediated public engagement with suffering.

No doubt, there are limits to the generalisations that can be made about the publics of different countries on the evidence from a dedicated, self-selecting, professional cohort in the Middle East. But this can be put another way: surely if the experiences of a group of professionals so palpably politically engaged and motivated can be full of pleasure and anguish and all the affective registers in between, then is audience engagement with mediated conflict also likely to look affectively diverse and not consistently sombre? This is by no means acquiescence in the face of apathy, but rather a reframing of what form an ethically defensible recognition of suffering takes in everyday practice. A phenomenological perspective goes further than the political theoretical postulation of what is expected of citizens according to the principles of cosmopolitanism (see e.g. Hannerz 2008), in that it starts by detailing how others appear to us in concrete, everyday contexts. It allows for a felt awareness that an individual's sense of self and their place in the world is not all or nothing – it needs to be practised iteratively, worked at in ordinary situations. This does not obviate solidarity. This kind of ambivalence towards, or even ironic distancing from, remote conflict sits well with a principle like solidarity once it is accepted that such principles are never straightforwardly expressed or enacted. Instead, they are sustained through routines of both media production and consumption that necessitate a certain detachment; an enduring awareness of their mundaneness ensures that everyday contexts never entirely withdraw.

Practically speaking, this means that there is little point in wringing our hands over the apparent fact that the ready visibility of conflict and violence does not seem to induce empathy in audiences, let alone solidarity. Neither is it logical to suggest that mediation is itself the problem, that visualisation perverts that which motivates it – either by hollowing out the ontological dimension of conflict or by marshalling the tropes and devices of performance. It also means arguing against Sontag's call for visual media in particular to try to break through the mediated fog that people are thought to wallow in, ultimately forcing them to realise that this is what violence really is and these are the real people experiencing it. There is nothing about mediation per se that makes that which is represented less real, though of course some accounts are better than others at conveying human experience. The flip side is that nor should media aim to break through whatever stands between viewer and viewed – complacency, distraction, cultural remoteness – to provoke some kind of revelatory recognition of the humanity of those depicted, since recognition is about iterative, embedded practices rather than eureka moments. Further, this approach offers a way around the politics of pity debate. For Hannah Arendt (1971: 300), pity reduces victims to 'nothing but men' or, in Jacques Rancière's (2009: 126) words, 'a monotonous moan', nothing but needs and lacks, wounds to be treated, mouths to be fed – the archetype of Foucault's biopolitics (2004). For Rancière as for Boltanski, the essential weakness of pity is that it prompts private responses to what should be recognised as public problems; Chouliaraki's (2006) second or 'emergency' response to distant suffering highlights the same issue with emotion sincerely felt, but that goes nowhere. Few argue these days that emotion should be totally excluded from public deliberation, but pity specifically is characterised as innately passive, an emotion without articulation to spheres of action. Butler counters in *Precarious Life* (2006) and elaborates in *Frames of War* (2010) that pity can be marshalled towards solidarity if we understand our own vulnerability to be the same as that of the victims on our screens; if we acknowledge not just the sad fact of a life lost but of the futures also extinguished, futures we can better imagine to be as precious as our own. However, this again relies on a breakthrough moment, the kind of lightning bolt of realisation that does not tally with the way in which recognition is felt, practised and embodied over time.

Since subjectivity is always a work in progress, there are always stakes involved in terms of how it plays out over time. Sense of self necessarily incorporates how that self is seen by others, and both are provisional and unresolved; maybe not often subject to thoroughgoing disruption or progressive evolution, but nonetheless temporally contingent. This means that encounters with conflict through either media production or consumption that appear superficial cannot be read as direct evidence of a lack of engagement with others; that is something worked on over time, not achieved in particular moments. This is categorically not to say that however people view mediated others is benign, but it means rethinking how recognition works. Recognition can be broken down into response practices activated by phenomenal stimuli, but individually such practices will appear stunted or simply misguided. But because these iterative encounters underpin a conscious experience that is for the most part seamless, they can sustain a relatively stable subjectivity over time – while I might not understand everything that is going on and while I might often be distracted, I am nonetheless compassionate – and that may also amount to solidarity as a durable orientation towards others. When someone fails to pay proper attention to a news item about a particular conflict, this will rarely undermine their sense of self as caring and principled, not because they are simply solipsistic, though that too is a possibility, but because the caring self is something achieved longitudinally. Those longer-term bearings towards others may or may not meet the scholarly criteria of engaged cosmopolitanism when subjected to scrutiny, but if it is a kind of engagement experienced as satisfactory and coherent by mediated publics, then it is just possible that our established norms of cosmopolitanism need rethinking.

Whatever this says about our theoretical models of social relations between mediated distant others, it has clear implications for media practitioners. The spectacularisation critique is compelling but ultimately inert, concluding in despair that there is nothing that can be done to break through the consumerist media bubble in which audiences are snugly ensconced. A lot of work has been directed towards coming up with ways of disrupting viewer complacency, though there is always the counter-argument that further mediations of conflict, however creative or counter-intuitive, will only contribute to the condition of generalised distraction that accompanies media saturation. Yet, this rests on the presumption that the subjectivities of those audiences have atrophied through comfort and have become impervious to disruption, protected by impenetrable layers of affective pleasures. It is plausible that complacency may well be endemic, but nonetheless there is an interest in ongoing subjectifying labour that might not look like much in observed behaviour, but is real enough considering what is at stake: a self that is liveable with. Viewers may respond to particular mediations of conflicts through acquired affective shorthand, registering a response of concern or horror before swiftly moving on, but the participants in this research demonstrate that substantive recognition and compassion can emerge through and not in spite of such affective habits. How media represents conflict to audience remains important, and media scholars should be quick to call out narratives and images that dehumanise, but to maintain that the wrong kinds of representation cause disengagement is as wide of the mark as the notion that the right representations will solve it.

Conclusion

This chapter has argued that recognition of the suffering other in mediated conflict is contingent not on intense confrontations revealing their undeniable, overwhelming humanity, but on a more generalised awareness of others' subjectivity and what their suffering means. Orientation towards others is usually experienced as instinct, but with some room for reflexive positioning. This might not amount to epiphany, and certainly not on an equal scale for all others encountered, but irony, ambivalence, resistance, annoyance and all the other conceivable responses to mediated conflict and violence may in habituated form afford sufficient space and solidity to sustain substantive recognition. This was certainly the case with the participants in this research, for whom there was no sense that the gravity of the events engulfing their worlds was lessened when they became the stuff of their work with all the petty affect that this entails. What we learn from these practitioners is that their political principles and moral values are not for the most part clinched in specific critical encounters, but are seen as ongoing work, experienced as a generalised orientation towards others sustained with less than intense engagements with others in the world, including those experiencing conflict, violence and deprivation. Rather than seeking out creative ways to disrupt the seamless life-worlds of media audiences, the same logic can apply here: what is needed is a sustained but uneven and even vague orientation towards the political and social phenomena transforming the lives of others for better or worse. This is not to suggest that both the invisibility of others' misery and its overfamiliarity cannot breed indifference, and, as such, thinking imaginatively and counter-intuitively about the representation of others in specific, concrete circumstances remains important. But engagement with the world around an individual is an incremental process, and giving them space to develop a principled, consistent and adaptable orientation to it means allowing for specific responses to conflict and violence that are ambivalent, or inconsistent, or that just do not amount to much. This is the way with most reactions to most encounters: they are just liveable with, enabling the individual to sustain a passably consistent idea of who they are and of the world they cohabit. It is not heartless, at least not seen in the round. It is how solidarity is lived, not usually as a full-throated declaration of one's humanity or global citizenship, or a decisive action that proves one's moral character, but as things to do and time to do them in. In a volume focussing on the lived reality of conflict, and particular one threaded through with a non-media-centric, practice theory approach to theorising media and conflict, this chapter has shown what an otherwise abstract principle like solidarity looks like on the ground, and what its affordances might be.

Tim Markham is Professor of Journalism and Media at Birkbeck, University of London. He is the author of *Media and the Experience of Social Change: The Arab World* (Rowman & Littlefield, 2017), *Media and Everyday Life* (Palgrave Macmillan, 2017) and *The Politics of War Reporting: Authority, Authenticity and Morality* (Manchester University Press, 2012), coauthor of *Media Consumption and Public Engagement: Beyond the Presumption of Attention* (Palgrave Macmillan, 2007, 2010) and coeditor of *Conditions of Mediation: Phenomenological Perspectives on Media* (Peter Lang, 2017).

Note

1. See also David Graeber's (2009) activist ethnographies.

References

Ang, I. 1991. *Desperately Seeking the Audience*. London: Routledge.
Arendt, H. 1971. *The Human Condition*. Chicago: University of Chicago Press.
Beck, U. 2002. 'The Cosmopolitan Society and its Enemies', *Theory, Culture & Society* 19(1–2): 17–44.
Blaagaard, B., M. Mortensen and C. Neumayer. 2017. 'Digital Images and Globalized Conflict', *Media, Culture & Society* 39(8): 1111–21.
Boltanski, L. 1999. *Distant Suffering: Morality, Media and Politics*. Cambridge: Cambridge University Press.
Bourdieu, P. 1990. *The Logic of Practice*. Stanford: Stanford University Press.
———. 1994. *The Field of Cultural Production*. Cambridge: Polity Press.
———. 1999. *The Weight of the World: Social Suffering in Contemporary Society*. Cambridge: Polity Press.
Butler, J. 1993. *Bodies That Matter: On the Discursive Limits of 'Sex'*. London: Routledge.
———. 2006. *Precarious Life: The Powers of Mourning and Violence*. London: Verso.
———. 2010. *Frames of War*. London: Verso.
Carruthers, S.L. 2008. 'No One's Looking: The Disappearing Audience for War', *Media, War & Conflict* 1: 70–76.
Chouliaraki, L. 2006. *The Spectatorship of Suffering*. Thousand Oaks, CA: Sage.
———. 2013. *The Ironic Spectator: Solidarity in the Age of Post-humanitarianism*. Cambridge: Polity Press.
———. 2015. 'Digital Witnessing in War Journalism: The Case of Post-Arab Spring Conflicts', *Popular Communication* 13(2): 105–19.
Cottle, S. 2007. 'Ethnography and News Production: New(s) Developments in the Field', *Sociology Compass* 1(1): 1–16.
De Beauvoir, S. 1948. *The Ethics of Ambiguity*. New York: Philosophical Library.
Foucault, M. 2004. *The Birth of Biopolitics: Lectures at the Collège de France 1978–1979*. New York: Picador.
Fraser, N., and A. Honneth. 2003. *Redistribution or Recognition? A Political-Philosophical Exchange*. London: Verso.
Giddens, A. 1984. *The Constitution of Society: Outline of the Theory of Structuration*. Oakland CA: University of California Press.
Goffman, E. 1959. *The Presentation of Self in Everyday Life*. Garden City, NY: Doubleday.
Graeber, D. 2009. *Direct Action: An Ethnography*. Edinburgh: AK Press.
Hannerz, U. 2004. *Foreign News: Exploring the World of Foreign Correspondents*. Chicago: University of Chicago Press.
———. 2008. 'Cosmopolitanism', in D. Nugent and J. Vincent (eds), *A Companion to the Anthropology of Politics*. Cambridge: Wiley, pp. 69–85.
Hegel G.W.F. 1979 [1803]. *Phenomenology of Spirit*. Oxford: Oxford University Press.

Heidegger, M. 1962 [1927]. *Being and Time.* Oxford: Basil Blackwell.
———. 1971. *Poetry, Language, Thought.* New York: Harper & Row.
Isin, E. 2002. *Being Political: Genealogies of Citizenship.* Minneapolis: University of Minnesota Press.
Levinas, E. 1989. *The Levinas Reader*, ed. S. Hand. Oxford: Blackwell.
Moeller, S.D. 1999. *Compassion Fatigue: How the Media Sell Disease, Famine, War, and Death.* New York: Routledge.
Morozov, E. 2009. 'From Slacktivism to Activism', *Foreign Policy* 5 (September). Retrieved 10 October 2019 from https://foreignpolicy.com/2009/09/05/from-slacktivism-to-activism.
Peters, J.D. 2001. 'Witnessing', *Media, Culture & Society* 23(6): 707–23.
Putnam, R. 2000. *Bowling Alone: The Collapse and Revival of American Community.* New York: Simon & Schuster.
Rancière, J. 2009. *The Emancipated Spectator.* London: Verso.
Rousseau, J.-J. 1968 [1758]. *Politics and the Arts: The Letter to M. D'Alembert on the Theatre.* Ithaca, NY: Cornell University Press.
Schatzki, T. 2005. 'Peripheral Vision: The Sites of Organizations', *Organization Studies* 26(3): 465–84.
Sennett, R. 1977. *The Fall of Public Man.* Cambridge: Cambridge University Press.
Silverstone, R. 2006. *Media and Morality: On the Rise of the Mediapolis.* Cambridge: Polity Press.
Smith, A. 1817. *The Theory of Moral Sentiment, or, An Essay Towards an Analysis of the Principles, by which Men Naturally Judge Concerning the Conduct and Character, First of Their Neighbours, and Afterwards of Themselves.* Boston: Wells and Lilly.
Sontag, S. 2003. *Regarding the Pain of Others.* London: Hamish Hamilton.
Taylor, C. 2004. *Modern Social Imaginaries.* Durham, NC: Duke University Press.
Tester, K. 1994. *Compassion, Morality and the Media.* Buckingham: Open University Press.
Von Engelhardt, J. 2015. 'Studying Western Audiences vis-à-vis Mediated Distant Suffering: A Call to Venture beyond Media Studies', *International Communication Gazette* 77(7): 695–707.

CHAPTER 5

Learning to Listen

Theorising the Sounds of Contemporary Media and Conflict

Matthew Sumera

What can we learn by listening to the relationship between media and conflict? This is the orienting question that informs this chapter and one that I will address through an examination of the sounds of various media as they are used in, reflect upon or in some other way are imaginatively connected to contemporary conflict and collective violence. My concern in doing so is animated first by my desire to argue for the importance of hearing and listening as critical tools in order to understand the complicated relationships between media and conflict. Second, and developing from the first, I am interested in focusing on the 'processual' nature of sound itself, a term I borrow from Keane (2005: 186), who uses it to explore the way 'signs give rise to new signs, in an unending process of signification'. As he argues, 'this point is important because it entails sociability, struggle, historicity, and contingency' (2005: 186). Simply put – and an issue I will return to throughout this chapter – sound is neither fixed nor static. Rather, it is an inherently event-oriented phenomenon (Altman 1992), opening up and revealing itself over time. This temporal quality of sound, in which it develops and unfolds, is a useful starting point for reflecting on sound's nature and for thinking about how the sounds of various media in conflict are used.

Time and temporality are therefore essential to my analysis. So too is space. For, to the extent that sound is always temporal, it is also always spatial, pointing to specific spaces or conceptions of space (real, virtual or otherwise), as well as filling them with auditory consequence and affect. As such, we might usefully think about the sound of media as a kind of Bakhtinian 'chronotope' in which 'spatial and temporal indicators are fused into one ... concrete whole' (Bakhtin 2008: 84).[1] In what follows, I will expand on this provisional definition as I explore the consequences of such chronotopes and their connections to media, sound and warfare.

While the notion of the chronotope helps emplace and situate the kinds of sonic deployments I explore below, I also work to think and write in ways that help rematerialise sound, reclaiming it from scholarly and popular discourses that too often describe the aural as fleeting, intangible and ethereal.[2] Rather, and as a number of scholars have been at pains to argue, sound is inherently material, a physical phenomenon of vibrational force (Altman 1992; Kapchan 2015; Petty 2015). Any analysis of media sound therefore needs to explain both recorded sound's representational qualities and its raw physical nature, a reverberational ontology increasingly seized upon to turn audio presence into haptic resource. Sounds are felt as much as they are heard, and the ability to make others feel (or succumb to) the force of sound is profoundly consequential. Indeed, largely because of sound's physicality, sonic media have been progressively weaponised over the last few decades, an issue I will take up in more detail below. For now, it is enough to note that if we only think about sonic media as heard, we significantly undertheorise a great deal of their potency.

This point was driven home repeatedly during my fieldwork, in which the purported content and semantic meaning of various media were often less crucial to my informants than their sheer volume or their ability to shake chests and vibrate bodies. The following chapter takes these lessons to heart and is the result of extensive fieldwork carried out between 2007 and 2012 with media producers and consumers alike, both online and in person in the United States.[3] During this time, I engaged with a wide range of individuals: active members of all branches of the U.S. armed forces, their family members and supporters, veterans, peace activists, video gamers, war film aficionados and others. The analysis that follows is based on thousands of hours of interviews, discussion board participation, email exchanges, game play and related activities. Throughout, my goal has been to work to understand the appeal and resonance of the sounds of various war media – what I elsewhere call 'war's audiovisions' (Sumera 2013b) – to those who choose to create, watch and listen.

This chapter is divided into two primary sections. In the first, I explore the weaponisation of recorded sound, reflecting on the ways in which new technologies have been used to amplify and direct sound in ways that imitate older models of sonic attack. In the second, I turn my attention to the related uses of media sounds as imaginative fields for affective and haptic engagement. My goal throughout is to explicate the connections between these sounds and armed conflict at the beginning of the twenty-first century, the timeframe in which I completed my research. In so doing, I argue that such sounds are less *about* conflict than part of it – they are co-constitutive, as Bräuchler and Budka argue in this volume – particularly in terms of the ways in which military personnel and developers come to understand, develop and deploy sounds.

Sonic Weaponry

Distanced Attacks

The weaponisation of recorded sound can be understood to operate in two primary fashions. First, we may think of practices in which loud sounds and music are projected across (sometimes great) distances at enemy combatants to irritate, disorient or otherwise intimidate. Such deployments may single out one individual or many and have been documented to last hours or even days. The most famous example remains the U.S. invasion of Panama between mid December 1989 and late January 1990, in which troops bombarded General Manuel Noriega (who at the time was held up in the Vatican Embassy) for three days with a range of heavy metal music as well as other songs chosen for their 'irony value, including "I Fought The Law" by The Clash, "Panama" by Van Halen, U2's "All I Want Is You", and Bruce Cockburn's "If I Had A Rocket Launcher"' ('Music Torture: How Heavy Metal Broke Manuel Noriega' 2017, quotes around song titles added by author). That Noriega, a known opera-lover, later referred to the music directed at him as 'scorching, diabolical noise' (Noriega and Eisner 1997: 181) only helped confirm the success of this tactic.

Harkening back to imaginative uses of recorded sound as weapons of assault – most famously depicted in the use of Wagner's 'Ride of the Valkyries', which blasts out of helicopters as the U.S. Calvary lays siege to a Vietnamese village in *Apocalypse Now* (1979) – the entire Noriega incident essentially functioned as a proof of concept for militaries and law enforcement worldwide. Numerous examples followed, from the 1993 FBI siege of the Branch Davidians in Waco, Texas – which included the weaponised projection of a number of sounds, such as dentist drills, sirens, crying babies and rabbits being slaughtered, as well as the music of Alice Cooper and Nancy Sinatra (Volcler 2013: 102) –

to the 2004 battle for control over Fallujah, Iraq, in which 'speakers mounted on [U.S.] Humvees bombarded the Iraqis with Metallica and AC/DC' (Ross 2016). In both scenarios, recorded sounds were seized upon for their power to unsettle, project, disorient and control.[4]

Importantly, each of these and countless similar sound events operate within a specific formulation of space-time (distances to be covered and duration to be performed), where music and sounds are harnessed for their semiotic qualities (particularly in terms of their indexicality, as seen in the Noriega example) and for their sonic materiality. It is worth reminding ourselves that most sounds do not respect windows or doors and that at certain decibels, all can penetrate walls, literally altering and occupying the spaces they encounter. As such, although individual deployments of these and similar sound events may be unique to their own space-times, we can also think of them as they coalesce into their own category of a chronotope of distanced attack, in which the portability of mp3 players (much like the acoustic musical instruments that performed similar functions in earlier times) have allowed for the weaponisation of the sonic, converting music and sound into combat assets.

Significantly, although these types of high-decibel sound events are relatively new, they nevertheless conform to a logic of practice that connects to a continuum Daughtry (2015: 3–5) has intriguingly labelled the 'belliphonic', a term he coins to think through the various sounds of warfare, including everything from weapons to loudspeakers to the various musical genres that are performed to memorialise the dead. To clarify this continuum, it is worth noting that although blasting an enemy with heavy metal may be a uniquely twenty-first-century practice, it does not differ radically from the role played by Protestant marching bands during the Troubles in Northern Ireland (between 1969 and 1997) or, for that matter, the role of ensembles like the Balinese *gamelan beleganjur* (which literally means the 'gamelan of walking warriors'), who in precolonial times were used to 'accompany Balinese soldiers as they descended upon their enemies' (Bakan 1999: 10). The harnessing and focusing of recorded sounds across distances to attack enemies has an important history (see Sumera (2013a) for an extended analysis of these connections).

Interrogation Sounds

If the first example of recorded sound as weapon is intended to cross distances to irritate or annoy as a combat practice, the second weaponisation operates in confined spaces, its deployment meant to psychologically break enemy combatants as a form of so-called 'no-touch torture'. Such uses have been thoroughly documented as part of the U.S.-led 'War on Terror'; they have also been adopted by other military and quasi-military organisations worldwide.[5] As early as May 2003, just a couple of months after the beginning of combat operations in Iraq, *BBC News* noted that 'uncooperative prisoners [were] being exposed for prolonged periods to tracks by rock group Metallica and music from children's TV programmes *Sesame Street* and *Barney* in the hope of making them talk' ('*Sesame Street* Breaks Iraqi POWs' 2003). A range of analyses by scholars, journalists and even the U.S. government followed,[6] and discussions and debates about the role of music as a form of torture were common for years after (see also Cusick (2006) for early, foundational analysis).

Such practices involved, at times, painfully loud music and sound effects that were blasted at detainees in coordination with sensory and sleep deprivation, shackling, the use of stress positions, reduced quality and quantity of food, etc. In addition, the repetition of 'specific music to signal to a detainee that another interrogation was about to begin' (United States Senate 2014: 429) was also common, in which music functioned to mark the social and corporal rhythms of interrogative practice. At other times, music would be played twenty-four hours a day at volumes that led to permanent hearing loss. The use of sound and music in such a fashion can therefore best be understood as defining an interrogative chronotope, a space-time of assault, trauma and increasing levels of confusion and hopelessness, even when, as in the cases of the use of theme songs from *Barney* and *Sesame Street* attest, these musical deployments also engaged in a kind of cloying, playful brutality.

The story of Algerian aid worker Laid Said, who was captured and transferred to a prison on the border of Malawi as part of the U.S. practice of extraordinary rendition, helps clarify these sonic deployments. As the *New York Times* reporters Smith and Mekhennet (2006) write:

> [He was] taken to what he described as a 'dark prison' filled with deafening Western music. The lights were rarely turned on.
>
> Men in black arrived, he said, and he remembers one shouting at him through an interpreter: 'You are in a place that is out of the world. No one knows where you are, no one is going to defend you.'

Typically, U.S. media accounts of musical interrogations offered little in the way of sustained critique, even as the brutal details of such practices were widely reported. Just the opposite, in fact, often occurred, as most state-side reporting led with tones of amusement, including, as just one example, the *Chicago Tribune*'s website that 'compiled readers' favourite 'interro-tunes' (Bayoumi 2005: 33). Indeed, it was common to see discussion boards filled with lists of the aesthetically worst songs readers could imagine, as the intensity of sonic materiality was ignored in favour of jokes about which song would 'break' a reader the fastest.

And yet, even as large swaths of the public initially dismissed the idea of music as torture, scenes of actual musical interrogations increasingly seeped into popular culture imaginings. Initially, such scenes were shown in passing, in seemingly relevant motion pictures like *The Men Who Stare at Goats* (2009), *Unthinkable* (2010), *Zero Dark Thirty* (2012) and the television drama *Homeland* ('Blind Spot' 2011). Later, however, audiences were exposed to extensive scenes of musical torture in, for example, an entire episode of *The Walking Dead* ('The Cell' 2016), in which taciturn hero Daryl Dixon is repeatedly subjected to the same song, 'Easy Street', at high volume. Indeed, the song functions as the primary orienting feature of the entire episode – its defining chronotope – and its sheer repetition is intended to show audiences just how much Daryl suffers. Tellingly, as one critic notes in an article entitled '"The Walking Dead" Tortured Daryl in the Most Cruel and Unusual Way', the use of the song in the episode made it 'truly painful to watch' (Aguilera 2016).

What is going on here? Most directly, such representations suggest a feedback loop between the militarised use of high-decibel music and sound in the interrogation centres and black sites of the U.S.-led global War on Terror and the imaginative practices of film and television producers, where certain belliphonics have been adopted as forms of drama and entertainment for the sheer horrors they manage to evoke. It is, of course, not at all unusual for fictionalised accounts to take inspiration from actual events and vice versa, but what is interesting about the cases noted above is that these practices, when they occurred to actual people, were often treated dismissively or made light of (as seen in the ranking of interro-tunes in the *Chicago Tribune* story noted above), while only later were their devastating impacts accepted and highlighted in more recent fictionalised accounts.

In such ways, we may think about the above uses of sonic media functioning as kinds of 'ordering' practices in which they 'anchor other practices through "authoritative" representations and enactments of key terms and categories' (Couldry 2010: 42). It is a concept worth considering, especially in light of sound events such as distanced attacks and the use of sound and music for interrogative purposes, practices that later show up in any number of war-themed media, from television shows and film to video games, as we will see below. Of course, as already noted, the reverse holds true as well, and earlier forms of media practices, such as the helicopter attack in *Apocalypse Now*, inform real-world combat too, something Anthony Swofford makes abundantly clear in his Gulf War-era memoir *Jarhead* (2003). Indeed, I argue that the battlefield and black site deployments of sonic media have functioned exactly as these kinds of anchoring practices for a number of contemporary media, and it is to these later practices that I now turn. In so doing, I seek to tie these earlier sound events to the ways in which a variety of contemporary media have been used to help people think through and 'feel' – albeit in a safe, controlled fashion – the sonic force of contemporary conflict.

Sonic Imagining and Affective Engagement

I have previously written about amateur war music videos and their role in the warscapes of the U.S.-led global War on Terror, principally as ways for creators and audiences to affectively engage with these conflicts (Sumera 2013a, 2013b). In what follows, I want to extend this critique through a sustained analysis of the actual bodies that are implicated in the circulation and reception of such media, the materiality of sound in these depictions, and the chronotopic nature of such representations. To do so, I will turn to these concerns in relation to the sounds of two very different sonic events – war films, particularly *Black Hawk Down*, and first-person shooter video games, specifically *America's Army*.

Black Hawk Down

Black Hawk Down (2001), the first major Hollywood film released after the 9/11 terrorist attacks, premiered a number of months earlier than planned as part of a direct attempt to sway public opinion. As Westwell (2006: 1) observes:

> Karl Rove, senior advisor to President George Bush Jr., met with several top Hollywood executives to discuss how the film industry might contribute to the 'war on terror'. As a result of this meeting *Black Hawk Down* (2001) and *We Were Soldiers* (2002), films with clear patriotic and pro-military tendencies, had their release dates brought forward in order to cash in on, and help to consolidate, post-11 September bellicosity.

An examination of *Black Hawk Down*'s sounds, music and reception will help provide some idea of the imaginative world in which the film is realised as much as the impact and effect its sounds have on those who watch and listen. In analysing these issues, my goal is to show how the film does indeed cash in on post-11 September bellicosity through its unique belliphonics. However, to do so, a quick detour through modern sound design is necessary.

In an important chapter about sound design in *The Silence of the Lambs*, Beck (2008: 77) argues that the contemporary film soundtrack, 'especially with the expanded frequency range of Dolby Stereo and its spatial dispersion of sound, buzzes with an intensity of its own'. He notes that isolating individual elements is increasingly difficult to do in analysis of recent film. To this end, he urges scholars to reconsider approaches to film sound, arguing that the 'multiplicity of sounds in the modern soundtrack begs for a new theoretical approach for categorizing sound as a transsensorial, polyspatial "event". And instead of describing the individual, hierarchically divided elements of soundtrack construction, it becomes beneficial to consider the function of the overall film sound design' (2008: 77). In place of three distinct areas of sound (historically understood as music, sound effects and dialogue), Beck argues that all coalesce into a fourth category, what he calls 'spatial ambience', an auditory assemblage 'that effectively traverses all of the classical divisions of sound mixing and dissolves the uniform segregations of contemporary soundtrack construction' (2008: 78).

What emerges from Beck's analysis is a direct call to retheorise film sound as a spatialised event, a cacophonous whole in which clear lines of distinction between discrete auditory features are understood in terms of their interweaving, and in which music and sound effects are neither distinct nor operate individually (see also Soberon, Smets and Biltereyst, this volume). Such spatialisation, as well as Beck's focus on the transsensorial, should, of course, call to mind the way I have written about chronotopes and sonic materiality above. In provocative ways, we may think about such space-time configurations as fashioned and operational while the film is projecting and a range of bodies are at attention. Conceptualised this way, it is useful – indeed, increasingly important – to understand the filmgoing experience as the rearticulation of specific areas of space not only into fictive environments but into haptic ones as well, places made sonically material by the high-fidelity, digital audio of the modern film as experienced in both commercial theatres and those at home, made operational (and increasingly loud) by sophisticated home stereo systems and more affordable sound bars.

Attending to a film like *Black Hawk Down* in this environment helps expand this assertion, for the entire film is little more than one long, loud combat sequence. Throughout, in addition to a heavy metal/oud (a plucked lute of Middle Eastern and North African origin), theme that develops as a way to indexically connect certain sounds to groups of racialised bodies (American soldiers are represented by the sound of heavy metal, Somali mercenaries are mapped to the sound of the oud), a number of other sonic-visual motifs are developed as well. Indeed, the entire film is defined by a near-constant bed of pulsating audition, in which auditory features reinforce or play against a range of visual elements. Importantly, within this cacophonous whole, the sounds of weaponry and musical instruments often merge, a productive practice that calls to mind the kinds of distanced attack noted above. In one notable sequence, for example, the sounds of a Black Hawk's rotor blades are suddenly replaced with what intriguingly resembles the sound of wire brushes (as used by jazz drummers) on a snare drum, frantically swishing away. This brush-like sound is seemingly intended to project the imaginative sounds of the helicopter blades (as we see them through screens located at central command), although this specific choice also makes them musical. At other times, drum rolls and cymbal crashes coincide with weapons fire, and it is unclear where one sound ends and the other begins. At yet other times, weapon fire sets up complex polyrhythms that function as counterpoints to other musical elements, all propelling the film forward.

What *Black Hawk Down* creates, then, is a kind of 'intensified audio-visual aesthetic' (Vernallis 2008: 278), in which visuals are developed in musical ways and in which audiovisual connections are deployed throughout. Indeed, there are few moments in the entire film devoid of such heightened aesthetics and, when attending to the film, one has the distinct impression of being constantly bombarded by the sheer intensity of such music/sound combinations – auditories of war that importantly function to drive the film's imagery forward. Fan reviews on a Netflix discussion board devoted to the film consistently comment on these sounds:

'Watching this on our big screen with Dolby 5.1 surround sound was overwhelming – I was in Somalia in the middle of a firefight.'

'Definitely an important war film of the last decade, which you should watch if you like the genre. If you don't, stay away. It is a long, loud, and dizzy film.'

'Gritty, loud, punishing, and sometimes oddly beautiful action picture.'

(Anonymous n.d.)

Two concepts emerge from these quotes. The first is the continuity of experience that connects *Black Hawk Down* with my previous analysis of musical torture. 'Overwhelming', 'loud', 'dizzy', 'gritty' and 'punishing' are not words we typically associate with film or entertainment. However, they are the exact kinds of descriptors one might expect to encounter in discussions of musical interrogation, and it is worth thinking through the aesthetics of the Kantian sublime implicit within their appeal, in which the real danger of sonic materiality is tamed and turned into sensual appeal. The disorienting, all-encompassing, even abusive materiality of sound here is rearticulated as a physical and aesthetic ideal, which presumably can only be appreciated if we know we can choose to get up and leave if we so desire. If not, we are even warned to stay away by one fan, in advice that directly acknowledges the film's devastating sonic potentials. Here, the earlier practices of sonic interrogation serve to anchor the filmic experience.

The second concept that emerges from these and other fan comments is how the sonic intensity of the film directly translates to ideas about the film's authenticity and verisimilitude. Indeed, fans see no disconnect between the obviously artificial filmic force, the hyperdeployment of film music/sound and the film's truth content; rather, all three work to buttress one another. Another reviewer writes, tying sound explicitly to the reality of the film:

> Buckle up! This thing rocks. Plus, some of the actual Rangers depicted in BHD acknowledge the film's authenticity. In which case, you definitely did NOT want to be anywhere near this mega-throwdown fire-fight. Just watch the movie and be glad somebody is out there watching your back.
> (Anonymous n.d.)

I want to suggest that we understand 'this thing rocks' as a direct reference to the intensified audiovisual aesthetics of the entire film and, indeed, the way in which such aesthetics create a chronotope of nationalistic credibility that helps tie the filmic narrative to the reality of individuals who are purportedly out there 'watching your back'. Films like *Black Hawk Down*, taking full advantage of the latest in audio sound and editing technologies, manage to produce overwhelming audiovisual aesthetics that call to mind both the raw physicality of contemporary auditories of war as well as feelings of patriotism and pride they connect to and bolster.

In the final section of my chapter, I explore one last sonic deployment, in which military funding, recruitment and interactive gaming research combine to create immersive environments for particularly meaningful aggregates of militarised play and aesthetic transport.

America's Army

First created by the U.S. Army in 2002 at a cost of $7.5 million, the video game *America's Army* is part of a 'larger military strategy to move from television ads to more cost-effective methods of recruiting' and to ensure that fewer new recruits 'wash out' during basic combat training (Stahl 2006: 123). Focusing on all aspects of Army life – training through deployment – to date there have been forty-one versions and updates of the game, including versions for all major gaming consoles, PCs, arcades and mobile technologies (for an important ethnographic analysis, see Allen (2017)).

In an attempt to understand the role of sound in the game as perceived by players, I spent several months during 2009 and 2010 on discussion boards, examining the role of music and sound in *America's Army* and other first-person shooters. Unlike some other war video games, *America's Army* is slightly unique in that it does not include a constant music bed during game play (although this practice has increasingly fallen out of favour). Rather, as one player notes, 'what America's Army chose to do was perfect. Music at the menu to ignite you to want to play again, brief emotional music at the end of each round/match. And no music played during gameplay. It's nice' (Anonymous *America's Army* Player One 2010).

However, this does not mean that players fail to conceptualise or engage in the sounds of *America's Army* in directly aesthetic ways. Indeed, explosions and gunfire themselves are often times understood in explicitly musical fashions, calling to mind the complicated blending of sound and music in recent filmic practices examined above. Comments by two players help clarify such theorisations. One notes that 'during the actual match, the music isn't on anyway, so during that time, I guess that gunshots and explosions are our music' (Anonymous *America's Army* Player Two 2010). Another writes:

> If by music you mean the sweet, sweet sound of the RPK [abbreviation for Kalashnikov rifle] echoing through the upper floor of SF_Hos [a hospital level in the game], or the spine-tingling 'CLICK' of the VOG round

[a fragmentation grenade] that's about to pound you to a paste, a sound which we will never, ever hear again, then I can honestly say yes. Songs where the only lyrics are 'Frag Out' [a phrase yelled just before a player throws a grenade into an enemy position to warn other players in campaign modes] and the OpFor [opposing forces] translation of 'Medic!' with the occasional 'WHAT ARE YOU DOING, SOLDIER?' then I'd have to say, absolutely. But the rest? No thanks. (Anonymous *America's Army* Player Three 2010)

At first, I understood this commenter's response as nothing more than a clever and witty comment. In short time, however, numerous other players chimed in with their support and I realised that this commenter, while being playful, was also serious. He had articulated a profound way in which gamers theorise the sound environments in which they operate. Indeed, players on a number of other gaming discussion boards confirmed such associations as they noted how they conceive of game sounds in similar fashions. In particular, numerous players I communicated with discussed their admiration for what they considered to be specifically evocative gunfire in both aesthetic and affective ways.

Players turn to war games, then, not only for what they perceive to be authentic combat experiences but also, and just as importantly, for their aesthetics, affect and haptics (an issue to which I will return shortly). This, of course, should not be surprising, as games are a powerful form of contemporary entertainment. Appealing games are exactly those that are repeatedly played, returned to again and again. As we see in the player quotes above, sound design is an essential part of a game's allure, and the careful development of evocative and feelingful (both literally and figuratively) sounds are crucial to gameplay and, consequently, game enjoyment. As such, the perceptual and discursive blurring of gunfire and music among these players is a natural engagement with in-game sound design.

Much like the increased blurring in Hollywood films between sound effects, dialogue and music, sound design in war video games increasingly relies upon the direct musicalisation of combat weaponry as part of its diegesis. This is something *America's Army* developers emphasised in the very first iteration of the game. In a piece entitled 'Introducing Emotion into Military Simulation and Videogame Design: *America's Army: Operations* and VIRTE', Army developers write about the role of sound and emotion in simulators and video games, noting that 'emotion is a critical component of learning in virtual environments' (Shilling, Zyda and Wardynski 2002: para. 3). They continue, positioning their work within the trajectories of sound design in the entertainment industry, stating that their goal is to produce 'systems that engage users on the visceral level as well as the intellectual. We also believe that it is critical to produce simulations that participants want to use and enjoy using' (2002: para. 3).

To this end, sound design principles related to weapons are especially important to game developers, and they spend considerable time creating sounds that are modelled 'for a combination of sonic accuracy and emotionality' (Shilling, Zyda and Wardynski 2002: para. 9):

> However, flat recordings of weapons fire were not used. Traditional recording and sound reproduction methods cannot capture the full dynamic range of high decibel weapons fire. A flat recording is not only emotionally flat; it also sounds unrealistic. Instead, flat recordings were mixed with other explosive sounds to compensate for the weaknesses of the reproduction media.

In this passage the aesthetics of weapon sounds becomes clear, as video game designers approach their work in highly musicalised fashions. Such sounds, in and of themselves, are consequently carefully designed, as are the sounds of their impacts, something game developers spend significant time perfecting – 'hence, we modelled the sounds of bullets whizzing by your ears, the sounds of bullet impacts in different types of materials (wood, metal, concrete, etc.), and the sounds of debris resulting from bullet impacts' (Shilling, Zyda and Wardynski 2002: para. 10). In creating the sonic world of *America's Army*, sound designers adopted techniques earlier explored by electronic and computer music composers such as additive synthesis, in which a number of discrete sounds are layered together to create more complex, timbrally rich aggregates (for more on this technique, see Manning (2013)).

As noted, sound design practices are undertaken to create both visceral and enjoyable games. When such sounds are developed, they also importantly create a specific kind of chronotope, defining the time-space of game play, one that increasingly relies upon sonic materiality for its immersion and affect. Indeed, while 5.1 surround sound systems are not at all uncommon among players, many others seek to amplify the materiality of sound even more through the use of sound system gaming chairs, in which speakers and subwoofers are embedded directly into the seat. Thus, the sounds of gunfire and explosions further act on the bodies of those playing, and sound's materiality is explicitly intensified for its haptic resource. We again need to situate such practices within the sound events explored at the beginning of this chapter, and it is useful to think about all such sounds as existing on Daughtry's

(2015) belliphonic continuum. These kinds of sonic events are valued not only for how they sound, but, equally as important, for how they make people feel.

Conclusion

In this chapter, I have explored a range of contemporary sounding practices, from the direct militarisation of sound in forms of distanced attack and sonic interrogation to the ways in which such practices have been referenced and implicated in both war films and video games. Throughout, the role of sonic materiality has been essential. Simply put, we cannot appreciate the significance of the sounds of contemporary media and conflict without understanding them as fundamentally physical. To do so, we need to retheorise sound as haptic, as a resource increasingly used to move and impact bodies, both willing and unwilling.

In the above, I have also attended to the ways in which such sound events create specific, potent chronotopes, combinations of sounded space-time that carry in them particular ways of knowing and being in the world. Again, issues of control are an essential part of the nature of these chronotopes; however, it is important to note that they exist on a continuum of sounding practice and reception. Sounds fill up spaces and mark time, and the contours of experience are largely dictated by the nature of these aggregations.

As noted at the beginning of this chapter, my primary interest in this work is to think through the implications of sound in terms of both how we understand and, increasingly, how we fight war. I seek to explore the practices addressed above as a way to argue that such sounds are less about war than they are part of it. In so doing, I am also interested in opening up a space for sound studies as an analytical tool for the study of media and conflict. In so doing, I challenge scholars to rethink how sound itself functions, particularly in terms of the ways in which people use sounds for specific imaginative and bodily purposes. Such an approach, itself leveraging the event-oriented nature of sound as defined by Altman (1992), helps us move from an overly interpretive model that understands media only as representation to highlight a range of deeply social, political and bellicose uses. Of course, as the editors of this volume importantly argue, we must also work to expand our analytical framework beyond Europe and America. To that end, I hope that the proceeding analysis will provide scholars working in other times and places with a number of practices to consider.

Matthew Sumera is a music and sound studies scholar who has published widely about the sounds and attendant uses of contemporary representations of war across a range of media. He is currently a visiting lecturer in sociocultural anthropology at Hamline University in St Paul, Minnesota. He has also taught at the University of Minnesota and the University of Wisconsin, Madison.

Notes

1. See Faudree (2012) and Harkness (2013) for other uses of Bakhtin's 'chronotope' in analyses of sound and music.
2. See Sterne (2003: 15–19) for a critique of what he calls the 'audiovisual litany', which works to ideologically position sound – conceptualised as immersive, interior, subjective, etc. – as the polar opposite of sight.
3. What follows focuses on U.S.-based media practices and attendant conflicts. It does not pretend to be comprehensive or representative of broader practices; rather, my goal is to speak to and theorise a set of specific auditory deployments that coincide with post-9/11 U.S. militarism. I also hope to suggest key themes that may be useful to scholars exploring the sound- and mediascapes of other conflicts.
4. While they are beyond the scope of this chapter, technologies like long-range acoustic devices (LRADs) are best understood to exist on a continuum of this kind of sonic weaponry. LRADs, also known as 'sonic cannons' or 'acoustic bazookas', create extremely concentrated sound beams that have the ability to produce instant migraines, knock people over or inflict permanent hearing loss (Volcler 2013: 109–11). Their use on battlefields and as an increasingly common method to disperse protesters is worth noting, pointing to the ways in which 'nonlethal' military technologies are also used to control civilian populations. The 2017–18 'sonic attacks' on U.S. diplomats in Cuba and China are additional examples of sonic weaponisation. See McLoughlin (2018) for a helpful overview of such uses.
5. The use of music in interrogation or as a form of torture has a much longer history and has been addressed by a number of scholars. See Grant and Papaeti (2013) for one important overview. Thanks to Oren Livio for his useful reminder.
6. The word 'music' appears a total of nineteen times in the United States Senate's (2014) official assessment report on the role of detention and interrogation practices in the War on Terror.

References

Aguilera, L. 2016. '"The Walking Dead" Tortured Daryl in the Most Cruel and Unusual Way – Relive the 4 Most Shocking Revelations!' *ET*, 6 November. Retrieved 14 October 2019 from http://www.etonline.com/

tv/202145_the_walking_dead_the_cell_daryl_tortured_dwight_negan_4_shocking_moments.
Allen, R. 2017. *America's Digital Army: Games at Work and War*. Lincoln: University of Nebraska Press.
Altman, R. 1992. 'The Material Heterogeneity of Recorded Sound', in R. Altman (ed.), *Sound Theory Sound Practice*. New York: Routledge, pp. 15–31.
America's Army. 2002. [Video game]. United States: United States Army.
Anonymous. n.d. *Black Hawk Down* [Online fan reviews]. Netflix.com. Retrieved 10 June 2010 from https://dvd.netflix.com/Movie/Black-Hawk-Down/60022056?strackid=35650114d5d36e96_1_srl&trkid=201891639.
Anonymous *America's Army* Player One. 14 December 2010. Americasarmy.com [specific webpage deleted during site redesign].
Anonymous *America's Army* Player Two. 14 December 2010. Americasarmy.com [specific webpage deleted during site redesign].
Anonymous *America's Army* Player Three. 14 December 2010. *Americasarmy.com* [specific webpage deleted during site redesign].
Apocalypse Now. 1979. [Film]. Francis Ford Coppola (dir.). United States: United Artists.
Bakan, M.B. 1999. *Music of Death and New Creation: Experiences in the World of Balinese Gamelan Beleganjur*. Chicago: University of Chicago Press.
Bakhtin, M.M. 2008. *The Dialogic Imagination: Four Essays*. Austin: University of Texas Press.
Bayoumi, M. 2005. 'Disco Inferno', *The Nation*, 8 December. Retrieved 14 October 2019 from https://www.thenation.com/article/disco-inferno.
Beck, J. 2008. 'The Sounds of "Silence": Dolby Stereo, Sound Design, and *The Silence of the Lambs*', in J. Beck and T. Grajeda (eds), *Lowering the Boom: Critical Studies in Film Sound*. Champaign: University of Illinois Press, pp. 68–86.
Black Hawk Down. 2001. [Film]. Ridley Scott (dir.). United States: Columbia Pictures.
'Blind Spot'. 2011. *Homeland*, Season 1, Episode 5. Showtime, 30 October.
'The Cell'. 2016. *The Walking Dead*, Season 7, Episode 1. AMC, 6 November.
Couldry, N. 2010. 'Theorising Media as Practice', in B. Bräuchler and J. Postill (eds), *Theorising Media and Practice*. New York: Berghahn Books, pp. 35–54.
Cusick, S.G. 2006. 'Music as Torture/Music as Weapon', *Revista Transcultural de Música/Transcultural Music Review* 10. Retrieved 2 January 2013 from http://www.sibetrans.com/trans/trans10/cusick_eng.htm.
Daughtry, J.M. 2015. *Listening to War: Sound, Music, Trauma, and Survival in Wartime Iraq*. Oxford: Oxford University Press.
Faudree, P. 2012. 'Music, Language, and Texts: Sound and Semiotic Ethnography', *Annual Review of Anthropology* 41: 519–36.
Grant, M.J., and A. Papaeti (eds). 2013. 'Music and Torture, Music and Punishment', Special Issue of *The World of Music* 2(1).
Harkness, N. 2013. *Songs of Seoul: An Ethnography of Voice and Voicing in Christian South Korea*. Berkeley: University of California Press.

Kapchan, D. 2015. 'Body', in D. Novak and M. Sakakeeny (eds), *Keywords in Sound*. Durham, NC: Duke University Press, pp. 33–44.

Keane, W. 2005. 'Signs are Not the Garb of Meaning: On the Social Analysis of Material Things', in D. Miller (ed.) *Materiality*. Durham, NC: Duke University Press, pp. 182–201.

Manning, P. 2013. *Electronic and Computer Music*, 4th edn. Oxford: Oxford University Press.

McLoughlin, I. 2018. 'Sonic Attacks in China and Cuba: How Sound Can Be a Weapon', *The Conversation*, 31 May. Retrieved 14 October 2019 from http://theconversation.com/sonic-attacks-in-china-and-cuba-how-sound-can-be-a-weapon-97380.

The Men Who Stare at Goats. 2009. [Film]. Grant Heslov (dir.). United States: Overture Films.

'Music Torture: How Heavy Metal Broke Manuel Noriega'. 2017. *BBC News*, 30 May. Retrieved 13 October 2019 from http://www.bbc.com/news/world-latin-america-40090809.

Noriega, M.A., and P. Eisner. 1997. *America's Prisoner: The Memoirs of Manuel Noriega*. New York: Random House.

Petty, K. 2015. 'Walking through the Woodlands: Learning to Listen with Companions Who Have Impaired Vision', in M. Bull and L. Back (eds), *The Auditory Culture Reader*. London: Bloomsbury, pp. 173–84.

Ross, A. 2016. 'When Music is Violence: From Trumpets at the Walls of Jericho to Pop Songs as Torture in the Iraq War, Sound Can Make a Powerful Weapon', *New Yorker*, 4 July. Retrieved 14 October 2019 from https://www.newyorker.com/magazine/2016/07/04/when-music-is-violence.

'*Sesame Street* Breaks Iraqi POWs'. 2003. *BBC News*, 20 May. Retrieved 14 October 2019 from http://news.bbc.co.uk/2/hi/middle_east/3042907.stm.

Shilling, R., M. Zyda and E.C. Wardynski. 2002. 'Introducing Emotion into Military Simulation and Videogame Design: *America's Army: Operations* and VIRTE'. *Paper Proceedings from GameOn 2002*. London: Westminster University.

Smith, C.S., and S. Mekhennet. 2006. 'Algerian Tells of Dark Term in U.S. Hands', *New York Times*, 7 July. Retrieved 14 October 2019 from http://www.nytimes.com/2006/07/07/world/africa/07algeria.html.

Stahl, R. 2006. 'Have You Played the War on Terror?' *Critical Studies in Media Communications* 23(2): 112–30.

Sterne, J. 2003. *The Audible Past: Cultural Origins of Sound Reproduction*. Durham, NC: Duke University Press.

Sumera, M. 2013a. 'The Soundtrack to War', in N. Whitehead and S. Finnström (eds), *Virtual War and Magical Death: Technologies and Imaginaries for Terror and Killing*. Durham, NC: Duke University Press, pp. 214–233.

———. 2013b. 'Understanding the Pleasures of War's Audiovisions', in C. Vernallis, A. Herzog and J. Richardson (eds), *The Oxford Handbook of Sound and Image in Digital Media*. Oxford: Oxford University Press, pp. 310–324.

Swofford, A. 2003. *Jarhead: A Marine's Chronicle of the Gulf War and Other Battles*. New York: Scribner.

United States Senate. 2014. *Report of the Senate Select Committee on Intelligence Committee Study of the Central Intelligence Agency's Detention and Interrogation Program.* Retrieved 12 April 2018 from https://www.intelligence.senate.gov/sites/default/files/publications/CRPT-113srpt288.pdf.

Unthinkable. 2010. [Film]. Gregor Jordan (dir.). United States: Sony Pictures Home Entertainment.

Vernallis, C. 2008. 'Music Video, Songs, Sound: Experience, Technique and Emotion in *Eternal Sunshine of the Spotless Mind*', *Screen* 49(3): 277–97.

Volcler, J. 2013. *Extremely Loud: Sound as Weapon*, trans. C. Volk. New York: The New Press.

Westwell, G. 2006. *War Cinema: Hollywood on the Front Line.* London: Wallflower.

Zero Dark Thirty. 2012. [Film]. Kathryn Bigelow (dir.). United States: Columbia Pictures.

PART IV
Mediated Conflict Language

CHAPTER 6

Trolling and the Orders and Disorders of Communication in '(Dis)Information Society'

Jonathan Paul Marshall

The phenomena known as 'trolling' appears within the normal 'ordering' and 'disordering' routines of 'information society'[1]. Trolling is generated by the social usages of information and communications technology (ICT) and by the consequences ICT has for social dynamics, through encouraging particular patterns of both media and political practice. These practices regularly extend and exaggerate features of 'ordinary' communication until a point of communicative and informational breakdown is reached. Conflict and misunderstanding is normal within people's everyday mediated life.

This chapter aims to help break down simplistic categorisations of media-conflict relations through a focus on the lived realities of conflicts within various overlapping media, and continues a long-term research project into the regular disorders of 'information society', which suggest that this form of society is better called '(dis)information society' (Marshall et al. 2015).

In this society, accuracy becomes less important than persuasion or the silencing of unwanted information and opponents. Politics routinely involves such actions as part of its campaigns (Ong and Cabañes 2018), and uses media to perpetuate and participate in conflict, not just report it. Indeed, conflict can attract audience and participants, or build names and loyal followers, so that successful media can be conflictual media. In which case, trolling is not a specific *disorder* of internet, or individual psychological life, but marks *orders* of life, including group allegiance, meaning-making and giving a sense of participation within this '(dis)information society'. In other words, this chapter aims to show that trolling behaviour is 'normal' and even encouraged by the system, no matter how much the trolling of others may be condemned as 'abnormal'. Trolling is integral to the co-constitutive forces of media and conflict.

Research for this chapter involved observing most of the material as it appeared, while looking for background comment and news. I did not participate in the discussions or speak to those involved, although I have participated in, and researched, trolling and online conflicts previously (Marshall 2007: 189–97). While my lack of direct participation increases risks of misinterpretation, general fit with the previous research reduces this possibility. After some background discussion on disorder, communication and trolling, the argument is illustrated by a short case study of celebrity trolling and retaliation, featuring the now-deceased Australian media personality Charlotte Dawson. These events occurred within the context of a mainstream Australian media campaign against online trolling from August to October 2012. Events flow across newspapers, television and online activity, as media are rarely isolated. These different media are vehicles for, and influence, communication, politics, conflict and social expression, while not always being equitable in the power relations they encourage. Behaviour that could be called trolling is present in most contemporary media and politics. Trolling is neither an integrating ritual of rebellion nor a sign of transformative class war; it is part of normal media experience. While Karmasin et al. remark that 'violence can be seen as being a specific form of communication' (2013: ix), here it is suggested that in (dis)information society, communication can become a form of violence.

Disorder and Communication

In complex mutually interactive systems (such as social systems), the results of interactions cannot be predicted in detail. Intense variability, flux, accident and surprise are standard and experiences of failure, error and disorder are normal (Doak et al. 2008; Marshall et al. 2015; Reice 2001). Social ordering constantly slips away and apparently separated areas of life interact unpredictably. People routinely do not know how people will respond to their attempts to communicate. Recognising this complexity, and the surprising results of attempts to order it, makes recognition of disorder and unintended consequences the centre of social theory. For example, communication depends upon, produces and is disrupted by noise, transmission errors, misinterpretation, ambiguity, deceit, incomprehension, threat, silencing and so on. Communication cannot occur without the possibility of disruption, and 'good' (or relatively accurate) communication is difficult. Human actors may also strategically increase the intensity of these problems to disrupt the communication and understanding of others (Marshall 2007: 13–30, 73–88), while hostility can produce the appearance of predictive order, recognition and involvement, all of which reinforce disruption of 'good communication'.

Problems in communication increase because meaning is not conveyed, or transmitted, but *interpreted*. Interpretation is influenced by the framings used to give messages context and reduce ambiguity (Bateson 1972: 184–92; MacLachlan and Reid 1994). Framings can be unstable, and groups may argue over the framings in play, as those who define the terms of communication are likely to win the argument (Lakoff 2014). For example, people can argue over what behaviour becomes framed as legitimate conflict or protest, and what becomes framed as criminal or disruptive, as with trolling. Framings can hide as well as illuminate intended meaning. When a group frames trolling in terms of mischief, art or the stupidity of victims, then they may not perceive the harm it does. Conversely, if people frame trolling as unacceptable online behaviour, then they may not perceive similar behaviour elsewhere.

A significant way of framing messages involves the practice of categorising those who emit the message as belonging to groups that have strong positive, or negative, connections to groups the interpreters belong to or would like to belong to. Imagined 'exemplary' connections to in-groups increase the persuasive effect of arguments, while 'negative' connections decrease that effect (Hopkins and Reicher 1997). Consequently, framing practices and processes are not only connected to general political conflicts, but are particularly important online, as people may have few other social ties to help them resolve and interpret meaning; categorisations deployed in framing do not have to be accurate in order to be effective. Online framing frequently seems motivated by political allegiances, gender constructions or ideas that the internet is a special place of freedom in which authentic/honest expression should reign without regard to personal hurt (Marshall 2007: 178–79).

Conflict arises, not only through incompatible framing, but also because communication is routinely about persuading other people to act, or think, in certain ways (Peckham 1979). Consequently, communication is embedded in wider relations of power, resistance and conflict, making use of practices such as misdirection, magnifying the volume and spread of some messages, and silencing opposition through violence or threat. These practices reinforce the probability of framings and miscommunication becoming disruptive, especially in a communicative environment where people: (a) routinely feel disempowered; (b) can find data to support almost any position; (c) can feel overwhelmed by the uncertainties and incompleteness generated by information overload; and (d) believe that most information is propaganda anyway (Marshall 2013). Abuse can both mark group boundaries and be used to attack people categorised as belonging to an out-group or associated with those held responsible for the in-group's supposed disempowerment and disorder. Attempted silencing of out-group members can become the (dis)ordering norm of practices, which attempt to reinforce informational and communicative social order.

Trolling in General

The term 'trolling' covers many behaviours. Herring et al. (2002: 375) identify the 'definitional criteria for trolls' as: (a) 'messages from a sender who appears outwardly sincere'; (b) 'messages designed to attract predictable responses or flames'; and (c) 'messages that waste a group's time by provoking futile argument'. Bishop (2013) further distinguishes twelve different types of trolling.

'Trolling' is clearly a word with a wide variety of possible interpretative usages, but despite these academic distinctions, the term 'trolling' is often used to refer to online harassment or disruption. Trolling can involve individuals or come from a group of people who seem to be at tempting to reinforce their own group bonds and superiority. Trolling can involve endless argument, abuse, the posting of 'shocking images' or death threats. Frequently, trolling attempts to punish out-group members for speaking. For example, after a person in Queensland was charged with racially abusing an Australian female Muslim activist in 2015, the U.S.-based white supremacist *Daily Stormer* webpage (2015) asked its readers to punish the activist by flooding her 'WITH RACIAL AND RELIGIOUS ABUSE, NOT WITH THREATS OF VIOLENCE', as she was 'subhuman vermin' who threatened their 'free speech'. The website stated: 'Stormer Troll Army, You Know What Must Be Done' (2015). Given the abuse commended, it is unsurprising that some people did make death threats. Here, silencing of racial abuse was seen as justification for attempting to silence the abused through more abuse. In response, other people organised Twitter hashtags supporting her, one of which reached the top ten trending hashtags (Stephens 2015).

One site of some importance to our general story is 4chan.org, the users of which have appeared to support group trolling. 4chan is an open 'bulletin board', with many different boards, the most famous being /b/, which (in 2012) encouraged random posts, anonymity, mutual abuse, the posting of notable or supposedly 'shocking' images, while apparently driving off people not conforming to their customs. While 'free speech' is a recurrent motif on 4chan, not all speech seemed acceptable at this time, especially speech framed by the supposedly feminine 'softer' or empathetic emotions (Manivannan 2013). Many users attacked people with that style of communication and 4chan was not quite the 'say anything zone' Coleman claims (2014: 41). Unconnected to 4chan, women online often report male attacks, patronisation and apparent attempts to re-establish gender hierarchies (Herring et al. 2002; Thacker and Griffiths 2012: 25). The trolling I described elsewhere strongly praised aggressive, 'emotionless' masculinity (Marshall 2007: 194–97), which seems a standard trope of right-wing politics (Kelly 2017).

Some academic analyses (Higgin 2013; Holmes 2013; Phillips 2011) claim that 4chan's unintentional politics liberate by making 'oppression' more obvious, and 4chan is often considered the birthplace of the loose association of leaderless online activists who called themselves 'Anonymous', who were famous for denial-of-service attacks on organisations that its 'members' of the day disapproved of (Coleman 2014: 4). However, 4chan users' politics primarily seem to celebrate their smartness, language conventions and insider knowledge, while spreading wariness of the group's supposed 'extremity'. 4chan activity is difficult to identify because it is hard to be certain who participates in that forum. This vagueness magnifies its effect (as activity can be attributed to 4chan when it is not present). However, users are reputed to flood Twitter hashtags, Facebook pages and so on with abuse and deliberately 'shocking' images, making response impossible. Their action tends to communicate that they are not interested in communicative exchange, just attack, silencing and showing the victims' lack of value to them. We could describe this behaviour as ritualised communication of noncommunication and superiority.

Trolls on Trolling

Trolling is often portrayed as a skill. One journalist (Feeny 2012) writing in the *Brisbane Times* and commenting on the Charlotte Dawson case describes the comments of a self-proclaimed troll:

[She] insists there's method to her meanness. She declares herself a performance artist ... [She says] Some people need to learn how to take criticism, especially on the internet. 'I also look at [trolling] as a form of culture jamming, in the sense that it can disrupt the status quo to hopefully stop and make people think for a moment ... I do it because I'd like them to see the hypocrisies of their and our ways ... If I've really offended people, it's probably because they deserved it and that's their own fault.'

On a television programme on Australia's Special Broadcasting Service (SBS) (Brockie 2012), part of the same anti-troll cluster of media events, another self-proclaimed troll states: 'I cause very large problems, social problems generally, for very powerful people. I like to think of trolling as a way of expressing working class discontent.' He argues that the people being trolled have to take some responsibility as 'it's impossible to do without the[ir] participation'. People should not be:

> insulated morons who can't ever hear anything that might hurt their feelings. Like get over it, get over it, grow up, grow up and learn to deal with people on the internet not liking you and if you don't like it shut down your Facebook page, make your Twitter private, don't engage in a public discussion and you'll never run into a conversation where I can say something that will hurt your feelings. (Brockie 2012)

This comment again suggests that self-identified trolls can feel that 'sensitive' or 'feminine' people should be silent if they don't want to be attacked. Here, trolling practices imply that trolls are more hip and savvy than people being trolled, with greater control over emotions and response. Some self-professed trolls see themselves as showing people the 'true reality' of internet order/culture and subverting stupidity and inertia; upset people don't get the joke. In this framing, becoming upset shows weakness, or lack of understanding, and results from a failure to embrace the true orderings and practices of those trolling.

Some trolls practice defacing online memorial sites (Phillips 2011). The 'RIP Trolls' Phillips talked with claimed antagonism towards 'grief tourists' with no relationship to the deceased. Not that the trolls had any association with the deceased either, but they practised the approved 'real/authentic' aggression rather than 'soft/inauthentic' sentiment. They also imply that if people declare grief or sympathy on a public discussion site, then they ask to be attacked and are only hurt if they choose to be. Silencing is part of troll order.

In this communicative environment, it is difficult to define the difference between practices of trolling and 'legitimate' political action. When people respond to a call to contact their local political representative, they become part of a group flooding that representative's email box, message bank, Facebook page or Twitter account, making it difficult for the victim to function, as with trolling. Some of those protests will undoubtedly be impolite, adding to the similarity, and a few people can pretend to be many to give force to their arguments (as when politicians claim support from 'silent majorities'). Rumours abound that some trolls are paid to promote political views, discredit hostile articles and make opposition painful. Government-paid trolls may likewise oppose those categorised as terrorists or political out-groups (Chen 2015; Greenwald 2014; Monbiot 2010). However, calling commentators 'paid trolls' frames critical comments as discredited, also bringing order to group communication and understanding (Manjoo 2012). Whether the term 'troll' is used to legitimate what appears to be attacking behaviour as 'just words' or 'a joke', or to discredit arguments one disagrees with, it is a practice of framing some communication as dismissible without consideration.

Usual Explanations for Trolling

Standard explanations assume trolling is disorderly and pathological. Fichman and Sanfilippo (2015: 163) begin with the assertion: 'Online trolling is a specific example of deviant and antisocial online behaviour.' Tom Postmes, a professor of social and organisational psychology, is quoted by *The Guardian* as saying: 'Trolls aspire to violence ... They want to promote antipathetic emotions of disgust and outrage, which morbidly gives them a sense of pleasure' (Adams 2011). Buckels, Trapnell and Paulhus (2014) identify trolling with sadistic, psychopathological and Machiavellian personality traits, through a survey that might be seen as inviting self-identified trollers to 'shock' the researchers. Trolling practices are often approached as unique phenomena of online life deriving from anonymity, identity deception, deindividuation or disinhibition of human aggression (Donath 1999; Suler 2004; Widyanto and Griffiths 2011: 15). However, nonanonymous aggression and abuse is common in mainstream media, with some media personalities making a career out of controversy, as will be discussed later.

Further, individual psychological factors such as disinhibition are not needed to explain some effects of trolling, only the *quantity* of action. If only 1 per cent of people are annoyed and act, then that can amount to a large number of people and a large amount of disruption. If, for instance, Dawson (as described below) had 22,000 followers, then 1 per cent of that is 220 people. If 220 people published abuse to her account in one day, then that could be an overwhelming amount of abuse for her to experience. It is also difficult for the victim to respond in kind, producing inequality of agency. This is a structural issue of practice, irrespective of whether disinhibition is involved or not.

The problem with online communication is not that identity is hidden (as suggested by the disinhibition thesis), but that people's identity categories are uncertain and that the practice of framing by attributing group membership to people, based on their remarks, has a routine uncertainty that can be exploited for acts of power and ordering. As described elsewhere (Marshall 2007: 89–92), quests for acknowledgement can result in people provoking abuse, and the many-to-many nature of online communication, together with the quantity of participants, implies that even if most people decide not to respond, then others will respond either in agreement or disagreement. It is hard for calm to erupt. Similarly, because of framing ambiguities, it is possible for well-intentioned people to be framed and attacked as trolls and, if those people were ambivalent about the group, this can confirm any previous bias they have against it (Marshall 2007: 180–88). This can then strengthen their framing of people they identify as coming from similar groups as inherently hostile, or stupid, and only worth interacting with through attack.

The Dawson Case

Research on trolling can be uncomfortable. There is always a risk of defaming people, as everything comes down to interpretation, which is neither stable nor sure. We cannot interpret another's condition or intention easily, yet such interpretive practices surround what we call trolling. Furthermore, if the volume, intensity or violence of messages is not shown, their effect is lost. However, displaying that violence may reward perpetrators by acknowledging them. Those defined as 'trolls' are difficult to interview as they are largely anonymous, and their responses could be a further troll. Furthermore, Charlotte Dawson, the focal person of this discussion, is dead and unable to correct any inaccuracies; as such, this chapter could be seen as an extended RIP troll. This and Dawson's obvious distress render the case problematic and even more painful to research. I kept the focus because these events are still referred to in Australian media (e.g. Lang 2018). I chose not to name people other than Dawson. Remarks quoted were available on publicly accessible websites, although some material has since disappeared. My research began, in early September 2012, in response to a media campaign for regulation of 'cyberbullying' and trolling. In this campaign, trolls were strongly categorised as a deviant out-group and were portrayed as socially inept, vicious losers or 'pissheads' (according to one academic) (Connelly 2012). Celebrity denunciations of trolls, and support for victims, was an essential part of the campaign, with Dawson being appointed an anti-bullying spokesperson from late June 2012.

Dawson lived in Australia, but was a New Zealand-born model and TV personality. She ran a voluble and quite heavily followed Twitter account with at least 22,000 followers depending on the source and date. She was known as an acerbic commentator online and on television. On the TV show *Australia's Next Top Model*, she was apparently known for telling young women they were too fat or unattractive. Impolite outspokenness is often thought to generate ratings and celebrities can depend on audience attention for their income. One year, she attacked the sixteen-year-old contestant who achieved second place in the competition, who had turned down a hefty contract in Paris. Her comments could easily be interpreted as aimed at destroying the young woman's career, saying she would 'end up being the poster girl for *Sunbury Centrelink*' (a local social security office) (Frockwriter 2009). Dawson was reported confirming she made these comments and did 'not see anything wrong with them … They're the sort of things I would say on the show … they're said with humour, not vitriol, and honesty' (Frockwriter 2009). She was reported as having described another woman, on her Facebook account, as a 'sad attention whore', a 'Westie scrag' and a 'suburban fattie with … a dirty crack pipe' (Reist 2010), but said 'it was joking no bullying' (Dawson, commenting in Reist 2010), showing both the troll-type joke defence and that media comments overflow the boundaries of that medium. Later Dawson claimed that the person she attacked probably did not exist and that the article reporting her comments was defamatory (Reist 2010). Her attacks led to other people calling Dawson a 'crack whore' and, when she complained, they likewise said 'Oh, we love you, we were just having fun', which she could not accept (Byrnes 2010). When it was proposed to her that fashion shows attack women's body image, she repeatedly replied along the lines of 'if you don't like the show then don't watch it' (see her comments on Reist (2010)). This resembles the troll argument that people choose offence by participating. In a conversation about fashion bloggers, she wrote: 'Somebody please kill "[X]" … Please please

please.' This was reported to the person in question as a death threat and he may have taken it seriously (Buchanan and Ellis 2012; Reality Raver 2012a). On television, Dawson dismissed the remark as a joke – 'we were having a light hearted conversation' – while implying 'X' had attempted character assassination of her (*Sunrise* 2012a). She did not appear to perceive her own remarks as having possibly unintended hurtful effects and tended to order her apparent attacks as jokes. She also did not apparently perceive the inequality of the interaction; as a paid celebrity, her remarks were more likely to be read than her victim's replies.

Dawson also regularly retweeted attacks on herself to her followers. Some perceived this as encouraging her followers to attack these attackers. The *Reality Ravings* site (2012a) quotes one person writing: 'Charlotte Dawson is a bully, she influenced her followers to attack me telling me to kill myself/get an eating disorder etc.' Another person, commenting on this story, claimed that Dawson responded abusively to tweets of his that had no connection to her: 'I had her followers telling me to "kill myself" among other things and I simply said to Charlotte that what she was doing was harassment'. He queried her credentials as an anti-bullying spokesperson (Reality Raver 2012a).

The events that drew the most media attention began some three months after the call to kill the fashion blogger, while Dawson was in New Zealand publicising her then forthcoming memoir. In an interview with a New Zealand newspaper (the *Herald on Sunday*), she stated that 'New Zealand is small, nasty and vindictive … [The book] does make New Zealand look pedestrian and stupid. But honestly, that was my experience' (Anstiss 2012). She was either unaware of the likely effects of her remarks or was, perhaps, practising a campaign of publicity through notoriety, setting up a conflict that might be reported in New Zealand and then reported in Australia. New Zealanders did respond on Twitter. She closed her account for twenty-four hours (*NZ Herald* 2012). However, when a person's main trade is celebrity and recognition, it is hard to be silent and she soon reopened it. A New Zealander, resident in Australia, responded: 'excuse me @MsCharlotteD on behalf of NZ we would like you to please GO HANG YOURSELF!!!' (apparently referring to an existing hashtag of that name). Dawson appears to have retweeted this tweet stripped of context. The remark offended a follower of hers whose fiancé had hanged himself, and afterwards this follower was abused by the person being retweeted (Lee 2012). The New Zealander *may* have apologised and *may* have said elsewhere that they were continuing to stir trouble (Reality Raver 2012b). The full context of messages is continually lost. Weeks later, Dawson discovered who this person was, rang her up at her work and reported her to her employer, leading to the troll's suspension. There is no real line between media and everyday life, and being framed as a troll can have hard offline consequences. Some people labelled Dawson's actions 'stalking' or 'bullying', while others praised her for confronting her attacker and thought that the attacker should be punished: 'It is time that these trolls learn that you aren't always safe hiding behind your computer screen, and I hope they get what's coming' (Whirlpool 2015). Dawson claimed she did not seek out the person and was not defending herself but her follower (Mark 2012). Differences of interpretation fed into the argument. Other people began to attack Dawson, especially for getting the attacker suspended. According to some reports, Dawson challenged 'trolls' to 'bring it on' (Whirlpool 2015).

Attacks escalated. It is hard to say how many attacks Dawson received, but they seem to have been largely monothemed, telling her to kill herself, creating a strong ambience of threat and rejection. Many of the more distressing messages (those with death threats, death images and sex threats) made references to the internet site/group 9gag. This becomes significant because some commentators suggest that Dawson had attracted the attention of people using 4chan, who, according to Whitney Phillips, had been blaming 9gag.com for anything 'horrible', likely to attract media attention, since late 2011 (Download This Show 2012). It is possible that someone posted to 4chan about Dawson 'persecuting' someone, stopping free speech or claiming she could defeat trolls, and this led to people trying to impose their worldview upon her 'in defence'. Keane (2012) claims that people did write things on 4chan/b/, like 'That was a great success. Vapid bitch deserved the raid' and: 'D-list celebrity retweets her nay-sayers (HURRDURRTROLLS) and publicly calls for them to take her on, saying on national TV that it doesn't faze her and "rolls off like water on a ducks back"'. Keane repeats assertions that much of 4chan/b/'s aggression seems directed at mainstream internet users, particularly women, unless they share the group's interests and customs (see also Download This Show 2012; Whirlpool 2015).

In the early morning of 30 August 2012, Dawson apparently tweeted: 'Ok NZ YOU WIN I GOT A FIST FULL OF VERY POTENT DRUGS! IM READY TO DIE!' (Reality Raver 2012b). There are claims she sent a tweet (possibly the one above) with a picture of a hand clutching a pill bottle, but soon deleted it. Her last tweets generally referred to in the media are 'Hope this ends the misery' and 'You win x'. She was then rushed to hospital after an attempted suicide (Hornery and Hall 2012). Sorrow and shock were expressed in mainstream media and offline.

Politicians intensified discussion of online regulation, and the New South Wales *Daily Telegraph* ran a 'News Limited want members of the public to help us identify trolls who threatened and harassed Dawson and other victims of harassment online' campaign (Connelly and Keene 2012). Tony Abbott, then Federal opposition leader, wanted tougher legal powers to order 'scurrilous' internet bullying attacks to be taken down. He said that online bullying was more disturbing than verbal attacks (Moses and Hornery 2012), possibly because he is renowned for his verbal attacks (which get repeated in many media forums). Similar remarks came from the government (Jones and Byrnes 2012). 'Experts' recommended that Dawson should have ignored or blocked the attacks, ignoring the difficulties involved, and reinforcing the troll idea that her distress was self-caused and that silence is a solution.

Cyberbullying became a catch-all phrase of denunciation. Right-wing radio personality Alan Jones accused people of cyberbullying when they ran a campaign to persuade companies not to sponsor him because of his personal attacks, on his radio show and elsewhere, on the Prime Minister Julia Gillard. In one of these attacks he called for her to be murdered and said she caused her father to die 'of shame' (Gardiner 2012). These attacks gave him recognition and publicity. One politician remarked: 'An airwaves troll trolling the digital trollers. We've come full circle' (Jones and Byrnes 2012). The Rupert Murdoch-owned *Daily Telegraph* newspaper, which was central to the media anti-troll campaign, has similarly fought for the right of its columnists to abuse people racially as a matter of free speech. It later published photoshopped front-page images with 'enemy' politicians in Nazi regalia and compared the national broadcaster to the Islamic State. It frequently uses abuse in support of its 'right-wing' political objectives. This trolling tendency was frequently recognised: 'If indeed these apparently evil perpetrators destroying society with these tweets should be named and shamed, jailed etc etc, then some of the radio and tabloid shock jocks should be sent to the gas chamber' (comment on Reality Raver 2012a).

As well as sorrow, cynicism was widespread, especially when Dawson left hospital for an interview with the Channel 9 current affairs programme *60 Minutes*, despite her doctors' advice (Moran and Reines 2012). On one discussion site (Whirlpool 2015), people wrote things like: 'Make no mistake, this is all about publicity for this D grade celebrity. Talk about trolls, she's the biggest one of all', and 'End of day she timed this stunt with her book release'. Other people remarked that by tweeting the suicide attempt, she was 'attention seeking' rather than serious (Whirlpool 2015). To my eyes, Dawson looked genuinely fragile in the interview. The interview only mentions her book because of allegations of publicity seeking, and she implies she could have found better publicity than this. The interviewer encouraged her to read some of the tweets, while seeming puzzled that Dawson kept on reading. The interviewer also appears to suggest that Dawson should get back online when she said she would stop using the internet (*60 Minutes* 2012).

Common tropes of anti-Dawson comment were that words and images cannot hurt anyone; she did not have to read her Twitter account if it upset her; she should not have given trolls publicity by retweeting; or she was oversensitive. A person, self-advertised as a 'social media influencer', wrote in a blog entry about Dawson: 'an outsider, a stranger I've never met, call[s] me stupid, unattractive or unknowledgeable? Pffft. Please' (Papworth 2012). Others alleged that people only felt sympathy for her because she was a celebrity and were therefore hypocritical, which resonates with disparagement of 'grief tourists' in RIP trolling. Supposedly, only people who knew Dawson intimately had any right to feel sympathy for her. The basic message was, yet again, that people with 'hurt feelings' are weak and their communication is framed as worthless. They should be silent and not disturb the genuine orders of authentic communication.

Dawson confronted some of the people who tweeted about her on a TV news item from 23 October 2012 on *Channel 7 News* (2012) followed by a recap on the morning *Sunrise* programme (2012b). It is unclear how Dawson gained the identities of the people she called 'online bullies'. In one confrontation, she responded to the allegation that she had posted where a troll worked 'to 22 thousand people' (clearly a message that could cause problems for the man's employer or cost him his job) by touching him and saying 'it's just exposing the nasty … it's not bullying you, its exposing you for what you are' (*Channel 7 News* 2012). These TV exchanges do not seem to exemplify equitable, 'nontrolling' or good communication. The 'trolls' seemed surprised, had no control over their message, little time to prepare a response, their words were likely to be edited and framed in a manner that was hostile to them, and the film of the programme with their names and faces could be online indefinitely, perhaps influencing the course of their lives. They were alone, outnumbered physically, by Dawson, another reporter, camera operator, sound technician, probably lighting people and other backup. These trolls were likely placed in a situation of much greater physical and emotional threat than she was. The programme finished with Dawson coming to 'understand' that trolls 'in real life' are pathetic, and cowardly; more silencing perhaps. These practices are similar to the way in which trolls 'proved' Dawson was inadequate. Both media and trolls worked within a framing of moral certainty and dehumanisation, making little attempt to sympathise with each other (Whelan 2013: 47). Annihilation was the order sought. Celebrities, like trolls, seek recognition, and shock or attack gives that recognition easily.

In February 2014, Dawson did commit suicide. She had been campaigning against government cuts in money for life-saving operations for cancer patients (Dawson 2014). Trolling occurred on other issues, but, judging by her surviving Twitter feed, seems minor. However, she was without work or income, and her home was being sold from under her. She was reportedly distressed by the prospect of a 'tell-all' interview on TV by her ex-husband. Media people knew she was suffering long-term depression and fighting alcoholism and that this interview would cause her great distress, but that did not stop them – the shock had to go on. In her last radio interview, she mentioned that her agency no longer wanted to represent her because of her depression. She also stated she left *Australia's Next Top Model* as she was worried about the message it gave to young women (KIIS 1065 2014). While quite a number of articles appeared to connect her death with trolling, none of the media reports I have seen blamed the precariousness of media/celebrity life and income, mainstream media action or the vagaries of Sydney real estate. Those factors did not involve an out-group or a despised and attackable minority, and were, as a result, perhaps invisible.

Conclusion

Trolling is not just about individuals being obnoxious or cleverly undermining the self-righteous, but about ordering communication in a particular context. It demonstrates the extent of conflict in people's mediated life. All the factors involved in trolling are present in ordinary communication, especially media communication, but are intensified by the patterns of online communication and by social conflicts in the wider world. Power struggles in communication easily shift into causing hurt, as force is both the ultimate basis of resolution of communicative ambiguity and of asserting 'correct' behaviours. Both online, and in offline media, disrupting people often gives response and recognition by others to the disruptors. Framing is important, and a common method of framing works through placing people into a social category; this 'reveals' what they intend and what they are doing, allowing their message to be dismissed or accepted. 'Sensitive' seems one framing category despised by trolls. 'Troll' seems another such category, despised by others. Such framing can place the person into a pattern of hostilities or collaborations, which exist more generally. Framings of hostility are easy to bring into play and reinforce inaccurate interpretation while intensifying splits. These framings can reinforce what the troller already suspects – that the out-group being trolled is closed, humourless, hostile, weak or overbearing. The resulting events largely confirm each side's sense of the other. In this case, Dawson appears to have seen trolls as villains, while the trolls appeared to see her as elite, humourless and overly sensitive. Order is asserted, at the cost of communication, through 'communication'.

Trolling is a *part* of the (dis)orders of information in an 'information society'. It is part of the way in which society both orders and disorders itself. Communicative trolling is also a normal part of media processes; it attracts attention, gains audiences, forms groups, threatens out-groups and prevents participants and audiences (however vague the separation) from listening to different ideas. Trolling, like many other forms of political communication carried into media, is not about encouraging diversity or balance, but about mocking or silencing other views. While some media organisations carried out campaigns against trolls, they legitimised and demonstrated trolling in the way they framed questions, presented evidence and abusively supported their own political ideals. In the campaign, ordinary (but not mainstream media) trolls were to be annihilated and punished. The ambiguity is shown by Dawson herself, who, as we have seen, was the 'nasty judge' on her modelling show and could define her attacks on people as part of that 'joking', recognition-seeking, celebrity persona. Media, as a vehicle of communication and modified by communication, is not separable from non-media life or everyday contexts, but is embedded within them, as shown when Dawson broke through into the offline lives of others as part of her 'news activity' and when the trolling magnified her depression. One reason why the distinction between public and private is being increasingly eliminated is that 'the private' expresses vulnerability and hence becomes a strategic target in such conflict.

While this chapter focuses on specific incidents, it merges with a more general argument I have made elsewhere (Marshall 2013, 2017; Marshall et al. 2015) that social practices in the 'information society' appear to encourage separation, rejection and refusal to communicate, as part of the way in which actors seek to bring order to communication and social relations. What is known as information society is more accurately labelled as '(dis)information society', based on a standardised breakdown of communication and information failure.

In this society, the use of media technologies to communicate is co-constitutive of conflict and misunderstanding.

Jonathan Paul Marshall is an anthropologist who has been studying life on the internet since 1992. He has been interested in questions of social control and how attempts to produce order produce disorder. He has held various research fellowships and jobs. He is currently researching the unintended consequences of climate technologies such as renewables, carbon trading, biofuels and geoengineering. He has edited numerous special issues, books and journals, authored *Living on Cybermind: Categories, Communication and Control* (Peter Lang, 2007) and coauthored *Disorder and the Disinformation Society: The Social Dynamics of Information, Networks and Software* (Routledge, 2015).

Note

1. The often-used term 'information society' implies that accurate democratic communication, networking and recognised knowledge are vitally important to social and economic processes in the contemporary developed world, with knowledge workers constituting a growing class almost everywhere. These propositions seem dubious (Marshall 2013; Marshall et al. 2015).

References

60 Minutes. 2012. 'Interview with Charlotte Dawson', Channel 9, 2 September. Retrieved 16 October 2019 from https://youtu.be/vFFftOoEaRs.

Adams, T. 2011. 'How the Internet Created an Age of Rage', *The Guardian*, 24 July. Retrieved 16 October 2019 from http://www.theguardian.com/technology/2011/jul/24/internet-anonymity-trolling-tim-adams.

Anstiss, C.D. 2012. 'Don't Call Charlotte a Kiwi', *New Zealand Herald*, 5 August. Retrieved 16 October 2019 from http://www.nzherald.co.nz/entertainment/news/article.cfm?c_id=1501119&objectid=10824673.

Bateson, G. 1972. *Steps to an Ecology of Mind*. San Francisco: Chandler.

Bishop, J. 2013. 'The Psychology of Trolling and Lurking: The Role of Defriending and Gamification for Increasing Participation in Online Communities Using Seductive Narratives', in J. Bishop (ed.), *Examining the Concepts, Issues and Implications of Internet Trolling*. Hershey: IGI Global, pp. 106–23.

Brockie, J. 2012. 'Trolls', *Insight. SBS*, 16 October. Retrieved 16 October 2019 from https://www.sbs.com.au/news/sites/sbs.com.au.news/files/transcripts/363601_insight_trolls_transcript.html.

Buchanan, M., and S. Ellis. 2012. 'A Big Day for … a Fashion Fatwa', *Sydney Morning Herald*, 9 May. Retrieved 16 October 2019 from http://www.

smh.com.au/entertainment/tv-and-radio/still-turned-on-by-sandilands-20120508-1yb5y.html.

Buckels, E.E., P.D. Trapnell and D.L. Paulhus. 2014. 'Trolls Just Want to Have Fun', *Personality and Individual Differences* 67: 97–102.

Byrnes, H. 2010. 'Australia's Next Top Blue as Charlotte Dawson Sues', *Daily Telegraph*, 7 August. Retrieved 16 October 2019 from https://www.news.com.au/entertainment/celebrity-life/australias-next-top-blue-as-charlotte-dawson-sues/news-story/b5bd11b517c73260ac23f8675beb5fe2.

Channel 7 News. 2012. 'Charlotte Dawson Tracks Down and Confronts Twitter Trolls', 23 October. Retrieved 16 October 2019 from https://www.youtube.com/watch?v=ASg8x9b2o0M.

Chen, A. 2015. 'The Agency', *New York Times Magazine*, 2 June. Retrieved 16 October 2019 from http://www.nytimes.com/2015/06/07/magazine/the-agency.html.

Coleman, G. 2014. *Hacker, Hoaxer, Whistleblower, Spy: The Many Faces of Anonymous*. London: Verso.

Connelly, C. 2012. '"It Just Makes Me Happy When I Can Make Someone Angry": A Special Investigation into the Dark World of Trolling', *Daily Telegraph*, 28 February. Retrieved 16 October 2019 from http://www.dailytelegraph.com.au/news/national/it-just-makes-me-happy-when-i-can-make-someone-angry-a-special-investigation-into-the-dark-world-of-trolling/story-fndo28a5-1226283852843.

Connelly, C., and N. Keene. 2012. 'Charlotte Dawson Twitter Attack Sparks Call for Changes to Laws against Cyber Bullying', *Daily Telegraph*, 30 August. Retrieved 16 October 2019 from http://www.dailytelegraph.com.au/news/charlotte-dawson-twitter-attack-sparks-call-for-changes-to-laws-against-cyber-bullying/story-e6freuy9-1226461809720.

Daily Stormer. 2015. Retrieved 16 October 2019 from https://dailystormer.name.

Dawson, C. 2014. Charlotte Dawson @MsCharlotteD. Retrieved 16 October 2019 from https://twitter.com/mscharlotted.

Doak, D.F. et al. 2008. 'Understanding and Predicting Ecological Dynamics: Are Major Surprises Inevitable?', *Ecology* 89(4): 952–61.

Donath, J. 1999. 'Identity and Deception in the Virtual Community', in P. Kollock and M. Smith (eds), *Communities in Cyberspace*. London: Routledge, pp. 29–59.

Download This Show. 2012. 'What Really Happened to Charlotte Dawson?', *ABC Radio National*, 6 September. Retrieved 16 October 2019 from http://www.abc.net.au/radionational/programs/downloadthisshow/ep34/4247094.

Feeny, K. 2012. 'Confessions of a Troll: "Trolling is an Art"', *Brisbane Times*, 16 October. Retrieved 16 October 2019 from http://www.smh.com.au/entertainment/tv-and-radio/confessions-of-a-troll-trolling-is-an-art-20121015-27n3f.html.

Fichman, P., and M.R. Sanfilippo. 2015. 'The Bad Boys and Girls of Cyberspace: How Gender and Context Impact Perception of and Reaction to Trolling', *Social Science Computer Review* 33(2): 163–80.

Frockwriter. 2009. '"We Don't Give a Shit": Charlotte Dawson on the Cassi Facebook Fallout', 30 July. Retrieved 12 February 2018 from http://frockwriter.com/2009/07/we-don-t-give-a-shit-charlotte-dawson-on-the-cassi-facebook-fallout.

Gardiner, S. 2012. 'Alan Jones Hits out at "Gutless" Mercedes Exec as Broadcaster Points Finger at Cyber Bullies', *Sydney Morning Herald*, 8 October. Retrieved 16 October 2019 from http://www.smh.com.au/entertainment/tv-and-radio/alan-jones-hits-out-at-gutless-mercedes-exec-as-broadcaster-points-finger-at-cyber-bullies-20121008-277tu.html.

Greenwald, G. 2014. 'How Covert Agents Infiltrate the Internet to Manipulate, Deceive and Destroy Reputations', *The Intercept*, 25 February. Retrieved 16 October 2019 from https://theintercept.com/2014/02/24/jtrig-manipulation.

Herring, S. et al. 2002. 'Searching for Safety Online: Managing "Trolling" in a Feminist Forum', *The Information Society* 18: 371–84.

Higgin, T. 2013. '/b/lack up: What Trolls Can Teach Us about Race', *Fibreculture Journal* 22: 133–46. Retrieved 16 October 2019 from http://twentytwo.fibreculturejournal.org/fcj-159-black-up-what-trolls-can-teach-us-about-race.

Holmes, S. 2013. 'Politics is Serious Business: Jacques Rancière, Griefing, and the Re-partitioning of the (Non)Sensical', *Fibreculture Journal* 22: 152–69. Retrieved 16 October 2019 from http://twentytwo.fibreculturejournal.org/fcj-160-politics-is-serious-business-jacques-ranciere-griefing-and-the-re-partitioning-of-the-nonsensical.

Hopkins, N., and S. Reicher. 1997. 'Social Movement Rhetoric and the Social Psychology of Collective Action: A Case Study of an Anti-abortion Mobilization', *Human Relations* 50(3): 261–86.

Hornery, A., and B. Hall. 2012. 'Top Model Judge in Hospital after Twitter Attacks', *Sydney Morning Herald*, 30 August. Retrieved 16 October 2019 from http://www.smh.com.au/lifestyle/private-sydney/top-model-judge-in-hospital-after-twitter-attacks-20120830-252b1.html.

Jones, G., and H. Byrnes. 2012. 'Time is up for Twitter Trolls and Bullies', *Daily Telegraph*, 11 September. Retrieved 16 October 2019 from http://www.dailytelegraph.com.au/time-is-up-for-twitter-trolls-and-bulllies/story-e6freuy9-1226472133504.

Karmasin, M. et al. 2013. 'Preface: Perspectives on the Changing Role of the Mass Media in Hostile Conflicts', in J. Seethaler et al. (eds), *Selling War: The Role of the Mass Media in Hostile Conflicts from World War I to the 'War on Terror'*. Bristol: Intellect, pp. ix–xv.

Keane, B. 2012. 'Celeb Tweeter Just Collateral Damage in Online War', *Crikey*, 3 September. Retrieved 16 October 2019 from http://www.crikey.com.au/2012/09/03/celeb-tweeter-just-collateral-damage-in-online-war.

Kelly, A. 2017. 'The Alt-Right: Reactionary Rehabilitation for White Masculinity', *Soundings* 66: 68–78.
KIIS 1065. 2014. 'Charlotte Dawson's Last Radio Interview', *Kyle & Jackie O Show*, 21 February. Retrieved 16 October 2019 from https://www.youtube.com/watch?v=AU8BO-AB-84.
Lakoff, G. 2014. *The ALL NEW Don't Think of an Elephant! Know Your Values and Frame the Debate*. White River Junction: Chelsea Green Publishing.
Lang, K. 2018. 'Cyber Trolls aren't Fringe Dwellers, They're Us', *Courier Mail*, 12 January. Retrieved 16 October 2019 from http://www.couriermail.com.au/rendezview/cyber-trolls-arent-fringe-dwellers-theyre-us/news-story/da5d19385b2acfdc2e99acb9aa8b217b.
Lee, J. 2012. 'Uni Staffer Suspended for "Go Hang Yourself" Tweet', *The Age*, 29 August. Retrieved 16 October 2019 from http://www.theage.com.au/victoria/uni-staffer-suspended-for-go-hang-yourself-tweet-20120829-25015.html.
MacLachlan, G., and I. Reid. 1994. *Framing and Interpretation*. Melbourne: Melbourne University Press.
Manivannan, V. 2013. 'Tits or GTFO: The Logics of Misogyny on 4chan's Random – /b/', *Fibreculture Journal* 22: 109–32. Retrieved 16 October 2019 from http://twentytwo.fibreculturejournal.org/fcj-158-tits-or-gtfo-the-logics-of-misogyny-on-4chans-random-b/.
Manjoo, F. 2012. 'Stop Calling Me a Troll: Just Because You Disagree with Me Doesn't Mean I am One', *Slate*, 5 December. Retrieved 16 October 2019 from http://www.slate.com/articles/technology/technology/2012/12/i_m_not_a_troll_why_does_everyone_on_the_internet_keep_calling_me_one.html.
Mark, D. 2012. 'TV Presenter in Hospital after Vicious Twitter Attacks', *PM*, 30 August. Retrieved 16 October 2019 from http://www.abc.net.au/pm/content/2012/s3579714.htm.
Marshall, J.P. 2007. *Living on Cybermind: Categories, Communication and Control*. New York: Peter Lang.
———. 2013. 'The Mess of Information and the Order of Doubt', *Global Media Journal Australian Edition* 7(1). Retrieved 16 October 2019 from https://www.hca.westernsydney.edu.au/gmjau/?p=308.
———. 2017. 'Disinformation Society, Communication and Cosmopolitan Democracy', *Cosmopolitan Civil Societies Journal* 9(2): 1–24. Retrieved 16 October 2019 from http://epress.lib.uts.edu.au/journals/index.php/mcs/article/view/5477.
Marshall, J.P. et al. 2015. *Disorder and the Disinformation Society: The Social Dynamics of Information, Networks and Software*. London: Routledge.
Monbiot, G. 2010. 'These Astroturf Libertarians are the Real Threat to Internet Democracy', *The Guardian*, 14 December. Retrieved 16 October 2019 from http://www.theguardian.com/commentisfree/libertycentral/2010/dec/13/astroturf-libertarians-internet-democracy.
Moran, J., and R. Reines. 2012. 'Charlotte Dawson Reveals How Twitter Trolls Sent Her into Spiral of Depression', *Daily Telegraph*, 2 September. Retrieved

16 October 2019 from https://www.news.com.au/tablet/charlotte-dawson-reveals-how-twitter-trolls-sent-her-into-spiral-of-depression/news-story/f5dc75476a1443630819a82cc11fe269.

Moses, A., and A. Hornery. 2012. 'Expert Says Dawson Broke the First Rule of Social Media: Don't Feed the Trolls', *Sydney Morning Herald*, 31 August. Retrieved 16 October 2019 from http://www.smh.com.au/technology/technology-news/expert-says-dawson-broke-the-first-rule-of-social-media-dont-feed-the-trolls-20120831-254b6.html.

NZ Herald. 2012. 'Charlotte Dawson's Web Overload', *New Zealand Herald*, 12 August. Retrieved 16 October 2019 from http://www.nzherald.co.nz/entertainment/news/article.cfm?c_id=1501119&objectid=10826305.

Ong, J.C., and J.V. Cabañes. 2018. Architects of Networked Disinformation. Newtontech4dev. Retrieved 16 October 2019 from http://newtontechfordev.com/wp-content/uploads/2018/02/ARCHITECTS-OF-NETWORKED-DISINFORMATION-FULL-REPORT.pdf.

Papworth, L. 2012. 'Charlotte Dawson, Cyberbullies and Social Media Pot and Kettle'. Retrieved 16 October 2019 from http://laurelpapworth.com/charlotte-dawson-cyberbullies-and-social-media-pot-and-kettle.

Peckham, M. 1979. *Explanation and Power*. New York: Seabury Press.

Phillips, W. 2011. 'LOLing at Tragedy: Facebook Trolls, Memorial Pages and Resistance to Grief Online', *First Monday* 16(12). Retrieved 12 February 2018 from http://firstmonday.org/htbin/cgiwrap/bin/ojs/index.php/fm/article/view/3168/3115.

Reality Raver. 2012a. 'Charlotte Dawson – Not Sure She Is the Expert on Twitter Etiquette'. Retrieved 12 February 2018 from http://www.realityravings.

———. 2012b. 'Charlotte Dawson Speaks out Shaken'. Retrieved 12 February 2018 from http://www.realltyravings.com/2012/09/03/charlotte-dawson-speaks-out-shaken-media-reporting-should-also-examine-the-national-vilification-of-tanya-heti.

Reice, S.R. 2001. *The Silver Lining: The Benefits of Natural Disasters*. Princeton: Princeton University Press.

Reist, M.T. 2010. 'Alex Perry and Charlotte Dawson's Anti Women Behaviour'. Retrieved 16 October 2019 from http://melindatankardreist.com/2010/07/how-can-sarah-murdoch-lend-her-good-name-to-this-toxic-show.

Stephens, K. 2015. 'Lawyer Mariam Veiszadeh Receives Message of Hope amid Tsunami of Anti-Islamic Hatred', *Brisbane Times*, 25 February. Retrieved 16 October 2019 from http://www.brisbanetimes.com.au/queensland/lawyer-mariam-veiszadeh-receives-message-of-hope-amid-tsunami-of-antiislamic-hatred-20150224-13ntqg.html.

Suler, J.R. 2004. 'The Online Dishibition Effect', *CyberPsychology and Behaviour* 7: 321–26.

Sunrise. 2012a. 'Twitter War Erupts', Channel 7, n.d. Retrieved 16 October 2019 from https://au.tv.yahoo.com/sunrise/video/watch/13638686/twitter-war-erupts.

———. 2012b. 'Charlotte Confronts Twitter Trolls', *Channel 7*, 24 October. Retrieved 16 October 2019 from https://www.youtube.com/watch?v=waSZ6yjeQfs.

Thacker, S., and M.D. Griffiths. 2012. 'An Exploratory Study of Trolling in Online Video Gaming', *International Journal of Cyber Behavior, Psychology and Learning* 2(4): 17–33.

Whelan, A. 2013. 'Even with Cruise Control You Still Have to Steer: Defining Trolling to Get Things Done', *Fibreculture* 22: 36–60. Retrieved 16 October 2019 from http://twentytwo.fibreculturejournal.org/fcj-155-even-with-cruise-control-you-still-have-to-steer-defining-trolling-to-get-things-done.

Whirlpool. 2015. 'Charlotte Dawson vs Twitter Trolls'. Retrieved 16 October 2019 from http://forums.whirlpool.net.au/archive/1972419.

Widyanto, L., and M.D. Griffiths. 2011. 'An Empirical Study of Problematic Internet Use and Self-Esteem', *International Journal of Cyber Behaviour, Psychology and Learning* 1(1): 13–24.

CHAPTER 7

'Your Rockets Are Late. Do We Get a Free Pizza?'

Israeli-Palestinian Twitter Dialogues and Boundary Maintenance in the 2014 Gaza War

Oren Livio

Much research in recent years has investigated the relationship between violent conflict and the internet in general, and conflict and social media in particular. Often associated with broader optimistic or pessimistic perspectives regarding the role of new media technologies in society, such studies have sometimes made far-reaching claims about the potentials of social media as either emancipatory or conservative: emancipatory due to their capacity for decentralised communication, ease of distributing information and democratising power (e.g. Castells 2012; Diamond 2010; Shirky 2011); conservative and supportive of the status quo due to increased possibilities for state surveillance, censorship and propaganda, as well as the willing subscription of citizens to such practices (e.g. Kuntsman and Stein 2015; Morozov 2011). Many of these studies have focused on the availability of internet platforms and the traffic they generate rather than on the meanings of online practices as experienced by users, leading to what Schoemaker and Stremlau (2014: 190) refer to as the 'blind alleys of normative approaches to technology and political analysis'.

Employing recent calls for a more contextualised, practice-oriented approach that focuses on what people actually do and how their activities are made meaningful, rather than on pre-established structures or systems (e.g. Couldry 2004; Postill 2010; Schoemaker and Stremlau 2014), in this study I examine a specific form of social media use during violent conflict: the use of Twitter for cross-national dialogue between a specific group of Israeli citizens and Hamas (the Islamist Palestinian organisation that has been the de facto governing authority of the Gaza Strip since 2007) during the 2014 Gaza War in Israel/Palestine. In what follows, I focus on Israeli left-wing activists for whom Twitter serves as an alternative arena for political conversation and mobilisation. This Twitter-based, loosely linked group is largely an outlier in the contemporary Israeli environment, which is characterised by increased ethnocentrism and nationalist sentiment. However, as I argue in this chapter, the supportive context available to left-wing users on Twitter provides more potential for cross-national dialogue that enables the examination of social media practices in conflict in ways that render more visible opportunities and limitations that may be more difficult to detect under circumstances involving a more varied group of users.

Social Media, Dialogue and the Israeli-Palestinian Conflict

Research on the role played by social media in conflict situations has explored diverse contexts such as popular uprisings and revolutions, religious and national conflicts, and wars (e.g. Bräuchler 2013; Faris 2008; John and Dvir-Gvirsman 2015; Kuntsman and Stein 2015). While findings have been mixed (see Schoemaker and Stremlau 2014 for a review), there seems to be a consensus that new information and communication technologies, when compared with more traditional media, potentially provide avenues for different communication patterns, but that these potentials are not necessarily realised in the same way or to the same extent across different contexts. Recent research has also emphasised that social media and conflict cannot be neatly separated, with one influencing the other unidirectionally, but rather that they are related dialectically: social media practices are shaped by the social, political and cultural characteristics of the conflict contexts in which they are embedded and, at the same time, they shape these very same characteristics. In addition, there is growing recognition that social media are only one part of a complex contemporary media landscape in which old and new forms converge to configure a hybrid media ecosystem (Chadwick 2013).

While recent years have seen an explosion of research on social media and war in relation to the Israeli-Palestinian conflict, a vast majority has focused on social media in the hands of state actors and in the service of power, with some studies also examining regular users as patriots conscripted to the national cause. Such research has demonstrated the ways in which social media are used to distribute and share information and propaganda in order to receive international support; to mobilise local and diasporic communities around themes of unity and resistance; and to influence traditional media coverage (e.g. Allan and Brown 2010; Kuntsman and Stein 2015; Seo 2014; Siapera 2014; Stein 2012; Zeitzoff 2016). In their comprehensive study of militarist social media practices in Israel, Kuntsman and Stein (2015: 6) refer to this coalescence of social media uses by different institutions and individuals in the service of state power as 'digital militarism': 'the process by which digital communication platforms and consumer practices have ... become militarized tools in the hands of state and nonstate actors, both in the field of military operations and in civilian frameworks'.

Research on the use of social media for cross-cultural conversation and dialogue by regular users is grounded in the rich body of literature on reconciliation-aimed Israeli-Palestinian encounters (see Maoz 2011 for a review). Initially built on Allport's (1954: 281) contact hypothesis, which suggests that negative intergroup stereotypes can be reduced through contact under conditions of equal status, ongoing personal interaction, cooperation towards a common goal and institutional support, such planned encounters have been carried out in Israel for several decades by various nongovernmental organisations (NGOs), nowadays also employing models that diverge from the Allport-inspired coexistence model (Maoz 2011).

Research on these encounters has produced mixed results (Kampf 2011; Maoz 2011), but more importantly for the purposes of the present study, most encounters studied to date have brought together Jewish and Palestinian Israeli citizens – and not Jewish Israelis and West Bank or Gaza Strip Palestinians (who do not have Israeli citizenship). As physical encounters of the latter type have become extremely difficult, in light of the renewed escalation of conflict since 2000, the possibilities engendered by social media (that do not require physical copresence for interaction) have received increasing attention (e.g. Ellis and Maoz 2007; Kampf 2011). However, to date, empirical research on this topic has been limited, with results not very promising. Conflict communication scholars Ellis and Maoz (2007), who analysed a computer-mediated dialogue project between Israelis and Palestinians carried out by the Israel/Palestine Center for Research and Information, found mostly dead-end arguments characterised by challenges and confrontations, with little productive argumentation. Other research on various internet platforms has found little sympathy among Jewish Israelis to Palestinian narratives of suffering, but more positive reactions to moderate voices emphasising the desire for peace (Mor, Ron and Maoz 2016).[1] Ruesch (2013: 22) quantitatively examined spaces potentially enabling unplanned contact between Israelis and Palestinians on Facebook and found 'a highly fragmentised, polarised virtual sphere with little intergroup interaction', with only 14 per cent of groups dedicated to dialogue and the rest to in-group mobilisation.

The 2014 Gaza War and Activist Israeli Twitter Users

My study builds on this previous research, but takes an ethnographic approach focusing on unplanned dialogue spontaneously occurring between Israeli activists and Hamas during wartime. My admittedly narrow focus on a subsection of Israeli Twitter users is strategic. Apart from the above-mentioned research on state-controlled initiatives on social media, Twitter in Israel has largely been ignored by scholars on account of its relatively small population of users: approximately 155,000 at the time of the Gaza War, compared with 3.9 million Facebook users comprising nearly half of the Israeli population (John and Dvir-Gvirsman 2015: 954). Yet for the purposes of this study, Twitter is of interest because it is this minority status that has rendered it something of a refuge for left-wing Israeli activists, who often explicitly link their political outsider status to their preference for the less popular, and thus allegedly less populist and nationalistic, social media platform (see Kuntsman and Stein 2015: 116; Livio 2019). While it is certainly not only voices of resistance that occupy Israeli Twitter – governmental, military and other institutional actors are present, alongside many media professionals and regular citizens – their proportion is sizeable when compared with other social media platforms such as Facebook, as acknowledged by both scholars and users (Kuntsman and Stein 2015; Livio 2019; Segal 2016); more importantly, at least some form a tightly knit group often extending beyond social media to physical space, as detailed in their online exchanges.

Twitter thus forms an important test case for examining the potentials of social media for unplanned cross-national dialogue in times of conflict that engages those whose proclivity towards such dialogue might be assumed to be higher than average. At the same time, it should be acknowledged that wartime in general is not very conducive to productive dialogue, characterised as it is by less tolerance towards the other side. On the Israeli side, the 2014 war specifically was with an enemy considered illegitimate even among much of the Israeli left (John and Dvir-Gvirsman 2015: 958), and many Israeli Twitter users were under regular threat of rocket fire and tweeted frequently about sirens and running to shelters.

The war lasted fifty days, from July to August 2014, and cost the lives of more than 2,200 Palestinians (mostly civilians) and seventy-two Israelis (sixty-seven soldiers), with many thousands injured, mostly on the Palestinian side. Between 300,000 and 500,000 Palestinians were displaced and a similar number needed food assistance (Bouris 2015: 111). Throughout this time, social media became an additional battleground used by both sides to distribute information, construct national solidarities and attempt to influence public opinion worldwide (e.g. Fowler 2014; Kuntsman and Stein 2015; Siapera, Hunt and Lynn 2015). While much of this activity was in English and targeted at a global audience, my focus here is on Hebrew language interaction between Israeli Twitter users and the official Hebrew account of the military wing of Hamas, @qassamhebrew, with which virtually all interaction with Israelis occurred. Hamas opened this account in February 2013, alongside its earlier (and frequently suspended) Arabic and English accounts, which had many more followers.

Not much is known publicly about the operator of the Hebrew account, but this account appears to have been controlled by one person, who according to speculation by Israeli sources had picked up his Hebrew while serving a term in an Israeli prison. Before the 2014 war, the account was used only sporadically and led to virtually no interaction with Israeli users. However, in the early days of the war and until the cessation of updates on 16 July 2014, Hamas used the account for more than 300 updates and conversations with Israeli Twitter users, who sent more than 1,600 tweets to the account or mentioned it in conversations among themselves. Most interactions occurred over a three-day period from 14 to 16 July, after the account became popular through word of mouth and mass media coverage (e.g. Barak 2014; Haaretz 2014; Mizrahi 2014). The account was suspended by Twitter on 19 July.

The analysis in this chapter is based upon my real-time and retrospective observation of these interactions. I had initially witnessed them as a regular follower of, and occasional low-key participant in, Israeli Twitter and particularly its activist branch. While I am not acquainted with most of these users offline, I have come to know many of them online as part of my ongoing work on protest discourse in Israel, and they formed the backbone of my local Twitter feed as a resident of Israel during the war. In addition to materials collected in real time, I later used Twitter's search engine for mentions of and interactions with

@qassamhebrew and followed threads that continued amongst Israeli users after direct interactions with the Hamas account had ended.[2] Overall, I collected more than 2,000 tweets, with a focus on users identifying with the Israeli left (based on my own previous knowledge and the content of their tweets). I gathered additional material from mainstream media coverage of the Hamas account in Israel and from posts on other social media platforms that were linked to the account by Twitter users.

Interacting with Hamas

Unlike the Hamas English Twitter account, which attempted to attract international support through a focus on Israel's destructive actions and Palestinian suffering (Seo 2014; Zeitzoff 2016), and its Arabic account, which was targeted at local and international speakers of Arabic and mixed national and religious inspirational messages with descriptions of heroic success on the battlefield, the Hebrew account targeted Israeli users and emphasised Hamas' military achievements. Tweets reported about rocket attacks and successful acts of resistance, and their tone was serious, confident and aggressive. This tone alone seemed to trigger ridicule on the Israeli side. Even as they were declaring their opposition to the war and criticising Israeli military actions, activist Israeli Twitter users' engagements with the operators of the Hamas account were full of sarcasm and condescension.

Although Israeli Twitter users are a diverse group, in general they are young, highly educated middle-class individuals well versed in contemporary digital culture vernacular (Coleman 2010; Kuntsman and Stein 2015: 116). Humour plays a central role in their social media practices and is often a standard for status – a phenomenon that has been observed from the early days of online communication scholarship (e.g. Baym 1995). In some respects, the use of humour in conversation with Hamas is thus characteristic of internet culture more generally and is shared by other Israeli users, including those holding mainstream political views. However, its use by activists appeared to be more frequent and reflected their regular tendency to employ such discursive strategies in their social media practices, as well as in contemporary offline protest culture more generally, as seen, for example, in the 2011 Israeli social protest movement (Livio and Katriel 2014).

Under normal circumstances, Israeli activists employ humour to construct themselves as different from – and superior to – the Israeli mainstream. By laughing at the banalities and clichéd thinking allegedly characteristic of dominant discourses, they position themselves as nonconformists possessing unique cultural capital and skills (see Zillien and Hargittai 2009: 287–89 for elaboration on social status and internet usage patterns). At the same time, this joint use of humour constructs a community of like-minded users for whom humour is also a form of escape from the disillusionments of their status as outsiders. Such everyday internet use thus reflects the complementary arguments of the superiority theory of humour, which claims that 'we laugh when we feel superior to someone', and the relief theory of humour, which suggests that 'people laugh to relieve psychological tension' (Sherman and Švelch 2014: 320).

During wartime specifically, the juxtaposition of the seriousness of war with the often playful, unserious tone of activist Twitter users enabled them to construct themselves as both oppositional to Israeli warmongering and superior (morally and intellectually) to Hamas. Of course, the use of humour for expressing resistance has been characteristic of protest movements long before the age of the internet, reflecting as it does incongruity theories of humour built upon the forging of unexpected links between seemingly incompatible elements (e.g. Sherman and Švelch 2014: 320). As this trend has migrated to contemporary digital culture, it has become a marker of cultural capital, as has been shown in diverse national contexts (e.g. Helmy and Frerichs 2013; Kuipers 2002). The recurring transition from seriousness to playfulness characteristic of activist discourse also enables users to construct their collaborative experience as *fun*, which, as Goffman (1972: 50–55) has demonstrated, serves as a form of interactionally achieved transgressive behaviour that is nevertheless temporary and safe, in that it does not permanently challenge the general seriousness associated with war and its costs.

I will now take a closer look at how the dual construction of group boundaries (versus mainstream Israelis and versus Hamas) took place, by focusing on three recurring forms of Twitter discourse: criticism of the Hamas' Hebrew, humorous requests and complaints directed at Hamas, and expressions of worry and concern over the account moderator's status. Thereafter, I will discuss wider implications for the potentials and limitations of social media in situations of violent conflict.

Hebrew 'Grammar Nazis' Go to War

One of the most common occurrences in the Twitter conversations was Israeli users commenting on the Hebrew used by Hamas. Customarily, this included corrections of faulty grammar and punctuation, although at times the Hamas account was also praised for its use of proper Hebrew. A general pattern of exchange emerged: following a message by Hamas about some battleground activity, Israeli users would completely ignore the content of the message and focus only on linguistic proficiency or the lack thereof. Thus, for example, after a garbled message about Hamas regiments clearing an area, one user replied 'you should say *xosfim* [clearing, plural form]. *Gdudim* [regiments] is plural' (@cyanidewand, 14 July 2014).³ In another case, when Hamas declared that it would attack Israel from all four directions, a user replied: '*arbaa kivunim* [four directions, masculine form], not *arba* [four, feminine form]. *Kivunim* is masculine not feminine' (@GiladIdisis, 14 July 2014). Some corrections focused more on punctuation: 'You have an extra period before the exclamation marks, [and] they should be inside the quotation marks. And it's *le-an*, not *li-an*. Proofread, baby, proofread' (@FtheBear, 15 July 2014); or 'in Hebrew you use three periods and not four [for an ellipsis], and you don't put a space between the word and the ellipsis. In general, in modern writing you avoid that' (@dvirsky, 15 July 2014b).

In some cases, the Hamas account administrator replied and thanked the users for the corrections. For example, on 14 July, the Hamas account reported about a text message sent to 500,000 Israelis via phone. In reply, an Israeli activist wrote: '*gdudim* is masculine. You should have written "The Al Qassam Brigades sent [*shalxu*, masculine plural form] a text message". You should also use a definite article for the word *text*: "and here is *the text*"' (@Elizrael, 14 July 2014a). The Hamas account manager replied: 'Hello. And thank you for your note. We wrote "the Al Qassam Brigades sent [*shalxa*, feminine singular form]". The word "sent" refers to the military arm [*zroa*, feminine] of Hamas, not to "Brigades". Thank you again' (@qassamhebrew, 14 July 2014, tweet no longer available). The activist replied: 'Oh, I understand. That's nice. You should have the same person in charge of the Twitter account responsible for the text messages, because the Hebrew in the text messages is really terrible and then it doesn't end up scary' (@Elizrael, 14 July 2014b).

The civility and politeness of such conversations are striking – one side thanking the activist for correcting their Hebrew and the other suggesting how Hamas could improve its propaganda. But these are obviously not the actual goals of the interaction. Rather, the use of humour and irony serves two purposes: it ridicules war through the incongruity between the seriousness of the original posts and the myopic focus on linguistic competence in the responses; and it displays superiority, as Israeli activists are shown to be both smarter and 'cooler' – as evidenced by their ability to treat the war as a diverting horror film. This construction ignores the asymmetrical power relations between the two sides in the conflict – both in terms of the much smaller danger faced by most Israelis in comparison with Palestinians and with regard to the fact that the corrections are in Hebrew, the native tongue of the Israeli users.

The use of humorous language management in internet culture as an instrument for social differentiation by so-called 'grammar Nazis' has been well documented (e.g. Sherman and Švelch 2014). Whereas this is usually accomplished *within* society, in this case the metalinguistic comments had three simultaneous target audiences, with different goals for each. The overt target audience was the Hamas account manager. In this avenue, condescension was clearly detectable. A second target audience was mainstream Israelis; in this arena, superiority was achieved by carrying out the conversation with Hamas 'above their heads'. The expectation was that these users would often miss the ironic undertones and thus strengthen their perception of leftist activists as colluding with Israel's enemies. This was indeed an accusation made by such users, and it was also referenced humorously by the activists among themselves, in statements such as 'can correcting proofreading errors be considered assisting the enemy?' (@dvirsky, 14 July 2014a).

The third target audience was the activists themselves. Conversations of this kind were usually followed by intra-group talk dealing humorously with questions such as what the monetary compensation for editing and proofreading should be. They were also commonly retweeted or posted on other social media platforms with headings such as 'probably my best trolling ever' (for a conversation shared 944 times on Facebook; Tsurkov, 15 July 2014; see also Marshall, this volume). Therefore, while seemingly conversing with Hamas, in practice the main goals of this type of conversation appeared to be in-group solidification and boundary marking, similar in some respects to Postill's (2008: 425–26) notion of 'web forum sociality', in which some online communication practices are targeted at achieving (in-group) conviviality and others at (out-group) confrontation and critique. As noted by Lionis (2016: 179), humour in this case 'forges a social bond between its participants [and] engenders a joint aggression against outsiders ... Those who remain ignorant of the cultural references that elicit humour are ... repositioned and reminded of their position as an outsider'.

Requests and Complaints

Another recurring phenomenon in dialogue with the Hamas account was making requests about rocket attacks or complaining when requests were not fulfilled. Here too, humour and irony served as the central strategies. Requests usually took the form of asking Hamas to avoid or postpone the firing of rockets, or else to fire rockets at certain times in order to assist the Twitter user in various ways. One user wrote: 'My Pilates tomorrow morning is cancelled (the teacher is sick). Planning to sleep late so no tricks, Okey Dokey?' (@RanLior, 10 July 2014). When Hamas promised rockets at nine, another user requested: 'Any chance you could postpone it till ten o'clock? I'm dying to take a shower. Thanks in advance' (@simontetros, 12 July 2014). Conversely, other users asked for rockets to be fired: 'What's the plan for tomorrow? Can we plan a siren for Tel Aviv at 8:30? I need to wake up early and that will be good' (@shyhalatzi, 14 July 2014); 'Hamasush [using an endearing suffix for Hamas], can you please fire some on Tel Aviv? I need a quiet break like before lunch' (@LiorZMan, 15 July 2014). In some cases, requests included details meant to ridicule the situation: 'Listen, my dog is sick and I cleaned up her vomit all morning … if you could send one in my direction – now's the time' (@ZSosenko, 15 July 2014); 'Hello, I haven't paid my apartment taxes for a few months and I'm embarrassed to meet Aliza the neighbour in the stairway. Any chance you could avoid rockets to the Jerusalem area?' (@radical_s, 16 July 2014). Initial requests were often followed up by conversations that were then retweeted for the entire group. Thus, for example, when Hamas' promise to fire rockets at a specific time failed to materialise, its account was bombarded with customer service-style complaints about being late, with demands for compensation in the form of a free pizza or garlic bread.

As in the previous examples, users here were poking fun at the seriousness of war and signalling their superior status by demonstrating that they were carrying on with their domestic routines even while being fired upon. At the same time, they were also referencing their own perception by mainstream Israelis as sympathetic to Hamas by ironically demonstrating their close relations (as evidenced by the use of endearing forms and slang), which enabled them to make such requests. This was even more noticeable in complaints, which often mockingly hinted at affinity and partnership: 'After all we've done for you, we didn't even get a text message' (@Talkoholic, 14 July 2014, protected tweet); 'No text messages, no rockets, I'm beginning to be offended by @qassamHebrew' (@Yashar2U, 15 July 2014); 'I'm really offended that you sent text messages to everyone but me. Do you want my phone?' (@ShaniAshkenazi, 16 July 2014b). Such self-effacing humour is a self-presentation strategy that demonstrates the quality of being able to laugh at one's shortcomings (Norrick 1993: 79) and is common in internet culture, particularly among youth, who use it 'to create a sense of community, a point of affective identification that crystallizes through the power of online address' (Szablewicz 2014: 268). In this case, this form of sociality was constructed as different from both Palestinians and their allegedly nonhumorous discourse, and from mainstream Israelis – who supposedly fail to distinguish between anti-war activists and Israel's enemies.

Expressions of Worry and Concern

A final common theme in tweets was the expression of concern over the wellbeing of the Hamas account administrator. This occurred mostly when the account was silent for several hours or, just before its suspension, for three full days. 'Qassamhebrew hasn't tweeted in nine hours. I wonder if something's happened to him', wrote one prominent activist (@ygurvitz, 16 July 2014), and many others followed suit: 'What's going on @qassamhebrew? Are you alive? Were you hit? We're worried about you here' (@orazon, 17 July 2014); 'Hello? We miss you a bit. Where have you vanished to? #worried' (@nirlivni, 17 July 2014); 'Why did you stop tweeting? I miss you' (@mtklng, 19 July 2014).

This mock-concern about the enemy is reminiscent of a cultural tradition in which stereotypical 'Jewish' anxiety is seemingly misdirected, expressed as a fool's concern for the plight of the enemy rather than for one's own suffering (e.g. Berger 2017: 83–96). It has been revitalised on the internet in the form of mock-identification with the ordinary sufferings of enemies. The most notable examples are probably the Hitler rant parodies, based on a scene from the German film *Downfall* (*Der Untergang* 2004). In the original scene, Hitler was seen fuming at his staff for their failures in the Second World War. Internet parodists have appended new subtitles to the scene, and Hitler's tirade now appears to be the result of a range of petty annoyances such as being unable to find a parking space or to obtain marijuana. While versions of these clips have been popular worldwide (e.g. Gilbert 2013), within Israel they have 'spread like wildfire', both in terms of the proportionate number of parodies made and the proportionate number of viewers (Steir-Livny 2016: 110). As such, they represent the use of humour as a defence mechanism based on shared reference to traumatic collective events in a way that is critical of hegemonic modes of collective remembrance (Steir-Livny 2016: 117). Similarly, Twitter users expressed their anxiety over the enemy's wellbeing, thereby simultaneously criticising war and constructing their own group boundaries through the repetition of a common (mock-)concern. At the same time, despite the humorous tone, there also appears to be genuine interest here. This arises from both the actual connection forged with the Hamas account operator, who generally conversed with Israelis politely, and from the operator standing synecdochally for all Palestinian casualties.

The recognition that the Hamas account administrator was in all probability an actual individual who may have been hurt was related to a broader concern expressed by Twitter users throughout the war regarding the authenticity of this operator. In many cases – for example, when the Hebrew seemed too proficient – activists expressed concern that they were being deceived by a fake account. Messages such as 'Tell me, is this account real or fake?' (@carmelva, 15 July 2014), 'Enough, that's too much. There's no chance in the world that this is a real account' (@dor_zach, 15 July 2014) and 'You've exposed yourself, no way is this account real' (@ShaniAshkenazi, 15 July 2014a) abounded. Indeed, finding out that the account was fake would have turned the entire performance of superiority on its head – the trolls having become trollees (see also Marshall, this volume). In fact, towards the end of the war, various fake accounts bearing names such as 'qazzamhebrew' and 'Qassamoriginal' were opened, and their operators attempted to lure activists into believing they were real. Activists responded to this by providing lists of fake accounts and evidence of the authenticity of the original account (such as the link from the official Hamas pages in Arabic and English) in order to ensure that members of the group would not be fooled. In a way, this practice echoes what Kuntsman and Stein (2015: 55–70) refer to as 'the politics of digital suspicion' or the attempt to employ digital tools to challenge and expose as fraudulent Palestinian claims regarding Israeli violence and Palestinian casualties. However, whereas mainstream Israelis mobilise this suspicion in the service of the national cause, here it was meant to protect the activists themselves.

Promising Possibilities, Problematic Affordances

In principle, social media seem to provide a unique opportunity for dialogue between groups who do not normally converse (Ellis and

Maoz 2007; Schoemaker and Stremlau 2014). Leftist Israeli activists, who have made Twitter a hotbed of resistant discourse (Livio 2019), might be expected to be particularly interested in such interaction with Palestinians. Indeed, during the war, there was more significant interaction on Twitter than on platforms such as Facebook, where activist networking tends to be intra-national, little cross-cultural conversation occurs and voices of resistance are often obscured by the sheer quantity of hegemonic discourse (Kuntsman and Stein 2015: 116; Ruesch 2013: 22). Nevertheless, most Twitter conversation that did occur between leftist Israeli activists and the official Hamas account during the 2014 Gaza War seemed to be invested more in establishing in-group solidarity than in meaningful political or interpersonal dialogue with Hamas. Some of this may be related to the specific nature of Twitter. In discussing the potential of computer-mediated communication for dialogue between adversaries, Ellis and Maoz (2007: 293) note that its limitless quality enables elaborate arguments. Twitter, which at the time had a 140-character limit (expanded to 280 characters in 2017; this may of course be extended by posting multiple tweets), is not very conducive to serious engagement with politics in this respect. And yet, these same users do succeed in utilising Twitter for political mobilisation at other times – prominent examples include the 2011 social protest and the 2017 anti-government demonstrations in Israel – so it is not merely a matter of technical constraints.

Indeed, as much research has shown, online platforms do not simply produce deterministic effects (e.g. Bräuchler 2013; Schoemaker and Stremlau 2014); they provide opportunities and contexts that are always in interaction with other relevant aspects of local culture, which in the case examined here includes both Israeli culture at large and the more specific nuances of online and activist culture. It appears that it is precisely the same affordances that have facilitated the establishment of an activist arena on Israeli Twitter that limit its potential for cross-cultural dialogue during violent conflict. In their everyday practices, activists are used to performing boundary maintenance work solidifying their outsider status and differentiating themselves from mainstream Israeli society. For this purpose, activists constantly mobilise (and sometimes transform) routine social media practices such as the use of humour and irony, trolling, digital suspicion and various forms of demonstrating cultural capital, including so-called 'grammar Nazism' (Sherman and Švelch 2014). These uses of social media vernacular normally serve as a means of resistance to – and displays of superiority over – dominant Israeli discourses and mainstream users of social media. In the case of war too, they are meant to resist and mock dominant ideologies regarding its necessity. However, at the same time, they largely leave Palestinians – and the opportunity for dialogue with them – out of the picture, neglecting real-world asymmetrical power relations in which treating war humorously and ironically is a privilege not shared to the same degree by all sides. While dialogue on Twitter is overtly carried out with Hamas, in practice it has three simultaneous audiences – Palestinians, mainstream Israelis and Israeli activists – with the assumption (and often the goal) that only the latter group will possess the cultural resources and skills to fully interpret the speakers' implicit intent.

Further reinforcing this inclination are the ways in which social media practices are intertwined with characteristics of (offline) local speech culture. As demonstrated by Katriel (2004), Israeli speech culture prioritises a quest for authentic dialogue as a means of constructing social affinity and solidarity, on the one hand, and social differentiation and exclusion, on the other. Finding its epitome in the *dugri* ethos associated with Israel's early years – the veneration of direct, explicit and nonmanipulative talk rather than politeness and restrictiveness – 'the vision of communication as "authentic dialogue" has played an important role in helping to cement group boundaries – for better and for worse' (Katriel 2004: 330). While the parameters of what is perceived as authentic talk have certainly changed over the years, Israeli speech culture continues to reverberate a complex individual/community dialectic and to associate specific ways of talking with collective and individual identities, which are also shaped by (and not only prefigure) these ways of talking (2004: 332–33). Activist Twitter users navigate this complex terrain in multifaceted and sometimes contradictory ways: they reject the manipulative character of much political talk and prefer to speak directly and in ways that are perceived as authentic. Yet, at the same time, they also reject what is perceived as the rude tone of much Israeli talk and often turn to irony and undertone to voice their critique; they are invested in the construction and celebration of sociality and affinity through repeated communicative rituals, but these are accomplished in order to position themselves as a group of like-minded (deliberate) outsiders within Israeli society, who are nevertheless distinct from external outsiders such as the Palestinians.

The findings of this study correspond to those of other examinations of the role of the internet or social media in violent conflict in Israel/Palestine and other national contexts. Thus, for example, Bräuchler (2013) has also demonstrated how instead of providing an opportunity for cross-cultural contact, Muslims and Christians in the

Moluccan conflict in Indonesia mostly use cyberspace for constructing and solidifying boundaries between their imagined communities, and, like Israeli users, they also employ conventional internet practices such as cross-posting and flaming to intensify rather than mitigate the conflict. Siapera (2014) and John and Dvir-Gvirsman (2015) have likewise shown how other social media practices such as the use of hashtags, retweets and unfriending were associated with constructing affective communities of solidarity and similarity rather than with productive engagement with others' views.

The fact that little meaningful dialogue between Israeli activists and Hamas was found in this study does not mean that this is a necessary or inevitable result of social media use in conflict. It does mean that in considering the relations between media and conflict, the nuances of different national, political and cultural contexts must be considered. While in some ways the context examined here led to expectations for a desire for contact, in other ways the situation was not particularly conducive to productive dialogue. Interactions occurred during a war that was extreme in its violence even by Israeli-Palestinian standards, and, while critical of the conduct of the Israeli government and military, Israeli activists – most of whom are secular – cannot be said to be sympathetic towards Hamas, which is considered by most of them to be a fanatical Islamist organisation involved in terrorist activities against Israeli civilians. Activists were under rocket fire, they were often condemned as traitors within Israeli society due to their peace activism, and the Hamas account they were interacting with broadcast mostly militarist messages targeting Israelis as a whole. Finally, the asymmetrical nature of the conflict was largely unrecognised in Israeli discourse, with mass media focusing on Israelis as victims rather than as perpetrators of violence.

The findings presented here should therefore be viewed cautiously: they show that *certain* affordances of *certain* social media under *certain* circumstances appear to encourage *certain* patterns of internal sociality and group boundary enforcement rather than opportunities for reconciliatory dialogue. But, more importantly, they illustrate that the complex sociocultural contexts in which social media practices are embedded can hardly be erased by the undeniable potentials of these media. At the same time, they show that these social media practices themselves help shape the contexts in which they occur – in this case, constructing (for the most part) a confrontational and condescending environment that reinforced, and perhaps exacerbated, existing divisions and power relations rather than potentially mitigating them.

Oren Livio is Senior Lecturer at the Department of Communication, University of Haifa. He received his Ph.D. from the Annenberg School for Communication at the University of Pennsylvania. His research focuses on discursive and cultural negotiations of national identity, militarism, civic participation and protest, particularly in the Israeli context. His work has been published in various books and journals, including the *Journal of Communication, Journalism: Theory, Practice and Criticism, Journalism Studies* and *Critical Studies in Media Communication*.

Notes

1. Allen (2009), focusing on earlier visual practices, demonstrates how Palestinian discourse has gravitated towards intensified bodily depictions of suffering, which is precisely what most Israelis are unsympathetic towards.
2. Hashtags were found to be unhelpful in searching for relevant data. While some exceptions do exist (e.g. the #J14 hashtag during the 2011 social protest and imported hashtags such as #MeToo), Twitter hashtag use in Hebrew appears to be relatively infrequent and unsystematic. When present, activist use in particular is often idiosyncratic and ironic.
3. All translations of Hebrew texts are mine.

References

Allan, D., and C. Brown. 2010. 'The Mavi Marmara at the Frontlines of Web 2.0', *Journal of Palestine Studies* 40(1): 63–77.
Allen, L.A. 2009. 'Martyr Bodies in the Media: Human Rights, Aesthetics, and the Politics of Immediation in the Palestinian Intifada', *American Ethnologist* 36(1): 161–80.
Allport, G. 1954. *The Nature of Prejudice*. Reading, MA: Addison-Wesley.
Barak, O. 2014. 'Talking with Hamas on Twitter: Threats and Also Mistakes in Hebrew', *Channel 2 News*, 15 July. Retrieved 20 October 2019 from https://www.mako.co.il/news-money/tech/Article-98c7506c53a3741004.htm.
Baym, N.K. 1995. 'The Performance of Humour in Computer-Mediated Communication', *Journal of Computer-Mediated Communication* 1(2). Retrieved 20 October 2019 from http://onlinelibrary.wiley.com/doi/10.1111/j.1083-6101.1995.tb00327.x/full.
Berger, A.A. 2017. *The Anatomy of Humour*. New York: Routledge.
Bouris, D. 2015. 'The Vicious Cycle of Building and Destroying: The 2014 War on Gaza', *Mediterranean Politics* 20(1): 111–17.
Bräuchler, B. 2013. *Cyberidentities at War: The Moluccan Conflict on the Internet*. New York: Berghahn Books.
@carmelva. 2014. Retrieved 20 October 2019 from https://twitter.com/carmelva/status/488942058199982085.

Castells, M. 2012. *Networks of Outrage and Hope*. Cambridge: Polity Press.
Chadwick, A. 2013. *The Hybrid Media System: Politics and Power*. Oxford: Oxford University Press.
Coleman, E.G. 2010. 'Ethnographic Approaches to Digital Media', *Annual Review of Anthropology* 39(1): 487–505.
Couldry, N. 2004. 'Theorising Media as Practice', *Social Semiotics* 14(2): 115–32.
@cyanidewand. 2014. Retrieved 20 October 2019 from https://twitter.com/cyanidewand/status/488705985909764096.
Der Untergang. 2004. [Film]. Oliver Hirschbiegel (dir.). Germany: Constantin Film.
Diamond, L. 2010. 'Liberation Technology', *Journal of Democracy* 21(3): 69–83.
@dor_zach. 2014. Retrieved 20 October 2019 from https://twitter.com/dor_zach/status/489162289174417409.
@dvirsky. 2014a. Retrieved 20 October 2019 from https://twitter.com/dvirsky/status/488838159925407744.
———. 2014b. Retrieved 20 October 2019 from https://twitter.com/dvirsky/status/489158478112382977.
@Elizrael. 2014a. Retrieved 20 October 2019 from https://twitter.com/Elizrael/status/488717989684862977.
———. 2014b. Retrieved 20 October 2019 from https://twitter.com/Elizrael/status/488805349969776642.
Ellis, D.G., and I. Maoz. 2007. 'Online Argument between Israeli Jews and Palestinians', *Human Communication Research* 33(3): 291–309.
Faris, D. 2008. 'Revolutions without Revolutionaries: Network Theory, Facebook, and the Egyptian Blogosphere', *Arab Media & Society* 6. Retrieved 20 October 2019 from http://www.arabmediasociety.com/?article=694.
Fowler, S. 2014. 'Hamas and Israel Step up Cyber Battle for Hearts and Minds', *BBC News*, 15 July. Retrieved 20 October 2019 from http://www.bbc.com/news/world-middle-east-28292908.
@FtheBear. 2014. Retrieved 20 October 2019 from https://twitter.com/FtheBear/status/488986534096281601.
@GiladIdisis. 2014. Retrieved 20 October 2019 from https://twitter.com/GiladIdisis/status/488835618860834816.
Gilbert, C.J. 2013. 'Playing with Hitler: Downfall and Its Ludic Uptake', *Critical Studies in Media Communication* 30(5): 407–23.
Goffman, E. 1972. *Encounters: Two Studies in the Sociology of Interaction*. Harmondsworth: Penguin.
Haaretz. 2014. 'Who Said You Can't Talk with Hamas?', 15 July. Retrieved 25 June 2018 from https://www.haaretz.co.il/captain/net/1.2377197.
Helmy, M.M., and S. Frerichs. 2013. 'Stripping the Boss: The Powerful Role of Humour in the Egyptian Revolution 2011', *Integrative Psychological & Behavioural Science* 47(4): 50–81.
John, N.A., and S. Dvir-Gvirsman. 2015. '"I Don't Like You Any More": Facebook Unfriending by Israelis during the Israel-Gaza Conflict of 2014', *Journal of Communication* 65: 953–74.

Kuipers, G. 2002. 'Media Culture and Internet Disaster Jokes: Bin Laden and the Attack on the World Trade Center', *European Journal of Cultural Studies* 5(4): 450–70.

Kuntsman, A., and R.L. Stein. 2015. *Digital Militarism: Israel's Occupation in the Social Media Age.* Stanford: Stanford University Press.

Kampf, R. 2011. 'Internet, Conflict and Dialogue: The Israeli Case', *Israel Affairs* 17(3): 384–400.

Katriel, T. 2004. *Dialogic Moments: From Soul Talks to Talk Radio in Israeli Culture.* Detroit: Wayne State University Press.

Lionis, C. 2016. *Laughter in Occupied Palestine: Comedy and Identity in Art and Film.* London: I.B. Tauris.

@LiorZMan. 2014. Retrieved 20 October 2019 from https://twitter.com/LiorZMan/status/488972910531710976.

Livio, O. 2019. 'Failure as Affordance: Why Has Twitter Become a Hotbed of Political Resistance in Israel?', *Comparative Media Studies in Today's World Conference, St. Petersburg, Russia, 16–18 April.*

Livio, O., and Katriel, T. 2014. 'A Fractured Solidarity: Communitas and Structure in the Israeli 2011 Social Protest', in P. Werbner, M. Webb and K. Spellman-Poots (eds), *The Political Aesthetics of Global Protest: The Arab Spring and Beyond.* Edinburgh: Edinburgh University Press, pp. 147–76.

Maoz, I. 2011. 'Does Contact Work in Protracted Asymmetrical Conflict? Appraising 20 Years of Reconciliation-Aimed Encounters between Israeli Jews and Palestinians', *Journal of Peace Research* 48(1): 115–25.

Mizrahi, A. 2014. 'The Tweet War: Hamas versus Israel', *Ynet,* 15 July. Retrieved 20 October 2019 from https://www.ynet.co.il/articles/0,7340,L-4543879,00.html.

Mor, Y., Y. Ron and I. Maoz. 2016. '"Likes" for Peace: Can Facebook Promote Dialogue in the Israeli-Palestinian Conflict?', *Media and Communication* 4(1): 15–26.

Morozov, E. 2011. *The Net Delusion: How Not to Liberate the World.* London: Allen Lane.

@mtklng. 2014. Retrieved 20 October 2019 from https://twitter.com/mtklng/status/490524111601270784.

@nirlivni. 2014. Retrieved 20 October 2019 from https://twitter.com/nirlivni/status/489870242600861696.

Norrick, N.R. 1993. *Conversational Joking: Humor in Everyday Talk.* Bloomington: Indiana University Press.

@orazon. 2014. Retrieved 20 October 2019 from https://twitter.com/orazon/status/489871076495618049.

Postill, J. 2008. 'Localizing the Internet beyond Communities and Networks', *New Media & Society* 10(3): 413–31.

———. 2010. 'Introduction: Theorising Media and Practice', in B. Bräuchler and J. Postill (eds), *Theorising Media and Practice.* New York: Berghahn Books, pp. 1–32.

@radical_s. 2014. Retrieved 20 October 2019 from https://twitter.com/radical_s/status/489418335914688512.

@RanLior. 2014. Retrieved 20 October 2019 from https://twitter.com/RanLior/status/487135925781032960.

Ruesch, M. 2013. 'A Peaceful Net? Intergroup Contact and Communicative Conflict Resolution of the Israel-Palestine Conflict on Facebook', in A. Ternès (ed.), *Communication: Breakdowns and Breakthroughs*. Oxford: Inter-Disciplinary Press, pp. 13–31.

Schoemaker, E., and N. Stremlau. 2014. 'Media and Conflict: An Assessment of the Evidence', *Progress in Development Studies* 14(2): 181–95.

Segal, A. 2016. 'A Story in More than 140 Characters: What's Really Going on with Twitter in Israel', 8 October. Retrieved 25 June 2018 from http://www.amitsegal.co.il.

Seo, H. 2014 'Visual Propaganda in the Age of Social Media: An Empirical Analysis of Twitter Images during the 2012 Israeli-Hamas Conflict', *Visual Communication Quarterly* 21(3): 150–71.

@ShaniAshkenazi. 2014a. Retrieved 20 October 2019 from https://twitter.com/ShaniAshkenazi/status/489167864453025792.

———. 2014b. Retrieved 20 October 2019 from https://twitter.com/ShaniAshkenazi/status/489379157193658368.

Sherman, T., and J. Švelch. 2014. '"Grammar Nazis Never Sleep": Facebook Humour and the Management of Standard Written Language', *Language Policy* 14(4): 315–34.

Shirky, C. 2011. 'The Political Power of Social Media: Technology, the Public Sphere, and Political Change', *Foreign Affairs* 90(1): 28–41.

@shyhalatzi. 2014. Retrieved 20 October 2019 from https://twitter.com/shyhalatzi/status/488823131415400448.

Siapera, E. 2014. 'Tweeting #Palestine Twitter and the Mediation of Palestine', *International Journal of Cultural Studies* 17(6): 539–55.

Siapera, E., G. Hunt and T. Lynn. 2015. '#GazaUnderAttack: Twitter, Palestine and Diffused War', *Information, Communication & Society* 18(11): 1297–319.

@simontetros. 2014. Retrieved 20 October 2019 from https://twitter.com/simontetros/status/488008556528926720.

Stein, R.L. 2012. 'StateTube: Anthropological Reflections on Social Media and the Israeli State', *Anthropological Quarterly* 85(3): 893–916.

Steir-Livny, L. 2016. 'Is It OK to Laugh about It Yet? Hitler Rants YouTube Parodies in Hebrew', *European Journal of Humour Research* 4(4): 105–21.

Szablewicz, M. 2014. 'The "Losers" of China's Internet: Memes as "Structures of Feeling" for Disillusioned Young Netizens', *China Information* 28(2): 259–75.

Tsurkov, E. 2014. Retrieved 20 October 2019 from https://www.facebook.com/photo.php?fbid=10152512760421358.

@Yashar2U. 2014. Retrieved 20 October 2019 from https://twitter.com/Yashar2U/status/488980991780716544.

@ygurvitz. 2014. Retrieved 20 October 2019 from https://twitter.com/ygurvitz/status/489485338843578368.

Zeitzoff, T. 2016. 'Does Social Media Influence Conflict? Evidence from the 2012 Gaza Conflict', *Journal of Conflict Resolution*. Retrieved 11 May 2017 from http://journals.sagepub.com/doi/pdf/10.1177/0022002716650925.

Zillien, N., and E. Hargittai. 2009. 'Digital Distinction: Status-Specific Types of Internet Usage', *Social Science Quarterly* 90(2): 274–91.

@ZSosenko. 2014. Retrieved 20 October 2019 from https://twitter.com/ZSosenko/status/489302064917278720.

PART V
Sites of Conflict

CHAPTER 8

What Violent Conflict Tells Us about Media and Place-Making (and Vice Versa)

Ethnographic Observations from a Revolutionary Uprising

Nina Grønlykke Mollerup

In this chapter, I theorise media as place-making in the context of conflict. This is a break with recent theorisations of media, which argue that the increasing mobility of media has entailed a decline in the significance of place in relation to media, creating a 'third place', a place distinct from the places of engagement with media (Miller and Sinanan 2014). It is also a break with earlier theories that originate in television studies and present media as an enabler of a 'doubling of place' (Scannell 1996). The notions of 'third place' and 'doubling of place' in a sense 'unplace' media by disintegrating people's engagement with them from the places they are in. These theorisations of media have grown out of studies that have not focused on violence. Studying media in the context of violent conflict invites a different understanding as violence highlights the significance of place to media. This chapter argues for the importance of understanding media as vitally emplaced in the phenomenological world alongside people and it uses violent conflict to develop this point (see also Markham, this volume). My understanding of place is inspired by the works of philosopher Edward Casey (1996), geographer Doreen Massey (2005) and anthropologists Sarah Pink (Fors, Bäckström and Pink 2013; Pink 2009, 2011, 2012; Pink and Mackley 2013) and Tim Ingold (2000, 2007,

2008, 2011, 2013). I thus take place to be primary to perception and agree with Casey (1996: 36, emphasis in original) that '*space and time come together in place*. Indeed, they arise from the experience of place itself'. The primacy of place over space is crucial to my argument as it is through place that media occur and are perceived.

This chapter is based on seven months of ethnographic fieldwork with activists and journalists in Egypt between 2012 and 2013, when the revolutionary uprising was still ongoing and protests and street clashes were common (see Mollerup 2015). On 25 January 2011, Egyptians took to the streets in unprecedented numbers, calling for bread, freedom and social justice, and, more specifically, for the end of military dictatorship, personified by the rule of Hosni Mubarak. Resisting the police's attempts at quelling protest, protesters conquered the streets through deadly battles. Most famously, at the end of January 2011, protesters took control of Tahrir Square, where an eighteen-day sit-in became the epicentre and imaginary of the uprising. Mubarak was forced to resign and the military announced that the Supreme Council of the Armed Forces (SCAF) would lead the country in what it purported to be a transition to democracy. The two and a half years that followed were genuinely revolutionary in the sense that while the military scrambled to regain control of the country, street protests, sit-ins and strikes continued to set new agendas and challenge authority. The military might never truly have been out of power, but the foundation of power was profoundly being shaken. In June 2012, Mohamed Morsi of the Muslim Brotherhood was elected President, but managed to satisfy neither the military generals nor the revolutionaries. After a year in office, on 3 July 2013, Morsi was ousted by the military after mass street protests against his rule. This signified the beginning of restoration of military dictatorship. As army chief, General Abdel-Fattah El Sisi was positioning himself as the next president of Egypt, hundreds of protesters were being shot dead in the streets by the army with impunity, harsh prison sentences were being handed out to revolutionaries, media outlets were shut down and journalists were being firmly instructed by the army in terms of how to present events in the 'interest of the nation'. The revolution had in effect been pushed back to the margins (Mollerup 2015: 28–39).

The attention to media in the context of the Egyptian uprising was immense. Mark Allen Peterson (2015: 509) remarks that: 'The multiple uses of social media during the Arab uprisings of 2011 drew global attention to the Middle East as a key site for understanding the relations between electronic networks and social networks, and for examining the ways in which information and communication technologies can be creatively put to use toward political and social goals'. However, he also laments that much of the work is 'anecdotal, assembled to support or contradict particular positions in an ongoing debate over technological contributions to global democratization' (2015: 509). While the polemics of this debate are unproductive, their premises are problematic. Discussions of 'the relevance of virtual ties for real ties' (Alterman 2011: 105) and arguments positing digital media against people physically being in the streets (see, for instance, Dajani 2012: 2) disregard the emplacement of people *alongside* media – digital or otherwise. I maintain that these understandings of media, similar to understandings of media as 'doubling place' or creating a 'third place', disregard the importance of place to media. The entanglement of violence and media can be used to assert this importance.

Proceeding in four sections, this chapter first grounds my argument in non-media-centric media studies and points to the importance of moving past the distinction between a symbolic and a material realm. Next, it develops an understanding of media as place-making and introduces the notion of presence to conceptualise the relationship of media and place. Subsequently, it discusses understandings of media as 'doubling place' or creating a 'third place', particularly pointing to the multisensoriality of perception. The conclusion reflects upon how an understanding of media as place-making might impact our understandings of conflict.

Movement and Entanglements

Violence played a significant role in the Egyptian uprising and highlights the predicament of underestimating the importance of the emplacement of media. Understandings of media as detached from the phenomenological world are challenged by protesters who wrote tweets and Facebook posts on their phones while participating in sit-ins in Tahrir Square, constantly threatened by imminent attacks of security forces. When a protester close to the frontline of a street battle tweeted that police were attacking protesters in Abd El Khaliq Tharwat Street and another protester around the corner in Shambilion Street read these tweets and used them to organise the delivery of rocks to the frontlines to keep police at a distance, media were vitally emplaced. When a journalist in an office in downtown Cairo saw images on Twitter of a peaceful demonstration that had suddenly come under attack from the army, with soldiers driving into and over crowds of people with Armed Personnel Carriers (APCs) (see Mosireen 2011a, 2011b), she walked the five-minute distance to investigate the massacre in person. Doing so, she was always already emplaced (Casey 1996: 18). Understandings of media as 'unplaced' are further challenged by two activists filming from a balcony above Tahrir Square. While documenting a military police officer dragging the body of Toussi, a dead protester, to a pile of trash, they exposed themselves to the danger of rooftop snipers, who particularly targeted photographers (see Mosireen 2012a). When activists shared these images on YouTube, Twitter and Facebook, the images arrived quickly by way of computers, cameras and phones, 3G networks, undersea cables and satellites in outer space, as well as meticulously developed networks of friends, followers and hashtags to screens in apartments nearby and across the world. As people saw these images, they were moved emotionally and physically. Some of them left their apartments and went to the same streets to join the protests and battles. Some lost their lives doing so. However, movement is a question not only of proximity, but also of engagement, embodied, for instance, by many Egyptian activists living abroad who left peaceful societies and boarded Cairo-bound planes to join the uprising after seeing images from the protests and battles. The movement of people and media is intrinsically entangled and bound up in the phenomenological world alongside planes, APCs, rocks dug out of concrete and the coffee next to the morning paper, resisting 'any neat analytical distinction between media and conflict' (Bräuchler and Budka, this volume).

Paying attention to the entanglements of people and things related to media, violence and conflict entails an insistence on the materialities of media. This is fundamental to a recognition of media as emplaced and encourages the study of media as they *occur*[1] in the world. This recognition of media goes well with media scholar David Morley's call for non-media-centric media studies:

> My argument is that we need a new paradigm for the discipline, which attends more closely to its material as well as its symbolic dimensions. If improvements in the speed of communications are central to the time-space compressions of our era, emphasis has recently fallen almost exclusively on the virtual dimension (the movement of information) to the neglect of the analysis of the corresponding movements of objects, commodities, and persons. (Morley 2009: 114)

Referring to Morley, Shaun Moores (2012a: 1) suggests that non-media-centric media studies entail an approach in which 'the distinctive characteristics and affordances of media are acknowledged, but also, crucially, in which day-to-day practices rather than media themselves are put at the centre of investigation'. Moores thus calls attention to media-related (Hobart 2010) or media-oriented practices (Couldry 2010; see also Couldry and Hobart 2010), which is significant to my endeavour. In his seminal chapter 'Theorising Media as Practice', Nick Couldry (2010: 36–37) suggests that the aim of theorising media as practice is 'to decentre media research from the study of media texts or production structures (important though these are) and to redirect it onto the study of the open-ended range of practices focused directly or indirectly on media'. Couldry (2010: 37) recognises that this approach places media studies within a broader sociology of action and knowledge or cultural and cognitive anthropology. It is not surprising, then, that media anthropologists, who have focused on people rather than texts, have contributed to theorising media as practice (see Bräuchler and Postill 2010). It must be emphasised, as John Postill (2010: 6) points out that '[s]ocial theorists agree that there is no such thing as a coherent, unified "practice theory", only a body of highly diverse writings by thinkers who adopt a loosely defined "practice approach"'. While I recognise the importance of the practice turn to media studies and its influence on media anthropology, I wish to draw attention not only to practices, but also to the emplacement of these practices in the phenomenological world and to people's sensory engagements with places.

With its aim to decentre media research from the study of texts and production structures, practice theory corresponds well with non-media-centric media studies, which I also find to be fundamental to an understanding of media as place-making. Non-media-centric media studies are a way of moving past the distinction between a symbolic and a material realm, a distinction that rests on the problematic assumption that media can have significance detached from their occurrence in the phenomenological world. The protesters battling or awaiting attacks in Tahrir Square do not leave this world to engage with media; in other words, we are never *not* 'offline'. This point is not an agreement with the 'widespread consensus that the online and offline are intermingled in intricate relations' (Lindgren, Dahlberg-Grundberg and Johansson 2014: 2). Rather, it disputes that the 'online' could ever exist devoid of its emplacement in the 'offline'. That is, the initial distinction between the two is artificial (see also Bräuchler 2013: 13–14). Our engagement with media, whether digital or not, remains intrinsically bound up with our being in places, which occur in the phenomenological world. This is particularly obvious when media are part of violent environments. Non-media-centric media studies avoid attempts at distinguishing between symbolic and material realms of communication as if a symbolic realm existed independent of the material realm and we could access this symbolic realm as an exclusive engagement of the mind, distinct from the body. Non-media-centric media studies, then, are both a methodological and a theoretical concern. Methodologically, they entail an engagement with the places, where media are significant to the people who engage with them. Theoretically, non-media-centric media studies entail an understanding of media as constituted by and constituent of the phenomenological world, including in the context of violent conflicts (see also Markham, and Bräuchler and Budka, this volume). Non-media-centric media studies, then, both theoretically and methodologically benefit from an anthropological approach to media with its attention to the study of media as entangled in people's lived realities (see, for instance, Ginsburg, Abu-Lughod and Larkin 2002; Peterson 2003; Postill and Peterson 2009). To characterise these entanglements, I explain my understanding of place and its relation to media in the following.

Media as Place-Making

I view media as communicative processes that occur *across* places and thus contribute to the making of other places. This is intentionally a broad definition that understands media as processes people engage in *in* places. Media, then, become an analytical category that cannot be defined *a priori*. Media are media only by people's engagement; it is a relational concept. What distinguishes media from other communicative processes is that they occur not only *in* places but also *across* places. My definition of something as media is thus dependent on an understanding of people's practices as communicative. Drawing on Moores (2005, 2012a, 2012b), I approach media as place-making, which acknowledges that media concurrently make and are made by places. In other words, I see media not as objects, which are closed in on themselves, but rather as open, in the world, among people, not detached from them (Ingold 2013). My notion of media is thus closely tied up with my notion of place.

Drawing on Casey, I have insisted on the primacy of place to perception and that space and time thus arise from the experience of place. Casey (1996: 18) further emphasises that: 'There is no knowing or sensing a place except by being in that place, and to be in a place is to be in a position to perceive it'. Ingold (2000: 192) complements this when pointing out that 'it is from the relational context of people's engagement with the world, in the business of dwelling, that each place draws its unique significance'. He further argues that '[a] place owes its character to the experiences it affords to those who spend time there – to the sights, sounds and indeed smells that constitute its specific ambience. And these, in turn, depend on the kinds of activities in which its inhabitants engage' (2000: 192). This understanding of place offers attention to movement and perception. I thus find it useful to employ Massey's understanding of place as event. Massey (2005: 130, emphasis in original) sees places 'not as points or areas on a map, but as integrations of time and space; as *spatio-temporal events*'. She elaborates that this is an understanding of place as 'open', 'woven together out of ongoing stories' and 'unfinished business' (2005: 131). Referring to Massey, Pink (2011: 349) describes place as 'composed of entanglements of all components of an environment' and explains that these elements should be understood as 'being in movement'. Places, then, do not exist as much as they occur and movement is an integral aspect of place. This leads me to highlight Casey's (1996: 46) point that place is constituted in relationality in that 'there is never a *single* place existing in utter isolation'. Let me now turn to the implications of media for place.

While I understand media as occurring *across* places, it is important to point out that I do not understand media as existing devoid of places. Rather, media always occur *in* places, as emphasised above. The videos of violence uploaded on YouTube by activists must materialise through lights in or on screens to occur in other places. In this way, media occur *in* places and *across* places. As they occur in places, they make places and are made by places through movement, which opens up places to each other. I suggest that the notion of presence provides a useful conceptualisation of the relationship of media and place. In other words, media enable a presence of elements of one place in other places and, by doing so, contribute to making places while they are simultaneously made, as they move and entangle with things and people in the places they move through. With this understanding, we can look at how media contribute to making places by bringing a presence of other places into a place without conflating or disregarding the significance of particular places. Presence, in this sense, is closely tied to having influence. Here it is crucial to emphasise that media are not necessarily reciprocal. Media can entail a presence that is not dependent on physical co-location and that may or may not be reciprocal.

While I understand media to entail a presence (of people, things and events) across places, we are never removed from the place of our physical location, however much the mediated presence might influence the places we inhabit. Participants in revolutionary street screenings in Tahrir Square during the July 2011 sit-in were not removed from the asphalt they were sitting on as they watched images of the historic battle that took place on 28 January the same year on the Qasr el-Nil Bridge, just a few hundred metres away (see Al Masry Al Youm 2011). As they watched these images, their emplacement on the asphalt in Tahrir Square was crucial for the way in which they made meaning of the images as well as for the danger they incurred from the imminent attack of the military (Mollerup and Gaber 2015). Ingold (2000: 166) contends that 'perceptual activity consists not in the operation of the mind upon the bodily data of sense, but in the intentional movement of the whole being (indissolubly body and mind) in its environment'. Whether in violent or peaceful settings, we perceive with our entire bodies; it is not just our minds engaging with a screen (see also Sumera, this volume). The division of media into a symbolic versus a physical realm implicit in many studies is a result of the division of body and mind to which Ingold objects. It is for this reason that I find the notion of presence useful. Presence points to a significance in our environments without separating body and mind and explains that violence can have an influence in places where people watch images of the violence without implying that the violence *occurs* in these places. The battle of Qasr el-Nil Bridge had a presence at the screening in July, but it did not occur there. Significantly, we are not in the place where the violence occurs when watching videos of this violence from other places. Violence might have a very significant presence in the places we inhabit when watching a video of violence. It might affect our lives and our actions dramatically, as protesters, who were killed in street battles they had joined upon seeing images of the violence, attest to.

Putting Media and Conflict in Their (Shared) Place

Having elaborated on my understanding of media as place-making, let me now return to my reservation with theorisations of media as 'doubling place' or creating a 'third place', which I understand to rest on a premise that disregards the emplacement of media. This allows me to further explore the significance of media as emplaced, not least by paying attention to the significance of multisensoriality. While my understanding of media as place-making is profoundly inspired by Moores, I significantly depart with him as he draws on Paddy Scannell (1996) to view media as a 'doubling of place'. Moores (2012b: 14) engages Scannell's (1996: 91) claim that television and radio provide listeners and viewers with the possibility of 'being in two places at once'. Moores (2012b: 14–15) explains that 'broadcasting permits a witnessing of remote happenings that can take listeners and viewers as "close" to those happenings, experientially, as they are to the goings-on in the physical environments'. He further engages Paul Adams (2009: 185) by holding that media enable their users to 'violate' the constraint that one can only be in one place at a time by bringing more places within the range of the senses (Moores 2012b: 15). Audiovisual media afford sights and sounds to people in places of viewings that are relatively similar to some of those seen and heard by people in the place of the recording. Yet seeing and hearing are only a part of our sensory apparatus and seeing a battle unfold does not entail the same sights as seeing a screen with images from that battle. As I have made clear, I understand our perception of the world as bound up with our being in the world. Casey (1996: 18) explains that: 'Knowledge of a place is not, then, subsequent to perception – as Kant dogmatically assumed – but is ingredient in perception itself'. He elaborates that 'to live is to live locally, and to know is first of all to know the places one is in. I am not proposing a merely mute level of experience that passively receives simple and senseless data of place. Perception at the primary level is synesthetic – an affair of the whole body sensing and moving' (1996: 18). This understanding of perception also challenges any attempt at a Cartesian division between body and mind. Ingold is a dedicated opponent to this division and his inspiration from psychologist James Gibson is substantial. Gibson (1979: 3) rejects the idea that 'sensory inputs are converted into perceptions by operations of the mind', as if the mind was, in Ingold's (2000: 3) words, 'a kind of data-processing device, akin to a digital computer'. Ingold (2013: 4–6) aspires to restore knowing at the heart of being and argues against 'the conceit that things can be "theorised" in isolation from what is going on in the world around us'. Most of Ingold's work revolves around one fundamental argument: that 'the person *is* the organism, and not something added on top' (2000: 3). This leads him to refuse any notion of knowing as detached from the environment. Much in line with Ingold, Michael Jackson (1996: 29) insists on 'locating knowledge, experience, and the person in the lifeworld. This implies that consciousness cannot be understood in isolation, as pure cognition or disinterested observation. Consciousness is engaged in the lifeworld'. We know from the inside, from being part of the world, not from standing outside looking in. Knowing, then, is movement (Ingold 2013: 1). This is well explained with Mark Harris' (2007: 1, emphasis in original) words: 'knowing is always bound up in one way or another with the world: a person does not leave their environment to know, even when she is dealing with the most abstract of propositions. Nor does she *stop* in order to know: she continues'.

With awareness of multisensoriality and the interdependence of place and perception, an understanding of media as emplaced emphasises that knowing with media is not a fundamentally different way of knowing; rather, knowing with media is knowing in engagement with the places we inhabit of which media are a part. Watching a video of a battle is an engagement with a very different environment from that of the battle. The way we move and sense in a battle is not the same as the way we move and sense in front of screens, removed from the battles. What we can know in these two places is different. Importantly, it is not a matter of one being a mental engagement and the other a bodily engagement; both are multisensory, bodily engagements with a place, but the places are very different. I watched many videos of violence from the Egyptian uprising while sitting in activist collective Mosireen's office in downtown Cairo, next to people who had filmed these videos. The visible marks of the violence on the body of one of those activists, Salma Said, after she had been shot with over 100 pellets by Central Security Forces while documenting street clashes after the Port Said Massacre, vividly reminded me of just how different these places were (see Mosireen 2012b). Watching videos of protesters engulfed in tear gas, at times even nerve gas while breathing the dusty, polluted Cairo air from the safety of distance, left me breathing with difficulty, but gratefully aware that I would not be choking. Violence can touch us deeply in very physical ways even when we are far removed from it (see also Markham, this volume). Yet being able to engage in sensory experiences of violence, which occur in other places, is not the same as inhabiting these places. It is not a 'doubling of place', but a presence of elements of one place in another.

While I thus do not find the notion of 'doubling of place' useful, I similarly have reservations about theorisations of media as creating a 'third place' distinct from the places where people engage with media (Miller and Sinanan 2014; see also Miller and Sinanan 2012). Based on Daniel Miller's (2011) study of Facebook in Trinidad, Miller and Jolynna Sinanan (2014: 82) argue that: 'Instead of thinking about them as instruments which connect separate locations, we may have reached the point where we should start to think of new media as places in which people in some sense live; a third place, distinct from the two offline locations'. This notion of 'third place', then, is very different from the notion put forward by Ray Oldenburg (1989) and Robert Putnam (2000), who argue that places where people can gather outside of home and work constitute 'third places'. Miller and Sinanan

(2014: 82) further contend that 'with mobile smart phones, it was no longer the case that specific location was of particular consequence'. I understand this as a break with Miller's earlier work, which argues that 'contrary to the first generation of Internet literature – the Internet is not a monolithic or placeless "cyberspace"; rather, it is numerous new technologies, used by diverse people, in diverse real-world locations' (Miller and Slater 2000: 1). As I described above, problematising the notion of a 'doubling of place', watching videos of violence does not bring a person to the place of the violence. In a similar fashion, recording a video of violence or tweeting a picture with violence does not remove a person from the place of this violence. Recording and tweeting might in many ways immediately influence the place of the violence, as activists and journalists have painfully experienced, since Egyptian police and military often target people for carrying a camera or in other ways documenting events. But recording or tweeting or in any other way engaging in media-related practices by no means removes them from the violence; it does not provide them with a 'third place' distinct from 'offline locations'. When people are targeted for documenting street battles, their emplacement in these battles, along with media and violence, is a matter of life and death. The horrid, last video filmed by photographer Ahmed Samir Assem of a sniper shooting him gruesomely attests to this (see *Huffington Post UK* 2013). The emplacement of media might seem less obvious in peaceful places, but violence, with its forceful and pervasive influence on the places it moves through, highlights the importance of the emplacement of media. We are never removed from the places we are in, however much our screens (and more) are part of it. We might have a sense of being 'there' or of being in a 'third place', when engaging with media, but theoretically the notions of 'doubling of place' and 'third place' are unhelpful. Media influence places through being part of them rather than multiplying them or enabling phenomenologically detached virtual places.

Conclusion

In this chapter, I have argued for an understanding of media as vitally emplaced in the phenomenological world. Using examples from the Egyptian uprising, I have shown how violence challenges understandings of media as a 'doubling of place' or creating a 'third place', particularly pointing to the importance of multisensoriality in our engagements with media. I have elaborated on how media have been entangled in the movement of people as they moved towards or away from violence and protests after seeing videos, images and tweets from violence around the corner or across continents. Thus, I have argued for the conceptualisation of media as place-making and I have focused on how media serve to open up places to other places by enabling a presence of elements of one place in others. I have analysed how both media and violence are co-constitutive of places and crucially entangled in the movement of people, rocks, snipers' bullets and more.

While violent conflict can thus be useful in the theorising of media, how does an understanding of media as place-making impact our understandings of conflict? First, emplacing media alongside violence entails that conflict cannot be divided in physical and information battles. This is, in my view, the essence of media being co-constitutive of conflict (see also Bräuchler and Budka, this volume) rather than something that is added to conflict. And, second, the opening up of places with media is significant to the way in which we can understand conflict, particularly as media devices become increasingly mobile and instantaneously connected. Empirically, this opening of places has an at times pervasive influence on conflict, like when people go to the streets to join protests and battles upon seeing images of violence, some being killed doing so. This should lead to an attention of how the opening up of places affects the scales and configurations of conflict. It is not only a matter of conflict having a presence in places far from the violence; it is also a matter of how the opening of places affect the way in which people engage with conflict from the respective places they are in – from close by or afar.

Nina Grønlykke Mollerup is postdoctoral researcher at the ethnology section of the Saxo Institute, University of Copenhagen. She was trained as an anthropologist and holds a Ph.D. in communication. Her research interests include journalism, activism, refugees, revolution, conflict, violence, technology and sustainability. Her work has mainly focused on Egypt, Syria, and Scandinavia. She has published in journals like *International Journal of Communication* and *Journalism Practice*.

Note

1. I use the verb 'occur' here in accordance with Ingold's (2011: 141, emphasis added) argument: 'persons and things do not so much exist as *occur*, and are identified not by any fixed, essential attributes laid down in advance or transmitted ready-made from the past, but by the very pathways (or trajectories, or stories) along which they have previously come and are presently going'.

References

Adams, P.C. 2009. *Geographies of Media and Communication*. Oxford: Wiley-Blackwell.
Al Masry Al Youm. 2011. '"thawrat al-ghaḍab" fī "qaṣr al-nīl"' ['"The Revolution of Anger" in "Qasr El Nil"']. Al Masry Al Youm YouTube Channel, 30 January. Retrieved 20 October 2019 from https://www.youtube.com/watch?v=PujwO_iY5BU.
Alterman, J.B. 2011. 'The Revolution Will Not Be Tweeted', *Washington Quarterly* 34(4): 103–16.
Bräuchler, B. 2013. *Cyberidentities at War: The Moluccan Conflict on the Internet*. New York: Berghahn Books.
Bräuchler, B., and J. Postill (eds). 2010. *Theorising Media and Practice*. New York: Berghahn Books.
Casey, E.S. 1996. 'How to Get from Space to Place in a Fairly Short Stretch of Time', in S. Feld and K.H. Basso (eds), *Senses of Place*. Santa Fe: School of American Research Press, pp. 13–52.
Couldry, N. 2010. 'Theorising Media as Practice', in J. Postill and B. Bräuchler (eds), *Theorising Media and Practice*. New York: Berghahn Books, pp. 35–54.
Couldry, N., and M. Hobart. 2010. 'Media as Practice: A Brief Exchange', in J. Postill and B. Bräuchler (eds), *Theorising Media and Practice*. New York: Berghahn Books, pp. 77–82.
Dajani, N. 2012. 'Technology Cannot a Revolution Make: Nas-Book Not Facebook', *Arab Media & Society* 15. Retrieved 7 February 2020 from https://www.arabmediasociety.com/technology-cannot-a-revolution-make-nas-book-not-facebook/.
Fors, V., Å. Bäckström and S. Pink. 2013. 'Multisensory Emplaced Learning: Resituating Situated Learning in a Moving World', *Mind, Culture, and Activity* 20(2): 170–83.
Gibson, J.J. 1979. *The Ecological Approach to Visual Perception*. Boston: Houghton Mifflin.
Ginsburg, F.D., L. Abu-Lughod and B. Larkin. 2002. 'Introduction', in F.D. Ginsburg, L. Abu-Lughod and B. Larkin (eds), *Media Worlds: Anthropology on New Terrain*. Berkeley: University of California Press, pp. 1–36.
Harris, M. 2007. 'Introduction: "Ways of Knowing"', in M. Harris (ed.), *Ways of Knowing: New Approaches in the Anthropology of Knowledge and Learning*. New York: Berghahn Books, pp. 1–24.
Hobart, M. 2010. 'What Do We Mean by "Media Practices"?', in J. Postill and B. Bräuchler (eds), *Theorising Media and Practice*. New York: Berghahn Books, pp. 55–76.
Huffington Post UK. 2013. 'Egyptian Photographer Ahmed Assem Shot by Sniper and Films His Own Death (GRAPHIC VIDEO)', 10 July. Retrieved 20 October 2019 from http://www.huffingtonpost.co.uk/2013/07/10/ahmed-assem-egyptian-photographer_n_3571460.html.

Ingold, T. 2000. *The Perception of the Environment: Essays on Livelihood, Dwelling and Skill*. London: Routledge.

———. 2007. *Lines: A Brief History*. London: Routledge.

———. 2008. 'Bindings against Boundaries: Entanglements of Life in an Open World', *Environment and Planning A* 40: 1796–811.

———. 2011. *Being Alive: Essays on Movement, Knowledge and Description*. London: Routledge.

———. 2013. *Making: Anthropology, Archaeology, Art and Architecture*. New York: Routledge.

Jackson, M. 1996. 'Introduction: Phenomenology, Radical Empiricism, and Anthropological Critique', in M. Jackson (ed.), *Things as They Are: New Directions in Phenomenological Anthropology*. Bloomington: Indiana University Press, pp. 1–50.

Lindgren, S., M. Dahlberg-Grundberg and A. Johansson. 2014. 'Hybrid Media Culture: An Introduction', in S. Lindgren (ed.), *Hybrid Media Culture: Sensing Place in a World of Flows*. London: Routledge, pp. 1–15.

Massey, D. 2005. *For Space*. London: Sage.

Miller, D. 2011. *Tales from Facebook*. Cambridge: Polity Press.

Miller, D., and J. Sinanan. 2012. 'Webcam and the Theory of Attainment', *Media Anthropology Network, European Association of Social Anthropologists (EASA) E-Seminar Series* 41: 1–16. Retrieved 20 October 2019 from http://www.media-anthropology.net/file/miller_sinanan_webcam.pdf.

———. 2014. *Webcam*. Cambridge: Polity Press.

Miller, D., and D. Slater. 2000. *The Internet: An Ethnographic Approach*. Oxford: Berg.

Mollerup, N.G. 2015. 'Media and Place in Revolutionary Egypt: An Anthropological Exploration of Information Activism and Journalism', Ph.D. dissertation. Roskilde: Roskilde University.

Mollerup, N.G., and S. Gaber. 2015. 'Making Media Public: On Revolutionary Street Screenings in Egypt', *International Journal of Communication* 9: 2903–21. Retrieved 20 October 2019 from http://ijoc.org/index.php/ijoc/article/view/3655/1460.

Moores, S. 2005. *Media/Theory: Thinking about Media and Communications*. London: Routledge.

———. 2012a. 'Loose Ends: Lines, Media and Social Change', *Media Anthropology Network, European Association of Social Anthropologists (EASA) E-Seminar Series* 40: 1–15. Retrieved 20 October 2019 from http://www.media-anthropology.net/file/moores_eseminar.pdf.

———. 2012b. *Media, Place and Mobility*. Basingstoke: Palgrave Macmillan.

Morley, D. 2009. 'For a Materialist, Non-media-centric Media Studies', *Television & New Media* 10(1): 114–16.

Mosireen. 2011a. 'Blood at Night, Grief by Day | Maspero 9/10 al-demā wa al-asá | masbīrū' ['Blood at Night, Grief by Day | Maspero 9/10 Blood and Sorrow | Maspero']. The Mosireen Collective YouTube Channel, 11

October. Retrieved 20 October 2019 from https://www.youtube.com/watch?v=Mh5F0ot_p3s.

———. 2011b. 'The Maspero Massacre | 9/10/11'. The Mosireen Collective YouTube Channel, 10 November. Retrieved 20 October 2019 from https://www.youtube.com/watch?v=00t-0NEwc3E.

———. 2012a. 'ākheretna al-zibālah? qiṣṣat tūsī | The Martyrs: Toussi' [Is our end in the garbage? The story of Toussi | The Martyrs: Toussi']. The Mosireen Collective YouTube Channel, 21 January. Retrieved 20 October 2019 from https://www.youtube.com/watch?v=Xz3Rg_heqAg.

———. 2012b. 'lam wa lan nestakhdem al-kharṭūsh: eṣābet salma saʿīd Salma Said [We have not and we will not use pellets: The injury of Salma Said Salma Said'. The Mosireen Collective YouTube Channel, 7 February. Retrieved 20 October 2019 from https://www.youtube.com/watch?v=7JhA4jIv4bk&t=210s.

Oldenburg, R. 1989. *The Great Good Place, Cafés, Coffee Shops, Bookstores, Bars, Hair Salons, and Other Hangouts at the Heart of a Community*. Cambridge: Da Capo Press.

Peterson, M.A. 2003. *Anthropology & Mass Communication*. New York: Berghahn Books.

———. 2015. 'New Media and Electronic Networks in the Middle East', in S. Altorki (ed.), *A Companion to the Anthropology of the Middle East*. Malden: Wiley-Blackwell, pp. 509–25.

Pink, S. 2009. *Doing Sensory Ethnography*. London: Sage.

———. 2011. 'From Embodiment to Emplacement: Re-thinking Competing Bodies, Senses and Spatialities', *Sport, Education and Society* 16(3): 343–55.

———. 2012. *Situating Everyday Life: Practices and Places*. London: Sage.

Pink, S., and K.L. Mackley. 2013. 'Saturated and Situated: Expanding the Meaning of Media in the Routines of Everyday Life', *Media, Culture & Society* 35(6): 677–91.

Postill, J. 2010. 'Introduction: Theorising Media as Practice', in J. Postill and B. Bräuchler (eds), *Theorising Media and Practice*. New York: Berghahn Books, pp. 1–32.

Postill, J., and M.A. Peterson. 2009. 'What Is the Point of Media Anthropology?', *Social Anthropology* 17(3): 334–44.

Putnam, R.D. 2000. *Bowling Alone: The Collapse and Revival of American Community*. New York: Simon & Schuster.

Scannell, P. 1996. *Radio, Television and Modern Life: A Phenomenological Approach*. Oxford: Blackwell.

CHAPTER 9

An Ayuujk 'Media War' over Water and Land

Mediatised Senses of Belonging between Mexico and the United States

Ingrid Kummels

A press conference was hurriedly convened on 6 June 2017, at the municipal building in San Pedro y San Pablo Ayutla, a Mexican village less than two hours by car from Oaxaca City, the state capital. The topic of the conference was the clash the previous day at a water source along the boundary between the villages of Ayutla and Tamazulapam del Espíritu Santo. Among the few press people in attendance were representatives of the communal radio station Jënpoj from a neighbouring village and the internet journal *@desdelasnubes* from Oaxaca City. On their way to the meeting, they passed the coffin of a young man from Ayutla, who had died in the clash. An eight-and-a-half-minute video projected at the press conference showed scenes from the front-line: a group from Ayutla fleeing the bullets of their persecutors and several of them – still bleeding from their wounds – escaping on the back of a pickup. Without further comment, the video displayed key images of the violent quarrel between members of the two village communities that belong to the same indigenous group, the Mixe or Ayuujk ja'ay.[1]

After the screening, the journalists sensed that this particular agrarian dispute had taken a new dimension, notwithstanding that skirmishes over water and land are quite common in Oaxaca. Normally the general public barely takes any notice. Neighbouring villages frequently belong to the same ethnic group and quarrel over municipal boundaries and the partitioning of natural resources. These conflicts are complex affairs and, in some cases, may hark back to the colonial period. At the same time, they are firmly embedded in the current situation of these villages, which for decades have expanded their economic basis from agriculture to other economic fields in larger regional, national and transnational settings. Besides, they persist because of discrepancies between the emic concept of community and the legal figure of the municipality imposed by the state (Romero Frizzi 2011: 68). In this particular case, digital means of communication became an integral part of the agrarian dispute: Ayutla's eyewitness video subsequently went viral, circulating on the websites of established national media and receiving over 250,000 clicks in total (see also Sumiala, Tikka and Valaskivi, this volume).

The novelty of the video triggered a similar media response from the opponent. Three days later, Tamazulapam also disseminated a nine-minute video on the web, although in a different, documentary-like style.[2] Instead of organising a press conference, Tamazulapam's municipal government chose to present its stance through this video, which begins with an image of the village emblem and a written statement in Spanish: 'The following video categorically rejects the accusation that Ayutla Mixe presented at the 6 June 2017 conference, in which it irresponsibly accuses Tamazulapam Mixe of an "ambush".' The video then focuses on a series of verbal exchanges that took place prior to the shooting. Scenes from several spontaneous mobile phone recordings are commented on with short texts, and are thus interpreted as evidence that the people of Ayutla intended to take Tamazulapam by surprise during its patron saint fiesta and that they also initiated the gunfight. The main injury documented is that of a Tamazulapam villager who is flown by helicopter to Oaxaca City after being shot. This video was likewise disseminated on the internet and received tens of thousands of hits.

Both videos were circulated via social media managed mainly by villagers and then were published on the websites of major regional and national newspapers and magazines. Diffusion through these two media circuits led to the agrarian dispute becoming the main news story in Oaxaca for the first two weeks of June. My Ayuujk interlocutors judged the public impact of both videos as a new form of mediatising the long-established agrarian disputes. They commented that for the first time, a 'media war' (*guerra mediática*) had broken out between their villages. By using this term, they referred to the fact that waging a conflict was now closely connected to the self-fashioned media environments of these villages. Local media-makers use video cameras, mobile phones and their personal Facebook pages to engage in cultural activism, communal politics, commerce or a combination of these fields (Kummels 2017). Since villagers primarily rely on Facebook to socialise with relatives and friends living far away (Ramos Mancilla 2015: 226, 238), it has become crucial for opening media spaces in a geographical, practice-oriented and imagined sense at the level of the village, the region or beyond. In recent years, highly educated, technically adept young media actors – both men and women – have emerged as public intellectuals engaging in social media who can be characterised as 'ethnic influencers' (Kummels n.d.). For the first time, they intervened in the quarrel via social media or were pushed into doing so by the authorities in their respective village.

The term 'influencer' is typically used to designate 'everyday, ordinary internet users who accumulate a relatively large following on blogs and social media through the textual and visual narration of their personal lives and lifestyles' (Abidin 2016: 3). They exert influence on consumer behaviour due to their strong presence and reputation in social media. In turn, I use 'ethnic influencer' for actors who use their narrative skills to influence followers in terms of cultural expressions and ideals considered characteristic of the ethnic group they identify with, in this case the Ayuujk ja'ay. Ayuujk ethnic influencers connect to diverse audiences. On the one hand, they have gained ground in the political sphere of the municipalities. On the other hand, their digital activism extends to nonethnic networks, such as those of academic circles and activists engaged in human, indigenous and gender rights. Justifying their ethnic interests via inalienable rights and a humanitarian cause enables them to disseminate narratives and images that appeal to a large audience (see also Adriaans, this volume).

It is precisely the role these emerging media actors play in mediatising the skirmishes between Ayutla and Tamazulapam that this chapter explores. This approach seeks to overcome the popular image, according to which these disputes are perceived as solely a source of village disruption and deemed a relic of the rural areas of Mexico – an image that has been used to stereotype indigenous people in general and Oaxaca as the Mexican state with the highest percentage of this population in particular. Instead, I scrutinise the potential of these disputes for reconfiguring social, cultural and political relations in the present. I argue that the current conflict actors still rely on traditional media to enforce territorial claims on village land that is intimately related to their communal way of life and politics. They formerly resorted to *lienzos*, colonial map-style paintings on canvas, to this end and on forms of 'visual warfare'. These media have long historical roots and remain embedded in Mesoamerican community culture (Kummels 2017: 40). At the same time, this chapter examines how the once intra-indigenous conflicts have been decisively modified through the transnationalisation of

Ayuujk villages and the new digital media strategies of many villagers. They now engage with wider audiences via social media by referring to larger issues such as gender equality, global human rights and Mexico's narco-violence.

Since the 1990s, people from the Mixe region have migrated in large numbers to the United States. As a result of their illegalisation and immobilisation, they rely heavily on long-distance communication to maintain social relations across the restrictive international boundary and develop 'mediatised' senses of belonging. I use the word 'mediatised' to emphasise the way in which stakeholders actively engage in a wide range of media – from maps to social media – to mobilise community affectively (Kummels 2016) and from different vantage points that may oscillate between local, regional, national and transnational levels of belonging. A case in point is the community governance (also called *usos y costumbres*), the grassroots democratic system according to which both litigant villages are governed. Decisions are taken by those attending a general assembly and municipal authorities onsite in the respective village. However, in recent years, village governance has been mediatised, so that even from a distance, community members can regularly participate. Ethnic influencers have created popular Facebook pages such as 'Asamblea Pueblo Tamazalupam Mixe' and 'Tukyo'm Ayuntamiento Ayutla Mixe' on their own initiative. Since the younger generation of 'digital natives' often debate crucial village issues such as agrarian disputes on these pages, they have become a kind of supplemental, unofficial virtual assembly that rally audiences beyond the local populations transnationally. These digital fora do not simply represent or double the traditional general assemblies, but instead reconfigure them and the agrarian disputes, as will be illustrated below.

Studying the Interdependence of Media and Conflict

Analysing this concrete case at the interface of conflict and media requires an approach based on the anthropology of conflict. I follow the school of anthropologists who contend that conflicts are nothing extraordinary: they are a component of everyday life that can have both disruptive and cohesive effects on social actors and groups (see e.g. Eckert 2004). Despite the impression of chaos that quarrels convey, the actors who intervene in them pursue them in view of concrete motives such as honour, power and material profit; they strategically (re)structure disputes by planning their logistics (Elwert 1999: 87). Actors who develop procedures for waging disputes can tap their potential to strengthen the social cohesion of the group through 'othering' the enemy and may even extend their political power beyond one group (Chassen-López 2004: 444; Gledhill 2012). Media-makers who convey local information on conflicts via the internet to a global audience or quarrel via social media for publicity also expand their radius of influence in a calculating manner, i.e. for the end of identity politics (Bräuchler 2013; see also Pype, this volume).

From a media anthropology perspective, I examine how politics and conflict are currently mediatised in Ayuujk villages. Focusing on social media like Facebook, YouTube and Twitter, I accompanied villagers who shaped the conflict in several places via their current media practices; that is, based on what they do and say in relation to media (e.g. Bräuchler and Postill 2010).[3] The appraisal of this particular quarrel as a 'media war' indicates that digital media literacy and creativity have become basic knowledge resources in negotiating agrarian conflicts. This prompted me to assess the new position and influence that emerging young actors – who are keen to experiment, social media-savvy and also critical of the reliability of the contents of such media – might be performing for agrarian disputes. The concept of 'mediatisation' refers to the more longlasting transformation of sociocultural institutions that result from the media practices used to shape them (Hjarvard 2008: 114). Actors who follow battles that are portrayed audiovisually online develop a 'sense of engagement' with that 'media event' as 'an ongoing and living event' (Hine 2000: 67). I therefore argue that these media or web events have become just as meaningful for the course of an agrarian conflict as the offline events from which they derive. Viewers are affected by and reposition themselves in relation to these mediatised battles of symbols and representations; that is, they become concerned with how battles are perceived by others (see Hoskins and O'Loughlin 2010: 4–5). But I also paid attention to the aspects of the agrarian conflict that were purposefully withheld from media diffusion. I contend that the comprehension of agrarian conflicts requires investigating both online and offline dimensions and the ways in which these practices are embedded in local settings and Ayuujk cultural forms (see Bräuchler 2013: 276).

Ayutla vs. Tamazulapam: Patterns and Media Innovations of Agrarian Disputes

Although the compact territory of the Mixe District is largely identified with the Ayuujk ja'ay as an ethnolinguistic group, the population's sense of belonging has long centred on the village, which the state recognises as an administrative unit or municipality. Ayutla is the seat of numerous institutions of the Oaxacan state and the most important administrative centre of the Mixe region. Since the Salesian mission has a stronghold there, most inhabitants profess Catholicism. Merchants, entrepreneurs and professionals, as well as the Spanish language, now dominate the village centre. Although Ayutla governs itself according to the communal *usos y costumbres* system (officially recognised by the Oaxaca state in 1995), a dissident faction favours Mexican party politics and the Partido Revolucionario Institucional (PRI), which has held power for decades. Since the 1960s, Tamazulapam has prospered by engaging in the coffee trade, transportation facilities and construction business. In 1991, it challenged its neighbouring village's predominance by establishing its own market place. Both Tamazulapam and Ayutla have migrant diaspora communities in Mexican and U.S. cities that operate taco restaurant businesses. Migrants' incomes are an important source of the hometowns' development. Tamazulapam too has maintained self-government according to the communal *usos y costumbres* system and is deemed more traditional in relation to Ayuujk religious beliefs, language and culture than Ayutla.

Ayutla and Tamazulapam, as well as the neighbouring villages, have long engaged in agrarian disputes according to a pattern of an argument 'among equals'. In other words, as municipalities they base their claims on communal land tenure, a legal form that requires them to provide evidence of historical occupation of the disputed terrain.[4] Agrarian disputes have become their established way of negotiating municipal boundaries and power relations. The patterns of waging them include ritualised political manifestations, such as erecting landmarks and sacrificing poultry in defence of one's territory (Kuroda 1993: 521–22). The state government largely recognises the autonomy of this internal procedure, since it only provides for intermediation between municipalities, whose task it is to convene reconciliation meetings and come to an understanding. On the other hand, this 'passive role' of the state is regularly questioned by the parties in conflict. Concerns that the state is actually pursuing its own interests or even conspiring with one party instead of mediating are often voiced.

By the 1990s, video had been appropriated in an innovative way for land disputes, such as the quarrel in which Tamazulapam and another neighbouring village, Tlahuitoltepec, engaged intensely between 1996 and 2000. Visualising land claims onsite was an important means of influencing the opponents' perception. Inhabitants of both villages massively reshaped the landscape through communal *tequio*-work, which they invested in erecting cement boundary markers and clearing forest aisles as a borderline to assert their respective land claims. These measures were meant to cause 'seeing that hurts', as several of my interlocutors remarked, and can therefore be characterised as a form of 'visual warfare'. The village taken by surprise respected these symbols on the ground as a partial victory of their opponents. Community media-makers from both villages used analogue video to record how the landscape was demarcated, thereby extending the 'visual warfare' on the ground (Kummels 2017: 183–84). However, the production of these videos was monitored by community governance and was used by municipal authorities exclusively for mobilising their own village's population during their screening at the general assembly. The visual evidence was not disseminated to a broader nonindigenous audience, based on the assumption that they did not factor into the outcome of the conflict.

At first, the dispute between Ayutla and Tamazulapam over the water source followed this established pattern. Only recently have participants began to embrace a nonindigenous audience to influence public opinion. The dispute has gone through four phases – 2004, 2015, 2017 and 2019 – which I will sketch briefly. According to my interlocutors, new layers have been successively added to the original bone of contention: the water source. In 2004, the dispute escalated when specific amounts of water had been assigned to each village by Mexico's national water authority. After Ayutla claimed the source in its entirety, villagers from Tamazulapam occupied the land on which the water source is located. Ayutla retaliated by blocking Tamazulapam's road access to the state capital. When both parties, armed with rifles, occupied the water source, the Oaxacan state police and the Mexican federal army were sent in. Municipal authorities from both villages subsequently met for reconciliation, but only reached a temporary agreement to work towards solving the conflict in further negotiations.

When the conflict broke out again in 2015, a new situation prevailed. In 2007, the five-village alliance that Ayutla, Tamazulapam, Tlahuitoltepec, Tepantlali and Tepuxtepec had once formed based on a colonial land title from 1712 was dissolved. While most of the villages demarcated individual municipal boundaries, since a change in agrarian laws now provided for better access to government funds, only Ayutla and Tamazulapam found it impossible to demarcate a final section of the border, a mere two kilometres in length. There lies the water source, which for both parties has a material and immaterial value. The growing population, agricultural projects with greenhouses and tourism enterprises require water; there is also speculation that Coca Cola is interested in exploiting this same water source. Besides, next to it is a cave, a site of the traditional Ayuujk religion sacred to both villages, which for Tamazulapam had become inaccessible when Ayutla built a water tank that enclosed it. In 2014, after Ayutla had erected a second, larger water tank, appropriating the water in its entirety, the dispute was further exacerbated by the issue of how to apportion land along the two-kilometre tranche. Members of both villages living at the tranche have intermarried and passed on land to their descendants or sold land to a member of the other village. Tamazulapam and Ayutla relied on different lines of argument to enhance their claims. Ayutla traces back its boundary markers to a remote past as testified through oral testimonies. Tamazulapam, in contrast, argues on the basis of land that was and still is actually ploughed by community members called *trabajaderos*, as evidenced by ongoing agricultural use.

In 2015, the authorities of both villages first engaged in joint talks they accorded mutually, but Ayutla cancelled a decisive meeting in September 2015. As the conflict escalated, both villages began erecting boundary markers. But this time, people from Ayutla did not recognise the markers of their opponents and simply destroyed them. In October 2015, Tamazulapam began clearing a forest aisle and traced it in such a way as to include the water source in its municipal territory. On 13 October, people from both villages gathered in the conflict zone and verbally attacked each other; bullets were fired in the air. Both parties documented the episode extensively with the support of their respective local media-makers, whom officials had commissioned. Interestingly, they relied on commercial fiesta videographers who are normally criticised for capitalising on their films (Kummels 2017: 11). These recordings were still dealt with as internal material and were not circulated beyond the respective village. Nevertheless, beginning in 2015 a decisive change took place: mobile phone recordings of the conflict posted by anonymous ethnic influencers emerged on YouTube (e.g. IMAGINA Explosión Creativa 2015).

On 18 May 2017, villagers from Tamazulapam destroyed homes that Ayutla residents had built on municipal land claimed by Tamazulapam and cut off their water supply. This triggered a wave of violence and in face-to-face conversations, people would comment: 'We are at war.' More online videos of crucial conflict moments were disseminated on YouTube. Representatives of Ayutla, accompanied by the state police, came to inspect the zone of conflict on 5 June, the Whit Monday Tamazulapam celebrates its patron saint fiesta of Espíritu Santo. According to the Tamazulapam video described above, snipers from both villages fired at each other, while the Ayutla video suggests that all the assailants were from Tamazulapam and that they fired at unarmed Ayutla villagers, killing one and wounding six. On 5 June, four women from Ayutla were arrested (according to Tamazulapam) or kidnapped (according to Ayutla) by Tamazulapam officials and released the next day. On 18 July, the parties began to attend reconciliation meetings moderated by the Oaxacan General Ministry. Each village sent a delegation of thirteen municipal authorities accompanied by village lawyers and other academics. Although a truce had been agreed upon, at the end of August 2017, the inhabitants of Tamazulapam dynamited the water tanks after a federal court ordered the restoration of Ayutla's water supply. Ayutla used a drone to record the opponent's activities and published the images on its municipal Facebook page.

In sum, media innovations have recurrently shaped agrarian disputes, and since 2015 a decisive change has taken place. Videoclips are now also produced and posted anonymously on social media to mobilise a wider audience. Ethnic influencers begin to factor in conflict dynamics.

Mediatising War in the Digital Era: Ethnic Influencers

I followed up on the media practices of Tamazulapam's transnational community in the aftermath of the recent skirmishes when I travelled to Los Angeles, Tamazulapam and Oaxaca City between July and October 2017. This was the most intensive period in the cyberwar. Most of my interlocutors from Tamazulapam's Los Angeles satellite community commented on the recent outbreak of the conflict by showing me scenes of the online videos described above, as well as the contents shared on popular Ayuujk Facebook pages. These web events became a defining moment and point of departure for political organisation offline. For the first time since 2004, the more than 400 people from Tamazulapam living in Los Angeles organised according to traditional community governance and began raising funds for their village of origin. This is noteworthy, considering that the majority of adults are undocumented due to their relatively late migration to the United States at the end of the 1990s, which basically inhibits the possibility of political organisation.

Several middle-aged members of Tamazulapam's satellite community commented on how scenes of the Ayutla video continued to make an unsettling impact on them and referred to the close-ups of people arguing and of the wounded from the opposing village. In general, they synthesised impressions based on the audiovisual material and texts posted by the competing parties as conforming to a single web event, which allowed them (and me as well) to relate to a common world of experience. One scene in the Ayutla video testifies to the imminent death of a man who had been shot in the forehead. The death of this young man of mixed Tamazulapam and Ayutla decent deeply disturbed them. In contrast to the impression conveyed by the Ayutla video, which clearly pinpoints people from Tamazulapam as the culprits, some of my interlocutors interpreted this and other scenes in a way that was critical of the reliability of media representations. They based their doubts on personal experiences (such as decades ago when they participated in skirmishes with Tlahuitoltepec) and referred to the former 'rules of the game' of an agrarian conflict. This led them to rate both the Ayutla and Tamazulapam videos as propaganda tools intended to convince public opinion in general, and thus not trustworthy with regard to what actually happened. As to the death of the young man (which was not recorded), it was assumed that he was killed by a Tamazulapam sniper, although his death was seen as unintentional. According to 'the rules of the game', bullets are never fired at the unarmed, but in the air as a form of deterrence. His death was deplored for two reasons: first, out of empathy for the tragedy of the young man; and, second, because it unequivocally conveys the impression that people from Tamazulapam are ruthless. Nevertheless, since the video emphasises this negative image, 'othering' Tamazulapam and subjecting it to public shaming, people from this village living in Los Angeles actually made it a reference point for solidarity.

Socialising through Facebook also transcends transnational village circuits. In particular, young Ayuujk professionals – many of whom no longer reside in these villages – have created very popular Facebook pages. In times of peace, they engage in Ayuujk cultural politics and promote its spoken and written language, its visual arts and its political models of *comunalidad* or Ayuujk communitarianism.[5] Some of these Facebook pages and Twitter accounts have become 'virtual' realms of experience in which Ayuujk creative people from diverse villages interact and also communicate with nonindigenous intellectuals in Mexican cities and beyond the country. Based on their status as public intellectuals in social media, these Facebook administrators can be characterised as 'ethnic influencers' (Kummels n.d.).

In the course of the intensification of the 'media war' or 'cyberwar' (a term that became popular in the context of neo-Zapatista uprising in Chiapas; see Froehling (1997)) in 2017, this young generation of professionals added a new dimension to the conflict by creating and responding to web events. Apart from the two main online videos, web events included the posting on 6 June 2017 of a televised interview with a woman from Ayutla who had summoned the PRI to help her municipality, a letter of solidarity with Ayutla signed by intellectuals from the Universidad Nacional Autónoma de México (UNAM) and the Universidad Autónoma Metropolitana (UAM), the publication of documents of sometimes questionable authenticity, such as the notebook an Ayutla official had allegedly lost during the skirmish, and 'newly discovered' 1907 maps of the territories of Ayutla and Tamazulapam. Media actors from both villages intervened via several new cyberstrategies. The Asamblea Pueblo Tamazalupam Mixe Facebook page designed by an ethnic influencer from Tamazulapam was shut down at a crucial moment – the dissemination of the Tamazulapam video – after its administrator was denounced for having created a fake profile. Flaming, solidarity campaigns to mobilise civil society and the revelation of confidential documents discrediting their opponents were also employed as cyberstrategies. My interlocutors often spoke of victories attained as 'he/she won on Facebook', which means that waging a successful media war was ascribed to a regular online presence in combination with the texting and imaging abilities to attract and convince many followers. The younger 'digital natives' experienced online battles just as exciting and fulfilling (or in the opposite case as frustrating) as battles on the ground that rely on land occupation and control of roads to regionally expand commercial power.

I will now discuss how the parties developed such strategies based on a new and diverging perception of the audiences they deemed relevant for influencing the outcome of the agrarian dispute. Young media-makers from Ayutla were the first to design web events based on global human rights and gender discourses in combination with public activities to stir Mexican civil society into action. This was consistent with the preference of Ayutla's municipality for solving the conflict beyond the regional level: with an appeal to the Mexican federal court in 2017 and through a petition to the United Nations in 2019 (see below). Tamazulapam actors, on the other hand, were critical of what they termed a 'media circus' (*circo mediático*), which they alleged Ayutla was staging for 'people outside'. They insisted on bilateral negotiations and concentrated on establishing good terms with 'people who know us' – coethnics of the region who interact face to face, in commerce or at fiestas, the traditional means of forging alliances in compliance with regional economic and political interests.

However, regardless of these diverging stances, authorities from both municipalities in fact directed their 'war' propaganda to an outside audience. They (re-)created press departments when the dispute escalated in October 2015 and ethnic influencers with persuasive Facebook pages as determined by the high number of followers – mainly intellectuals with university training – were integrated into community governance as official delegates. Initially they created Facebook pages as an alternative to the cultural and political activities common to their villages, but when conflict escalated the ethnic influencers were co-opted by the respective municipal authorities. This 'roping in', as insiders called it, of these media actors was remarkable, because some had been harshly criticised by the authorities for their deviations from the village's ideal of grassroots democracy, since they created Facebook accounts now perceived as representative of the village without first seeking approval from its general assembly. It is even more remarkable that established communal media, which for decades had been conceptualised as the villages' only assembly-based and legitimate media outlets, were not given this press relations role.[6] Ethnic influencers took their liberty to produce web events according to their personal likings that included art, literature and music fads. As they began to actively express themselves behind the façade of Facebook pages and Twitter accounts representing their villages, municipal authorities tried to keep a tight rein on their media activities.

However, the ethnic influencers introduced a new angle by resorting to the academic knowledge they acquired and the networks they fostered with Mexican civil society. Contrary to what happened during previous agrarian disputes, arguments were now frequently based on international human, women's and indigenous rights. Ayutla women who possess land at the disputed boundary rose to prominence on 31 May 2017 in relation to the following web event: at a press conference in Oaxaca City, their spokeswoman deplored Tamazulapam's destruction of houses and crops, which she alleged had been specifically directed against women. At the subsequent press conference on 6 June, she emphasised the gender-based aggression by Tamazulapam, accusing it of 'irrationality' (Martínez 2017). These declarations were not only disseminated by established press outlets in Oaxaca, but also by national networks of women's social movements such as the SemMéxico (Servicio Especial de la Mujer) website. On 27 June, a group of twenty-one intellectuals, including linguists and feminists from the UNAM and the UAM, declared their solidarity with Ayutla and accused the Oaxacan state government of 'not having advised detention orders with regard to the depredation of the land of community members, in their majority women' (La Jornada 2017, my translation). The orchestration of this web event was attributed to a particular academic activist from Ayutla who has become a public intellectual in Mexico and is perceived as a spokesperson of the Ayuujk people in general. The impact of the event was based on nonindigenous academics from highly respected universities clearly siding with Ayutla in an otherwise intra-indigenous conflict.

The 'Ayutla Mixe en Hermandad' Facebook page is an example of how an older medium, the *lienzo*, and traditional 'visual warfare' strategies were resignified through a social media event. In the past, both villages based their land claims on their individual painted copies of the same colonial *lienzo*, a map of communal land drawn on canvas. Each village had complemented its *lienzo* with written explanations to meet its own needs (Kummels 2017: 188). The Ayutla Facebook page reported the 'discovery' of maps of Ayutla and Tamazulapam dating from 1907 that supported Ayutla's claim to the contested water source as part of its 'ancestral territories'.[7] The accompanying text in Spanish specified that 'we count on the support of expert anthropologists and historians who step by step gained insight into the heart of the current situation in our village'. The map of Ayutla was interpreted as its municipality including not merely the water source, but most of the Tamazulapam settlement known as Tierra Blanca. Moreover, the page claimed that international law allegedly favoured Ayutla, referring to the Indigenous and Tribal Peoples Convention No. 169 (International Labour Organization 1989), which endorses indigenous people's rights of ownership and possession of lands they traditionally occupy, despite the fact that Tamazulapam could have used the same argument to substantiate its own claims. The wider audience the site addressed would probably not perceive this inconsistency. Thus, this Facebook page renewed the traditional medium of legitimating resource ownership by digitally publishing and interpreting a *lienzo*-like map. It translated traditional 'visual warfare' into terms that were culturally legible for the broader audience of the digital era.

Hence, 'weapons' such as university training and the expertise of anthropology, history and other disciplines played a vital role in waging a cyberwar. International human rights were redirected towards a purpose for which they had not been designed: intervillage and intra-ethnic conflict. New intra-social differentiations based on higher education, as well as shifts in the framework of cultural definition and political power, are not merely additional layers to the conflict. All these layers are in fact enmeshed with the current dynamics of 'war' being handed over to a younger, university-trained generation that makes its own sense of it. For this reason, ethnic influencers who carry out verbal battles on their Facebook pages also discuss academic expertise and social networks as new defining elements of being Ayuujk. They are effective resources in extending control over water and land, and gaining political power within the confines of the municipality and beyond. Experts in Amerindian languages, sociologists, political scientists and lawyers have emerged in both municipalities in recent decades. In several instances, people specifically chose these degree programmes to advance municipal issues such as water and land claims.

At the same time, many conflict strategies on the ground were not dealt with in the realm of digital advocacy. This includes the reconciliation meetings moderated by the Oaxacan General Ministry, which began taking place in June 2017 and mounted up to sixty-two meetings over the next two years. The compromises reached at these meetings were documented in short minutes and were discussed by the municipal authorities of Ayutla and Tamazulapam with their respective general assemblies. These compromises ideally serve to pave the way for a larger agreement. However, in parallel to these negotiations, both villages first blockaded roads leading to Oaxaca City, imposing controls through armed municipal sentinels and affecting the entire Sierra Norte region for months. Gaining control of the roads is one of the traditional strategies to increase a village's commercial influence throughout the region. Yet, ethnic influencers did not address these issues online. Nor did they mention that each village intensely engaged in sacrificing poultry at its boundaries, since a broader audience has little comprehension of ritualised politics. Furthermore, they were silent about daily routines in both villages being substantially altered during the conflict, since municipal authorities imposed rigid requirements that community members participate in *tequio* work shifts and become part-time sentinels as well as contribute financially to the logistics of the agrarian dispute. Virtually none of this appears on video or on the internet, since ethnic influencers may not want to interfere in the reconciliation work of municipal authorities, although by omitting mention to their efforts, they may also bypass and override them. Nevertheless, both groups, which differ with regard to age, gender composition, education and professional background, now decisively influence the more general dynamics of agrarian conflicts in the twenty-first century. Meanwhile, other stakeholders such as most village peasants either have less access to media technology or may choose to abstain from 'media warfare', measuring their actions carefully in view of having to face the consequences onsite.

Preliminary Conclusions in Light of the Conflict's Latest Turnaround

In accordance with the ongoing character of the conflict, this chapter can only offer a provisional balance on how media and conflict are now mutually constituted in a longstanding agrarian dispute. When I revisited Oaxaca in February and March 2018, I was able to experience several outcomes of the cyberwar. The general assemblies of both villages had elected women (for the first time in Tamazulapam and the third time in Ayutla) to the highest municipal offices in 2018, in the expectation that these women would be capable of settling the dispute. At a reconciliation meeting in late August 2017, both villages came to an agreement on reconnecting the water. Nevertheless, Ayutla's water supply was not restored in 2018.

The 'media war' was temporarily abandoned and to date (December 2019) people from Tamazulapam no longer appear to be participating in it. The public perceived an academic activist from Ayutla as the main actor behind events, particularly between March and May 2019. At the end of April 2019, she filed a complaint with the United Nations Special Rapporteur on the Rights of Indigenous Peoples, asserting that Ayutla's human right to access water was being violated and accusing the Oaxacan state government of 'negotiating with the aggressors' (Flores 2019), that is, of siding with Tamazulapam. #AguaParaAyutlaYa became a trending topic. This line of argument was now supported by nonindigenous media actors like Mexican writer Emiliano Monge (2019), who alleged that due to their own interest in the water source, 'armed groups related to drug trafficking' had allied with Tamazulapam, which was a new version of the conflict. The original arguments that led to the dispute and its many layers were not mentioned in his article.

Unexpectedly, on 13 May 2019, the top regional news story was that the agrarian conflict had been solved. Oaxacan newspapers featured PRI state governor Alejandro Murat posing in the middle of municipal authorities from both villages, declaring that they had come to a final agreement and that the water supply would be reinstalled to both parties on equal terms. A two-minute video of this proclamation was broadly spread through the governor's Twitter account. However, in an official letter dated 15 May, Ayutla's municipal authorities denied that any agreement had been reached. In successive articles in Oaxacan newspapers, the many layers of the quarrel once again came to the fore: that is, that the fifty-fifty solution for water distribution was being rejected because the issue was intertwined with land claims of both villages along the two-kilometre tranche, causing the municipal authorities to intervene.

Despite the impression of chaos – or precisely because of it – I would like to offer a preliminary assessment of the lasting effects of this cyberwar on agrarian strife in light of the theories of the anthropology of conflict and media that were my starting point. Agrarian disputes have remained a component of everyday life. Although this has been elaborated on by conflict anthropologists, in the present case, this holds true even in the course of a generational change. New social media actors now address various audiences to mobilise mediatised senses of belonging, which for the first time transcend the level of the transnational village to include a nonindigenous audience and even nonindigenous conflict actors. Ethnic influencers have not only invested new resources such as their fluency with social media and knowledge of its wider private enterprise-based structure into their Facebook and Twitter accounts and the recruitment of followers; they have also paved the way for reconfiguring existing conflict strategies, such as maps and 'visual warfare' in digital spaces, while abandoning earlier 'rules of the game', which restricted frontline images to members of their respective villages. At the same time, because of the influence of these young media actors, consensual discourses on gender, human rights and narco-violence appeal affectively to a wider community to ally against the 'other'. 'Othering' the enemy online now includes novel 'elements of surprise' such as conflating the opponents of the neighbouring village with national villains, for example, the drug mafia and the PRI state government. Some ethnic influencers have been promoted to official community delegates in ongoing conflict negotiations.

Several new opportunities for conflict appeasement have opened up – or closed – in this context. Information and disinformation on the dispute now flow in a more accessible way to both the younger generation of social media users and an international audience. Opening up a media space for these quarrels allows anyone on social media to partake in a common world of experience that incorporates key Mesoamerican symbols such as maps in a way that not only represents but is also constitutive of a village's territory and conflict itself. However, this exchange via social media privileges the few villagers, mainly academics, who are able to influence national and international audiences due to their knowledge of global discourses on indigeneity that they have integrated into the logic of agrarian conflicts. In an initial phase, they were 'roped in' by municipal authorities, but subsequently they rushed ahead of the slower-paced decision-making processes of the villages' respective general assemblies. The strategy of disengaging from the 'media war' tends to give greater weight to the temporalities of face-to-face reconciliation meetings as well as of established communal media outlets.

Nevertheless, Oaxacan agrarian disputes are now waged with regard to mediatised senses of belonging by imagi(ni)ng and mobilising different vantage points via digital media practices. Multiscale 'warfare' is embedded by young social media actors in the *longue durée* of Mesoamerican media and community culture. At the same time, the current mediatised ways of highlighting water and land claims also increase the field of tension to which village governance and communal decision-making processes are exposed in times of transnationalism. Ending this agrarian conflict – which is what most of those involved are striving for – will depend on how the rationale and intricacies of on-the-ground conflict negotiations are made accessible to an extended audience. It will also depend on opening media spaces to a greater diversity of voices from the villages themselves.

Ingrid Kummels is Professor of Cultural and Social Anthropology at the Institute for Latin American Studies at Freie Universität Berlin. She has conducted long-term ethnographic research in Mexico, Cuba, Peru and the United States, focusing on transnational community building from the perspective of media and visual anthropology. On the topic of indigenous people's use of media, she has published *Transborder Media Spaces: Ayuujk Videomaking between Mexico and the US* (Berghahn Books, 2017).

Notes

1. The Ayutla video was first posted 6 June 2017 on the website of Radio Jënpoj as 'Version of the community of Ayutla Mixe on the situation of 5 June'; see Radio Comunitaria Ayuujk (2017).
2. The Tamazulapam video was first published on 9 June 2017 on YouTube by the anonymous BAjo El CIeLO MIxE (2017).
3. I studied these topics during my ethnographic research from 2015 to 2019, primarily in Tamazulapam and its satellite community in Los Angeles. My information on Ayutla stems from individual villagers living in Oaxaca City. This imbalance implies that I mainly followed media practices and mediatised senses of belonging with regard to Tamazulapam. I have avoided naming or giving pseudonyms to my interlocutors since I am primarily concerned with analysing the agency of conflict actors in general.
4. More than 50 per cent of land possessions in the state of Oaxaca are recognised as communal (*bienes comunales*). Municipalities claiming *bienes comunales* may rely on a colonial land title or previous court decisions that defined municipal boundaries for justification (Moreno Derbez 2010: 9, 27).

5. The intellectuals who coined the notion of *comunalidad* in the 1980s engaged in village movements that relied on the then-novel technology of analogue video to revitalise Ayuujk and Zapotec culture. Floriberto Díaz from Tlahuitoltepec conceptualised *comunalidad* partly during the period of quarrel over land with Tamazulapam.
6. For example, the Ayutla communal radio station Konk' Anaa did not attend the municipality's press conference on 6 June. In the neighbouring village of Tlahuitoltepec, Radio Jënpoj provided no further coverage after the onset of the dispute, since Tlahuitoltepec municipal authorities were anxious to avoid any involvement in the dispute.
7. The 1907 map is not an original land grant map. For the fundamental difficulties of determining municipal boundaries based on historical maps, see Romero Frizzi (2011: 74–76).

References

Abidin, C. 2016. '"Aren't These Just Young, Rich Women Doing Vain Things Online?": Influencer Selfies as Subversive Frivolity', *Social Media + Society* 2(2): 1–17.
BAjo El CIeLO MIxE. 2017. 'Video del enfrentamiento que sostuvieron tamazulapan mixes y ayutla en el manantial'. YouTube, 7 June. Retrieved 18 October 2019 from https://www.youtube.com/watch?v=7zHlzxzIT9I.
Bräuchler, B. 2013. *Cyberidentities at War: The Moluccan Conflict on the Internet*. New York: Berghahn Books.
Bräuchler, B., and J. Postill (eds). 2010. *Theorising Media and Practice*. New York: Berghahn Books.
Chassen-López, F.R. 2004. *From Liberal to Revolutionary Oaxaca: The View from the South. Mexico 1867–1911*. Pittsburgh: Pennsylvania State University Press.
Eckert, J. 2004. 'Einleitung: Gewalt, Meidung und Verfahren: Zur Konflikttheorie Georg Elwerts', in J. Eckert (ed.), *Anthropologie der Konflikte: Georg Elwerts konflikttheoretische Thesen in der Diskussion*. Bielefeld: transcript, pp. 7–25.
Elwert, G. 1999. 'Markets of Violence', in G. Elwert, S. Feuchtwang and D. Neubert (eds), *Dynamics of Violence: Processes of Escalation and De-escalation in Violent Group Conflicts*. Berlin: Duncker & Humblot, pp. 85–102.
Flores, R. 2019. 'Denuncian la ineficacia y negligencia del gobierno de Oaxaca', *Oaxaca Media*, 25 April. Retrieved 20 October 2019 from http://www.oaxaca.media/portada-2/mixes-llevan-a-la-onu-el-caso-de-violacion-de-su-derecho-al-agua.
Froehling, O. 1997. 'The Cyberspace "War of Ink and Internet" in Chiapas, Mexico', *Geographical Review* 87(2): 291–307.
Gledhill, J. 2012. 'Violence and Reconstitution in Mexican Indigenous Communities', in W.G. Pansters (ed.), *Violence, Coercion, and State-Making in Twentieth-Century Mexico*. Stanford: Stanford University Press, pp. 233–51.

Hine, C. 2000. *Virtual Ethnography*. London: Sage.
Hjarvard, S. 2008. 'The Mediatization of Society: A Theory of the Media as Agents of Social and Cultural Change', *Nordicom Review* 29(2): 105–34.
Hoskins, A., and B. O'Loughlin. 2010. *War and Media: The Emergence of Diffused War*. Cambridge: Polity Press.
IMAGINA Explosión Creativa. 2015. 'Dialogo Bienes Comunales "Ayutla-Tama"', *YouTube*, 13 October. Retrieved 18 October 2019 from https://www.youtube.com/watch?v=pS7QTdZrL_s.
International Labour Organization (ILO). 1989. 'Indigenous and Tribal Peoples Convention, 1989 (No. 169)'. Geneva.
Kummels, I. n.d. 'Archivar aspiraciones entre México y EE.UU.: influencers étnicos y el archivo dancístico zapoteco online', in I. Kummels and G. Cánepa Koch (eds), *Antropología y archivos en la era digital: usos emergentes de lo audiovisual*, vol. 2. Lima: IDE/PUCP.
———. 2016. 'Introducción', in I. Kummels (ed.), *La producción afectiva de comunidad: los medios audiovisuales en el contexto México-EE.UU*. Berlin: Edition tranvía, pp. 9–39.
———. 2017. *Transborder Media Spaces: Ayuujk Videomaking between Mexico and the US*. New York: Berghahn Books.
Kuroda, E. 1993. 'Los Mixes ante la Civilizacion Universal: Reseña de las Observaciones y Reflexiones sobre los Cambios de la Sierra Mixe en los 1990s', *Bulletin of the National Museum of Ethnology, Japan* 18(3): 495–531.
La Jornada. 2017. 'Denuncian ataque a Ayutla Mixe y exigen justicia', *El Correo Ilustrado*, 27 June. Retrieved 18 October 2019 from http://www.jornada.com.mx/2017/06/27/correo.
Martínez, I. 2017. 'Acusan mujeres de Ayutla violencia de género en conflicto', *Hoja Pública*, 6 June. Retrieved 6 June 2017 from http://www.hojapublica.com/2017/06/06/acusan-mujeres-ayutla-violencia-genero-conflicto.
Monge, E. 2019. 'Ayutla mixe se ahoga de sed', *El País*, 30 May. Retrieved 18 October 2019 from https://elpais.com/internacional/2019/03/30/actualidad/1553900472_626842.html.
Moreno Derbez, C. 2010. *Conflicto agrario y organización campesina: los cambios al artículo 27 constitucional en el Estado de Oaxaca*. Oaxaca: Delegación Estatal de la Subsecretaría de Educación Media Superior.
Radio Comunitaria Ayuujk. 2017. 'Versión de la comunidad de Ayutla Mixe, sobre los hechos del 5 de junio'. YouTube, 6 June. Retrieved 18 October 2019 from https://www.youtube.com/watch?v=st8jY7ttk1g.
Ramos Mancilla, O. 2015. 'Internet y pueblos indígenas de la Sierra Norte de Puebla, México', Ph.D. dissertation. Barcelona: University of Barcelona.
Romero Frizzi, M. 2011. 'Conflictos agrarios, historia y peritajes paleográficos. Reflexionando desde Oaxaca', *Revista Estudios Agrarios* 47: 65–81.

PART VI

Conflicts across Borders

CHAPTER 10

Transnationalising the Nagorno-Karabakh Conflict

Media Rituals and Diaspora Activism between California and the South Caucasus

Rik Adriaans

The commercial break is interrupted by an explosion. A wall of flames emerges, in front of which black-and-white photos of the Armenian Genocide of 1915 perpetrated by the late Ottoman Empire are screened. A bright blue background appears, colourful scenes of folk dances and state celebrations are shown, metamorphosing into black-and-white footage of soldiers celebrating victory in the Karabakh War with Azerbaijan of the early 1990s. The video finishes with military drills in Yerevan with the nation's tricolour in the background. As these images appear on the Armenian television channels of Los Angeles, a narrator reads the following text:

> A hundred years ago, they destroyed us. They tried to make us go extinct. But we lived, we grew stronger and today we have a free and independent Armenia.
>
> Twenty-three years ago they came with a war. Again, they wanted to conquer our ancestral lands. But we won as a nation. And today, Nagorno-Karabakh is ours!
>
> This year they tried to pierce through our borders. They wanted to provoke us. But the Armenian soldier protected our fatherland like a lion, and the enemy retreated in panic!

Me! You! Every Armenian is responsible for the fate of Armenia! Participate in the attempt to strengthen our fatherland. Join the national Telethon!

Thanksgiving Day, November 27th, 8 AM on channel 17 in the Los Angeles area.

Hayastan All-Armenian Fund. One nation, one fatherland. (ArmeniaFundUS 2014)

I first witnessed this promotional video during my fieldwork in Los Angeles in the autumn of 2014. It advertises the Armenia Fund Telethon, an annual fundraising television marathon that gathers diasporic funds to build infrastructure in the unrecognised Nagorno-Karabakh Republic on the internationally recognised territory of Azerbaijan. In the late 1980s, the Karabakh Armenians began petitioning the Soviet authorities to secede from Azerbaijan and join Armenia, and anti-Armenian pogroms soon ensued in Azerbaijan. The conflict escalated into a full-scale war in the early 1990s, which as the video showcases was widely perceived in the diaspora as a continuation of the 1915 Genocide. At the time of the ceasefire in 1994, it had led to a loss of around 30,000 lives and the proclamation of a nominally independent Armenian-controlled de facto state (de Waal 2003). Two years after the ceasefire, in coordination with the governments of Armenia and the post-war de facto state, the first Armenia Fund Telethon was organised to fund a highway connecting Armenia to Nagorno-Karabakh (Adriaans 2019: 81).

Broadcast annually on Thanksgiving Day from Los Angeles and collecting an average of U.S.$20 million in donations per year from diaspora households and benefactors around the world, the event has for almost two decades been perceived mostly as an apolitical humanitarian initiative. However, recent years have seen the appearance of critical voices that use participatory media, from call-in television shows to social media campaigns, to question the politics of the fundraising spectacle. Diaspora activists in Los Angeles call for a boycott because they believe that the media event sponsors and legitimises an oligarchic state complicit in corruption, tax evasion and the mismanagement of funds. On Thanksgiving Day in the autumn of 2013, they organised a competing parallel live television broadcast during the Armenia Fund Telethon, named the Pan-Armenian Tell-a-Thon, on a cable channel that was scheduled to screen the regular event. While the traditional broadcast solicited donations for a new road it optimistically dubbed 'the road securing long-lasting peace', this simultaneous event suggested a complicity of oligarchs and diasporic elites in preserving a status quo of 'neither peace nor war'.

In this chapter, I theorise how the parallel transmission of these competing broadcasts alters the politics, framing and scale of the Karabakh conflict. I draw on my fieldwork with diaspora activists in Los Angeles to analyse the entanglement of media rituals (Couldry 2003, 2012) with the interests of the U.S. diaspora and post-Soviet oligarchs in the Caucasus. The annual telethon operates by institutionalising media rituals that tie diaspora wealth to de facto state formation, while framing the Nagorno-Karabakh War victory as transforming Armenia from a genocide victim into a resurrected victor nation (Kolstø and Blakkisrud 2012: 144). The competing Pan-Armenian Tell-a-Thon, by contrast, sought to dismantle the diaspora's ritualised engagement with the Karabakh conflict by framing the telethon as driven by the personal interests of Armenia's ruling oligarchs. This form of activism has proven to be highly controversial to many diasporans, which leads me to pose two questions: what is the significance of the media rituals surrounding the Karabakh conflict for Armenian institutions and diasporic identity in Los Angeles? And how do activist media practices, such as the broadcasting of confrontations with elites and the dissemination of corruption reports, alter the diaspora's relation to the conflict in the Caucasus?

My analysis of the complex interplay between diasporic media rituals, activist practices and homeland conflict unfolds in four main sections. First, I outline how the mediatisation of the Karabakh conflict has become central to the cordial ties between the post-Soviet Armenian state and diasporic elites in Los Angeles. Second, I unpack how the annual telethon creates a transnational humanitarian sphere of media rituals (Couldry 2003, 2012; Malkki 2015), which turns materialising an Armenian-controlled Nagorno-Karabakh into a humanitarian cause central to diasporic identity (Adriaans 2019). Third, I locate the counter-telethon's activist media practices, which engage both media objects and media subjects (Mattoni and Treré 2014), in discontent over the post-1998 alliance between the diasporic establishment and the two Karabakh-born presidents of Armenia. The capturing of abuses of power across the Armenian world in raw form is central here, as media activists juxtapose homeland witnessing videos with recordings of tense encounters in Los Angeles (McLagan 2003, 2006; Razsa 2014). Lastly, I reflect on the limits and possibilities of diaspora activists to challenge the ritualisation of the conflict through media. On the one hand, the increasing transnational outreach of grassroots digital journalism from Yerevan energises the campaign to deritualise long-distance intervention in the Karabakh conflict through media rituals.

On the other hand, the unexpected sudden outbreak of the Four-Day War with Azerbaijan in the spring of 2016 made it more difficult than usual to challenge the ritualised media power of Armenian transnational elites, as its suffering rendered questioning the role of oligarchs in the humanitarian fund inappropriate.

Taken together, these four sections shed a new light on the relation between media and conflict by showing how the ritualisation of an ethnoterritorial conflict in a diasporic media ecology affects popular understandings of the nature of that conflict, which in turn reconfigures transnational practices of generosity. Previous takes on the relationship between media, ritual and conflict have inquired into how ritualisation and mediatisation work together to amplify or resolve a conflict (Grimes et al. 2011). My contribution to this debate lies in showing how the same conflict can, through ritualisation and mediatisation, shift from a humanitarian frame of victimhood vis-à-vis an ethnic other to an intra-ethnic political dispute over economic interests. Ruling powers that benefit from the nonresolution of the war (Liakhov 2016) utilise media rituals in the diaspora to monetise the unresolved conflict's nationalist appeal, their interests hidden behind the affective shocks sent by mediatised eruptions of armed violence. But recent changes in media connectivity allow activists to challenge ritualised participation and make space for more informed diaspora engagements with homeland conflict.

The Karabakh Conflict and Diaspora Politics in Los Angeles

Los Angeles is widely considered the global capital of the Armenian diaspora (Fittante 2017). The area is composed not only of an unmatched variety of subethnic, political and religious factions, but is also home to a complex Armenian media ecology. Until the early 1980s, the majority of Armenians in the area could trace their ancestry to present-day Eastern Turkey, often arriving in the United States via the Middle East where they had found refuge after the 1915 Armenian Genocide. The 1980s, by contrast, saw a large influx of newcomers from the Soviet Union, initially often dismissed by the diasporic establishment as undeserving economic migrants. This era also saw a proliferation of transnational media ties to Soviet Armenia, largely established in response to the catastrophic 1988 Spitak Earthquake that killed an estimated 25,000 people and left a half million homeless. The Karabakh War (1988–94) further amplified the presence of the homeland, as diaspora organisations used television fundraising to aid the militants who fought the Azerbaijanis and to rebuild infrastructure (Adriaans 2019).

Two decades since independence, the control of diasporic media in Los Angeles has largely moved from the institutions that had arrived in the United States from the Middle East to media conglomerates originating in Yerevan. But the last decade has also seen the rise of a third segment in the diaspora's media ecology: anti-government voices that engage in heated debates on the future of the homeland while recirculating content created by Armenia's investigative journalists, drawing on the rapid rise of independent online media since the late 2000s. It is in this emergent transmission of oppositional media that newcomers tend to find their views reflected, as those who came from Armenia tend to blame not the Ottoman Turks, but the oligarchic government in Yerevan for their exile. This trend by and large provides the fuel for new activist initiatives such as the boycott targeting the Armenia Fund Telethon.

However, the efficacy of such activist campaigns remains compromised by divisions between the older diaspora and newcomers from Armenia, largely shaped during the transition years. As in other post-Soviet countries that underwent neoliberal shock therapy, there emerged in Armenia an oligarchic capitalism in which the state apparatus and the economy are thoroughly interwoven through patron–client networks (Adriaans 2017; Derluguian 2005). Yet, more troubling to the older diasporic establishment in Los Angeles were reports on the first independent government's pragmatism vis-à-vis neighbouring Turkey and Azerbaijan. Levon Ter-Petrosyan, the first President of Armenia, became disliked for his prioritising of economic ties and stability over recognition of the Armenian Genocide and territorial claims in Karabakh. His unpopularity was sealed when the Armenian Revolutionary Federation, the most influential political party in the diaspora both in Los Angeles and globally, was banned as a terrorist organisation in 1994.

The two presidents who followed Ter-Petrosyan are often referred to in Armenia as the 'Karabakh clan', a term denoting both their origins in the disputed region and the perceived abuses of political power for the economic benefit of friends and relatives. However, among the diasporic elites in the United States, these presidents have been perceived much less negatively than their predecessor, due to the carefully cultivated image they project with regard to contentious issues of genocide recognition and the conflict with Azerbaijan. While their prestige was eventually tainted by post-election state violence in 2008 and a reconciliation attempt with Turkey in 2009, the Nagorno-Karabakh

Republic retains an almost sacred quality of national resurrection for those diasporans who trace their past to the 1915 Genocide (Kolstø and Blakkisrud 2012). It is this affective appeal that is monetised in practices during the annual telethon, which I conceptualise in the next section as a transnational humanitarian sphere of media rituals.

Media Rituals in the Armenia Fund Telethon

The Armenia Fund Telethon is the signature event of the Hayastan All-Armenian Fund, a transnational organisation governed by a board of trustees that includes the presidents of Armenia and the Nagorno-Karabakh Republic, the two head patriarchs of the Armenian Apostolic Church, and the leadership of the main political parties and charitable organisations in the diaspora. While the fund also realises projects in Armenia proper, no less than seventeen out of the twenty annual editions of the telethon since 1996 have been marketed to the diaspora with a Karabakh-related theme. The fund's most publicised projects have been the roads that connect Armenia to Nagorno-Karabakh through the occupied Azerbaijani regions of Lachin and Kelbajar, as well as Karabakh's North-South highway, which has led to the road network of the de facto state being almost entirely diaspora-funded. The fund has also raised money for other types of infrastructure, such as water pipes, electricity networks, hospitals as well as free housing provided to large families as a demographic stimulus to increase the Armenian population of Nagorno-Karabakh.

In the weeks prior to the annual media event, Armenian schools, churches, sport clubs and cultural organisations around the world incentivise young diasporans to gather donations by staging fundraising events, joining phone marathons, and informing relatives and acquaintances about the theme of the year's telethon broadcast. In Los Angeles County, particularly in the city of Glendale with its Armenian-majority population and unmatched number of diaspora institutions (Fittante 2017), such practices take place in anticipation of public display on a global media stage. During the broadcast, pupils from the Armenian schools and cultural organisations of Southern California recite patriotic slogans dedicated to compatriots in the Caucasus, announce the collected sums, and volunteers pick up the telephone in the studio for pledges made during the broadcast. Other routinised practices around the time of the event include sharing pictures with hashtags such as #NKpeace and #ArtsakhStrong[1] on Facebook and Instagram, or decorating donation boxes with the de facto state's flag. In Los Angeles, this extends to the fund's organising of events where diasporans can meet the political elite and clergy of the unrecognised republic, who are flown over to California for the telethon. Those who donate during the broadcast also receive gifts by mail, such as CDs with the fund's anthems or a DVD entitled *Welcome to Nagorno-Karabakh*, promoting diaspora tourism to the conflict zone.

The aforementioned practices, taking place in diaspora communities around the world in anticipation of and with dedication to the annual Armenia Fund Telethon, show the centrality of embodiment and routinised media practices in the structuration of diasporic time-space (Postill 2010: 12). In one way or another, they all link the Nagorno-Karabakh conflict to what Nick Couldry has called media rituals (2003, 2012). Media rituals, in Couldry's (2003: 29) words, are 'formalised actions organised around key media-related categories and boundaries, whose performance frames, or suggests, a connection with, wider media-related values'. More recently, Couldry (2012: 62) has also suggested to analyse the workings of such media rituals 'beyond the media's concentration of symbolic power' and in a variety of geographical settings. It is in this latter sense that the Armenia Fund Telethon makes for an insightful case, as the recurring media rituals surrounding the event by no means emerge spontaneously in response to the broadcast.

By and large, the actions organised around the telethon all perpetuate the notion that participation in the annual media event is essential to the flourishing of the Karabakh Armenians in the unresolved conflict with Azerbaijan. 'Every Armenian is responsible for the fate of Armenia!', as the promotional video put it (ArmeniaFundUS 2014). But its symbolic power is itself not concentrated in media; rather, media practices are 'ritualised' by a network of hegemonic diaspora institutions that reproduce nationalist discourses on the conflict. These institutions make use of the well-established link between broadcasting and cyclicity (Moores 2005: 16), generating annually recurring concern for the Karabakh issue. Of primary importance are Armenian primary and high schools, sports and scouting clubs and cultural associations, as well as church organisations and political parties. The event also draws on an older ritualisation of media in the United States that links Thanksgiving Day to charity telethons (Longmore 2016). Taking these layers into account exemplifies how a non-media-centric approach (see Bräuchler and Budka, this volume) reveals media and conflict to be unpredictably embedded in localised institutional histories, none of which are reducible to any logic inherent to media themselves.

Malkki (2015) provides a helpful way of thinking about how the relatively non-media-centric ritualisation of telethon fundraising establishes unexpected moral resonances between popular philanthropy, oligarchic interests and armed conflict. She argues that the global circulation of images and figurations of children between charity organisations and donors, from photos and knitted dolls to handwritten letters, leads to the constitution of a transnational ritual sphere of humanitarianism. She insists on using the term 'ritual', on the one hand because of the conventionalised nature of contemporary humanitarian practice and on the other hand because of its capacity to render 'apolitical, even suprapolitical' practices that 'clearly have political effects' (2015: 79). Taking my cue from Malkki and Couldry, I argue that the Armenia Fund Telethon enlists diaspora Armenians across the world in the Nagorno-Karabakh conflict through a transnational humanitarian sphere of media rituals. In the process, questions on the potentially counter-productive consequences of building infrastructure in a depopulated conflict zone claimed by both Armenians and the Azerbaijani state are sidelined, and internal political disputes over oligarchs and corruption make way for a pan-Armenian celebration of humanitarianism.

The possibility of generating the telethon's transnational ritual sphere depends not only on a complex institutional network that ritualises participation in the media event, but also hinges on the willingness of the Armenian television channels across the world to give up twelve hours of their regular broadcast time to the Hayastan All-Armenian Fund once per year. It is this traditional cooperation of the broadcasters that was broken for the first time in the event's history in Los Angeles on Thanksgiving Day in 2013. The opening up of ritualised broadcasting time to grassroots media activists in Los Angeles enabled a one-time counter-telethon that sought to 'deritualise' the habitual participation in the telethon, arguing that it is thoroughly entangled with the instrumental reason and accumulation projects of the so-called 'Karabakh clan' oligarchs. In the next two sections, I examine how this challenge to the Hayastan All-Armenian Fund's transnational media power (see Bräuchler and Budka, this volume; Couldry and Curran 2003) articulates with internal diasporic and international conflict.

From 'Peace Road' to 'Business Road'

The 2013 and 2014 editions of the Armenia Fund Telethon were dedicated to the construction of a new highway connecting Vardenis in Armenia to Martakert in Nagorno-Karabakh. As Armenia and the former Nagorno-Karabakh region of Soviet Azerbaijan are not geographically contiguous, this new road also runs through the Kelbajar region, the status of which remains highly contested due to the large number of Azerbaijani refugees with hopes to return there one day (Broers and Toal 2013). While in the telethon's promotional materials, the new highway is optimistically presented as a patriotic, pan-Armenian 'peace road', illustrated with humanitarian imagery of white doves, it is thus at the same time also an occupational infrastructure. However, in the weeks prior to the 2013 telethon, reports appeared on diasporic television in Los Angeles arguing that the new road that the diaspora was asked to fund is, in fact, neither a peace road nor a road to irredentist success, but instead an oligarchic 'business road'.

The circulation of these critical reports was the initiative of two middle-aged Armenian-American entrepreneurs from the old, post-genocide diaspora. Each of them hosts a weekly Los Angeles cable television show on Armenian topics, entitled *Return to Armenia* and *The Truth Must Be Told*, which broadcast and discussed reports made by independent journalists in Armenia and Karabakh to argue that the Vardenis-Martakert highway is primarily an instrument for the accumulation of resources by oligarchs. Their activism was made possible by two key developments: on the one hand, participatory media, and the smartphone in particular, made it possible for them to closely monitor and record their encounters with diasporic elites in Los Angeles; on the other hand, the increase in transnational connectivity, making available online, oppositional news outlets from Armenia, provided them with footage showing the critical views of inhabitants of the region, which would have never made it on to the official telethon.

For example, one report showed a settler surrounded by goats in the mountains of Kelbajar, with imagery cutting to the transport of raw materials from mines, giving a monologue explaining why the planned route of the road does not serve the Armenian repopulation of the area. Juxtaposed with commentaries from the hosts, an argument was made that the main purpose of the new road is the transport of copper, gold, molybdenum and coal from Karabakh to Armenia, with new mines recently opened in Kashen and Maghavuz near Martakert. Texts by investigative journalists from Armenia were read on air to fortify the claim that the business transporting the raw materials is owned by the President's nephew, Narek Sargsyan. The hosts also played interviews and reports on environmental activism. These reports highlighted the toxic pollution caused by the mining operations of the Vallex Group, the company behind the new venture in Karabakh (Return to Armenia 2013). In particular, they exposed the bad track record of the Vallex Group concerning the environment in its exploitation of the Teghut mine, protests against which had become a potent symbol of resistance for a generation of civic initiatives in the homeland (Ishkanian 2014, 2016). As the momentum of the boycott campaign grew, a town hall meeting for the Armenian community was organised on 23 November 2013 in the Glendale Public Library. During the event, Zaruhi Postanjian, an opposition MP from Yerevan, joined via Skype to voice her support for the activists, and reports of the meeting were broadcast on the television shows and disseminated through the YouTube channels of the two hosts.

To understand how this culminated into a competing Thanksgiving broadcast that sought to 'deritualise' the regular telethon, it is necessary to take a closer look at the activist media practices of the host of one of the shows. Activist media practices, as defined by Mattoni and Treré (2014: 259), are 'creative social practices' that engage media objects, 'such as mobile phones, laptops, pieces of paper' to disseminate activist messages, as well as 'interactions with media subjects', such as journalists, broadcasters and public relations managers, who can open up the media realm to activists. The boycott campaign in Los Angeles did not merely relay video messages from Armenia to diasporic television, but also drew on more explicit activist practices, turning interactions with persons personifying media power into mobilising media messages.

Born in the United States, the human rights activist Ara Manoogian lived for almost a decade in the Nagorno-Karabakh Republic, migrating to the unrecognised republic in the early 2000s. Manoogian is widely respected as the grandson of Shahan Natalie, the principal organiser of the celebrated campaign in the 1920s to assassinate the perpetrators of the Armenian Genocide who had fled Turkey after being sentenced to death. Already an active blogger while living in Karabakh, he has been an especially prominent diasporic media producer since his return to Los Angeles, using his on-the-ground connections to gather data with which to inform diasporans about the political realities of the Caucasus. He has also organised protests, debates and a hunger strike in response to political developments in the homeland. Among his long-term projects, the most relevant one for this chapter is a periodically updated white paper on corruption in the Hayastan All-Armenian Fund, entitled 'To Donate or Not to Donate', which argues for the complete separation of state power from the charity organisation (Manoogian 2015).

In late November 2013, Manoogian attempted to distribute printed copies of this corruption report at the Glendale Hilton, the hotel in which a large number of honorary guests, including the President and Archbishop of the Nagorno-Karabakh Republic, were staying to take part in the Armenia Fund Telethon. As he entered the hotel lobby together with his son, Manoogian encountered the permanent representative of the unrecognised republic for the United States and Canada, as honorary guests were just leaving a gala banquet dinner. When the sheriff's deputies in charge of securing the de facto state's politicians began to question Manoogian about his presence, the activist sensed that trouble might start and, as is his usual practice when confronting those in power, he began to record videos of the unfolding situation. He was almost immediately ordered to leave. 'We know who you are. People say you're here to create problems', a sheriff's deputy told him. Asking for clarification, he was accused of trespassing and of threatening the representative of the Nagorno-Karabakh Republic (Manoogian 2013b).

Countering that these charges were made up, Manoogian continued recording and calmly explained that he was only in the hotel to inform people about corruption and tax evasion by the politicians governing the Armenia Fund. In response to this, one of the sheriff's deputies made a surprising formulation: 'Our job is to protect our president [i.e. Bako Sahakyan, President of the Nagorno-Karabakh Republic]. We're not saying you are armed, but we know your file. You tried to disturb the All-Armenian Fund's functions!' (Manoogian 2013b). The video also shows a woman from the gala banquet trying to make Manoogian leave with reference to kinship codes: 'You are dishonouring your family's reputation by coming here. Please protect the honour of your grandfather and your grandmother. We revere them!' – a reference to his grandfather's organising of the assassinations of the Ottoman triumvirate (2013b). After being threatened by one of the sheriff's deputies that he would be sent to jail for trespassing and would have his son taken away from him as soon as the Glendale police arrived, Manoogian kept recording audio and video, but finally left the hotel, which had flags of the United States and the Nagorno-Karabakh Republic waving in unison for the telethon. The video footage shows no less than five police cars arriving to the hotel (2013b). The following day, the activist returned after having booked a room for the purpose of doing an onsite live broadcast of his television show, but he was again forced to leave before he could set up his equipment, this time by the hotel manager.

By creating audio and video recordings of these tense encounters, Manoogian sought to challenge the media power of the transnational elite of the Armenian world, lifting the polite veil of patriotism and philanthropy from the annual telethon. The central claim that these recordings carried is that the post-Soviet state's power to mute, censor and intimidate civic initiatives is no longer limited to the homeland, but now also reaches the heart of the diaspora (see Adriaans 2017). His capturing how he was hindered from handing out corruption reports by a public servant of the California state who refers to the Nagorno-Karabakh President as 'our president', juxtaposed with footage of the flags of the United States and the de facto state waving in unison, seemed to suggest as much. 'This is happening in Glendale! This is not Yerevan!', the activist stresses agitatedly whenever broadcasting such material. As is common in human rights media, the stylistics of representation uses video as a technology of witnessing (McLagan 2003, 2006; see also the chapters by Markham, Meis and Mollerup, as well as Sumiala, Tikka and Valaskivi, in this volume), the confrontations being partially provoked for their media appeal. 'Go ahead, arrest me for trespassing', Manoogian tells the sheriff's deputy in the video, evoking in the viewer anticipation of further escalation and a curiosity as to just how far these powers will go to silence their critics (Manoogian 2013b). Together with the homeland witnessing videos, such as those of the Kelbajar settler denouncing the highway as a business road and the environmentalists testifying to the risks of mining, these tense mediatised encounters are part of an affective pedagogy that seeks to inculcate a homeland engagement that is less mediated by state power than the ritualised telethon engagements (Razsa 2014: 497).

Using the persuasive appeal of these recordings, Manoogian called in the help of a fellow host of a cable television show and of the owner of Armenian Media Group of America (AMGA), one of the channels that was scheduled to broadcast the official Armenia Fund Telethon on Thanksgiving Day. Emerging from the collaborative efforts of unaffiliated broadcasters in the 1980s, AMGA has the reputation of being the last independent Armenian cable television channel in the Los Angeles diaspora. It belongs neither to the traditional, political faction-dominated outlets nor to the newer post-Soviet networks. In the weeks prior to the 2013 telethon, the station had received anonymous calls criticising its broadcast of activist media shows promoting the boycott campaign. When it became clear at the last minute that AMGA had not yet received the U.S.$12,000 from the Armenia Fund for relaying its telethon, the owner sold the broadcast time to the boycott campaign instead. This led to the ad hoc production of the twelve-hour Pan-Armenian Tell-a-Thon – a simultaneous, competing broadcast urging the Armenians of Los Angeles *not* to donate to the Hayastan All-Armenian Fund. People who expected to tune in to the official Armenia Fund Telethon were treated instead to discussions of corruption and environmental problems caused by Armenia's post-Soviet oligarchs.

During this Pan-Armenian Tell-a-Thon, viewers called in to express their agreement that the Armenia Fund Telethon was but a smokescreen for the governments of Armenia and Nagorno-Karabakh. The discourse of those who joined the discussion had two recurring themes: first, a claim that the 'old diaspora' was falling for the telethon because it lacked genuine insight into the political and economic situation of the homeland; and, second, a criticism of the ritualised nature of participation in the media event, particularly by children. One activist made a statement live on air combining both critiques, addressing the diasporic establishment's complacency with the oligarchs with much agitation:

> We all know how you operate. You are bringing some innocent children from our Armenian schools to your Telethon and force them to say that 'we love Armenia!' But what do these children know about Armenia? What do they know about what is happening there!? Why do we continue to give ten, twenty or thirty dollars to our children when they go to school? Isn't it just for your oligarch rulers to run their mines and put this money into their own pockets? This is not a matter of twenty dollars, or even a hundred dollars. This is a matter of dignity! (Manoogian 2013a)

The twelve-hour broadcast saw a continuous flow of call-ins from viewers who expressed their appreciation of the surprise broadcast, stating their discontent with the Armenia Fund Telethon, with the recurring idiom that it is a shameful form of beggary (*muratskanutyun*). There were occasionally also more negotiated positions: viewers who agreed that the presence of oligarchs on the fund's board was problematic, but believed that it was nevertheless the duty of every diasporan to contribute to safeguarding the security of the Karabakh Armenians.

These activist media practices illustrate how two key changes in the diasporic media ecology have made it possible to challenge the Armenia Fund Telethon. First, the rise in online journalism in the homeland, particularly prominent following the launch of YouTube in 2005, provided activists with audiovisual materials to persuade viewers of the necessity of the boycott. Second, the simultaneous availability of new participatory media technology, and smartphones in particular, made it possible for activists in Los Angeles to capture evidence of how they are treated by the diasporic establishment. Taken together, these practices make legible the mechanisms behind the routinised structuration of diasporic time-space and the cyclicity of donations for Karabakh. In the next section, I examine how unexpected eruptions of homeland violence nevertheless alter and limit the persuasive appeal of activist initiatives in the diaspora.

Homeland Violence and the Need to Help

While the promotional video with which this chapter began solicited donations from the Los Angeles diaspora with stock footage of flames and explosions, public life in Yerevan was interrupted by real explosives during the 2014 telethon. As Armenian children left their family's Thanksgiving dinner table to represent their school in the television studios, and AMGA returned to broadcasting the event, citizens in Yerevan were posting pictures on social media of the seven cars owned by well-known activists and opposition members that had been firebombed during the night (Aslanyan 2014). One young activist was beaten up by masked men on the street (Movsisyan 2014). Such attacks have not been uncommon during the civic initiatives challenging state power in the early 2010s (Adriaans 2017: 153). The consensus among the activists posting from Yerevan was that the government was to blame, using such attacks to intimidate civil society. The dramatic news was spread mostly online, as broadcast media remained silent.

The timing of the attacks allowed the transnational activist group Armenian Renaissance, an offshoot of a Yerevan-based nationalist group known as the Sardarapat Movement (Adriaans 2017: 146), to target the diaspora with a call for another boycott of the Armenia Fund Telethon. Warning against falling victim to 'fake patriotic slogans', the group stated in its social media communications that the diaspora would better provide donations to support activists in Armenia. An announcement posted on activist Facebook groups (such as 'Diaspora Armenians Support the People's Movement', 'Armenian Renaissance Los Angeles Chapter' and 'The Centennial Without the Regime') asserted:

> We hope that our compatriots, instead of donating their funds to the Pan-Armenian Fund, serving the corrupt dictatorial regime, will support us and transfer their funds to the Rights and Support Foundation, which will be able to compensate the losses of the citizens who suffered as a result of these terrorist acts and to ensure the further struggle of civil society. (Sefilyan 2014)

In spite of this strategic attempt to use the coinciding of the violence against activists with the Thanksgiving broadcast, the impact of these calls for solidarity was almost negligible in Los Angeles, reaching no more than a few dozen shares within a familiar, prestructured sphere of circulation. Unlike in 2013, AMGA returned to broadcasting the regular telethon, as the Armenia Fund overbid the activist attempt to get air time for another counter-telethon. While the new wave of civic activism and independent journalism in Armenia since the late 2000s has a strong online presence, the demographic most critical of the Armenian government in Los Angeles consists not of tech-savvy youth, but of middle-aged exiles and first-generation pensioners whose internet usage is mostly limited to Skype calls with relatives abroad. Whereas the 2013 Pan-Armenian Tell-a-Thon circumvented this problem by having its hosts act as 'cultural brokers' (Andén-Papadopoulos and Pantti 2013) translating between independent online media from Armenia and diasporic television in California while providing a stage for call-in discussions, the lack of activist broadcast time made it difficult to overcome the diaspora's digital divide in 2014.

The affective resonance of homeland violence in the diaspora was a different matter when armed conflict between Armenia and Azerbaijan reignited during the Four-Day War in the spring of 2016. With an estimated death toll of no less than 100 on both sides and fears that the de facto state would suffer significant losses to Azerbaijan, it is not surprising that the scale of circulation for this violent episode far exceeded that of the firebombing of cars and the beating-up of an activist in Yerevan. In this most dramatic escalation of the Karabakh conflict since the Armenia Fund Telethon began in 1996, the 'peace road' from Vardenis to Martakert became a strategic asset to transport military personnel and arms. It thus became hard for the media activists of the boycott campaign to argue that the road was *exclusively* a 'business road', regardless of the profits reaped by oligarchs from their mining ventures in Karabakh.

When after a few days a new ceasefire had been reached, an emergency Armenia Fund Telethon was organised in Los Angeles for the conflict's victims (Asbarez 2016). Although dedicated to reconstruction and recovery, the humanitarian tone was now supplemented by a rather strong militarism. One woman representing the Armenian Relief Society, a charity organisation, told the viewers that she hoped the Karabakh Armenians would not invest the diaspora's funds solely in reconstruction efforts, but would also use some of the money to buy better arms. Unlike at the annual Thanksgiving telethons, this time there were no gala dinners for the transnational elite of the Armenian world, and the boycott campaign remained silent. The dying out of the receptivity for grassroots media initiatives against the Armenia Fund Telethon in Los Angeles thus correlates, on the one hand, with the increased real security risks to Nagorno-Karabakh and, on the other hand, with the sense that when the homeland is in crisis, one cannot do nothing. In this situation, the media event's mix of humanitarian and political elements was reconfigured, muting the internal conflicts and contradictions of the diaspora as well as the problems of homeland state repression by an encompassment in external conflict.

The shifting receptivity for diasporic activist attempts to 'deritualise' the media power of transnational elites marks the instability of relations between media, ritual and conflict (Grimes et al. 2011) in tense moments of rupture. It shows how ritualisation and deritualisation are 'fluctuating processes that occur in degrees' (Grimes 2011: 20) in a messy, unpredictable counterpoint to the acutely felt shocks of mediatised homeland violence. We have seen that the rise of online journalism in Armenia has led to an increasing availability of critical accounts of oligarchic capitalism, which, coupled with activist media practices in Los Angeles, energise activist attempts to deritualise the post-Soviet state's transnational media power. But the affective resonance of the 2016 Four-Day War in the diaspora made the 'invisible hand' of the government in the event even less apparent than it is in the regular telethons. The indisputable suffering caused by the violence made debates on the politics of fundraising impertinent. The shock waves sent by the homeland violence thus consolidated the transnational ritual sphere that turns the interests of the oligarchic state and its diasporic allies into a humanitarian cause.

Conclusion

In this chapter, I have analysed how ritualised practices surrounding the Armenia Fund's fundraising telethons in the diaspora alter the politics of the Nagorno-Karabakh conflict. The institutionalisation of media rituals throughout the worldwide diaspora generates a transnational ritual sphere dedicated to the materialisation of an Armenian-controlled Nagorno-Karabakh Republic, uniting a large segment of the global diaspora around the promise of infrastructure to strengthen claims on the disputed territories. While the Pan-Armenian Tell-a-Thon of 2013 resonated with an oppositional segment in the diaspora by revealing the links between routinised media power and elites, its attempt at deritualisation was compromised by a lack of institutional power to change the structuring practices that constitute the annual event.

In spite of these constraints, the activists' counter-telethon did spark new debates in Los Angeles on the merits and flaws of the telethon tradition. At least one Armenian school abandoned the tradition of giving extra credit to pupils in exchange for their telethon donations, and an Armenian student association at an elite university in Los Angeles that I observed during my fieldwork became divided over continuing its participation. But the almost complete cessation of the boycott campaign in the aftermath of the Four-Day War of 2016 suggests that the affective resonance of violence in the homeland, with its sense of immediate urgency to 'do something', sets firm limits to the deritualisation of media power. In a dynamic of scalable animosity that is familiar to anthropologists since the work of Evans-Pritchard (1940), the internal conflicts of the diaspora were sidelined for a higher level of external conflict (see Baumann 2004).

The link between media and conflict in the two competing Armenian broadcasts in Los Angeles is by no means a simple one-way movement in which the one merely amplifies the other. Rather, it is the complex entanglement between institutionalised media rituals and the affective resonances of armed hostilities that modulates the extent to which the Karabakh conflict is experienced exclusively in terms of a humanitarian ethos against external enemies, or can also be related to as a site of intra-ethnic political struggle. Equipped with participatory media technologies to capture abuses of power, media activists can increasingly reveal how oligarchic elites and their diasporic allies instrumentalise the Karabakh conflict for their own benefit. But the periodic eruption of violence resulting from the conflict's nonresolution, in tandem with the ritualisation of transnational media power, does pose limits to the receptivity for their message.

Rik Adriaans is Teaching Fellow in Digital Anthropology at University College London. His research examines the interfaces between image production, technological mediation and diasporic recognition struggles in the transnational circuits that connect post-Soviet Armenia to the Armenian diaspora in Los Angeles. He also maintains an ongoing interest in the politics of Armenian popular music. His articles have appeared in *Identities: Global Studies in Culture and Power*, *Social Analysis*, *Nationalities Papers* and *Caucasus Survey*.

Note

1. Artsakh is the medieval Armenian name for the Nagorno-Karabakh region that has come into popular use since the end of the war with Azerbaijan over the region in 1994, as the 'nonindigenous' Russian, Turkish and Persian etymologies of the toponym Nagorno-Karabakh are considered undesirable by Armenian nationalists. It has become the de facto state's official name after a constitutional change in 2017, reflecting its territorial ambitions that stretch out into the occupied regions of Azerbaijan beyond the former Soviet region of Nagorno-Karabakh proper.

References

Adriaans, R. 2017. 'Dances with Oligarchs: Performing the Nation in Armenian Civic Activism', *Caucasus Survey* 5(2): 142–59.

——. 2019. 'The Humanitarian Road to Nagorno-Karabakh: Media, Morality and Infrastructural Promise in the Armenian Diaspora', *Identities: Global Studies in Culture and Power* 26(1): 69–87.

Andén-Papadopoulos, K., and M. Pantti. 2013. 'The Media Work of Syrian Diaspora Activists: Brokering between the Protest and Mainstream Media', *International Journal of Communication* 7: 2185–206.

Antonyan, Y. 2016. 'Being an "Oligarch" in the Armenian Way', in Y. Antonyan (ed.), *Elites and 'Elites': Transformations of Social Structures in Post-Soviet Armenia and Georgia*. Yerevan: ASCN, pp. 110–71.

ArmeniaFundUS. 2014. 'Armenia Fund Telethon 2014 – One Nation, One Homeland'. YouTube. Retrieved 20 October 2019 from https://www.youtube.com/watch?v=qQSvrXTghls.

Asbarez. 2016. 'Armenia Fund Raises $1.1 Million during Emergency Artsakh Telethon', *Asbarez*, 19 May. Retrieved 20 October 2019 from http://asbarez.com/150645/armenia-fund-raises-1-1-million-during-emergency-artsakh-telethon.

Aslanyan, K. 2014. 'Yerevanum hrkizum en enddimadirneri yev qaghaqatsiakan aktivistneri meqenanere', *Azatutuyn*, 27 November. Retrieved 20 October 2019 from https://www.azatutyun.am/a/26713666.html.

Bakalian, A. 1993. *Armenian-Americans: From Being to Feeling Armenian*. New Brunswick, NJ: Transaction Publishers.

Baumann, G. 2004. 'Grammars of Identity/Alterity: A Structural Approach', in G. Baumann and A. Gingrich (eds), *Grammars of Identity/Alterity: A Structural Approach*. New York: Berghahn Books, pp. 18–50.

Broers, L., and G. Toal. 2013. 'Cartographic Exhibitionism? Visualizing the Territory of Armenia and Karabakh', *Problems of Post-Communism* 60(3): 16–35.

Couldry, N. 2003. *Media Rituals: A Critical Approach*. London: Routledge.

——. 2012. *Media, World, Society: Social Theory and Digital Media Practice*. London: Routledge.

Couldry, N., and J. Curran (eds). 2003. *Contesting Media Power: Alternative Media in a Networked World.* London: Rowman & Littlefield.

Derluguian, G. 2005. *Bourdieu's Secret Admirer in the Caucasus: A World-System Biography.* Chicago: University of Chicago Press.

De Waal, T. 2003. *Black Garden: Armenia and Azerbaijan through Peace and War.* New York: New York University Press.

Evans-Pritchard, E.E. 1940. *The Nuer: A Description of the Modes of Livelihood and Political Institutions of a Nilotic People.* Oxford: Clarendon.

Fittante, D. 2017. 'But Why Glendale? A History of Armenian Immigration to Southern California', *California History* 94(3): 2–19.

Grimes, R.L. 2011. 'Ritual, Media, and Conflict: An Introduction', in R.L. Grimes et al. (eds), *Ritual, Media, and Conflict.* Oxford: Oxford University Press, pp. 3–33.

Grimes, R.L. et al. 2011. *Ritual, Media, and Conflict.* Oxford: Oxford University Press.

Ishkanian, A. 2014. 'Self-Determined Citizens? New Forms of Civic Activism and Citizenship in Armenia', *Europe-Asia Studies* 67(8): 1203–27.

———. 2016. 'Challenging the Gospel of Neoliberalism? Civil Society Opposition to Mining in Armenia', in T. Davies, H. E. Ryan, and A. M. Peña (eds), *Protest, Social Movements and Global Democracy Since 2011: New Perspectives.* Bingley: Emerald, pp. 107–36. Kolstø, P., and H. Blakkisrud. 2012. 'De Facto States and Democracy: The Case of Nagorno-Karabakh', *Communist and Post-Communist Studies* 45(1–2): 141–51.

Liakhov, P. 2016. 'Behind the Four-Day War', *Jacobin Magazine*, 13 April. Retrieved 20 October 2019 from https://www.jacobinmag.com/2016/04/armenia-azerbaijan-nagorno-karabakh-war.

Longmore, P. 2016. *Telethons: Spectacle, Disability and the Business of Charity.* Oxford: Oxford University Press.

Malkki, L. 2015. *The Need to Help: The Domestic Arts of International Humanitarianism.* Durham, NC: Duke University Press.

Manoogian, A. 2013a. 'Hamahaykakan Khosaton – Mas 3-rd'. YouTube. Retrieved 20 October 2019 from https://www.youtube.com/watch?v=r-jq297nKCI.

———. 2013b. 'Human Rights Activist Threatened by Persons Claiming to Be Sheriff's Deputies'. YouTube. Retrieved 20 October 2019 from https://www.youtube.com/watch?v=s35QWLAxBXk.

———. 2015. 'To Donate or Not to Donate? A White Paper on "Hayastan" All-Armenian Fund'. Shahan Natalie Family Foundation. Retrieved 20 October 2019 from http://www.thetruthmustbetold.com/wp-content/uploads/haaf-en-2015.pdf.

Mattoni, A., and E. Treré. 2014. 'Media Practices, Mediation Processes, and Mediatization in the Study of Social Movements', *Communication Theory* 24(3): 252–71.

McLagan, M. 2003. 'Principles, Publicity, and Politics: Notes on Human Rights Media', *American Anthropologist* 105(3): 605–12.

———. 2006. 'Introduction: Making Human Rights Claims Public', *American Anthropologist* 108(1): 191–95.

Migliorino, N. 2008. *(Re)constructing Armenia in Lebanon and Syria: Ethno-cultural Diversity and the State in the Aftermath of a Refugee Crisis*. New York: Berghahn Books.

Moores, S. 2005. *Media/Theory: Thinking about Media and Communications*. London: Routledge.

Movsisyan, H. 2014. 'Hardzakman e yentarkvel Nakhakhorhrdarani andame', *Azatutyun*, 27 November. Retrieved 20 October 2019 from https://www.azatutyun.am/a/26713947.html.

Postill, J. 2010. 'Introduction: Theorising Media and Practice', in B. Bräuchler and J. Postill (eds), *Theorising Media and Practice*. New York: Berghahn Books, pp. 1–32.

Razsa, M.J. 2014. 'Beyond "Riot Porn": Protest Video and the Production of Unruly Subjects', *Ethnos* 79(4): 496–524.

Return to Armenia 2013. 'Armenia Fund 2013: A Critical Evaluation and Questions'. YouTube. Retrieved 20 October 2019 from https://www.youtube.com/watch?v=VcYwYhOii2c.

Sefilyan, J. 2014. 'We Expect Solidarity and Civic Courage from All Armenians for the Sake of Our Homeland and Its Liberation'. Facebook, 28 November. Retrieved 20 October 2019 from https://www.facebook.com/Jirayr.Sefilian/posts/656488341136126.

CHAPTER 11

Stones Thrown Online

The Politics of Insults, Distance and Impunity in Congolese Polémique

Katrien Pype

This chapter investigates an emerging culture of violent texts, so-called diatribes, in the Congolese online sphere. These invectives are known as *mbwakela*, a Lingala term for 'something that is thrown to someone' (plural: *bambwakela*). Lingala is the lingua franca in Kinshasa, capital of the Democratic Republic of the Congo (DRC), and for large segments of the Congolese immigrant community. In its initial form, *mbwakela* is a genre of camouflaged insults exchanged indirectly between cowives or female rivals in the colonial context of Léopoldville (as Kinshasa was called then). Nowadays,[1] *mbwakela* also appears on the internet, has become more direct and explicit, and has been inserted into political protest emanating from the Congolese diasporas. The emergence and transformation of *mbwakela* into digital political contestation are set against the background of a double transformation in Congolese society: the lowering of internet fees has made interactions between the home country and diasporic communities more intense, even instantaneous, while at the same time, the Congolese nation has been experiencing severe uncertainty regarding its political future.

As from 2002, when President Joseph Kabila came to power, a new political wind blew through the nation. For a few years, a general mood of hope and anticipation was observable in Kinshasa. Many Kinois (inhabitants of Kinshasa) anticipated a genuine democratic future. However, nearly a decade later, repetitive political nondemocratic interventions mounted frustrations among Kinshasa's population and also among Congolese in the diasporas. During Kabila's regime (which ended in January 2019), the growing availability of the internet as a space to voice political opinions was welcomed by Congolese in the DRC and abroad. Many Congolese residing abroad (some still holding Congolese citizenship, while others may have given it up) frequently posted rants and diatribes on websites and social media platforms addressed to the President and his entourage. Anti-Kabila sentiment in the diaspora was mainly expressed through a leaderless movement known as the Combattants (French for 'fighters'; 'those who resist').

Anthropologists understand conflict and violence as social performances, practices embedded in competition and 'the product of a historical process that may extend far back in time and that adds by virtue of this capacity many vicissitudes to the analysis of the conflictive trajectory' (Schröder and Schmidt 2001: 3). In the introduction to this volume, Bräuchler and Budka argue in a similar vein that 'conflict and its resolution can take on very different shapes and scales, depending on the actors [and collectivities that get] involved'. In this chapter, I will focus on the paradigmatic and syntagmatic dimensions of Combattants' digital political protest. The study of the insults will bring to the fore collective political subjectivities and the historicity of forms of conflict and their social consequences, among others schisms, but also social costs and impunities. It is exactly attention to these sociocultural contours of verbal attack in the digital world that allows us to understand ways of negotiating political identities, aspirations and responsibilities in an increasingly interconnected world. Today, diasporic communities are intimately, and often instantaneously, connected to people in the home country (Bernal 2014). Their engagement in domestic politics in their home country can take various forms, of which, as will be shown in this chapter, some are traceable to other worlds of rivalry and competition.

Obviously, violence, competition, conflict, protest and rivalry depend to a great extent on words. Language as a medium itself is at the centre of various forms of conflict and violence. 'Disorderly discourse' (Briggs 1996) and violent speech genres are characterised by particular linguistic forms and sociopolitical frames of reference that co-create the conflict-inciting potential of verbal behaviour and social interaction. Protest songs and cartoons constitute genres that anthropologists have been keen to study as an entry into the political imagination of a particular group (Isbell 1998; Jackson 2013; Mbembe 1997).

Rants and insults, examples of 'disorderly discourse' (Briggs 1996), are opposed to more familiar speech genres in sociolinguistics and anthropology such as praise poetry and flattery. My take on media and conflict is inspired by anthropologists such as Karin Barber and Judith Irvine, who have carried out research on the social contours of texts such as praise singing in Nigeria (Barber 1991) and insult poetry in

Senegal (Irvine 1993). Flattery and praise singing very much make personhood, as Barber's (2007) analysis of praise singing in three different contexts of African societies shows. These are at the centre of the processes through which reputations are made. In rants and insults, reputations are contested and challenged (see Irvine 1993).

If reputations can be made or broken via insults, then unsurprisingly, rants and other invectives are not simple, banal forms of electronic interaction, but can gain a prominent place in political communities and debate. We need to inquire further into the sociopolitical codes that guide responses, which undermine or neutralise the risky nature of violent expressions and discursive provocations in the digital world. This chapter sets out to do this by offering anthropological attention to the aesthetics and generic features of political protest within the Combattants movement (see also Meis, this volume). In particular, I will show that the online invectives are part of a culture of *polémique*, a Kinois term that speaks to the cultivation of opposition, debate, provocation and insults. *Polémique* is considered a central characteristic of Kinshasa's social universe: in the city, jealousy, lies, adultery, fraud, and other so-called 'anti-valeurs' lead to conflict, disagreement, insults and provocation. *Polémique* is arguably one of the basic axes on which Kinshasa's public culture thrives, as it is a label assigned to discursive conflicts between political opponents, leaders in the world of sports and popular culture, but also quarrels and fights within families or compounds. Questions to ask are: what happens when a genre such as *polémique* appears in the digital world? What are the consequences of digitality? And how is it situated within the larger field of political communication and political constituencies?

Within the scope of this chapter, it is impossible to provide deep answers to these questions. The analysis here will be limited to an exploration of the affordances of the digitalisation of the *mbwakela*. My argument is twofold. First, I argue that when one particular form of communication, *in casu* verbal attack, is mobilised for new purposes (political protest) and is expressed in a new space (the internet), it meets significant differences along the line of impunity. Second, I argue that the *mbwakela* case study showcases how mediatisation of conflict uses distance as a productive aesthetic device in violent encounters. The online *mbwakela*, expressed by the migrant community and circulating online, plays with two forms of distance: first, the linguistic and poetic displacement of the initial forms of *mbwakela*; and, second, the migratory distance. In my view, it is exactly the combination of these two forms of dislocation (metaphor and spatial difference) that explains the appeal of the online *mbwakela* to Combattants. As will become clear, the *mbwakela* has always played with indirectness and metaphors, mobilising a gap between the discourse and the referent. Digitally mediated conflict has widened this gap as the insertion of a medium seemingly increases distance between the aggressor and the target, which provides new opportunities for the expression of disagreement, attack and other forms of discursive violence (see also Marshall, this volume). The online sphere thus not only allows for different forms of verbal attack to appear and to circulate among larger publics, but also sets forth a changing range of opportunities, impunities and targets. This chapter will therefore also be attentive to the historicity of addressees in the *mbwakela*.

I will first analyse the main aesthetics of the online *mbwakela* as expressed by Combattants. This will be followed by a comparison with other social realms in which the *mbwakela* appears. Attention will be mainly oriented to the aesthetics (especially in terms of directness and concealment), interlocutors and impunities. Thus, this chapter offers history in terms of a changing range of opportunities and targets. This follows the emergence of innovations in cultural expression of conflict as genres travel through time (*in casu* from the colonial to the postcolonial era) and space (here, from an urban centre to the diaspora) (see also Mollerup, this volume).

The material for this chapter derives from more than fifteen years of research on Kinshasa's media worlds. Ever since my initial fieldwork in Kinshasa in 2003, I have observed Kinois dialoguing over various media devices with relatives, friends and strangers abroad, and have interviewed them regarding their stances towards *bato ya libanda* ('people outside', i.e. immigrants). Especially since 2009, I have also become interested in diasporic media engagements with Congolese at home and in migrant communities. In order to understand how media and migration intersect in the Congolese community, I have carried out participant observation in Europe (Brussels, Paris, Rotterdam, London and Birmingham) and the United States (Boston, Washington DC, Silverspring, Chillum and Hyattsville) among Congolese migrants and visitors (tourists, expats, traders), and have conducted formal and informal conversations in these cities. Additional data were collected online via Facebook, WhatsApp and Instagram pages.

Solidarity and Contestation

The Combattants movement, operating in the diaspora and in particular known as such since 2010, is a response to the Kabila regime in the homeland (2002–19) and has significantly reshaped the political interactions between 'home' (*mboka*) and 'abroad' (*libanda*). The movement is best known for protest marches it organised around the world (Toronto, Johannesburg, Brussels, etc.) in the aftermath of presidential elections held in the DRC in November and December 2011. Yet, Combattants were also active at other moments – for example, they occupied public spaces in front of hotels or meeting spaces when Kabila and other political rulers visited New York, Brussels and elsewhere. For many Kinois, the Combattants movement was a matter of contention because of its self-imposed embargo on live performances of Congolese dance music in the diaspora communities.[2] The symbolic role of Congolese rumba for national unity is strong: for many, Congolese rumba music is the export product of Congolese society par excellence. Apart from being a source of national pride, since Mobutu (President from 1965 to 1997), Congolese rumba music has also been one of the most important 'binding' forces at the national level. Combattants thus attacked the familiar aesthetics of postcolonial Congolese leadership.[3]

The internet was first of all an important space for communication among Combattants residing in Paris, Cape Town, Montreal, etc., to organise the protest and to create solidarity among the Congolese diaspora. Yet, the digital world also constituted a space to express their political stances, especially anti-Kabila opinions, to attack or threaten those they considered to be pro-Kabila – musicians included. Some examples of websites on which these forms of community-making and contesting were acted out and which were run by Combattants are Banamikili.skyrock.com, talatube.com and congokioskque.forumgratuit.eu (literally translated from slang Lingala 'ChildrenofEurope.skyrock.com; channeltowatch.com; and congokiosk.freeforum.eu'), though Combattants were also vocal on social media such as YouTube and Facebook.

The following anecdote illustrates how these various internet platforms were important in the organisation of this global anti-Kabila movement. In early March 2014, Pitshou,[4] a Congolese man who arrived in Belgium in the mid 1980s and is now a Belgian citizen, was excited about the fact that a few days earlier, pastor Pascal Bakole, commonly known as Sans Rival (French for 'unrivalled'), living in Johannesburg, had been arrested for the second time in one month. Sans Rival, known for his political anti-establishment statements, can be termed 'un pasteur combattant', in contrast to 'les pasteurs collabo' or 'pasto collabo', who were said to be 'collaborating' because they were assumed to be supporting the current Congolese government (see also Garbin 2014; Garbin and Godin 2013). The pastor was arrested by the South African police after a complaint made by the producer of Ferre Gola, one of the Congolese rumba music stars. On 26 January 2014, the pastor had released footage on YouTube in which he warned Ferre Gola, whose concert in Johannesburg was scheduled for 14 February 2014 (EDTV-richetempete 2014). In the YouTube clip, Sans Rival challenged Ferre Gola and warned him 'he would meet the Combattants' (EDTV-richetempete 2014). Combattants living in and around Cape Town encouraged their fellows in Johannesburg and challenged those living in Paris claiming 'that Ferre Gola was not going to perform' (EDTV-richetempete 2014). Adopting military language, they argued that 'Cape Town will not fall'. I quote (my translation): 'Despite the police [*mbila*] and the helicopters [referring to state surveillance], Ferre will see. We are here in South Africa. We are together here. What are we afraid of? Of the police? Are you wondering whether we have all the required documents? Don't worry. We have them' (EDTV-richetempete 2014). The provocation ended with a message to all Combattants: 'We need to be united, we need to fight on various fronts, but we are together. The survival of our nation depends on it' (EDTV-richetempete 2014). In the end, Ferre Gola did not perform. A few days before the concert was supposed to take place, an announcement on Gola's Twitter account informed his followers that the concert was cancelled, with no explanation given as to why. As Gola's Twitter account shows, followers immediately assumed that he had been intimidated by the Combattants. Some fans cheered for this alleged victory of the Combattants, while others regretted this action, saying that 'Ferre Gola had given in to the Combattants' (Gola 2014).

Pitshou had followed a video on the website nouslescombattants.com (literally 'wethefighters.com') containing YouTube footage showing another Congolese man calling out to the larger Congolese diasporic community (so also beyond those in Johannesburg) to help the pastor's relatives both financially and morally. What is exciting here is the transnational communication through the internet and, in particular, the mobilisation of money and affect (solidarity) across the globe, but still circulating within the political community of Congolese – from South Africa to France and elsewhere. Camera men and image editors who identified as Combattants filmed Combattants' activities, interviewed people on the scene (during their meetings), posted the footage online and, if required, made copies so that the interviewed could add the footage to their files, e.g. when applying for political asylum. All of the editing happened in the homes of Combattants and with very basic computer infrastructure (a desktop and FinalCutPro software). These images were uploaded onto websites such as those mentioned above, on internet TV stations (congomondetv.com, congomikili.net) and on YouTube.

It is important to bear in mind that these digital texts did not stand in isolation, but dialogued with other internet-texts without which accusations, rants and provocations would not make sense. As such, a chain of digital texts emerged, in which provocations were followed by reactions, counterchallenges and new insults that had online and offline repercussions. On Facebook, Instagram and YouTube, users could participate in these conflicts, thus extending them into larger social worlds, while at the same time also giving them a form of fixity, to be consulted, reread, copied, remediated and commented on, very much like what Pitshou did when he called me and thus stirred my interest in this topic.

Combattants, living in migrant cities such as Montreal, Brussels and Johannesburg, thus performed patriotic obligations, not only by sending remittances home or by assisting relatives in the paperwork for visa applications, but also by engaging with the Congolese leadership, and critiquing and denouncing bad governance. The digitally remediated insults and threats were inspired by a moral and political duty towards their families and friends, though were part of a larger array of violent actions, such as kidnapping Congolese politicians when they arrive in Europe, invading the Congolese embassy in Paris, destroying its furniture and beating up the Congolese ambassador, preventing *pasto collabo* from organising cults and prayer sessions in the diaspora, and blocking concert venues, thus preventing Congolese rumba musicians from performing live.

Politics, religion, music and digital media came here together within the Congolese migrant community and speak of frictions (Tsing 2004) within the Congolese nation at large. For the Combattants movement, the internet was a space of voicing threats against the political establishment and a space in which unity of and difference within the movement was expressed. The internet was thus not only a space of representation of conflict, but the space through which conflict took shape. Resistance can be as violent as the oppression it opposes, including resistance expressed digitally (see Bräuchler 2013).

The Form of an Insult

The digital *mbwakela*, the hallmark of the Combattants' protest, offers us unique insights into forms of diasporic protest, engagements between diasporas and the home country, and, more generally, the aesthetic and ethic processes that people constitute and employ to act in their world. One of the loudest voices in the Combattants' world was Boketshu I ('Boketshu premier', translated as 'Boketshu the first'; 'Boketshu' and 'Boketshu I' are used interchangeably), a former musician now in his mid fifties. He arrived in Brussels in the early 2000s, and very soon his wife and children joined him. Today, all of them have become Belgian citizens. Due to health issues, he is never called in anymore by the Brussels public service of social support (CPAS) to work, and he and his wife receive a monthly allowance by the state, which allows him, as he said during an interview conducted on 19 January 2016, an easy life. One of his children is still attending secondary school, while the older ones are undergraduate students. Very proud of his children who will become *des diplômés* (people who have obtained a degree), Boketshu's life is primarily oriented towards the DRC. He is a central figure in the Congolese milieu in Brussels, follows the news about Congolese politics with a keen eye, enjoys dressing sharply (each time, our meetings started with a discussion of the clothes he was wearing), insists on eating Congolese food such as *fufu* and peanuts, and is in touch with relatives in Kinshasa on a daily basis.

Yet, Boketshu I occupies an ambivalent position within Congolese society at large. On the one hand, he still has many fans due to his previous life as a successful musician in the DRC. They offer him services and gifts, like free drinks and food whenever he brings a guest along. Yet, others in the Congolese diaspora have a more critical perspective towards him, as they do not agree with his rants against the Congolese leadership. Their rebuttal is not necessarily informed by a different political position, but rather by the style of his political protest, which some esteemed to be vulgar.

Despite this ambivalent position, Boketshu I remained a central character within the diasporic protest movement. The following is a description of a YouTube video (Banamboka 1 2013) from Combattants entitled 'Boketshu and Jannot Kabuya Attack JB Mpiana, Didier Reynders and the Invitation for Kabila'. Uploaded on 28 September 2013 by Banamboka 1 (Lingala for 'Children of the Country', meaning 'Congolese citizens'), the clip takes twelve minutes and includes a seven-minute rant by Jeannot Kabuya (the man on the left) and Boketshu I (the man in a red vest). The footage starts with an identification of one of the protagonists: Jeannot Kabuya is said to be a 'journalist of the Combattants' and part of the 'active, conscious youth'. A following slide says in capital letters 'It is time to cut' (*tokomi na tango ya papakopapa*). The Lingala verb *kopapa* is used, an onomatopoeia that evokes the sound of a machete in use, thus suggesting that 'it is time to kill'.

These images are followed by some excerpts of the upcoming rant, as in previews, in which Boketshu I names a few Congolese big men (politicians, commercial entrepreneurs, musicians) and threatens them. Another short sequence shows the two protagonists being greeted by (presumably Congolese) passers-by patting them on the shoulder – as a gesture of support. These previews are interspersed by short shots of a music video clip of Boketshu I dancing in a nightclub while singing the same phrase *eza tango ya kopapapa* ('it is time to cut and kill') and dancing (his arm movements imitating the movement of a cutting machete).

At 2:58, the rant starts. The two men, standing on the pavement in the Brussels area of Matonge (known as the African neighbourhood of the city), are fulminating against the Congolese President, politicians, musicians and a Belgian politician (Didier Reynders). At 10:00 the rant is over, followed by a two-minute song by Boketshu I praising Alain Moloto, a deceased Congolese gospel singer, accompanied by pictures of a group of six young men, stern faced as if ready to take on provocations and to fight. The choice of public space in Matonge (Brussels) as a setting for the clip, in contrast to a living room, for example, is not accidental, as it suggests that the rabble-rousers feel totally at ease there due to, one assumes, the freedom of speech that is supposed to protect people in Europe, in contrast to the dictatorial regime in the home country. For over a minute (5:04 until 6:15), one can see Belgian policemen in the background, who seem to be totally unaware of the defamation going on in an (for them) unintelligible language. The following is a translated transcript and description of one minute of the rant (5:00–6:00), which I deem to be representative of the whole clip, and indeed of the main themes and style of Combattants' protest:

> Hyppolite Kanambe, you are Rwandese. If you come to Belgium, be aware ... I know that you were here recently and that you met Didier Reynders [Belgian Minister of Foreign Affairs] at the airport. I learned about that meeting. But if you come back to Belgium things will heat up. Your shit! Your Mother! Rwandan! Moron! Congo does not belong to you. Wait, I will take off my glasses [which he does]. Henri Hyppolite Kanambe; Mende [Congolese Minister of Information]; Kengo Wa Dondo [Congolese President of Parliament]. Since your birth, Congo has 'made' you. And what did you do for Congo? Animal. Moron. Animal. You are playing with Congo. Do you really care about Congo, the country of Kimbangu? And also, I have a message for JBira [J.B. Mpiana; see below]. JBira, do you think the fight we are conducting is funny? Really? Are you making fun of us? Go and do your humanitarian work somewhere else, not in Poto

[Europe]. Go and do humanitarian work in Bandundu, in Mbandaka, in Kisangani [Congolese province and cities]. You will die on the podium here, JBira. I am telling you. If the fight that I am fighting is right, and you set foot here, [incomprehensible speech], you will die. They killed Floribert Chebeya [an activist journalist, killed in June 2010, assumed to have been killed by the authorities]. You, JBira, Werera [Werrason], Papario [Papa Wemba] you drink champagne in Paris. JB, if you set foot here, you will die. (Banamboka 1 2013)

This excerpt offers us an interesting entry point into the audiovisual aesthetics and the discursive forms – in particular, some linguistic strategies of Combattants' digital protest.[5] The first linguistic action is morphological: the use of the suffixes 'ira/era' added to personal names or place names. These can be called 'suffixes of belonging' as they suggest an intimacy with Rwanda, a neighbouring country with which the DRC is officially at war. In the excerpt above, Boketshu I spoke about the Congolese musicians 'JBira, Werera [Werrason], Papario [Papa Wemba]'. The '-ra' is a suffix that evokes Kinyarwanda, national language of Rwanda. By calling J.B. Mpiana 'JBira' and Werrason 'Werera', an intimacy or affinity is suggested between these musicians and Rwanda. This linguistic strategy resonates with the political anxiety that gained much currency in the opposition movement, i.e. that Rwanda is occupying the DRC, even the capital city (and thus even were decisive in instating Joseph Kabila as President of the DRC).

Second, when speaking about President Joseph Kabila, Combattants consistently refused to address him as such and persistently spoke about him as 'Hippolyte Kanambe'. One could think that, here, in the digital rants, the usage of 'Hyppolite Kanambe' instead of Joseph Kabila was a 'line of retreat' (Irvine 1993: 106), i.e. a protective linguistic device in order to render the insult deniable. However, Combattants called Kabila an 'imposter' and claimed that his *real* identity was 'Hippolyte Kanambe', as one would hear time and again when Combattants spoke about Kabila. The pseudonym was thus not a linguistic strategy to reference the same person; rather, it was part of the politics of accusation. Combattants actively deployed this name to 'uncover' his Rwandan identity. 'Kanambe' rhymes well with 'Kagame', the last name of the Rwandan President, Paul Kagame. Significantly, both linguistic devices (pseudonym and suffixes of Rwandese belonging) mobilised by Combattants produced social and political distance between the Congolese population (to which Combattants feel they belong as well, even if they have obtained Belgian or French citizenship, or are trying to do so) on the one hand and Kabila's leadership on the other.

These linguistic strategies evoking a sense of betrayal on the part of Kabila towards the Congolese population were embedded in a whole sphere of communication in which one could read, for instance, about an assumed real biography of Kabila (printed on stencils and sold on Kinshasa's streets) or find video-letters circulating in the European diaspora in the early 2000s in which Etienne Kabila, from South Africa, speaks about the 'real' biological parents of Joseph Kabila (e.g. RD Congo CultureK 2008; Ngandu 2011). Online, one can also find documents rephrasing Kabila's biography in light of a deliberate, subtle and internationally accepted domination by the Rwandese President (e.g. Bisonioso CongoRDC 1 2017). It is argued that Kabila is a mere puppet of Kagame, who tried to overhaul the country. These audiovisual and digital texts claim that the ruler is the stranger and that the musicians who praise him are traitors.

Conflict Genres

Mbwakela is a form of indirect communication. At its root is the verb *kobwakela* (Lingala), which means 'to throw something towards or in front of someone'. In the context of communication, *kobwakela* refers to a discursive act, 'to throw [sentences] to someone', though usually while using metaphors, proverbs or other forms of suggestion, insinuation and camouflage.

From a social perspective, *mbwakela* is commonly perceived as a form of conflict dominating in the milieu of musicians and of women. Songs play an important role in the production of conflict, as, for example, very early on in colonial times, political critique was voiced through music (Gondola 1997). For most Congolese nowadays, the paradigmatic example of protest music is the 1978 song 'Le Tailleur' by Franco, which supposedly is a critique on the General Attorney Sakombi and the President Mobutu who blocked some of his songs and dances due to alleged obscenity. In the song, Franco chants about how the 'owner of the needle' has taken away the 'needle' of the 'tailleur' (tailor), thus depriving him of his working utensils.

It is argued that Franco actually learned the art of *mbwakela* from his mother, who was a *ndumba* (an unmarried woman) in Léopoldville. Still today, violence and conflict are easily associated with women. However, in this context of diatribes among female 'rivals' (*mbanda*), i.e. women who fight over the affect and economic power of the same man, then the label of 'pamphlet' will be used. Usually *pamphlets* are expressed through intermediaries such as children, neighbours or relatives because these women tend to avoid one another; in the event of physical proximity (e.g. if they happen to live in the same compound), music can be inserted into their conflict. This was the case, for instance, in a conflict I observed in a compound with five households. One of the married women suspected a girl in her twenties, also living in the compound and actually the daughter of the compound owner, of sleeping with her husband. While the married woman tried to keep her composure for most of the time, at certain moments conflict erupted. One morning, the married woman had put on a song by Kofi Olomide, in which he sings about a love rival. The girl who was addressed by the song woke up and felt attacked. She stormed out of the house and entered into an argument about the insinuations, which the whole compound could easily follow.

Mbwakela thus originally refers to a culture of metaphors, indirect communication, and is embedded within conflict between people with a power difference. The one with less power is provoking or challenging someone with more power, though does so in a subtle, deniable fashion. One of the most important elements of what we could call a 'classic *mbwakela*' is exactly its convolutedness and indirectness. Responding to the insinuations is a form of confirming the information communicated in the rant and is thus a form of self-accusation. People know that the best way to respond to a *mbwakela* is simply ignoring it. Targets of *mbwakela* are entitled to act as if it is not addressed to them. The 'classic *mbwakela*' is commonly explained as 'a stone thrown in the dark' (*lihanga ya molili*) and my interlocutors would go to explain that 'if one says "ai", it means he or she has been touched' (*soki otchie ai, oyo akotch, eza ezui ye*). By running into the courtyard and shouting out, the girl was saying 'ai'.

Genres are of course never static and can undergo changes. Since the late 1990s, the *mbwakela* has transformed into more violent, immediate aggressive insults, commonly called 'krètch' or 'polémique'. The world of rumba musicians is an important space for these recent transformations. In the *krètch* or culture of *polémique*, the *porte-parole*, the spokespersons of musicians are responding on behalf of their patrons. *Porte-paroles* occupy particular roles at the margins of music bands: they are not formal members of the music orchestras, but usually travel together with the lead singer(s) and the musicians to concerts or live performances. They are also standing in for the lead musicians in radio and TV shows (*variété*), where they are invited to give an update on the progress made for a new music album, or to deny or confirm certain rumours. Usually, the *porte-parole* takes advantage of the media space to attack their musician's opponents, e.g. patrons who have stopped sponsoring the band, musicians who have left the band and so on. The following week, the journalist is usually obliged to invite the *porte-parole* of the opponent to give a reply, which then leads to new insults and accusations. The *porte-paroles* thus move between sycophancy and defamation. They flatter and praise their patron, often in exaggerated ways, and are as extreme in the insults towards their patron's opponents. All of these accusations or rebuttals are eagerly followed by the spectators, who take up these rivalries in the streets, in the homes and on social media.

Just like *mbwakela*, *krètch* and *polémique* are discursive practices that also occur outside the space of music production. Within the family, the compound, the neighbourhood, an association, sports and politics, gossip and critique are very often couched in the form of *krètch* or *polémique*. These forms of verbal aggression comprise social contexts of opposition and attacks on the opponent's reputation, and usually occur in public.

The main goal of the *krètch* is to attack one's reputation (*kosambwisa*) and to diminish the other's following. In a society run by 'big men' (*patron*, *bato ya kilo*), i.e. people who are able to attract a large group of followers (fans, clients, members), attacking or confirming one's reputation is an important maker or breaker of leadership. Both sycophancy and *krètch* constitute discursive spaces of belonging in which ties between individuals are named and qualified. Significantly, it is the *porte-paroles* who engage in *krètch*. While the musicians might limit themselves to *mbwakela* in their songs, *porte-paroles* are often very explicit in their verbal attacks. This is part of a culture of leadership, in which the leader usually remains silent, hardly says a word and has other people actually speaking for them (Yankah 1995).

Polémique then stands in opposition to the notion of *palabre* ('palaver'), which commonly refers to conversations with the aim of conflict resolution, finding solutions to problems and restoring harmony. In the Kinois imagination, palaver is a discursive performance mainly carried out by (social) elders, i.e. heads of families or representatives of lineages. By contrast, *polémique* is usually seen as a performance by youth and women – social categories perceived as people who do not behave as 'responsible people'. While in a *palabre*, interlocutors are expected to behave in a composed manner, respond to a discipline of the self and speak in a calm, clear and slow manner, often using proverbs and allowing for time so that interlocutors can reflect on the suggestive language; those who engage in *polémique* avoid silence, shout, use lewd language, gesticulate nervously with their limbs (often pointing a finger to someone – usually seen as a major insult), and speak quickly and erratically.

Mbwakela, *krètch* and *polémique* (but also *pamphlet*) are different but interrelated forms of verbal attack and speak – each in their own ways – to a culture of conflict and competition. Yet, these are more than just labels for discursive acts. Rather, these concepts reference social practices that, at the same time, articulate oppositional positions and unite people around a controversy; they require listeners to take a stance, to defend one party or the other. These verbal attacks can be considered as social drama arenas, in a similar vein as Postill and Epafras (2018) have recently described for religious conflict played out in the Indonesian online sphere. Drawing on Turner's theory of arenas, they (2018: 108) argue that: 'In a social drama arena nothing can be left unsaid or "merely implied" ([Turner] 1974: 134).' Rather, as Postill (2011: 96) wrote in his *Localizing the Internet*, 'all actors drawn into the drama … must state publicly where they stand on the dispute at hand'. In line with the intertwining of politics and music in Congolese society, Boketshu I and other ranting Combattants expressed not only their anti-Kabila sentiments, but also forced other Congolese to position themselves within this antagonism. Insofar as *mbwakela* is usually articulated from a 'powerless position', i.e. from the position of someone who actually should not manifest disagreement (see above with regards to Franco's song, women and their rivals, the *porte-parole* vis-à-vis leading musicians), Combattants attacked the highest political leader, the President. However, while Franco and women can take recourse to denial because of the convolutedness, and the *porte-parole* is backed by his own patron (a leading musician), Combattants' backing came from their positionality in the diaspora. Outside of the national territories, criticisers of the Kabila regime were deemed to be safe.

Conclusion: Distance and Digital Protest

This chapter has shown how digital invectives are embedded in sociocultural histories of popular forms of opposition. Very much like kinship opposition in lineages, *polémique* and *krètch* produce boundaries between groups of people: between fans of music bands, football teams, political parties and individual leaders. Yet, these forms of verbal attack generate dialogue and provocation. In this sense, as communicative practices, *mbwakela*, *krètch*, *pamphlet* and *polémique* literally connect people (see also Livio, this volume). Opponents and enemies become interlocutors in a violent conversation.

I have formulated two arguments at the beginning of this chapter. First, I argued that verbal attack appears in various forms in different social spaces and enjoys different forms of impunity. The second argument relates to the productive work of distance. We can now combine these and answer the question about the permissibility of voicing aggressive or negative attacks on others. In 'old' *mbwakela*, the veil of indirection and allusion allows insults to be expressed. Even though everyone knows who is being targeted, the attack is not explicit, but relies on intelligent uptake. In *pamphlet*, indirection is provided by intermediaries or the disguising medium of song. In *krètch*, the impunity for the *porte-parole* is warranted by the powerful patron. In diasporic mediatised polemic, then, discursive distancing (see the above-mentioned linguistic strategies) and the sheer (transnational) distance, both providing impunity, combine here into a strong technology of protection.

Distance also becomes an important producer of meaning in the online *mbwakela* on another level. In the short description of an online *mbwakela*, Boketshu I and Kabuya are standing on a street in Brussels, with two policemen behind them, probably in a kind of fortuitous coincidence. This décor is significant: by situating themselves in the public sphere and backed by Belgian policemen, the aggressors communicated to their target that they are in a safe space. This display of security contrasts with the reputation of the DRC as a space where oppositional voices and political protest are violently repressed by the state and Congolese policemen in particular. It is then also not surprising to understand that political protest, often initially planned in Kinshasa, became 'diaspora only events' after city governors prohibited the rallies (Garbin and Godin 2013). Online representations of anti-Kabila discourse thus signalled the huge rift between citizens' safety at home and abroad.

The online *mbwakela* mediates social and political forms of distance, as expressed in the indirectness of the genre, embodied in migrants' living bodies and emphasised by the digitality of the *mbwakela*'s circulation. It is exactly this affordance of distance preservation that pushed Combattants to produce online *mbwakela*. In this way, the material shows the ambiguity of the spatial work of media in the generation of conflict. Instead of compressing space by virtually connecting distant spaces, online media can also emphasise and allow people to take advantage of distance and dislocation by emphasising these.

Finally, how did 'home', in particular President Kabila and Congolese in the DRC, react to these digital insults? Respecting the rules of the *mbwakela*, President Kabila never responded to the online *mbwakela*. Rumours travel around Kinshasa that Kabila once asked: 'Who is Boketshu I?' This question does not necessarily diminish the power of the *mbwakela*; rather, it suggests that the President knew the speech genre and its social possibilities. Many Kinois had an ambiguous stance towards the Combattants' activities and verbal attacks. The safe distance of the online *mbwakela* was a matter of contention for people in Kinshasa, who urged Combattants to repeat their invectives in Kinshasa rather than from afar.[6] Of course, this was a challenge Combattants – even when visiting briefly Kinshasa during holidays or for a family event – could not take on. Physical distance became a condition *sine qua non* for the possibility of political *mbwakela*.

Katrien Pype is a cultural anthropologist who has been studying Kinshasa's media worlds since 2003. Her research on the production of television serials, politics and propaganda, old age in a heavily mediatised society, and ICT and urbanity has been published in, among others, *Journal of the Royal Anthropological Institute, Ethnos, Africa: Journal of the International African Institute, Journal of African Media Studies, Journal of African Cultural Studies* and *Visual Anthropology*. She is the author of various book chapters on the topics and of the monograph *The Making of the Pentecostal Melodrama: Religion, Media, and Gender* (Berghahn Books, 2012).

Notes

Data for this project have been collected during fieldwork trips funded by an FWO ERC Runner Up Grant (FWO GA.0.0.05.14N) and an Odysseus Grant (FWO G.0.E65.14N), and by the Research Council of Norway (New Media Practices in a Changing Africa, P.I. Jo Helle-Valle). I gratefully acknowledge the comments made by Karin Barber and the editors of this volume on drafts of this chapter.

1. This chapter is based on ethnographic research during the Kabila regime (from 2002 to January 2019). At the time of finalising this chapter, we were only a few months into the new regime (with President Felix Tshisekedi). The anti-Kabila movement in the diaspora (the so-called 'Combattants movement') is still reconsidering whether its actions need to continue or not. I prefer to see this chapter as situated within a particular history (the Kabila regime) rather than making any assumptions on the future of the Combattants movement in the diaspora. Therefore, the chapter is written in the past tense.
2. The embargo was on live performances within the Congolese migrant community. Combattants did not ban the Congolese rumba music and kept on listening to and dancing on recorded music (CDs, USB sticks and music video clips). Combattants argued that the Congolese community was mourning, as the country was 'dead', so festive live performances were not appropriate.
3. Examples are Papa Wemba, Werrason, Fally Ipupa and Ferre Gola, but also Christian musicians such as Lor Mbongo.
4. Most names used in this chapter are pseudonyms.

5. Similar strategies were used in internal conflict among Combattants (e.g. Congoeuro bis Pierre Mike Mulowayi 2014).
6. See Gilbert (2018) for an incisive exploration into the ways in which young women in Nigeria's Calabar use distance and cellular communication in order to form new social bonds and opportunities.

References

Banamboka 1. 2013. 'Boketshu et Jannot Kabuya attaquent JB Mpiana, Didier Reynders et l'invitation à Kabila'. YouTube. Retrieved 19 October 2019 from https://www.youtube.com/watch?v=h8dz7XEgeMs.

Barber, K. 1991. *I Could Speak until Tomorrow: Oriki, Women, and the Past in a Yoruba Town*. Edinburgh: Edinburgh University Press.

———. 2007. *The Anthropology of Texts, Persons, and Publics*. Cambridge: Cambridge University Press.

Bernal, V. 2014. *Nation as Network: Diaspora, Cyberspace, and Citizenship*. Chicago: University of Chicago Press.

Bisonioso CongoRDC 1. 2017. 'Paul Kagame ayebisi Kabila alonguate et abomelaye ne Muanda Nsemi'. YouTube. Retrieved 19 October 2019 from https://www.youtube.com/watch?v=NJqDBcU6j8s.

Bräuchler, B. 2013. *Cyberidentities at War: The Moluccan Conflict on the Internet*. New York: Berghahn Books.

Briggs, C.L. 1996. *Disorderly Discourse: Narrative, Conflict, and Inequality*. Oxford: Oxford University Press.

Congoeuro bis Pierre Mike Mulowayi. 2014. 'Combattants de Paris en colère contre MUYAMBO ET JEANNOT Kabuya, Boketshu 1° Papytsho, CONGOEURO'. YouTube. Retrieved 19 October 2019 from https://www.youtube.com/watch?v=lH1nknfvVNQ.

EDTV-richetempete 2014. 'Ferre Gola Défie les Combattants d'Afrique Du Sud'. YouTube. Retrieved 19 October 2019 from https://www.youtube.com/watch?v=96IWqSt106g.

Garbin, D. 2014. 'Regrounding the Sacred: Transnational Religion, Place Making and the Politics of Diaspora Among the Congolese in London and Atlanta', *Global Networks* 14(3): 363–82.

Garbin, D., and M. Godin 2013. 'Saving the Congo: Transnational Social Fields and Politics of Home in the Congolese Diaspora', *African and Black Diaspora* 6(2): 113–30.

Gilbert, J. 2018. '"They are My Contacts, Not My Friends": Reconfiguring Affect and Aspirations through Mobile Communication in Nigeria', *Ethnos* 83(2): 237–54.

Gola, Ferre. 2014. Personal Twitter account: posting on 13 February 2014. Retrieved 19 October 2019 from http://twitter.com/ferregola/status/433902412131082240.

Gondola, C.D. 1997. 'Popular Music, Urban Society, and Changing Gender Relations in Kinshasa, Zaire (1950–1990)', in M. Grosz-Ngaté and O.H. Kokole (eds), *Gendered Encounters: Challenging Cultural Boundaries and Social Hierarchies in Africa*. London: Routledge, pp. 65–84.

Irvine, J. 1993. 'Insult and Responsibility: Verbal Abuse in a Wolof Village', in J.H. Hill and J. Irvine (eds), *Responsibility and Evidence in Oral Discourse*. Cambridge: Cambridge University Press, pp. 105–34.

Isbell, B.J. 1998. 'Violence in Peru: Performance and Dialogues', *American Anthropologist* 100(2): 282–92.

Jackson, J. 2013. *Political Oratory and Cartooning: An Ethnography of Democratic Process in Madagascar*. Malden, MA: Wiley-Blackwell.

Mbembe, A. 1997. 'The "Thing" and Its Double in Cameroonian Cartoons', in K. Barber (ed.), *Readings in African Popular Culture*. Oxford: James Currey, pp. 151–63.

Ngandu Bukasa, E. 2011. 'Preuve irréfutable: Hyppolite KANAMBE alias "Joseph Kabila"'. Forum Udps Belux. Site des combattants UDPS BELUX. Retrieved 19 October 2019 from http://udps.be/beluxx/viewtopic.php?t=1979.

Postill, J. 2011. *Localizing the Internet: An Anthropological Account*. New York: Berghahn Books.

Postill, J., and L.C. Epafras 2018. 'Indonesian Religion as a Hybrid Media Space: Social Dramas in a Contested Realm', *Asiascape: Digital Asia* 5(1–2): 100–23.

RD Congo CultureK. 2008. 'Etienne Kabila Taratibu parle de Joseph Kabila'. YouTube. Retrieved 19 October 2019 from https://www.youtube.com/watch?v=yKvH2o3FTX4.

Schröder, I.W., and B.E. Schmidt 2001. 'Introduction. Violent Imaginaries and Violent Practices', in B.E. Schmidt and I.W. Schröder (eds), *The Anthropology of Violence and Conflict*. London: Routledge, pp. 1–24.

Tsing, A.T. 2004. *Friction: An Ethnography of Global Connection*. Princeton: Princeton University Press.

Turner, V.W. 1974. *Dramas, Fields and Metaphors: Symbolic Action in Human Society*. Ithaca, NY: Cornell University Press.

Yankah, K. 1995. *Speaking for the Chief: Okyeame and the Politics of Akan Royal Oratory*. Bloomington: Indiana University Press.

PART VII
After Conflict

CHAPTER 12

Mending the Wounds of War

A Framework for the Analysis of the Representation of Conflict-Related Trauma and Reconciliation in Cinema

Lennart Soberon, Kevin Smets and Daniel Biltereyst

War destabilises society, shatters national infrastructure and emotionally scars its involved parties. The impact of war and other types of armed conflict goes beyond the realm of physical harm into different aspects of the social life. Not only are conflicts themselves wholly traumatic periods in the history of nations, they are also the catalyst for many individual and collective traumas. This chapter is interested in the afterlife of such conflicts and it explores these issues by looking at the wounds opened up by war and the mechanisms of mourning, processing and ritualistic remembering stemming forth post-conflict. More specifically, we investigate how such traumas are represented in cinema and how these films can contribute to transnational discourses of remembrance. Whether didactically, politically or commercially motivated, in representing trauma histories, films co-constitutively interact with a wide space of memory and they are powerful tools for the invention, documentation and crystallisation of conflict. Departing from the perspective of memory studies, this chapter considers film to be a locus for storing and communicating such traumatic histories. While films dealing with conflict-related trauma do mostly tackle individual traumatic experiences – and often trauma is conceptualised through a psychoanalytical framework that highly favours the individual level – the events undergone always relate to the collective (see Ashuri 2010). Being a form of mass media communication distributed transnationally, cinema has powerful symbolic potential in establishing cultural identities and a belief in certain rules of law (Everett 2009). Although taking certain cinematic representations and stylistic strategies as starting points in our discussion, we shy away from employing a media-centric textual perspective. Rather, we are concerned with how this amorphous body of conflict and trauma films can be understood as part of broader (collective) practices of remembering and dealing with trauma. As such, our perspective is informed by the practice approach in media sociology (Couldry 2004), and more broadly the interest in media practices shared by media anthropologists (Igreja 2015; Pedelty 1995; Postill 2010). As this volume aims to take an anthropologically informed practice approach to the terrain of media and conflict relations, we specifically want to address how this plays out in relation to cinema.

Furthermore, since the films under scrutiny base themselves on contexts of conflict, some still being waged, they can have wider implications for how parties, nations or ethnic groups are perceived as victims and perpetrators of atrocities. Therefore, we adopt media anthropological notions of collective memory that relate to how such media representation can contribute to different forms of remembering and help shape new collective identities in post-crisis periods. Special attention should also be paid to how these representations enter within a wider transcultural space of production structures and audience practices. In that respect, we are sensitive to the representation of trauma in the context of specific textual codes and sociocultural contexts (see also Sumiala, Tikka and Valaskivi, as well as Markham, this volume). In doing so, we tackle 'trauma cinema' both transnationally and across genres. The arguments we present are structured in three main parts. First, we will theorise cultural trauma within global cinema in relation to memory and ideology. This positioning is followed by outlining the types of trauma representation and the debates currently dominant within trauma theory. We conclude with a critical suggestion of how trauma cinema, as a category of films and as a field of study, can evolve in perceiving these films as a tool of remembrance and reparation in post-conflict societies.

Trauma Theory and Collective Memory

Conceptualising trauma as 'an overwhelming experience of sudden or catastrophic events in which the response to the event occurs in the often delayed, uncontrolled repetitive appearance of hallucinations and other intrusive phenomena', Caruth (1995: 11) considers trauma as stemming from the dynamics of the event and the witness. Unable to forget or cognitively place the atrocities lived, the witnesses cannot fully assimilate the experience and are forced to experience it belatedly. Because the traumatic event cannot be experienced fully, a compulsion is felt to revisit the trauma, to represent it as it were. Trauma victims are forced to relive the experiences they underwent and do so in a manner that is prone to distortions and emotional reinterpretations. While trauma was initially understood as an inherently individual experience, it can also carry across individuals and be conceived as something collective; entwined with wider social groups or national identities (Assman 2006: 210–11). Amongst others, LaCapra (2014: 78) writes of 'historical trauma', theorising trauma as manmade historical atrocities such as conflicts, genocides and oppression with a lasting impact on the identity of both individuals and communities. Trauma seems to be contagious (Crownshaw 2013: 170): it cannot be fixed or contained to one location, but rather spreads through the likes of language and representation. This is why, according to Kaplan (2005), focusing on the relationship between trauma and media is important. In reproducing discourse and public reflections, mass media representations of trauma have implications as to what is understood as traumatic collectively and how these events fit within a wider historical framework. As such, representation contributes to how a collective defines itself as 'injured' or 'traumatised'. Or, in the words of Meek (2011: 34): 'Whenever we hear the phrase "traumatic event" we need to ask: for whom is the event traumatic? If we assume events and their representations are not traumatic in themselves, we need to critically examine the role media plays in reproducing traumatic effects and traumatic structures of memory and forgetting.'

Alexander (2004: 7–8) takes this mediation argument further and states that events in themselves are never traumatic, but that trauma can be considered mostly a 'socially mediated attribution'. This of course does not mean that he believes such traumas to be stemming from nonexistent events; he simply points out the 'imagined' dimension to trauma, in the sense that what is being referenced to as traumatic can be easily distorted, exaggerated and, in some cases, completely fabricated. To Alexander (2004: 1), cultural trauma occurs 'when members of a collectivity feel they have been subjected to a horrendous event that leaves indelible marks upon their group consciousness, marking their memories forever and changing their future identity in fundamental and irrevocable ways'. Collective trauma is thus very much in line with Bal's (1999) conception of cultural memory. Bal (1999: viii) understands memory as the 'product of collective agency rather than the result of psychic or historic accident'. Assmann and Czaplicka's (1995) writings investigate how the institutionalised formation of collective memories contributes to a kind of historical canon. How meaning and memory are constructed from such a historic event therefore becomes a struggle of meaning, a 'trauma process' (Alexander 2004: 27) in which discourses on the self and the other are solidified through collective representation. The implications of this trauma process are many-sided. Not only do they aid in the remembrance and general acknowledgement of the events, but under the symbolic marker of 'trauma', they memorialise such events (Blake 2008: 3). To an extreme extent, such commemoration can lead to an aura of afterthought that understands remembering as a moral demand. Besides such sentiments, conceptions of historical trauma can easily function as signifiers for collective identity, such as nation states, ethnic groups and religious communities (Meek 2011: 1). These markers in the history of the nation have wider consequences and can lie in the self/enemy/victim structure attributed to the events. In representing such series of events, moral judgement is often made and perpetrators identified. Moreover, these historical passages are commemorated and imbued with cultural significance. The commemoration of national trauma provides a powerful and ideologically stable frame of reference for the nation, aiding in the construction of collectives. This chapter is particularly interested in how such frames relate to structures of exclusion and enemy-making, since the collective identity stemming from such types of trauma work is often achieved at the expensive of an enemy perpetrator. Film is but one of many sites through which such traumas are socially mediated, and have the possibility to reproduce or resist a dominant reading of events as traumatic.

Tackling Trauma on Screen

As a shared conceptual space, cinema is a powerful tool in sustaining or disrupting reflections of, and about, the past (Bronfen 2012: 2). Through narrativised accounts of events, cinema gives collectives a way to address the traumas haunting them. Not only do films serve as mnemonic aids in processes of commemoration and trauma construction; film narratives can also be considered a form of memory in their own right (Landsberg 2004). Furthermore, being products of popular entertainment and mass media, such narrativised accounts of conflict enter a wider intertextual environment and interact with other forms of war framing. Pedelty (1995: 22), for example, uses the example of

Salvador (1986) as an illustration of how films can be an interpretative framework for conflict reporters and American audiences alike. By using an America photojournalist as a point of view to represent the Salvadoran Civil War, *Salvador* encouraged audiences not only to reflect on the violent events that were taking place, but also on how American news framing offered a biased perception of the conflict. By considering cinema as a site of memory, we are particularly interested in how traumatic histories of conflict are established, sustained, subverted and reinterpreted within the medium. Typologies of the representation of trauma in cinema might be divided in a reworking of conflict-related trauma as: (a) backstory; (b) subject matter; and (c) aesthetic. These suggested categories can be seen as part of what Erll (2008: 285) describes as 'intra-medial strategies' in the making of memory: 'modes of representation which may elicit different modes of cultural remembering in the audience' (2008: 290). Each in their own manner, films belonging to this tripartite try to formally engage the spectator in a position of vicarious witnessing.

The first category relates to how film-makers tap into traumatic histories as a way to flesh out the film's characters and establish motivation. Trauma as backstory is in line with so-called 'backstory wounds' (Elm, Köhne and Kabalek 2014: 5), in which individual trauma is translated into the narrative unit of the flashback. Such traumas are often hegemonically acknowledged as 'historical traumas' by the intended audiences and film-makers engage with these historical passages because of their dramatic power. In the Hollywood superhero film *X-Men: First Class* (2011), for example, Magneto, one of the story's protagonists, has lived through the trials and tortures of Auschwitz. This event is referenced to by way of flashbacks and serves no particular point other than to establish the antagonistic relationship between Magneto and the story's chief villain Shaw, who was the camp doctor responsible for his hellish childhood. Adapted from American comic books, this part of the character's backstory is based within this historical passage not out of a will to inform an audience about the atrocities of the Holocaust, but because the genocide works as a powerful historical referent, efficiently delivering dramatic set-ups and affective tensions.

The second category of films is didactically motivated since they often stem from the will of the film-maker to inform the public and (re)tell traumatic narratives. As Terry George, director of *Hotel Rwanda* (2004), says: 'I'm not trying to blow a trumpet for *Hotel Rwanda*, but I don't think people had a sense of it until the movie came out, particularly in the United States where the film had a big impact' (Fleming 2016). Other examples of this category of movies are *Schindler's List*

(1993), *Katyn* (2007), *12 Years a Slave* (2013) and *Son of Saul* (2015). These examples can be subtle or exploitative, politically motivated or commercially oriented. However, they all affectively link the spectator to a protagonist who undergoes a traumatic passage. One way in which films on conflict often attempt to make claim for authenticity is through their opening credits (Pötzsch 2012: 313).

The third category relates to conflict-related trauma as aesthetics. A considerable amount of literature on post-conflict trauma in cinema has focused on this category, which supposes a conception of trauma cinema as an entirely different form of film. Walker (2005: 19) writes on the genre of 'trauma cinema' as a category of (documentary) films that reject a realist mode and attempt to subvert the dominant narrative and aesthetic discourses within cinema through strategies of disruption and fragmentation. Alain Resnais was one of the first directors to investigate the dubious relationship between trauma and remembrance in films such as *Nuit et Brouillard* (1955) and *Hiroshima, Mon Amour* (1959). Building on modernist stylistic strategies of disturbance and fragmentation, Resnais contributed to a form of trauma representation that not only tackles the traumatic events lingering in our collective memory, but first and foremost provides a critical reflection of our relation to such traumatic remembrance. Such representations go beyond establishing an event or series thereof as a period of historical trauma, and question the authenticity of the structures of memory. In many ways, this is similar to Hirsch's (2002: 142) concept of 'posttraumatic cinema' as a kind of film defined 'by the attempt to discover a form for presenting that content that mimics some aspect of post traumatic consciousness itself'.

While we have to be critical towards considering Western modernist reflexes and avant-garde traditions as a superior type of trauma representation, this final type provides the most interesting examples when adopting the viewpoint of media anthropology. By refusing the notion of an authoritative retelling of events and embracing the gaps and distortions that characterise processes of remembrance, a type of self-reflective trauma work is undertaken. Many film-makers have continued this project and, as documentary films such as *Waltz with Bashir* (2008) show, film-makers keep finding new ways to involve spectators in precarious relations of witnessing. For example, by departing from dreams and inconclusive instances of remembrance, instead of the events themselves in his recovery of memory of the Sabra and Shatila massacre (the 1982 killing of Palestinians and Lebanese Shiites in a refugee camp by a Christian Lebanese militia under the eyes of their Israeli allies), its director Ari Folman refuses the illusion of total recall.

In offering a traumatic remembering characterised by subjectivity and incompleteness, our position as vicarious witness is problematised, therefore contributing to a more ambiguous treatment to our relation of the past and position as makers of memory and meaning. Films such as *The Act of Killing* (2012) and *The Missing Picture* (2013) also stress the indeterminateness of remembrance by involving perpetrator and victim in performances of mediation and remediation. In *The Act of Killing* (2012), for example, militia that aided in the Indonesian mass killings (in 1965–66) are asked to fictionally stage their own actions by way of acting and directing a film based on the events. As such, it demonstrated how these war criminals have narrativised the genocide and how generic and formal codes of cinema are brought into negotiation with the mechanics of remembering. These strategies organise the likes of history and personal experiences in ways that do not dictate a specific narrative, but rather create a liminal space for the interaction of a multitude of narratives – collective and individual – relating to past, present and future (Torchin 2014).

Memory Wars

However, the different types of trauma in films are only one aspect of cinema's role in traumatic remembrance and reconciliation. Perhaps rather than asking how, we should ask who this position of witness is precisely directed towards. As Caton (1999) asserts, spectator positions are essential when trying to understand the wider role of representations. Because of cinema's potential in acknowledging and prioritising different forms of trauma, we must also be critical of how these representations travel and to whom they are directed. As cultural products, these types of representation do not exist in a void, but can be considered as both expressions and reproductions of meaning in a wider sociocultural and political landscape. Just as conflicts themselves, these films too can be seen to possess an extensive afterlife.

Since they occupy a place in discursive networks, economic structures, geopolitical formations, technological innovations and global flows, a treatment of trauma in cinema requires an acknowledgement of the transnational nature of these films. These films have the capability to engage in a reaffirmation of already-established traumas, rectify forgotten or unacknowledged ones or contradict previous historic accounts. Herman (1992: 47) articulates a 'dialectic of trauma', in which traumatic experiences are always struggling between oblivion or intrusion. Processing the likes of historic trauma is thus always a matter of balancing between the need to articulate these events and the inexpressibility of them. As a mass medium and global industry, cinema has the potential to reveal traumatic narratives that remain unacknowledged to a transcultural audience. Moreover, film can go beyond informing audiences and can emotionally involve them through wider politics of identification. Such vicarious witnessing and affective involvement can influence the patterns of remembering and recovery. Not only does bearing witness constitute 'a specific form of collective remembering that interprets an event as significant and deserving of critical attention' (Zelizer 2000: 52), but this process also contributes to post-conflict societies because it 'brings individuals together on their way to collective recovery' (2000: 52). Nevertheless, these wounds of war have to be acknowledged before they can be properly treated, and it is therefore important to take into account the global power dynamics and structural imbalances at play in this commemoration.

As Rothberg (2009: 3) argues, memory is subject to ongoing negotiation, cross-referencing and borrowing. Despite the fact that all narratives on historical trauma stemming from conflict contribute to the cultural discourse on these events, it is safe to say not all narratives have the same potential to help sustain or subvert such dominant historical readings. Some historical trauma enters a cycle of almost ritual remembering, such as the Holocaust, while other conflicts remain at risk to be symbolically annihilated and retracted from the likes of history writing. From a political-economic point of view, we can argue that the cinematic sustainment or disruption of a memory hegemony is dependent on the production and distribution infrastructure of the industry that supports said narratives. Such representations should be considered as part of the logics of wider media industries. The unbalanced flow of international capital not only leads to an underexposure and overexposure of certain subjects, but when applied to the likes of trauma also distributes a commercial worth to the representation of such subjects. Films that tackle the Cambodian, Rwandan and Armenian genocide, to name but a few, appear in far smaller numbers than those dealing with the Holocaust, the Vietnam War and 9/11. We argue that this cinematic remembering has nothing to do with the severity or geopolitical importance of the event in itself, but much more with the Western cultural proximity towards such events, together with the already-established hegemonic acknowledgement of what happened as a political fact.

This illustrates what Margalit (2003: 80) called 'the danger of biased salience'. Because Euro-American traumas have had more exposure and are well known, these events are deemed morally more significant than atrocities elsewhere. When expanding upon the example of the

Armenian Genocide, which is still being contested by Turkey despite being widely acknowledged by the international community, a kind of lifeline of cinematic trauma becomes evident. As the Armenian Genocide has gained greater acknowledgement, this historic trauma progressed along the lines of cinematic visibility. While it is evident that these stories are near-impossible to tell in Turkey, gradually international film-makers from, among others, the United States and Europe have started tackling these events for international distribution. The representation of the genocide went through stages of European arthouse films such as *The Cut* (2014) and independent productions starring American A-list actors, *Triage* (2009), before becoming increasingly recognised as a possible subject matter for mainstream film-makers. With the recent release of the first big-budget Hollywood periodpiece *The Promise* (2016), it can be argued that, as a site of trauma, the Armenian Genocide has entered a new circle of postmemorial work.

How Trauma Travels

Occupying a place in transcultural spheres, these films offer multiple levels of identification, be it regional, national or transnational. Yet, it is essential to understand to which type of audience this position of vicarious witnessing is structured, whose trauma is specifically voiced and where these notions proliferate. A prevailing implication with the production and dissemination of non-Western traumas is the reproduction of certain ethnocentric discourses. The cinematic representation of events such as the Rwandan and Cambodian Genocides might be a transnational matter, but these representations often remain embedded in an American-centric and Eurocentric worldview and/or Western production context and cast. As Elsaesser (2016: 16) points out, it is not uncommon for media to involve the suffering of others in a process of commodification. Conflict-related traumas are a locus for drama and many film-makers use these films as background, topic or form in an attempt to tap into their topicality and intensity, albeit for a wide number of reasons. Occupied with the consumption of trauma as spectacle, Kaplan and Wang (2004) meticulously investigate how trauma can be repackaged as popular fiction. Their concern is that such representations lead to a trivialisation of such events. Aiming for collective identification, these films try to involve the spectator in the experience of witnessing. Ellis (2000: 11) conceptualised this experience as one of 'separation and powerlessness'. Films play on these feelings of powerlessness or, as Elsaesser (2016: 16) notes: 'It is such combinations of victimhood and power – in short, of negative agency – which make certain post-conflict situations both topical and of general interest, but also morally volatile, historically specific and politically precarious; and perhaps especially under these aggravated conditions, they become topics fit for the cinema.' For Kaplan and Wang (2004), the identification we are meant to feel, is a morbid one. Real historic trauma is moulded into spectacles through myths and narratives that are set to excite. Such obsession fits in a wider 'wound culture' (Seltzer 1997: 253), one where 'the very notion of sociality is bound to the excitations of the torn and opened body, the torn and exposed individual, as public spectacle'.

However, some authors see constructive potential in these mediated renderings of trauma and believe that the representation of trauma has the power to generate a new type of memory, one that transcends national boundaries and the conceptions of the self and 'the other'. Writing that 'in a catastrophic age ... trauma might provide the very link between cultures', Caruth (1996: 18) is in search of a type of humanist commonality stemming from a shared memory across groups of people who might be seen as different communities. History thus becomes an interconnected cultural product in which we all have the power to participate (Leys 2000: 285). In the same vein, Levy and Sznaider (2002) argue that Holocaust discourse has been responsible for establishing a type of 'cosmopolitan memory'. This remembering extends the group memory to citizens of the world. This global diffusion of memory should, according to them, be evaluated positively since it can enhance the respect for democracy and human rights. Starting from Landsberg's (2004) nominal concept of 'prosthetic memory', one could be optimistic about this type of cross-cultural memory. Landsberg notes that as transnationally distributed mass media, cinema offers experiential sites for the processes of exploitation and commercialisation, but also, and more importantly for our argument, of remembrance and commemoration. These films offer the spectator a site of identification with histories that are not their own, and therefore take away memory from a particular social context. Films contribute to a prosthetic remembrance, a site of memory somewhere between the individual and the collective. In this process, an empathic link is formed with traumatised subjects, one that can potentially contribute to political and ethical action.

While this discourse on the symbolic importance of cross-cultural identification features heavily in trauma theory, it has received a great deal of criticism. There are structural problems to the symbolic extension Caruth (1996) offers. It is debatable to what extent Holocaust discourse has contributed to a more war-weary world instead of offering states an interpretive frame through which pre-emptive action can be legitimised (Meek 2011). Alexander (2003: 54) makes reference to the Holocaust as now functioning as an almost globally acknowledged 'sacred-evil' myth. The use of Nazi comparisons of George W. Bush before the invasion of Iraq, and the literal equating of Saddam Hussein to Adolf Hitler, are just two examples of how the memory of the atrocities of the Second World War could be incorporated into jingoist political rhetoric, with grave results. Thus, such a reference point only reiterated an understanding of conflict as consisting of monster perpetrators that need to be fought. While the belief in the unifying power of shared understanding stemming from trauma is well-meant, by starting from the self-evidence and objectivity of the pain of others, and taking the identification with culturally specific situations for granted, it is easy to relapse into melodramatic sentiments (Kaplan and Wang 2004: 15). In this respect, Kaplan and Wang (2004: 9) warn of the eliciting of 'empty' empathy, in which feelings of misery are decontextualised and are used for little more than cheap sentiment. If inciting social action is the goal of these films, more is needed than isolated images of injustice, violence and cruelty. Moreover, the belief in universalised culturally specific trauma always runs the risks that it 'flattens difference, history, memory, and the body into an abstract, pleasing mold' (Kaplan and Wang 2004: 11). This can lead to a 'cinema of indifference', in which conflicts, and their related traumas, become almost interchangeable (Smets 2015: 2443).

While it is true that, as Elsaesser (2016) argued, representing trauma can lead to narratives of 'universalisation' by functioning as a symbolic referent to the value of human life and the wickedness of man, there are structural indifferences that cannot be ignored. One such problem is that historic trauma is very much treated from a Western perspective. Not only can 'the "iconic" traumas of modern media – Vietnam, the Holocaust, 9/11 – ... be understood as symptoms of a deeper crisis emerging from the historical impact of imperialism, colonialism and globalization' (Meek 2011: 28), but our theorisation of trauma is also very much a Western conception (Craps 2012: 4). Therefore, several authors such as Craps (2012) and Visser (2011) set the goal to decolonise trauma theory. Both in cultural production and in scholarly research, the traumatic experiences of non-Western cultures are greatly marginalised. Craps (2012: 3) is mostly frustrated with the universal validity implied in our conceptualisation of trauma, without critically acknowledging that it stems from the history of Western modernity. He rightfully notices that 'hegemonic definitions of trauma have been criticized for being culturally insensitive and exclusionary, and charges of cultural imperialism have been levelled at the uncritical cross-cultural application of Western trauma concepts in the context of international humanitarian disaster relief programmes' (2012: 3). A notable exception is the work of Lester (2013), who provides an overview of a critical anthropology of trauma in ongoing, developing human relationships. Considering the capacity to relate to others 'beyond the specifics of the trauma or their "damaged" identity' (Lester 2013: 760) as a core component in post-traumatic reconciliation, he opts to connect classic anthropological concerns in relation to trauma and social organisations with a political economic perspective on the commodification of victimhood.

Nevertheless, there is still a great deal of bias and misrepresentation concerning non-Western trauma. Often, when represented at all, such events are treated as regressive chapters in history (Kaplan and Wang 2004: 18) and it is not uncommon for films dealing with such non-Western trauma to take a white Western protagonist (e.g. the journalist, human aid worker or peacekeeper) as an entry point into foreign conflict. Films as *The Killing Fields* (1984), *Salvador* (1986) and *Darfur* (2009) and many more offer non-Western conflict as a kind of transitory space through which white heroes tackle personal feelings of responsibility and regret, before finding redemption. Thus, reaching out to our cultural 'others', as Caruth (1996) intended, can lead to the appropriation of their suffering (Craps 2012: 3). Nassar (2002: 27–28) goes as far as to speak of a 'colonisation' of memory. However, as we will discuss further on, some films try to actively resist this commodification and appropriation of trauma by distancing themselves from the belief of giving an objectivity account of events.

Cinematic Recall and Conflict Reparation

Another such criticism lies in the filmic treatment of historic trauma as individual experiences of isolated events, thus failing to acknowledge structurally embedded, everyday forms of traumatising violence. Films such as *The Battle of Algiers* (1966) and *Chronicle of the Years of Fire* (1975) are involved in a form of trauma work that somewhat resists classical categorisations. Tackling longer periods of colonial oppression and political persecution, these films succeed in reconceptualising historical trauma so as to include periods of colonial rule. As Craps (2012: 72) argues, the academic conception of trauma as isolated and event-like has led to trauma theory failing to acknowledge wider regimes of oppression – such as many passages of Western colonial rule. It is therefore no coincidence that the systemic atrocities perpetrated in or against colonies and minority communities take a back seat in favour of historic tragedies enacted within or against Western Europe and the United States. In this way, structural inequalities are further obscured and the hegemonic conception of history obeyed. There is also a great lack of dialogue in the remembrance of events. Too often dominant notions of traumatic passages in history get reiterated in the process of commemoration, leading to a reaffirmation of hegemonic remembering. Furthermore, using claims of authenticity and historicity as ways of enacting authority upon the spectator, trauma films enforce an aura of truthfulness upon the spectators concerning the perception of these passages. Yet, as Alexander (2004: 118) points out, there is always a process of interpretation present in the representation of trauma. Events can get misrepresented or facts misconstrued, and it is easy to see how a lack of diversity in perspectives can contribute to a narrow remembering of events. The shortage of films on the Vietnam War told from the viewpoint of Vietnamese soldiers and civilians, let alone produced in Vietnam, could be considered as attributing to a more rigid mode of remembrance. The same can be said of many types of conflicts in which the United States was involved and that were subsequently appropriated for dramatic and commercial purposes. Moreover, because these histories are greatly narrativised along the lines of the dominant Hollywood narrative structure, the greater forces at play in the realisation of conflict-related atrocities get reduced to interpersonal conflict between individuals with different political agendas (Elsaesser 2016: 16).

Conflict-related traumas are thus reshaped into relations of little more than victims and villains, in the process denying the remembering of these events a complexity they require. Therefore, we are in need of counter narratives that attempt to subvert the memories solemnly held. In relation to the reparation of post-conflict societies, such systematic representations of victim and villains could be problematic because they persist in the construction of the very antagonism between parties that often leads to trauma in the first place (Cairns, Niens and Tam 2005). As Worthington and Aten (2010: 56) assert: 'Forgiveness and reconciliation help heal past memories, restore present trust, and thus pave the way for breaking future cycles of trauma.' If we are to renegotiate trauma work in a manner that does not give rise to ongoing hostilities, sentiments of forgiveness and moral inclusion must also persevere cinematically. However, in a post-conflict context, it is not uncommon to hold on to the binary distinction of victims and villains. According to Elsaesser (2016: 22), such distinctions are 'preliminary crucial but subsequently problematic and controversial' – crucial because it is important for the survivors for their suffering to be acknowledged and guilt attributed, but problematic because such one-sided attribution fails to acknowledge the traumatic experiences of the perpetrators.

Because of the accumulation of injustices, cruelty and grief during violent conflict, the parties involved often perceive themselves as victims. Denying the enactors of traumatic experience any sense of victimhood is to deny them any real history, which can be particularly problematic in a post-conflict society because all parties eventually have to be peacefully reintegrated into society (Martz 2010: 12; see also the chapters by Oldenburg and Bräuchler in this volume on the challenges of transforming and reconciling identities in post-conflict societies). Freedman (1998: 200) conceptualises reconciliation as the societal restoration of violated trust amongst actors. When inner-group/outer-group distinctions are equated with that of victim and perpetrator, and these negative associations persist in post-conflict contexts, they have the potential to pave the way for a new generation of conflict and trauma. Worthington and Aten (2010: 64) argue that in order to build lasting structures of peace, it is essential that 'both parties or groups need to consider the others' experiences of threat and sense of injustice'. Cinema can be an important attribute in moulding the memories of such traumatic events, and in helping new generations interpreting these events as either a Manicheist testament to the cruelty of the 'other' or a complex entwinement of tensions and misperceptions resulting in conflict.

If cinema is to contribute to processes of reconciliation, the generic inclination to demonise and provide an easy antagonist should be resisted by film-makers. Whilst the recognition of suffering is a crucial first step in the representation of conflict-related trauma, it is of prime importance for films in the aftermath of trauma to move past such tense divisions and attempt to offer a wider understanding of the historical forces, and arbitrary difference, that lie at the root of these traumas. Joshua Oppenheimer's now widely renowned *The Act of Killing* can be considered a rare example of a film that successfully negotiates notions of perpetrator and victim roles in a post-conflict society. Identifying the perpetrators of the Indonesian killings in order to attribute guilt is not Oppenheimer's main objective, mostly because these figures are already exposed, not to mention considered notable by many, and also because he attempts to resist a sense of indignation built around these actions. Rather than offering a portrait of monsters, the banality of evil is here investigated by making the Indonesian war criminal complicit in peeling away the layers of self-righteousness and mechanisms of legitimisation that made them capable of such horrific crimes. If trauma disrupts our notions of self, as conceptualised by Caruth (1996) and LaCapra (1996), we have to be thoughtful of how these notions of identity are to be reconstructed and which place former enemies and cultural 'others' hold in this redefinition (see also Bräuchler 2015).

It has to be stressed that cinematic representations are not the only way to learn about such violent passages of history. As Paramaditha (2013: 48) argues in relation to the post-conflict work of *The Act of Killing*, instead of demanding these films to count as the conclusive testament of the events that took place, they should foremost be considered as a starting point. Cinema has the potential to identify how such memories are being handled and how national and international communities alike can still work towards the recognition, rectification or atonement of these traumatic histories. *The Act of Killing* in this sense did not close one fixed narrative as many films on conflict-related traumas attempt to do; alternatively, it opened up the conversation. Moreover, the film itself remains an entry point into an otherwise difficult-to-access part of Indonesian history, for young Indonesians and international citizens alike. As was stated earlier, trauma travels and as long as film-makers conscientiously work with events, the medium of cinema will continue to form a suitable channel for the transcultural expeditions of these private and collective histories.

Conclusion

Olweean (2003: 271) rightfully states that 'communal psychological wounds are one of the most – if not the most – powerful fuel of war and violent conflicts'. In this chapter, we offered a theoretical introduction into the representation of conflict-related trauma in cinema. Considering cinema as a symbolic battleground through which different types of remembering are crystallised, subverted and negotiated, we have illustrated the potential of films in the commemoration and reconciliation of conflict-related trauma. This two-tier theoretical overview into trauma films as cultural products and as an academic field thus provided a framework through which the relationship between trauma representation and memory construction can be better understood. By going through the dominant modes of cinematic treatment of conflict-related atrocities and trends in trauma theory, this chapter has therefore tried to raise questions and incites readers into further investigation.

Questions of ethics, representability, agency, identification and universalisation still occupy the field, and while scholarly investigation is expanding, there remains a lot of work to be done. Considering the debate on how filmic narratives interact with the wider space of memory, we theorised how such narratives can interact with conflict reconciliation and cross-cultural solidarity. Films aid in the specific remembering of events, but are far more than mnemonic devices in the representation and conveyance of memory. As has been illustrated, some authors share a belief in the representation of trauma as spreading cross-cultural solidarity and aiding in the formation of a global community. However, these claims have to be approached with caution because they leave us at risk of instrumentalising the suffering of 'others' and neglecting what these events meant for a particular group of people at a particular time. Working with an exclusively Western conception of historic trauma has led to the structural neglect of specific passages of history and to a narrow conceptualising of trauma. Instead of the individually focused, event-obsessed treatment of historic trauma, cinema should grasp the opportunity to reveal and deconstruct the structural, pervasive dimensions of such atrocities, and deliver narratives that break the victim/villain binary that is so heavily established within these films. If we agree that media are co-constitutive of conflicts, the role of cinema and the responsibilities of film-makers deserve the full consideration of scholars working on conflict and its transformations across different contexts.

Lennart Soberon works as a researcher and teaching assistant for the Department of Communication Sciences at Ghent University, where he is a member of the Centre for Cinema and Media Studies. His research concerns the representation of contemporary conflicts in cinema and focuses on the construction of enemy images in American war and action films.

Kevin Smets is Assistant Professor at the Department of Communication Studies, Vrije Universiteit Brussel and postdoctoral fellow of the Research Foundation Flanders, affiliated with the Department of Communication Studies at the University of Antwerp. His main research interests are media, conflict and migration, and Middle Eastern and diasporic media cultures.

Daniel Biltereyst is Professor in Film and Media History and director of the Cinema and Media Studies research centre at Ghent University, Belgium. Besides exploring new approaches to historical media and cinema cultures, he is engaged in work on film and screen culture as sites of censorship, controversy, public debate and audience engagement. He has published widely on these matters in edited volumes and journals. He is now working on *The Routledge Companion to New Cinema History* (with R. Maltby and P. Meers) and on *Mapping Movie Magazines* (Palgrave Macmillan).

References

12 Years a Slave. 2013. [Film]. Steve McQueen (dir.). United States/United Kingdom: Fox Searchlight Pictures.

The Act of Killing. 2012. [Film]. Joshua Oppenheimer. dir. Norway/Denmark/United Kingdom: Dogwoof Pictures.

Alexander, J.C. 2003. *The Meanings of Social Life: A Cultural Sociology*. Oxford: Oxford University Press.

―――. 2004. 'Toward a Theory of Cultural Trauma', in J.C. Alexander et al. (eds), *Cultural Trauma and Collective Identity*. Berkeley: University of California Press, pp. 1–30.

Ashuri, T. 2010. 'I Witness: Re-presenting Trauma in and by Cinema', *Communication Review* 13(3): 171–92.

Assmann, A. 2006. 'Memory, Individual and Collective', in R.E. Goodin and C. Tilly (eds), *The Oxford Handbook of Contextual Political Analysis*. Oxford: Oxford University Press, pp. 210–24.

Assmann, J., and J. Czaplicka. 1995. 'Collective Memory and Cultural Identity', *New German Critique* 65: 125–33.

Bal, M. 1999. 'Memories in the Museum', in M. Bal, J.V. Crewe and L. Spitzer (eds), *Acts of Memory: Cultural Recall in the Present*. Lebanon: Upne, pp. 171–90.

The Battle of Algiers. 1966. [Film]. Gillo Pontecorvo. dir. Italy/Algeria: Rialto Pictures.

Blake, L. 2008. *The Wounds of Nations: Horror Cinema, Historical Trauma and National Identity*. Manchester: Manchester University Press.

Bräuchler, B. 2015. *The Cultural Dimension of Peace: Decentralization and Reconciliation in Indonesia*. Basingstoke: Palgrave Macmillan.

Bronfen, E. 2012. *Specters of War: Hollywood's Engagement with Military Conflict*. New Brunswick, NJ: Rutgers University Press.

Cairns, E.H., M. Niens and U.T. Tam. 2005. 'Intergroup Forgiveness and Intergroup Conflict: Northern Ireland, a Case Study', in E.L. Worthington (ed.), *Handbook of Forgiveness*. London: Routledge, pp. 461–76.

Caruth, C. 1995. *Trauma: Explorations in Memory*. Baltimore: JHU Press.

―――. 1996. *Unclaimed Experience: Trauma, Narrative, and Memory*. Baltimore: JHU Press.

Caton, S.C. 1999. *Lawrence of Arabia: A Film's Anthropology*. Berkeley: University of California Press.
Chronicle of the Years of Fire. 1975. [Film]. Mohammed Lakhdar-Hamina (dir.). Algeria: Arab Film Distribution.
Couldry, N. 2004. 'Theorising Media as Practice', *Social Semiotics* 14(2): 115–32.
Craps, S. 2012. *Postcolonial Witnessing: Trauma out of Bounds*. Basingstoke: Palgrave Macmillan.
Crownshaw, R. 2013. 'Trauma Studies', in P. Wake and S. Malpas (eds), *The Routledge Companion to Critical and Cultural Theory*. London: Routledge, pp. 167–76.
The Cut. 2014. [Film]. Fatih Akin (dir.). Canada/France/Germany/Italy/Poland/Turkey: Bombero International.
Darfur. 2006. [Film]. Uwe Boll (dir.). United States: Phase 4 Films.
Ellis, J. 2000. *Seeing Things: Television in the Age of Uncertainty*. London: I.B. Tauris.
Elm, M., K. Köhne and J.B. Kabalek. 2014. *The Horrors of Trauma in Cinema: Violence Void Visualization*. Newcastle: Cambridge Scholars Publishing.
Elsaesser, T. 2016. 'Paradoxes and Parapraxes', in D. O'Rawe and M. Phelan (eds), *Post-conflict Performance, Film and Visual Arts: Cities of Memory*. New York: Springer, pp. 15–36.
———. 2016. 'Post-conflict Cinema', in A. Martins, A. Lopes and M. Dias (eds), *Mediations of Disruption in Post-conflict Cinema*. Basingstoke: Palgrave Macmillan, pp. 21–42.
Erll, A. 2008. 'Literature, Film, and the Mediality of Cultural Memory', in S. Young (ed.), *Cultural Memory Studies: An International and Interdisciplinary Handbook*. Berlin: De Gruyter, pp. 389–98.
Everett, D.A. 2009. 'Public Narratives and Reparations in Rwanda: On the Potential of Film as Promoter of International Human Rights and Reconciliation', *Northwestern Journal of International Human Rights* 7(1): 103–31.
Fleming, M. 2016. 'Hotel Rwanda's Terry George Looks at Armenian Genocide with "The Promise": Toronto Q&A', *Deadline*, 11 September. Retrieved 22 October 2019 from http://deadline.com/2016/09/terry-george-armenian-genocide-wwi-turkis-government-the-promise-toronto-hotel-rwanda-1201817135.
Freedman, L. 1998. 'The Changing Forms of Military Conflict', *Survival* 40(4): 39–56.
Herman, J. 1992. *Trauma and Recovery: The Aftermath of Violence, From Domestic Abuse to Political Violence*. London: Pandora.
Hiroshima, Mon Amour. 1959. [Film]. Alain Resnais (dir.). France/Japan: Pathé Films.
Hirsch, M. 2001. 'Surviving Images: Holocaust Photographs and the Work of Postmemory', *Yale Journal of Criticism* 14(1): 5–37.

———. 2002. 'Posttraumatic Cinema and the Holocaust Documentary', *Film & History: An Interdisciplinary Journal of Film and Television Studies* 32(1): 9–21.
Hotel Rwanda. 2004. [Film]. Terry George (dir.). United Kingdom/South Africa/Italy: Lionsgate Films/United Artists.
Igreja, V.M. 2015. 'Media and Legacies of War: Responses to Global Film Violence in Conflict Zones', *Current Anthropology* 56(5): 678–700.
Kaplan, E.A. 2005. *Trauma Culture: The Politics of Terror and Loss in Media and Literature.* New Brunswick, NJ: Rutgers University Press.
Kaplan, E.A., and B. Wang. 2004. *Trauma and Cinema: Cross-cultural Explorations.* Hong Kong: Hong Kong University Press.
Katyn. 2007. [Film]. Andrzej Wajda (dir.). Poland: ITI Cinema.
The Killing Fields. 1984. [Film]. Roland Joffe (dir.). United Kingdom: Columbia-EMI-Warner.
LaCapra, D. 1996. *Representing the Holocaust: History, Theory, Trauma.* Ithaca: Cornell University Press.
———. 2014. *Writing History, Writing Trauma.* Baltimore: JHU Press.
Landsberg, A. 2004. *Prosthetic Memory: The Transformation of American Remembrance in the Age of Mass Culture.* New York: Columbia University Press.
Lester, R. 2013. 'Back from the Edge of Existence: A Critical Anthropology of Trauma', *Transcultural Psychiatry* 50(5): 753–62.
Leys, R. 2000. *Trauma: A Genealogy.* Chicago: University of Chicago Press.
Levy, D., and N. Sznaider. 2002. 'Memory Unbound the Holocaust and the Formation of Cosmopolitan Memory', *European Journal of Social Theory* 5(1): 87–106.
Margalit, A. 2003. *The Ethics of Memory.* Cambridge, MA: Harvard University Press.
Martz, E. 2010. *Trauma Rehabilitation after War and Conflict: Community and Individual Perspectives.* Berlin: Springer.
Meek, A. 2011. *Trauma and Media: Theories, Histories, and Images.* London: Routledge.
The Missing Picture. 2013. [Film]. Rithy Panh (dir.). Cambodia/France: Les Acacias.
Nassar, I. 2002. 'Reflections on Writing the History of Palestinian Identity', *Palestine-Israel Journal of Politics, Economics, and Culture* 8(4): 24–54.
Nuit et Brouillard. 1956. [Film]. Alain Resnais (dir.). France: Argos Films.
Paramaditha, I. 2013. 'Tracing Frictions in *The Act of Killing*', *Film Quarterly* 67(2): 44–49.
The Promise. 2016. [Film]. Terry George (dir.). United States: Open Road Films.
Rothberg, M. 2009. *Multidirectional Memory: Remembering the Holocaust in the Age of Decolonization.* Palo Alto, CA: Stanford University Press.
Olweean, S.S. 2003. 'When Society is the Victim: Catastrophic Trauma Recovery', in S. Krippner and T.M. McIntyre (eds) 2003. *The Psychological Impact of War Trauma on Civilians: An International Perspective.* Westport: Greenwood, pp. 271–76.

Pedelty, M. 1995. *War Stories: The Culture of Foreign Correspondents*. London: Routledge.

Postill, J. 2010. 'Introduction: Theorising Media and Practice', in B. Bräuchler and J. Postill (eds), *Theorising Media and Practice*. New York: Berghahn Books, pp. 1–32.

Pötzsch, H. 2012. 'Framing Narratives: Opening Sequences in Contemporary American and British War Films', *Media, War & Conflict* 5(2): 155–73.

Salvador. 1986. [Film]. Oliver Stone (dir.). United States: Hemdale Film Corporation.

Schindler's List. 1993. [Film]. Steven Spielberg (dir.). United States: Universal Pictures.

Seltzer, M. 1997. 'Wound Culture: Trauma in the Pathological Public Sphere', *October* 80: 3–26.

Smets, K. 2015. 'Cinemas of Conflict: A Framework of Cinematic Engagement with Violent Conflict, Illustrated with Kurdish Cinema', *International Journal of Communication* 9(1): 2434–55.

Son of Saul. 2015. [Film]. László Nemes (dir.). Hungary: Mozinet.

Torchin, L., 2014. 'Mediation and Remediation: La Parole Filmée in Rithy Panh's *The Missing Picture (L'image Manquante)*', *Film Quarterly* 68(1): 32–41.

Triage. 2009. [Film]. Danis Tanović (dir.). Ireland/France/Spain: Parallel Films.

Visser, I. 2011. 'Trauma Theory and Postcolonial Literary Studies', *Journal of Postcolonial Writing* 47(3): 270–82.

Walker, J. 2005. *Trauma Cinema: Documenting Incest and the Holocaust*. Berkeley: University of California Press.

Waltz with Bashir. 2008. [Film]. Ari Folman (dir.). Israel/Germany/France: Sony Pictures Classics.

Worthington, E.L., and J.D. Aten. 2010. 'Forgiveness and Reconciliation in Social Reconstruction after Trauma', in E. Martz (ed.), *Trauma Rehabilitation after War and Conflict: Community and Individual Perspectives*. Berlin: Springer, pp. 55–72.

X-Men: First Class. 2011. [Film]. Matthew Vaughn (dir.). United States: Marvel Entertainment.

Zelizer, B. 2000. *Remembering to Forget: Holocaust Memory through the Camera's Eye*. Chicago: University of Chicago Press.

CHAPTER 13

Going off the Record?

On the Relationship between Media and the Formation of National Identity in Post-Genocide Rwanda

Silke Oldenburg

On 3 May 2013, during a conference on the occasion of the World Press Freedom Day, I observed three young journalists approaching a professor of Kigali's School of Journalism and Communication asking for an interview. 'What do you think of the latest figures of Reporters without Borders?', the professor was asked. Then one of the aspiring journalists, lowering his voice, continued: 'You can answer off the record, of course.'

—Fieldnotes, 3 May 2013

The gap between what can be said and what appears to be taboo in Rwanda's media sector, between the 'off' and the 'on'-the-record, is striking, particularly when related to external critics such as Paris-based Reporters without Borders (RsF). The professor frowned, criticising the journalist for his unprofessional behaviour and answered on-the-record: 'Who is about to judge us? Where do they get their information from?' (Fieldnotes, 3 May 2013).

Media, production of knowledge and figurations of power are highly interrelated in Rwanda and play strongly into the formation of a national identity. Building on the numerous studies that focus on the role of the radio in the evolution of the Rwandan Civil War (from 1990 to 1994), particularly during the devastating genocide[1] (1994), this chapter zooms in on the little-investigated post-genocide media realm. It analyses the challenges, understandings and visions of today's media practitioners and therefore contributes to an ethnographic lens on (post)conflict practices of social transformation and their interplay with Rwanda's highly volatile media environment.

'I want to mention some few points "off-the-record"', 'I remind you that this is off-record', or a continuous look at the recording device conveyed to me the impression that my interlocutors were on guard. The request to discuss topics 'off-the-record', a confidential sigh when I switched off the recording device, or a completely different version of events while being in the office than while being in the pub, struck me on several occasions. Obviously, interviews are moments of performance, and the discrepancy between what is speakable and what should not be said is relative and context-specific. However, the brief utterance to answer 'off the record' became a mantra during my research[2] and will serve in this chapter as a point of departure to provide insights into a particularly sensitive realm of Rwanda's nation-building endeavour: the media after genocide.

After the genocide in 1994, Rwanda faced challenges in all societal realms. The reconstruction of the state, the re-establishment of sovereignty, the provision of security and justice, unity and reconciliation present only some of the most important domains in which the state engaged with a vision and a hard hand. With the government's vision of the future, Rwanda advanced quickly to become a 'donor darling' partly because of its ability to invest and control foreign aid efficiently due to its authoritarian top-down nature (Buckley-Zistel 2009; Purdeková 2011). This led to unprecedented economic growth and the implementation of technocratically 'good governance'.

Today, Rwanda's media landscape is presented by Rwandan official sources as vibrant and plural. At the same time, the national media scene still remains at the bottom of the RsF index, ranked number 156 out of 180 countries in 2018 (Reporters without Borders 2018), while other ranking houses such as the Freedom House ranking of Global Press Freedom continues to classify Rwanda as having 'no free press' in 2017 (Freedom House 2017). In the rationale of rankings and measurements and the importance people ascribe to them in their efforts to 'influence their social worlds' (Guyer et al. 2010: 36), the media environment appears to be a failed one, portraying the Rwandan government as oppressive to journalists and curtailing media freedom in general. Yet, Rwandan media practitioners feel mischaracterised by external critics and confidently refute any interference, as seen in the brief ethnographic vignette above. However, how does this reflect the plea to answer 'off-the-record' and what does this reveal about the formation of national identity after genocide?

The transformation but also the future of the Rwandan route to national unity can be described and interpreted by the media scenery. This chapter is based on the idea that the analysis of how people talk or remain silent about politics, and how different actors, particularly the state, shape these voids respectively voices, provides information about historical dynamics and the transformation of the state within the last twenty years and its contribution to collective identity formation. Nevertheless, it is apparent that the media sector in Rwanda is still trying to come to terms with its historical legacy. In the frame of this chapter, I therefore follow Elwert's (2004) conceptualisation of conflict with a particular focus on everyday practices of avoidance (see also Alber 2004; Häberlein 2007; Scott 1985; Thomson 2014). Merging a conceptual take on social practices of avoidance with a practice approach (Bräuchler and Postill 2010) helps to make sense of experiences in an uncertain and volatile political context. This angle allows in the following to open up a discussion on changing professional identities, practices of meaning-making of the historical legacy, and media ethics among media practitioners in Rwanda.

This chapter briefly traces the historical background of Rwanda's media landscape (with a focus on 'traditional' media such as radio and newspapers) and presents recent developments in media regulation in the post-genocide era. In this context, I reflect on Straus' provocative study (2007), which countered the omnipotent explanation of the importance of hate media. His study does not downplay the deadly impact of 'Radio Machete', but shows that its often assumed central role is debatable. The following sections engage empirically with everyday practices of dealing with this highly ambivalent context. Together with an unevenly distributed access to knowledge, these different social practices aim to draw attention to the complexities and interconnectedness of the media and the political realm in Rwanda. Finally, the historical legacy of the genocide, the authoritarian nature of the current government and the lack of a 'culture of debate' flow together in what I coin an 'off-the-record' culture.[3]

Histor(ies) of Media and Conflict in Rwanda

The biggest difference between our country and others is the culture of discussion. In other countries they scream and yell at each other. Not in Rwanda. Even during the genocide, people were silent. They used the machete but were not shouting. After three months you had a million deaths and there was still a big silence. You can say that we don't have a proper democracy, that we don't have a proper opposition, but you have to understand why.

—Policy-maker/Media High Council staff, personal communication, 12 May 2013

Between April and June 1994, an estimated 800,000 Rwandans, primarily Tutsi but also politically moderate Hutu, were massacred in a state-sponsored, 100-day-long genocide in Rwanda. In an effort to bring stability and reconstruction to the country, the government led by the victorious Rwandan Patriotic Front (RPF) pursued numerous goals since 1994: most importantly transitional justice, a comprehensive agricultural reform and a large project of 'social engineering', which means 'mold[ing] the culture, norms, identities and behaviour of Rwandans' (Straus and Waldorf 2011: 15).

Among these objectives, the government adopted a policy of 'national unity' and abolished ethnicity as an official factor in bureaucratic life, while trying to construct a shared historical narrative of unity among the Rwandan ethnic groups of Hutu, Tutsi and Twa (Burnet 2009: 86). Implementing policies without much space for dissent, the state's reach in today's Rwanda leads to effective political control, strong surveillance and little counterweight (Purdeková 2011: 476).

The quote at the beginning of this section reflects on an omnipresent culturalist argument uttered by a member of the Media High Council (MHC), the official institution that regulated the Rwandan media landscape from 2003 to 2013.[4] He framed the historical context as pivotal in understanding today's media scenery and, by alluding to 'silent' Rwandans and a lacking 'culture of discussion', he picked up on a culturalist approach that silences questions of structural inequality and political economy (Zorbas 2009a: 100). In fact, at the end of the 1980s and the beginning of the 1990s, Rwanda experienced, like many other African countries, a liberalisation process both in the political and the media realms. The admission of new political parties and the creation of private media implied more competition for followers and scarce resources: Already in 1991, more than fifty new newspapers and journals emerged, a lot of them with a strong focus on journalists' and other contributors' 'opinions' (Chrétien 1995). That means that the first phase of press freedom did not follow a professional journalistic logic, but focused on exercising one's right to express oneself (Frère 2011: 23). A decisive feature of popular culture and academic research on Rwanda embraces the pernicious belief in the radio, often labelled as 'hate media', 'hate radio' or 'Radio Machete', played in inciting violence and committing atrocities by using this freedom of expression.

Radio Télévision Libre des Milles Collines (RTLM)[5] apparently exemplified the dangers of media liberalisation (Carver 2000). However, according to Straus (2007: 610), there has been 'little sustained social scientific analysis of radio media effects in the Rwandan genocide'. Without rejecting the openly inflammatory form of incitement of this radio station, he puts RTLM's impact into perspective. Picking up on the already introduced omnipresent culturalist approach, he engages in countering narratives that deny the listeners' agency and that portray them stereotypically as poorly educated people who follow orders blindly (2007: 615). He convincingly fleshes out that 'the bulk of violence' occurred before the most inflammatory broadcasts and regionally far from them.[6] Hate radio 'only' constituted one dimension by which hardliners achieved dominance and persuaded individuals to join in attacks against Tutsi civilians. Finally, he concludes that hate radio mattered a lot in Rwanda, but the dynamics of genocide are considerably more complex than the popular image of 'Radio Machete' suggests (2007: 100). This observation is interesting as it reveals the interests of governmental policies in remaking and engineering the media realm, and can be read with Elwert's (2004) concept of conflict as a field of embedded social action. Avoidance is one of four poles that are characterised by differing levels of violence and embeddedness in social institutions (Elwert 2004: 30). As in the case of Rwanda, practices of avoidance are a particularly relevant way of navigating a highly restricted environment.

Different scholars have made use of Scott's famous 'weapons of the weak' (1985), zooming into processes of reconciliation and justice and demonstrating how, in their studies, peasants were able to articulate dissent by social practices of avoidance. Bodily experiences of violence and uncertain structural conditions made people wary of how to navigate shaky terrains (e.g. Newbury 2011; Thomson 2014; Zorbas 2009b). This avoidance is highly palpable in the media realm too, trying to find a way to engender media freedom while preventing hate speech. Nevertheless, even if direct censorship in the aftermath of genocide has loosened and changed to an allegedly self-regulated media body, alternative accounts within the political arena are still rarely heard (Straus and Waldorf 2011: 7). In Elwert's (2004: 30–36) conceptualisation of conflict, avoidance is defined as of little innovative potential as avoidance strategies are characterised by relatively weak embeddedness in social action. Practices of avoidance allow for individual coping, as is the case for the media practitioners, yet the causes of conflict remain untouched and perpetuate, with the potential to explode (Elwert 2004: 31). Reconnecting these theoretical reflections to the Rwandan policy-maker quoted at the beginning of this section provides insights into the practices of an enforced formation of collective identity in Rwanda. Cultural approaches that generalise about a lacking 'culture of discussion' frame a relatively restricted space of expression for media practitioners and civil society as they purport assumed guidelines for reporting. However, this space can obviously be challenged; given the authoritarian nature of the Rwandan state, the room for manoeuvre is limited, which favours practices of avoidance in general.

Rewriting the Past with the Help of Media

When in 1994, the RPF took power, Rwanda and its media sector were devastated: more than fifty journalists were killed, others had fled or went to prison under the RPF's regime. Printing houses were heavily damaged and the whole press sector only slowly recovered between 1994 and 2001 (Frère 2011):

> After 1994 it was really difficult. We had only the national radio and only some few journals. All of what happened around the media before, now complicates the way for us journalists today. We are the new generation of journalists (laughter). Really, for the new media the situation presented itself as chaotic. We were afraid of getting into trouble. As RTLM [radio station] and Kangura [journal] had their weird role in the genocide, the government said that the media is not serious. We had to start in the media sector from scratch ... After the genocide everybody mistrusted the media as they were used during the genocide as tool for mobilisation. And you need to know that the mentality of us Rwandans is, you know, if you listen to the radio, they think, 'ah, this is true'. But during the genocide it was not the media, it was the journalists who did all the bad things. So after the genocide it was very difficult to find independent media. Every news, everything was revised again and again until it was purified. Not easy at all. (Media practitioner/radio journalist, personal communication, 14 June 2013)

This statement by a radio journalist who had worked for the Rwandan state hints at the way in which many journalists appropriated and experienced this process of transformation. My interlocutors often alluded to themselves as a 'new generation' that emerged out of the void of role models and are still seeking tentatively their position in today's media sector. Commentary on patron–client relations, paternal rhetoric and relations of dependency came up in many conversations I had with different media practitioners (either working for state media, private enterprises or international nongovernmental organisations (NGOs)) who described the Rwandan media landscape as in 'its infancy', 'lacking mothers and fathers' and 'waiting for maturity'. This exhibits the nexus between feelings of belonging and citizenship with the prevalent political regime. However, in informal talks, journalists often voiced how they felt used as *abamotsi*[7] (figuratively 'mouthpiece') while they wanted to be 'watchdogs of democracy' (Fieldnotes, 14 April 2013). Nevertheless, most Rwandan media practitioners acknowledge the specific situation of the media, and that it requires them to accept that some issues are taboo. Here, the rewriting of the past is closely connected to everyday realities of Rwanda's media sector.

The Official Part of the Record

The regulation of media has changed from the government to, at least in principle, a self-regulatory body in 2013; however, the state still shapes Rwanda's voices and the way in which media practitioners talk and remain silent. In Rwanda, freedom of the press and freedom of expression are not considered to be an absolute right, but rather a context-specific and conflict-sensitive right. According to Reyntjens (2010: 3), policy circles argue that the 'political framework of liberalisation at the start of civil war favoured the mobilization towards genocide'. In this line of argumentation, the implementation of censorship was a necessary means to reduce the potential of new ethnic fighting and preserve the population from manipulation. Referring to the liberalisation of the media landscape in the beginning of the 1990s, many policy-makers stated that 'too much freedom made people "tell whatever they wanted"' (Reyntjens 2010: 3). After the genocide, this legitimised the restrictions on the media sector and the suppression of civil society.

An independent media with a plurality of vibrant and accessible voices is propagated by the various institutions related to media in Rwanda (government institutions and NGOs alike). However, open venues for discussion are very limited, still referring to the particular historical context. A foreign journalist working in the Rwandan NGO realm with a local newspaper states:

> Normally, freedom of the press is a human right, anchored in the UN's Article 19 and as universal human right it should be universal and NOT context-specific. In Rwanda, the government officials emphasise that

there is no censorship, and they keep on saying that it's the journalists' fault if they do not dare to speak out or restrict themselves. They call it a 'virus in the profession'. I don't think this is the case. Of course, self-censorship exists, but certainly it is because of experiences of repression. It's not that journalists tend to declare 'OK, I know I am free but for the nation's sake this cannot be published'. This is nonsense. I experience this frequently in our editorial meetings. The journalists themselves state 'No, we can't bring this or that story'. So the argumentation of the government is not false and journalists commit self-censorship before problems and involvement may arise. So to say it's the journalists' fault is a perfidious argumentative strategy because the fear of journalists stems from somewhere. They are not stupid or prefer to restrict themselves even if not necessary, but because they know and fear what may happen. ((Foreign) NGO staff, personal communication, 29 April 2013)

That 'what may happen' refers to official policies that relate to the 2001 law on 'divisionism' (i.e. sectarianism), the 2003 law criminalising 'negationism' (i.e. the denial or minimisation of genocide) and the 2008 law criminalising 'genocide ideology',[8] which are also reflected in the Media Laws of 2003, 2009 and 2013 (Maina 2010). Within the framework of 'divisionism', 'negationism' and 'genocide ideology', the elimination of dissident voices and the imposition of the RPF's reading of history and truth was implemented in order to overcome the divisions of the past and construct a new Rwandan collective identity. Alternative accounts from inside or outside the country were heavily attacked (Buckley-Zistel 2009). Charges on 'genocide ideology' are defined broadly and inhibit any criticism of the government due to fear that the morale of the country would be undermined and would leave a void for political manipulation (Waldorf 2009: 118). Therefore, even if censorship has transformed into self-regulation or self-censorship, alternative accounts and the negation of ethnic diversity might bring about future problems (such as prison sentences) as potential public resentment is not articulated, but silenced away. Interestingly, this repeats Straus' (2007: 613) comment that in many cases, the Rwandan (rural/poor) population has been denied agency and has been criticised as believing everything they hear. This means that freedom of the press and freedom of speech remain suspicious. As a member of the MHC explained:

Integrating Article 19 is one thing, but implementing it is another. Media cannot flourish unregulatedly because of our past. Ideas can be more dangerous than guns. Media is a power, which needs to be regulated. Freedom of expression has to be exercised within the limits of the law; that is why media have the obligation of criticising positively and using freedom responsibly. (MHC staff, personal communication, 24 April 2013)

An academic expands on the same point during a conversation we had – that teaching theoretically about freedom of the press is a rather ambivalent experience as students tend to be stopped by their editors in practice when approaching a sensitive issue.

One of the most important points among the issues central to the reforms was the transformation of the state broadcaster (Office Rwandais d'Information (ORINFOR)) into a public broadcaster (Rwanda Broadcasting Agency (RBA)) and the enactment of the Access to Information Law, which had been adopted by the cabinet and put into effect in February 2013. In addition, a new media policy focusing on and supporting media self-regulation was passed with the stated intention of increasing the communication from the government and enhancing media development and capacity-building through the MHC. This was seen as promoting independence of the media and as an essential component of good governance and a precondition for durable economic, social and political development. Many journalists, policymakers and media trainers frequently state that they perceive progress in the media sector, and that regarding the country's legacy, they consider themselves on the right track. However, as a Rwandan NGO staff put it, 'the Rwandan mentality is still the mentality of the Legislator that still does not want to lose its grip on the media'. He considers this attitude as highly exaggerated as 'the genocide involved all sociopolitical realms, not only media. All the ministries, the police, the military, everybody was involved, not only media. I think the law is still too strict. However, I see light; the media sector is opening up a bit' (Rwandan NGO staff, personal communication, 20 May 2013).

The modified legal framework for the media, and most importantly for journalists, the shift from regulation to self-regulation includes more responsibility and professional work ethos. However, one of the major accusations of the legislator is that journalists lack skills (Frère 2007: 111). In capacity workshops, organised either by the MHC, NGOs or within the framework of academic training institutions, journalists 'learn' how to produce a balanced and objective story. Furthermore, this is enhanced through invitations to public institutions such as the National Unity and Reconciliation Commission (NURC):

> Q: When do you decide to have press conferences?
>
> A: When we prepare a big event. But as well when something happens we can't swallow, when people tell rumours. Last year for example, a newspaper published an article with a kind of discrimination. So, we invited all the journalists to a press conference and asked them to avoid similar publications which might promulgate discord, discrimination and divisionism.
>
> Q: Have you invited the journalist or the people who produced the newspaper?
>
> A: Unfortunately, the chief editor was already in prison, so there was nobody who could participate.
>
> Q: But what happened to the newspaper? Was it closed down?
>
> A: No, they just arrested the person who was responsible for this piece of divisionism. (NURC interview, 21 June 2013)

Meandering between media freedom on the one hand and the fight against genocide ideology and hate speech on the other hand leaves media practitioners in a shaky field. Even if officially, the government gave up its hard grip, broadly defined policies that lead to hard punishment might intimidate journalists. Sanctions mostly imply incarceration. However, there are many rumours about disappearances or even selective murders that cause fear and create a climate of suspicion among media practitioners. As the broad framework of these policies is flexible and open to interpretation, imagined consequences might surpass actual ones. Capacity trainings about producing balanced and objective stories offered by state institutions or (international) NGOs are therefore very much adjusted to what can be said and written upon in the local context – rewriting history while pretending peace, stability and reconciliation 'on' the record is complemented by everyday comments 'off-the-record'.

Everyday Routines of Self-Regulation and Self-Censorship

> Self-regulation is as old as media itself, but regulation is new and comes from history. Self-regulation comes from fear of media because of those in power. Don't criticize MTN (Mobile Telephone Networks group), it's our main sponsor. Don't criticize the government, you'll lose your accreditation. Journalists are still careful what they say publicly.
>
> —Media practitioner/newspaper journalist, personal communication, 24 May 2013

Obviously, journalists themselves are very much aware of the boundaries between what should be 'on' and what should remain 'off'-the-record. Referring to their stock of knowledge and to the 'doxa' that characterises everything that is taken for granted makes media practitioners (and ordinary people alike) evaluate which information can be shared with whom. Applying Bourdieu's appropriation of the phenomenological concept 'doxa' makes it possible to assess the ways in which power relations are maintained and normalised (Bourdieu 1977). Focusing on everyday practices from a background of practice theory provides a useful means of examining and understanding the meaning-making routines of media practitioners (Postill 2010: 19). Media practitioners' experiences of sanctions and intimidations make them cautious to expose themselves in openly critical stances. These would be laughed at by certain media practitioners loyal to the government, who would mock them for not being professional. Such discrepancies reveal ongoing tensions between the immediate and the imagined:

Q: What do you think about self-censorship?

A: Personally, I would say that there is more self-censorship than censorship. The people practice too much self-censorship because they are afraid of themselves. Everything is a taboo, everything is dangerous, you can't touch it, it's like fire. With our talk show, we demonstrated that everything is possible if the programme is designed properly. If you do it right, you can discuss. And we received a lot of calls from the authorities that we should continue, that people in Rwanda need this. So you see, everything seems to be a taboo but in reality it isn't. During the talk show we talked about 'Hutu' and 'Tutsi'. But we did it in a constructive manner. So, there is space to express oneself, but you have to take it, or better: you need to know how to take it. But sometimes people are manipulated. Everything is manipulated, so people fear. (Rwandan NGO staff, personal communication, 10 April 2013 – the interviewee was trained as a journalist but never practised the job and asked me to continue 'off-the-record')

'Self-censorship' alludes in this quote to 'lack of skills' of journalists, not trusting their own capacities, a lack of professionalism and social responsibility. But, as the NGO staff tries to demonstrate, if you organise a programme properly, everything can be realised 'constructively'. Interestingly, the journalist reiterates the official version, thereby reproducing the public agenda, but then asks me to continue talking 'off-the-record' and affirms unconsciously another kind of 'self-censorship': avoidance. Imagining future challenges, many media practitioners intentionally opt for the practice of avoidance, which is framed by one broadcast journalist as follows:

> Another strategy is avoidance. You will see that many journalists don't deal with politics. They prefer to report on sports or leisure. You cannot critique openly, you have to use codes and hide your critique. I mean, you can't say it frankly and address somebody directly. No, you have to do it in an indirect manner. But we can speak out even if we try not to get exposed too much. (Radio journalist, personal communication, 3 June 2013)

Most journalists therefore practise self-censorship and strategies of avoidance – which belong to the same social register – before serious threats may occur. Here, practices of avoidance could be read in Scott's sense (1985: 29) as weapons of the weak that 'represent a form of individual self-help' and help to avoid 'any direct confrontation with authority or with elite norms'. Avoidance may here reflect past experiences of violence and may deal with uncertain futures of imagined punishments in the case of disobedience or disagreeing with public transcripts. For example, in order to avoid problems but keep on performing the profession, many media practitioners chose a niche such as sports reporting that does not lead them too closely to politics. This underlines the co-constitution of media and conflict as these individual practices of avoidance in the media realm do not change the underlying conflict causes, but might perpetuate negative feelings or perceptions and inhibit a climate of reconciliation.

As the Rwandan media environment is vibrating, many new actors enter the stage and perceive the media mainly as an income-generating opportunity. A potentially delicate political agenda is substituted here by mere economic business interests. This shapes processes of collective identity formation profoundly as critical topics like structural inequalities are not tackled. The manifold perspectives on today's media sector by diverse social actors and audiences are represented in the following statement by a media manager from Radio Rwanda:

> We lent a hand in destroying our own country, we have seen that the people don't have faith in us because of what we did to them but we are coming a very long way … It's still a long journey, because most newspapers that you meet across the country are newspapers that just want to sell. They are not into helping our population to go past our history, educate them. But every time I meet with my newsroom, this is one thing I tell them 'hey you guys, every time you go to look for a story, remember

that you are going to report this story also to your parents ... Would it impact them negatively or would it kind of twist their mind or improve their living standards?' ... If I write to advocate for people to get access to water, electricity, roads, to make them form decisions, why would I tell them that the army is going to break down in the next two or three days? Why would I tell them there is a coup d'état? Why would I tell them to revolt against their government? I really want to report to them stories that really help them improve their living standards, get access to markets, infrastructure, those kind of things people want to hear ... But when you talk about politics, nobody cares ... It doesn't affect their daily lives directly. But if you tell them there is a new fertiliser coming to their area, everybody will send messages 'how can we get access, how can we meet this woman'. We really need to focus on these kinds of stories, none of them is scandalous and that is what people want. Let them think for themselves and let them get what they want. So it's a process we just need to teach, and experience is the best teacher. (Media manager, personal communication, 21 June 2013)

This quote forcefully demonstrates the official direction of the Rwandan media landscape: towards depoliticisation and a rewriting of history. The argument of taking listeners' feedback and interests seriously appears to be progressive, but is somewhat twisted as it omits to mention that the discussion of a plural political realm still appears to be a taboo and that listeners from the rural context avoid commenting on politics as much as other people. However, at the same time, this excerpt provides subtle and important insights from a practice approach. Even in uncertain times, an all-too-often silenced group chooses when and where to get 'on' the record by calling in to radio shows or sending text messages asking for further information on certain topics. That not all topics are equally desirable seems to confirm a difficult walk on the tightrope of media practitioners and audiences alike.

Visions and Velocity

Culturalist approaches, that is to say focusing on seemingly culturally shaped traits, are dominant in Rwanda in terms of blaming a 'Rwandan culture of obedience' for leading to the genocide (Zorbas 2009a: 99, 226). However, as Straus and Waldorf (2011: 9) state, the RPF government's dynamics of social engineering and intimidation have strongly contributed to maintain these routines of obedience, avoidance and silence. This demonstrates the interplay between media and conflict on social practices in the media realm where many hidden transcripts prevail. As the media sector is particularly exposed, critics are harsh and punishment is severe, there is not much leeway in expressing one's dissent. A small glimpse into media practitioners' worlds of understanding and experience has shown in this chapter how the plea to answer 'off-the-record' indicates a fast-shifting social and political environment where one's framework of interpretation is to be carefully adjusted. In order to approach uncertain conditions, a practice approach proves highly relevant to analyse the subtle ways of knowledge production and the different ways in which everyday uncertainty is dealt with.

In the aftermath of genocide, the Rwandan government has developed many answers to the challenges the country has faced, bringing international acclaim to President Kagame for being a 'visionary leader' (Tony Blair) or being 'one of the greatest leaders of our time' (Bill Clinton) (Smith 2012). The development and implementation of original and transformative policies have boosted many sectors of the country. Promoting democratic governance in a post-conflict society entails re-creating a wide array of institutions against the backdrop of sociopolitical polarisation. Rwanda has been undergoing a process of rapid economic development often praised by international donors as 'exemplary' and 'visionary'. In this scenario, the media hold significant potential for encounter and a critical discussion of 'national unity' (Frère 2007: 3) and with the new media laws, the sector is booming.

However, one of the biggest challenges remains how to engage in media freedom while preventing hate speech. Here, the recent shift towards a conducive political and legal environment – from strict regulation of the media to the recently adopted self-regulation of journalists and from censorship to journalistic self-censorship as rhetoric of social responsibility – is only one example of a seeming opening of Rwanda's media realm. Yet, despite a massive change in regulations, only very few alternative voices can be heard. This is reflected in the fact that many journalists avoid covering the political realm critically, regarding it as too risky. Control over local voices as well as the mantra that media freedom can never be 'absolute' in order to avoid a new genocide hinder a frank dialogue in Rwanda. Self-censorship in this regard has to be read as a way of protecting oneself. This makes a far-reaching transformation of the media landscape towards international standards doubtful, as the majority of well-trained journalists leave the profession due to frustrations caused by political pressure and/or better earning opportunities in NGOs, the PR sector or governmental institutions. Nevertheless, media observers and media professionals in Rwanda note a slow but steady evolution of the local setting. Particularly pointing at the new media laws, some journalists feel like vanguards, stating that they want to be remembered for leaving 'marks not scars', while considering the media landscape as 'virgin territory' and 'plein de possibilités' (full of possibilities). Yet, the fluidity and velocity with which people get nominated to new positions, the realities and restrictions of doing one's job and following one's passion in an economically precarious context where journalists switch from 'on' to 'off-the-record' in case of doubts, where doors are closed, voices lowered and political topics avoided, suggest that the media environment still faces many challenges.

In this sense, approaching perceptions and experiences of Rwanda's media practitioners ethnographically has demonstrated how their lifeworlds are shaped by and simultaneously shape practices of avoidance on an everyday basis. The practice approach proves useful in terms of shedding light on the discrepancies between the seemingly successful recovery of the Rwandan post-genocide state, while revealing some tensions between the immediate and the imagined. Finally, the theorisation of conflict and media from a practice perspective helps us to get a grip on questions of continuity and change, indicating that processes of social transformation and reconciliation face a difficult future as their social embeddedness is rather weak in the Rwandan context.

Silke Oldenburg is Senior Lecturer at the Institute for Social Anthropology at the University of Basel. She obtained her Ph.D. from the University of Bayreuth, and held postdoctoral and visiting fellowships at the University of Boulder and Columbia University. Her research interests include the anthropology of media and journalism, urban anthropology and political anthropology, with a particular focus on aspects of everyday life within contexts of protracted violent conflict. Her ethnographic work concentrates on the Great Lakes Region (Democratic Republic of Congo and Rwanda) and the Andes (Colombia and Venezuela).

Notes

1. The genocide of 1994 was the endpoint of a deadly four-year civil war between the two dominant ethnic groups of Hutu and Tutsi. Without having the space to elaborate on the genesis of genocide and conflict dynamics, most authors chime in with strong local mobilisational capacity and history of the ethnic categorisation between the two ethnic groups of Hutu and Tutsi, and uncertainty and fear in a situation of economic scarcity and regional antagonism (e.g. Chrétien 1995; Hintjens 1999; Newbury 1988; Pottier 2002). The literature on the role of the media in instigating and fuelling genocide is vast, with a particular focus on the role of the radio (e.g. Kirschke 1996; Li 2004; McNulty 1999; Thompson 2007).

2. Ethnographic fieldwork was carried out between March and June 2013, mainly in Kigali. The material derives from interaction with media practitioners in the broad sense: journalists, policy-makers, national and international NGO staff, and academics teaching and studying journalism and communication at university level. I gathered the material during workshops and conferences, social gatherings and by accompanying journalists on their reportages and consulting documents in media-related public institutions. The empirical data in the form of interview quotes or fieldnotes are rendered anonymous and contain the positions of my interlocutors. Specific to Rwanda's context is that many trained journalists entered alternative employment. I made this visible in highlighting my interlocutors' professional identities at the end of the respective extract. The scope of my data is exclusively on 'traditional media' (e.g. newspapers and radio). It would be interesting to see how the use of social media has altered the Rwandan media landscape in the last five years.
3. This lacking 'culture of debate' has been raised in many studies (e.g. Prunier 1995: 245; Willame 1995: 108; Zorbas 2009a: 211–237). Often it is referred to as a particular 'Rwandan tradition of obedience' (e.g. Zorbas 2009a: 5).
4. In March 2013, President Kagame assented to a new media law that introduced the principle of media self-regulation (with the print media entirely self-regulated and the broadcast media partially self-regulated). This means that ten years after its creation as High Council of the Press in 2003, the MHC is virtually out of media regulation but enhances its capacity-building activities.
5. RTLM was a private broadcast radio, operating from 1993 to 1994.
6. He shows the radio's 'marginal impact' close to Rwanda's capital Kigali and the reinforcement of stereotypical ethnic divisions.
7. The *abamotsi* was the herald to the former Rwandan kings and was frequently translated to me as 'mouthpiece' in today's media landscape.
8. Divisionism is treated in Law N° 47/2001, *Official Gazette of the Republic of Rwanda*, 15 February 2002, 'genocide ideology' Law N° 18 of July 2008 and 'negationism' in Law N° 33, September 2003. Genocide ideology is defined as 'a set of ideas or representations whose major role is to stir up hatred and create a pernicious atmosphere favouring the implementation and legitimization of the persecution and elimination of a category of the population'.

References

Alber, E. 2004. 'Meidung als Modus des Umgangs mit Konflikten', in J. Eckert (ed.), *Kultur und soziale Praxis. Anthropologie der Konflikte: Georg Elwerts konflikttheoretische Thesen in der Diskussion*. Bielefeld: transcript-Verlag, pp. 169–85.

Bourdieu, P. 1977. *Outline of a Theory of Practice*. Cambridge: Cambridge University Press.

Bräuchler, B., and J. Postill (eds). 2010. *Theorising Media and Practice*. New York: Berghahn Books.

Buckley-Zistel, S. 2009. 'Nation, Narration, Unification? The Politics of History Teaching After the Rwandan Genocide', *Journal of Genocide Research* 11(1): 31–53.

Burnet, J.E. 2009. 'Whose Genocide? Whose Truth? Representations of Victim and Perpetrator in Rwanda', in A.L. Hinton and K.L. O'Neill (eds), *Genocide: Truth, Memory, and Representation*. Durham, NC: Duke University Press, pp. 80–11.

Carver, R. 2000. 'Broadcasting and Political Transition: Rwanda and Beyond', in R. Fardon (ed.), *African Broadcast Cultures: Radio in Transition*. Oxford: James Currey, pp. 188–97.

Chrétien, J.-P. 1995. *Rwanda: Les Médias du Génocide*. Paris: Karthala.

Elwert, G. 2004. 'Anthropologische Perspektiven auf Konflikt', in J. Eckert (ed.), *Anthropologie der Konflikte: Georg Elwerts konflikttheoretische Thesen in der Diskussion*. Bielefeld: transcript, pp. 26–38.

Freedom House. 2017. Rwanda Country Profile. Retrieved 22 October 2019 from https://freedomhouse.org/report/freedom-press/2017/rwanda.

Frère, M.-S. 2007. *The Media and Conflicts in Central Africa*. Boulder, CO: Lynne Rienner.

———. 2011. 'Covering Post-conflict Elections: Challenges for the Media in Central Africa', *Africa Spectrum* 1: 3–32.

Guyer, J. et al. 2010. 'Introduction: Number as Inventive Frontier', *Anthropological Theory* 10(1–2): 36–61.

Häberlein, T. 2007. 'Das abgewandte Gesicht: Konflikt und Meidung in Zuunchangai Sum (Mongolei)', *Zeitschrift für Ethnologie* 132(2): 287–314.

Hintjens. H.M. 1999. 'Explaining the 1994 Genocide in Rwanda', *Journal of Modern African Studies* 37: 241–86.

Kirschke, L. 1996. *Broadcasting Genocide: Censorship, Propaganda and State Sponsored Violence in Rwanda, 1990–1994*. London: Article 19.

Law N° 04/2013 of 08/02/2013 Relating to Access to Information, Article 1. Official Gazette N° 10 of 11 March 2013.

Li, D. 2004. 'Echoes of Violence: Considerations of Radio and Genocide in Rwanda', *Journal of Genocide Research* 6(2): 9–27.

Maina, H. 2010. *Legal, Policy and Regulatory Framework for the Media in Rwanda*. London: Article 19.

McNulty, M. 1999. 'Media Ethnization and the International Response to War and Genocide in Rwanda', in T. Allen and J. Seaton (eds), *The Media of Conflict: War Reporting and Representations of Ethnic Violence*. New York: Zed Books, pp. 268–86.

Newbury, C. 1988. *The Cohesion of Oppression: Clientship and Ethnicity in Rwanda, 1860–1960*. New York: Columbian University Press.

———. 2011. 'High Modernism at the Ground Level: The *Imidugudu* Policy in Rwanda', in S. Straus and L. Waldorf (eds), *Remaking Rwanda: State-Building and Human Rights after Mass Violence*. Wisconsin: University of Wisconsin Press, pp. 223–39.

Postill, J. 2010. 'Introduction: Theorising Media and Practice', in B. Bräuchler and J. Postill (eds), *Theorising Media and Practice*. New York: Berghahn Books, pp. 1–32.

Pottier, J. 2002. *Re-imagining Rwanda: Conflict, Survival and Disinformation in the Late Twentieth Century*. Cambridge: Cambridge University Press.

Prunier, G. 1995. *The Rwanda Crisis: History of a Genocide*. London: Hurst.

Purdeková, A. 2011. '"If I am Not Here, There are So Many Eyes": Surveillance and State Reach in Rwanda', *Journal of Modern African Studies* 49(3): 475–97.

Reporters without Borders. 2018. 'Rwanda'. Retrieved 22 October 2019 from https://rsf.org/en/rwanda.

Reyntjens, F. 2010. 'Constructing the Truth, Dealing with Dissent, Domesticating the World: Governance in Post-genocide Rwanda', *African Affairs* 438: 1–34.

Scott, J.C. 1985. *Weapons of the Weak: Everyday Forms of Peasant Resistance*. New Haven: Yale University Press.

Smith, D. 2012. 'Paul Kagame's Rwanda: African Success Story or Authoritarian State?', *The Guardian*, 12 October. Retrieved 22 October 2019 from https://www.theguardian.com/world/2012/oct/10/paul-kagame-rwanda-success-authoritarian.

Straus, S. 2007. 'What Is the Relationship between Hate Radio and Violence? Rethinking Rwanda's "Radio Machete"', *Politics and Society* 35(4): 609–37.

Straus, S., and L. Waldorf. 2011. 'Introduction. Seeing Like a Post-conflict State', in S. Straus and L. Waldorf (eds), *Remaking Rwanda: State-Building and Human Rights after Mass Violence*. Wisconsin: University of Wisconsin Press, pp. 3–21.

Thompson, A. 2007. *The Media and the Rwandan Genocide*. London: Pluto Press.

Thomson, S. 2014. *Whispering Truth to Power: Everyday Resistance to Reconciliation in Postgenocide Rwanda*. Madison: University of Wisconsin Press.

Waldorf, L. 2009. 'Revisiting Hotel Rwanda: Genocide Ideology, Reconciliation, and Rescuers', *Journal of Genocide Research* 11(1): 101–25.

Willame, J. C. 1995. *Aux Sources de l'Hécatombe Rwandaise*. Paris: L'Harmattan.

Zorbas, E. 2009a. 'Reconciliation in Postgenocide Rwanda: Discourse and Practice', Ph.D. dissertation. London: LSE.

———. 2009b. 'What Does Reconciliation after Genocide Mean? Public Transcripts and Hidden Transcripts in Post-genocide Rwanda', *Journal of Genocide Research* 11(1): 127–47.

CHAPTER 14

From War to Peace in Indonesia

Transforming Media and Society

Birgit Bräuchler

Johan Galtung and others have argued that reconciliation and peace have attracted much less attention from the media than war and conflict (e.g. Cottle 2006).[1] Taking the Moluccan society's transition from violent conflict to peace, this chapter[2] discusses how media in Indonesia can contribute both to the fragmentation and the unification of society. It illustrates how society and media are interdependent, and how not only conflict and media but also media and peace are co-constitutive, and it provides a comprehensive analysis of these processes based on a context-oriented, integrative and agency-oriented approach to media studies.

Indonesia's Transforming Media Scene

In an archipelagic nation like Indonesia, the media are a key element in creating and sustaining a national identity. As Anderson (1983) has prominently argued, the rise of print media played a primary role in the formation of the nation as 'imagined community'. Under the authoritarian Suharto regime, news media in Indonesia were subjected to strict control and censorship. They served to promote the government's and the military's idea of a 'national culture' and their interpretation of news, history and the state (Sen and Hill 2000). After the regime's step-down in 1998, the Department of Information was closed and the freedom of the press was enacted as an essential part of the democratisation of the country (Pemerintah Republik Indonesia

1999). The loosening of authoritarian constraints upon the media and its subsequent liberalisation resulted in an explosion in the number of dailies, journals, radio and TV stations throughout the country. In addition, internet access rapidly increased. Such advances have 'dramatic consequences for the political and social fabric of Indonesia and Southeast Asia as a whole' (Woodier 2006: 42) and can challenge established power structures and authorities. But the new developments fostered not only democratisation, but also competition and social fragmentation. Media – the former cornerstone of national unity – became increasingly used by different interest groups and as weapons in the many regional conflicts in the post-Suharto era. 'Media is a double-edged sword' (Howard 2005: 21).

Media, Conflict and Peace

The marriage of conflict and media has been a quite happy and successful one for many decades now. Media can be used in various ways and for various objectives. The coverage in local, national and international media decisively influences local conflicts and mass violence, and the way in which outside observers perceive and react to them (see e.g. Allen and Seaton 1999; Hudson and Stanier 1998; Knightley 1975). Media can be used to deceive the public about a conflict's 'real' causes and to construct a unified narrative (Pottier 2003). The rise of new media technologies has even transformed conflicts into global spectacles: images of conflicts from all over the world are brought right into homes, be it on TV or the internet, in the newspaper or on the radio.[3] But media are not only used to report about conflicts; they are increasingly employed as weapons by warring parties.[4] Cottle's term 'mediatized conflicts' tries to express the multiplicity of these media processes in which 'conflicts are variously defined, framed and visualized, elaborated, narrativized and evaluated; moralized, deliberated and contested; amplified and promoted or dampened and reconciled; conducted and symbolized; enacted and performed' (Cottle 2006: 185). Importantly, and as emphasised in the Introduction to this volume, 'mediatised' needs to be understood not in the sense of how media do things with conflicts, but how media are co-constitutive of conflict. As I will show, the internet and 'small media' such as leaflets, graffiti and locally produced video CDs play as much of a role in those 'mediatised conflicts' as the more conventional mainstream media. They enable common people, beyond the mainstream media conglomerates, to participate in media production and participation, a trend that has increased tremendously through the advent of the following web generations and social media.

The news media pay much less attention to reconciliation and peace than to conflict (Cottle 2006: 100). Images of conflict seem to be much easier to convey than images of reconciliation and peace. Similarly, very few scholars have analysed how media may be used to foster or are co-constitutive of peace. Nevertheless, media can demonstrably be an important means in peace and reconciliation processes. As Howard et al. argue, media are an 'extremely versatile *tool*' that can be used not only 'to deconstruct and break down and indeed demolish existing structures', but also 'to construct and repair and rebuild' (Howard et al. 2005: 81). 'Peace journalism' was a term introduced by Galtung in the 1960s and then further developed in the following decades (see e.g. Lynch and McGoldrick 2001). Galtung criticised the prevailing style of journalism that focused on violence and the negative side of conflict, and was thus more one-sided propaganda than a neutral means to convey 'the truth' about a conflict. Peace journalism, on the contrary, is supposed not to differentiate between 'us' and 'them', but to rehumanise people and emphasise that all had suffered in the conflict, and that it was now time to consider how to solve the conflict and the problems that triggered it. Peace journalism tries to explore the conflict's dynamics, uncover the truth on both sides, highlight integrative initiatives that secure common ground between the parties and thus foster dialogue and peace.[5] Most of the literature on peace journalism and related topics is highly policy-oriented and application-oriented.

As in the study of media and conflict (see Bräuchler and Budka, this volume), a major shortcoming in the studies on peace journalism is that they typically focus on one type of media and, at least at the time of writing the original version of this chapter, institutionalised media structures and rarely include grassroots agencies into their analyses. What I want to argue for in this chapter, using the Moluccan case, is a more integrative perspective on local media that emphasises the link between the various media and the active appropriation of the media by a broad variety of actors, including traditionally media-affine people such as journalists and ordinary citizens – a trend that has been further intensified through social media.

Integration, Agency and Communication

A study that only focused on one type of media would run the risk of not appreciating the complex media environment in situations of conflict and peace-making; it might also fail to capture the impact of those people who have access to some media, but not to the specific form of media under analysis. At the time of writing this chapter (but with similar trends today), many studies researching conflict and media focused on news media, the press, radio or TV stations, to which most local people might have no access (see e.g. Allen and Seaton 1999; Hussain 2016; Vladisavljević 2015). Although these (often) national media do exert their influence on local conflicts, in an archipelagic state like Indonesia, local media play a much bigger role in conflicts carried out far away from the centre – in particular in a pre-social media era. Gatekeepers of local media such as local newspapers and radio stations are often embedded in the local population and thus are much more empathetic to their aspirations. Other local media such as leaflets, graffiti, posters and video CDs are practically available to anybody.

We not only need to consider the mainstream media and new media technologies, but also 'the potential of alternative "old" media' (Cole 2006a: 118). The differentiation of media producers, media activists and (passive) recipients of media messages is rather counterproductive in contemporary contexts of conflict. As the 'practice turn' in social theory (e.g. Ortner 2006; Schatzki, Knorr Cetina and Savigny 2001) and its growing influence on media anthropology (e.g. Bräuchler and Postill 2010) suggest, common people are not locked up in predetermined and fixed media structures and hierarchies, but can creatively appropriate media and shape the media space. Moreover, media-oriented practices are inseparably linked with other social practices, in our case in conflict and peace processes (for a more in-depth discussion, see Bräuchler and Budka, this volume). As Couldry argues, a main objective of a practice-oriented media anthropology is 'mapping the complexity of media-saturated cultures where the discreteness of audience practices can no longer be assumed' (Couldry 2004: 115). This is not to say that power and hierarchy no longer have a role to play when it comes to media access, but we have to investigate also how 'the resource-poor and institutionally powerless ... are apt to resort to creative tactics and/or turn to new media and modes of communication in their bid to gain media space and symbolically counter ingrained imbalances of power' (Cottle 2006: 2).

Media are part of a much larger communicative repertoire (*kommunikativer Haushalt*; see Luckmann 1988) that is heavily determined by local collective memories, the local sociocultural context and its interplay with the broader national and international environment. To achieve peace, conflicts have to be transformed through the mobilisation of other registers of the communicative repertoire. The most important aspect is how one group identifies itself and then refers to their opponent in a conflict. To overcome a conflict, the practices of how to address and characterise 'the other' have to be altered, and a sense of shared interest and commonality created.[6] Peace journalism builds on this transformative potential. However, not only journalism but also the whole media scene has to undergo this transformation.

For the rest of this chapter, we turn to the Moluccas (or Maluku in Indonesian) to understand the role that media and various media actors played in the conflict and peace process, how they interacted, and how transformations within society and media are interlinked.

The Moluccan Conflict

Following a quarrel between a Christian bus driver and a Muslim passenger in Ambon City on 19 January 1999, a violent conflict was fought in Maluku from 1999 until 2003. While the exact number of deaths (estimated between 8,000 and 15,000) may never be known, around 700,000 people – almost a third of the Moluccan population – had to flee temporarily, and hundreds of churches and mosques were destroyed. Although scholars like Aditjondro (2001) and Tomagola (in Salampessy and Husain 2001) suspect that members of the former Suharto regime and the military whose political influence was curbed after Suharto fell were the driving force behind the Moluccan conflict, the clashes were generally depicted as framed with religious symbolism from the beginning. The incident described above took place on Idul Fitri, the end of the Muslim fasting month of Ramadan, and shortly after that, rumours spread that the biggest mosque and largest church on Ambon Island had been set on fire. In 2000, the radical Muslim Communication Forum of the Followers of the Sunnah and the Community of the Prophet (Forum Komunikasi Ahlus Sunnah wal Jama'ah – FKAWJ) sent its military wing, the Laskar Jihad (Holy Warriors), to Maluku in order to help their coreligionists, preserve them from their alleged extinction and fight Moluccan separatism that the FKAWJ equated with the Moluccan Church and Christianity.[7] This further contributed to the oversimplified depiction of the Moluccan conflict as a religious war, and reinforced a widespread image of fundamentalist Islam, resurgent worldwide. Moluccan society became divided along religious lines between Muslims and Christians. Neutrality was interpreted as betrayal and was thus often fatal.[8]

Media in the Moluccan Conflict

The media became a crucial factor in enforcing the religious dichotomisation of Moluccan society.[9] Newspapers, radio and TV stations were either classified as Muslim or Christian. With a few exceptions (e.g. Bräuchler 2003, 2013; Joseph 2000; Spyer 2002b),[10] in the Moluccan context, scholars have paid very little attention to the role of media as an important means to enforce conflict lines and trigger new clashes – be it through the expansion of the conflict into the internet, the local press, TV or radio stations, books or tabloids, pamphlets or graffiti, pictures or videos. Through media, people involved in the conflict could express their emotions and fight each other; media became tools to manipulate people and thus influence the conflict dynamics – clear evidence for the co-constitutiveness of media and conflict.[11]

The general explosion of media in the post-Suharto era coincided with the outbreak of the Moluccan conflict. Immediately before the start of the conflict there was only one daily newspaper in Maluku, *Suara Maluku* (*SM*). *SM* had been published with intermissions since 1953. It was incorporated into the Jawa Pos Group in 1993, leaving the consortium in 2003 (Passal 2007: 23). In the first year of the conflict, two new dailies emerged: *Ambon Ekspres* (*AE*) in July 1999 and *Siwalima* (*SL*) in October 1999. *SM* was located in a Christian area, which made it difficult, if not impossible, for its Muslim staff to come to the office during the conflict. At the same time, the remaining Christian journalists could not get access to events that took place in the Muslim area or to Muslim informants. This necessarily resulted in a one-sided, Christian-focused reporting. That was when Dahlan Iskan, chief of Jawa Pos Group, decided to start a new daily in Ambon, *Ambon Ekspres*, to give Muslim journalists the chance to work and write about the situation in Maluku.[12] The reporting in *SM* and *AE* became increasingly divergent. *Siwalima* was set up few months later in the Christian area but with the intention of providing a unifying peace press and to unite Christian and Muslim journalists. However, this proved to be rather unfeasible and *SL* turned into the most polarised of these three dailies, clearly siding with the Christians.[13] *SM* and *SL* became the mouthpiece for the Christians, *AE* for the Muslims. As some of these dailies' journalists later put it, these media not only heated up the conflict, but also turned it into a war between journalists. Despite their often good intentions, the journalists could not manage to bridge the religious divide. In part this may have been because the process of training quality journalists could not keep up with the post-Suharto media boom. Most journalists in these newspapers had little media experience and underwent no professional training prior to joining the papers. They were trained briefly by the more senior staff and then left to learn on the job. In a conflict situation where it was a challenge for even trained journalists to provide neutral reporting, this lack of experience proved destructive.

Muslims reproached the national television station TVRI (TV of the Republic of Indonesia) and the national radio station RRI (Radio of the Republic of Indonesia) for being pro-Christian; yet, although both stations had their main offices in Christian areas, they tried hard to cover the Muslim perspective. RRI tried to keep in touch with Muslim colleagues by telephone; TVRI continued to have a Muslim and a Christian crew. But the conflict conditions and the strict boundary lines between communities made it very difficult to cover both sides comprehensively (for the media landscape, especially the press, during the conflict see Eriyanto 2003; Joseph 2000; Southeast Asian Press Alliance 2002). The government even made efforts to use television as a peace medium by sponsoring the so-called *Obet-and-Acang* spot, which was broadcast on national TV and several commercial channels in 1999 a short while after the conflict had broken out (Spyer 2002a: 29). The narrative of this *Obet-and-Acang* reconciliation 'advertisement' focused on the violent disruption of a friendship between two Ambonese children whose names – and nicknames – reflect their different religious affiliations – Robert ('Obet') and Hasan ('Acang'). They search for each other in the smoke and eventually, find and embrace each other. But the spot did not have the desired effect: 'Instead, "Obet" and "Acang" have become Maluku's favourite slang for "Christian" and "Moslem", a hostile shorthand to delineate us and them', which are used next to the slang 'whites' (Muslim) and 'reds' (Christian), after the headdresses the fighters wear, or the sarcastic local jibes 'Israeli' (Christian) and 'Palestinian' (Muslim) (International Crisis Group 2000: 4).

During the conflict new radio stations emerged, the most prominent being the extremely provocative and radical station run by the FKAWJ in Ambon on 105.5 FM: Suara Perjuangan Muslimin Maluku (SPMM – the Moluccan Muslims' Voice of Struggle). SPMM was on air daily from 10 p.m. until 7 a.m., broadcast news every half hour and otherwise recitations of the Koran (mostly verses that legitimised the Laskar Jihad's mission in Maluku) and lectures on religious issues very much coloured by the FKAWJ's ideology. The predecessor of SPMM was Gema Suara Maluku (GSM – Reverberation of the Muslim Voice), the first radio station of the Muslim community in Ambon City that was initiated in August 2000 by the Chief of the Information Department of the FKAWJ, Abdul Hadi, together with local Muslims in order to counter what they regarded as the mischievous information offered by existing Christian private radio stations, TVRI, RRI, *Siwalima*, *Suara Maluku* and even *Ambon Ekspres*. According to the FKAWJ, GSM provided Muslims with another effective weapon in their struggle against the Christians. It was used not only to provide information for the Muslims, but also to broadcast Friday speeches from the famous Al-Fatah mosque in Ambon City and speeches given by the FKAWJ's leader, Ja'far Umar Thalib. When SPMM took over from GSM, the programme was even more radicalised. The station called upon the whole Muslim community to refrain from any interactions whatsoever with Christians and to join the jihad against a worldwide Judeo-Christian conspiracy and the (Christian) South Moluccan Republic (RMS) militia allegedly destroying the Indonesian state.[14]

The Christian side got extremely worried about the highly provocative character of SPMM and asked the local government to shut it down, but in vain. Some of SPMM's equipment was destroyed in a military raid, but shortly after, the station was back on air. The radio was most popular among uneducated Muslims, who often gathered in the streets and cafés to listen to SPMM's news. The FKAWJ considered media most important for its missionary, social and educational endeavours, its information politics in the Moluccan conflict and as a weapon against the Christians. In order to cover all levels of society and to reach as many people as possible, the FKAWJ spread its messages not only via radio, but also on the internet,[15] via a tabloid called *Laskar Jihad Ahlus Sunnah Wal Jamaah*,[16] bulletins and leaflets,[17] booklets and books (e.g. Syafruddin and Prasetyo 2001; Thalib 2000, 2001).[18] These books were sold at newspaper stalls in Muslim areas together with the publications of Rustam Kastor, a former general who was the main local ideologue behind the Muslims' accusation against the Christians and the Church, regarded by him as seeking a separate Moluccan state. Leaflets were also used by other people or groups to spread their views and, along with rumours, often triggered new waves of violence (e.g. Spyer 2002a). The most prominent example is a leaflet, distributed in Tidore in North Maluku in November 1999, allegedly written by a pastor who 'revealed' in it the plan to Christianise North Maluku. Although both the church and the pastor repeatedly rejected these accusations, the deceptive leaflet triggered massive acts of violence against the local Christian population in the north (see Nanere 2000).

The FKAWJ's deployment of the media reflects the Moluccan conflict's multifaceted media scene, in which 'small media' (e.g. Ginsburg, Abu-Lughod and Larkin 2002) and the internet play as big a role as the daily newspapers. Ambon City and conflict-affected villages were plastered with graffiti, scrawled on the walls of destroyed buildings. 'Making the stones speak' (Peteet 1996: 144) became a very effective and visible means of expressing one's feelings, to discredit and insult the other side, and to provide symbols with which one can identify or that depict the artist as part of a wider community that could protect him or her in the conflict. There were, for example, slogans insulting Jesus or Mohammed, such as *Jesus pemabuk* (Jesus is a drunkard) or *Mohammed berzina* (Muhammed commits adultery), which would not only offend Moluccan Christians or Muslims, but also Christian and Muslim communities worldwide. The same applies to inscriptions that attack the religious 'other', such as *Islam Muka Lonte* (Islam has the face of a whore), or depict the Moluccan Christians as *kafir* (infidels). Muslim murals regarding *satu ummat* (one community) imply that Moluccan Muslims are part of an Islamic world community to which they can turn for support. Depictions of the Star of David in Christian areas compare their situation with the Jews in Israel.

In a much more direct though not as accessible way, the parties to the conflict visualised their experiences, their sufferings and the other side's cruelty and viciousness through locally produced and distributed videos.[19] Pictures used in these videos and on the internet often depicted the physical destruction of the conflict and pictures of victims: bloody images with often badly mutilated bodies. These pictures are much more effective in arousing emotions than words and would have never been accepted for publication in the mainstream Indonesian press. As Cottle (2006: 95) argues, 'showing images of body horror' does not automatically 'produce anti-war sentiments', rather the opposite. Pictures of a massacre of hundreds of Muslims who had sought refuge in a mosque in North Maluku when circulated on Java massively angered the Muslim community there and prompted the FKAWJ to send the Laskar Jihad to Maluku. More generally, as Spyer (2002a: 24) suggests, 'too little heed is given to the work of the imagination and the construction of knowledge in all of this and, specifically, to how these compel and propel particular actions and shape those who carry them out'. The various media not only refer to what happened, but also appeal to people's fantasy and imagination regarding what might (or is about to) happen, thus increasing tension and a dangerous alertness that can easily turn into another cycle of violence.

Conflict videos were produced not only as propaganda material to split society further and legitimise more violence, but also as part of campaigns to seek outside help to stop the conflict. Masariku Network was set up by a group of (Protestant) Moluccans in Jakarta and Ambon in order to document the violence, exchange information among their members in Maluku and abroad, deliver proof of who is involved in the violence (such as the Laskar Jihad and the military), raise international awareness of what is happening in Maluku, and thus build an advocacy and fundraising network that could help end the conflict and reconcile the parties. Masariku set up an online mailing list, collected eyewitness reports, went to many hot spots, took thousands of pictures, put them online, circulated them on CD and also produced documentary campaign videos under conditions that were often very dangerous. Although these videos try to take an objective stance by emphasising the suffering of the whole Moluccan population, the role of the military and of outsiders in triggering the conflict and setting Christians and Muslims against each other, they inevitably represented a Christian perspective.

The Catholics also actively used the media to circulate information about the violence locally as well as internationally, and to seek support, particularly after the arrival of the Laskar Jihad. The Crisis Centre of the Diocese of Ambon (CCDA) first used faxes and then the internet to spread their almost daily (English) reports on the conflict to an international (mostly Christian) audience. Like the Laskar Jihad and the Crisis Centre of the Protestant Church, the CCDA was confronted with an increasing number of daily requests and enquiries, and the only way to deal with these in an effective way was the internet. It is fast, has a global reach, is cost-effective and interactive, and is thus an ideal means for the people involved in the conflict to provide a voice for their respective communities. In order to make this information available as well to the local population that had no internet access, the Catholic Church also included summaries of these reports in its monthly Pastoral Newsletter (*Warkat Pastoral – Warta Keuskupan Amboina*) that was distributed to all Catholic churches in the Diocese of Ambon.

These various media and their depictions do not, of course, exist in isolation from each other; rather, they refer to each other, react to each other's reporting, emerge because of each other, and are thus part of a vicious cycle that is hard to break. *Ambon Ekspres*, for instance, emerged to balance *Suara Maluku*'s reporting. *Siwalima* was established to reconcile the media split. The FKAWJ claims that their radio station and their website were set up in reaction to Christian-biased local press and radio stations and the prominent Christian Ambon Berdarah Online website (ABO)[20] that was strongly promoting the Christian cause. Graffiti 'communicated' or more accurately battled with each other as well as the varied internet projects in a series of actions and reactions, to give just a few examples.

Cross-media references were common on all sides of the conflict. The media of the Laskar Jihad, Radio SPMM, was promoted on their website and in their tabloid. Speeches broadcast via SPMM were also put online. The website advertised books published by the Jihad Press and new editions of the tabloid. In the tabloid, one could find information about the websites and the radio station. The leaflets provided email and web addresses, and reproduced graphics used on the webpage. The bulletins reproduced excerpts from the tabloid, the websites and the financial reports of the Laskar Jihad. Photos of graffiti were put online by Masariku as well as the FKAWJ; reports from *Siwalima* were forwarded to and circulated via the Masariku-Mailing-List and ABO; Masariku contributions were integrated into ABO; *Siwalima*, *Suara Maluku*, RRI and TVRI were used as sources for the reports of the Crisis Centre of the Diocese of Ambon and so forth. Media on all levels were thus involved in the conflict. All tried to advance their group's cause (some more and some less consciously) and pick up common themes of the warring parties' identity schemes, thus reinforcing them.

The Moluccan media thus became a constituent part of the conflict's dynamics (and vice versa) and the establishment of 'divided memories' (Giesen 2004). The strategic use and the 'power of images' were decisive (Frey 1999). Religious symbols played an important role and provided the media players with the chance to connect to a wider religious community, its values, its prayers and its funding opportunities.

Although the influential role of the multifaceted media is more than obvious, it was neglected for a long time by local authorities, and no preventive measures were taken at the local or the national level. It was possibly the simultaneous explosion of the conflict in Maluku and the media in Indonesia in general that made the situation so difficult and unpredictable. Only from the beginning of 2001 did the then Moluccan governor, Saleh Latuconsina, begin repeatedly warning the population not to be provoked by the reporting in the local and national newspapers, TV and radio stations (see e.g. *The Jakarta Post*, 28 February 2001 and *satunet.com*, 27 March 2001).[21] At the same time, he urged the media to provide neutral coverage of events and also took concrete measures to control media representatives. His first plan to shut down SPMM was never realised. He put more effort into his second plan: to ban any reporting on FKM activities from August 2001 onwards. Associations such as the Indonesian Alliance of Independent Journalists (Aliansi Jurnalis Independen – AJI) and Reporters without Borders (Reporters Sans Frontières – RSF) were extremely worried about press freedom during civil emergency rule. As if to confirm these worries, the military took Latuconsina's reporting ban as a reason to beat up two journalists (from *SL* and *SM*) simply because they were on their way to the same meeting as the FKM's leader in Waisarissa on Seram, which was meant to promote reconciliation.[22] While increasing attention was paid to the print media, small media and the role of the internet were not considered at that stage.[23]

Transforming the Media Scene, Transforming Society

The rising awareness of the influential role of the media resulted in the establishment of the Maluku Media Centre (MMC) in early 2001. The MMC was one of the many conflict solution, peace and reconciliation efforts initiated after the outbreak of the conflict. It became an important factor in the peace dynamics in Maluku. The MMC was established after AJI had organised a meeting of journalists and leaders of Moluccan and North Moluccan media (mainly newspapers) in Bogor, West Java. To lend more weight to this initiative, the governor of Maluku was also invited, after which he finally started to raise community awareness about the role of the media in the conflict.[24] Being located right at the border between a Christian and a Muslim area in Ambon City, the MMC initially functioned primarily as a place where journalists from both sides could meet in the midst of the conflict situation, hold discussions, try to produce more balanced news and thus contribute to solving the conflict.

Over time, the MMC developed from being a neutral meeting point into a centre that organised skills trainings for journalists, workshops, discussions, research, monitoring and advocacy for press freedom and the rights of journalists, who were still severely underpaid and who were often physically threatened if covering sensitive topics like corruption (see e.g. Maluku Media Centre 2007a). These were also the objectives of a webpage the MMC maintained (until 2005) and its monthly magazine *Tabaos*. From the MMC's perspective, it was critical to replace 'war journalism' (*jurnalisme perang*) with the introduction and teaching of peace journalism (*jurnalisme damai*) (see the contributions in Maluku Media Centre 2007c). The MMC's main goal was capacity-building and increasing media professionalism in Maluku to equip journalists better for their tasks in any future conflict, as a preventive force. With the support of AJI and the international Media Development Loan Fund (MDLF),[25] in 2005 the MMC extended its training activities beyond Ambon Island, organising a big meeting in Namlea town on Buru Island, which had the largest number of journalists after Ambon. In 2007, it held training programmes in

Southeast Maluku. It also extended its training activities to TV and radio journalists.

The MMC was one of the decisive factors triggering a transformation of the conflict-oriented media scene in Maluku into a peace-oriented one. The reporting style in the dailies changed radically as reports and editorials tried to avoid simplified dichotomisations of society and started using unifying symbols. Importantly, they focused on reporting peace efforts instead of war events. Moreover, the organised media tried to rebalance the religious composition of their staffing. The MMC managed to create immense solidarity and cooperation among journalists, thus setting a good example for the Moluccan population at large and triggering other media initiatives for peace.

In February 2001, even before the official launch of the MMC, *Radio Suara Pelangi* (103.5 FM) was set up in the border area, using the callsign *The Reconciliation Station*, with the aim of countering one-sided reporting of the conflict. Through its news and partly interactive programming, it aimed to foster dialogue and integration, thereby contributing to the reconciliation process. The initiative was supported by the government as an effort to 'counter' the Laskar Jihad's SPMM station and to 'neutralise' community tensions. As an indication of the connections between local media, the director of Radio Pelangi was also head of *Siwalima*. Radio Pelangi employees also underwent training organised by the BBC and *Internews*,[26] among others, for media staff in conflict areas throughout Indonesia.

Other reconciliation media projects evolving in the transition from conflict to peace in Maluku included the travelling library (*perpustakaan keliling*) of the National Library in Ambon City, which delivered books to remote areas and villages on Ambon and neighbouring islands by truck and boat. This was interrupted by the conflict and revived in 2002. Other reconciliation activities initiated by the National Library, which is ideally located in a Christian-Muslim border area, were exhibitions, readings, recitation and storytelling competitions, and a letter-writing competition for International Peace Day in 2003. Christian and Muslim teenagers from all levels of society were asked to express their feelings about the conflicts in letters to the government. These were then published as a book (Saya 2003).

Since the revival of tradition is an important means for the Moluccan people to build interreligious bridges and create sustainable peace (for an extensive account, see Bräuchler 2015), video CDs of the conflict were replaced by videos of installation ceremonies of traditional village heads, celebrations of the renewal of interreligious village alliances (*bikin panas pela*), the performance of rituals that had been postponed during the years of conflict, or regionally important celebrations, such as the anniversary of the Pattimura revolt against the Dutch on Saparua Island (Central Maluku) in 1817. Many of these ceremonies and rituals brought Christians and Muslims together and were thus a means for reconciliation. Their recording on CD provided abiding symbols of historical moments of unity.

By 2008, although much graffiti remained from the heights of the conflict, the street scene, at least on Ambon, seemed to be increasingly marked by posters and banners promoting peace (*spanduk damai*), reconciliation and the unification of Moluccan society through cultural activities and values. During the campaigns for local and regional elections (specifically the elections of the mayor in 2006 and of *Bupati*, or district head, in 2007), election posters dominated public space in Ambon City and the villages. Great care was taken that each pair put up for election (consisting of the candidate plus a deputy) included one Muslim and one Christian, which was assumed to guarantee balanced policies. Candidates depicted individually on election posters included integrative election slogans. For example, Muhammad Umarella, a *Bupati* candidate, adopted the slogan *Agama boleh beda–Kita Satu dalam Budaya & Adat Istiadat* ('Our religions may differ, but we are united through culture and tradition'). In early 2007, the governor of Maluku, together with his wife, appeared on oversized posters next to images of the Protestant Silo Church, the Al-Fatah Mosque and the Catholic Cathedral, the three most important buildings in Central Maluku representing the three major denominations. On their posters, they wished the community 'Happy Maulid' (for the Prophet Muhammad's birthday) and 'Happy Easter', while also including the unifying slogan *Bersama Membangun Maluku* ('Developing Maluku Together').

In line with the rapid growth of media throughout Indonesia, the number of dailies and weeklies in Maluku also increased. Some survived, while others closed after a short time. But all tried to balance the numbers of Christians and Muslims on their staff. By May 2007, there were twenty radio stations in Ambon compared to only a handful before the conflict (Maluku Media Centre 2007d). Two local TV stations emerged in Ambon: Ambon TV and Maluku TV. The former was founded one week before the 2006 local elections (*Pilkada*) and was owned by the then deputy governor, Muhammad Abdullah Mehmed Latuconsina; the latter was established in 2007 by the governor of Maluku, Karel Albert Ralahalu, and several businessmen.

While this chapter celebrates the role of media in the transition to peace in Maluku, the increasing link between politics, politicians and the media requires a more cautionary note. Politicians routinely used television to promote their causes. Regional and local politicians were involved in the executive committees of some local newspapers and some members of parliament were professional journalists. Media can thus easily become a political instrument. During the 2006 mayoral elections in Ambon City, many journalists were involved in candidates' campaign teams. As a consequence, their reporting was biased and gave the impression that each newspaper had its favourite candidate. Reporting in several newspapers became quite tendentious, due to political rather than religious affiliations.[27]

Conclusion

I have attempted to reflect on new directions for media anthropological research, to promote a more practice-oriented approach to media research and dismiss the producer–audience divide for such conflict settings (even though this took place in a pre-social media era). Only when we develop an integrative perspective, that is, when we analyse the media scene as an integral part of its sociocultural context and also analyse the relationship between different media, can we appreciate its dynamics and its influential role in peace *and* in conflict and the co-constitutive nature of conflict/peace and media. Such analysis requires long-term studies of an area and its evolving local mediascape.

During the Moluccan conflict, different kinds of media were used at all levels of society, on both sides of the divide: the press, radio, TV, photos, videos, leaflets, books, letters, the internet, graffiti, bulletins, etc. After the conflict, a lot of effort has been put into the creation of a 'unifying' media. Each type of media works differently; they are used by different kinds of people, they cater to different people and have a different reach, they require different agencies, but they all refer to each other, communicate with each other, react to each other and make use of a symbolism that is understood across diverse media and on both sides of the conflict. Although class, power and hierarchy influence who has access to which media, all levels of society can still contribute to shaping the Moluccan mediascape; they can ignore certain media messages, they can creatively appropriate media space, invent new media and thus produce their own messages. As Warde (2005: 148) notes, 'no matter where a practice fits in a hierarchy of prestige, there are internal goods to be derived from it for individual practitioners'. All the various media practices contribute to the conflict and peace dynamics and are integral parts of the societal transformation process. Media discourses decisively shape communication processes, social memories, individual agencies and collective identities in a society, and, conversely, cultural communication patterns, social memories (of conflict, of a shared past, of a common culture, etc.), individual agencies and collective identities shape the way in which media are appropriated and used. It is the perspective of practice that helps us to 'address how media are embedded in the interlocking fabric of social and cultural life' (Couldry 2004: 129).

Postscript

The aftermath of the Moluccan conflict saw the proliferation of social media in the area. Social media were used to spread rumours that almost led to renewed violence, but were also strategically used to successfully counter such trends and maintain and 'provoke' peace. In September 2011, for instance, a Muslim motorcycle driver died in a Christian area – according to some, an accident, according to others, murder. The incident immediately caused the circulation of rumours and the arson of dozens of Christian and Muslim houses, thus triggering fears that violence might escalate again. Peace activists set up an information filter team, checked rumours through social media, telephone and SMS, and pressured the national media through journalist networks to stick to the facts and not provoke further unrest. As a result, the situation was quelled and no more incidents of extraordinary violence followed. These people called themselves *provokator damai* or peace provocateurs – an idea that soon attracted national and international attention. It is meant to give expression to their proactive support and facilitation of grassroots reconciliation and peacebuilding in everyday life, where peace does not come about naturally, but everyone is asked to contribute whatever he or she can to foster societal transformation and change.

Media, again conceptualised in a broad sense, played and still play important roles in these transformations, to help Moluccans restore social relationships and consolidate peace. Moluccan films on local peace initiatives, such as the award-winning *Provokator Damai* (Husain and Salay 2013), and poetry collections or stories from conflict survivors and peace activists, such as *Basudara Stories of Peace from Maluku* (Manuputty et al. 2014, 2017), prove to be highly influential, locally, nationally and internationally. The Peace Provocateur Movement also utilises social media such as Facebook and Twitter and a website to provide information about peacebuilding, reconciliation and interfaith dialogue, and how others can learn from the Moluccan experience.[28]

Several creative communities emerged in Maluku over the last decade, including blogging, IT, film, hip-hop, literature, theatre, tourism and environment, photography and painting. These social media-savvy youth come together to be creative, have fun and take responsibility for the reintegration of society and the restoration of Moluccan values, the decline of which had fostered the outbreak of violence. They see themselves as a social movement reaching out for a broader public through activities and a broad variety of media such as street theatre, concerts, poetry readings, photography and social media. Through their music, poetry and painting, they express Moluccan voices, feelings and realities. They give voice to the unheard, and key peace activists, national artists and their international networks make sure that these voices are heard. The long-term goal of some of the initiators is a youth movement that builds and maintains peace in creative and nonviolent ways, through continuous activities, regular meetings and strategic media usage.

Birgit Bräuchler is Senior Lecturer in Anthropology at the School of Social Sciences, Monash University, Melbourne. Her research interests include media anthropology, conflict and peace studies, protest movements, human and cultural rights, anthropology of law and religion; Southeast Asia, especially Indonesia. Among others, she is author of *Cyberidentities at War* (transcript, 2005/Berghahn, 2013), *The Cultural Dimension of Peace* (Palgrave Macmillan, 2015), editor of *Reconciling Indonesia* (Routledge, 2009) and coeditor of *Theorising Media and Practice* (Berghahn, 2010, with John Postill) and has published widely in peer-reviewed journals.

Notes

This is a slightly revised version of Bräuchler, B. 2011. 'The Transformation of the Media Scene: From War to Peace in the Moluccas, Eastern Indonesia', in K. Sen and D.T. Hill (eds), *Politics and the Media in 21st Century Indonesia*. London: Routledge, pp. 119–40. Many thanks to Krishna, David and Routledge for their permission to reprint.

1. Johan Galtung is one of the founding fathers of modern peace and conflict research and a strong promoter of the concept of '"positive peace" ... built around such ideas as "harmony", "cooperation" and "integration"', opposed to "negative peace", the mere absence of violence' (Galtung 1985: 145). For an earlier example of this kind of thinking, see Galtung (1964). As will be outlined later, Galtung has also developed the concept of 'peace journalism'.
2. The conflict and the related research took place in a pre-social media era. However, findings about the important role of media in the transition from

conflict to peace, the co-constitutiveness of conflict and media, but also peace and media, are relevant until today. Moreover, studies that follow the often long-winded transition from conflict to peace within a specific context are still rare. Research in the area was continued by the author and a new postscript and a few (but certainly not exhaustive) additional references to this chapter provide insights into some of the more recent developments.

3. Since the internet demonstrably played a decisive role in planning the 9/11 attacks on the Twin Towers in New York, increasing attention was then paid to a rising fusion of media, conflict and terror, which also resulted in a boom of scholarly publications on the topic (see e.g. Cole 2006b; Cottle 2006; Kavoori and Fraley 2006; Knorr Cetina 2005; Latham 2003; Thrall 2000).

4. For example, the so-called 'hate media' in Rwanda, fax wars in Saudi Arabia and the expansion of the Moluccan conflict on to the internet (see Bräuchler 2003, 2013; Eickelman and Anderson 1999; Marks 2005).

5. See e.g. Galtung (1998) and Transcend International at http://www.transcend.org (last retrieved 27 October 2019).

6. For a comprehensive study on the complexity of communication and how it determines the emergence, the perpetuation, the understanding and the solving of conflicts, see Ellis (2006).

7. This accusation became an essential part of the Moluccan Muslims' interpretation and explanation of the conflict. Turning into a self-fulfilling prophecy, an Ambonese doctor, Alex Manuputty, in December 2000 founded the Moluccan Sovereignty Front (FKM – Front Kedaulatan Maluku) in order to re-establish independence proclaimed in 1950 by the South Moluccan Republic (RMS). According to Manuputty, since the Indonesian government was not able to put an end to the conflict, this was the only way to stop the fighting and the abuse of human rights in Maluku. However, contrary to what the Laskar Jihad and Manuputty himself claimed, the FKM only had a handful of followers in Maluku and the Netherlands. Some observers even claimed that the FKM was a provocation by the military to give them an excuse to intervene in Maluku.

8. The scale of violence that erupted in January 1999 and went on for almost four years took most observers by surprise, as Maluku and its roughly half-Christian (by majority Protestant), half-Muslim population used to be praised for interreligious harmony in a majority Muslim country. To understand fully why religion could become such a driving force in Maluku, it is necessary to consider regional and national developments over previous decades, such as the Suharto government's Islamisation policy in the 1990s and its transmigration policy. Through these programmes, more and more (Muslim) migrants came to Maluku, and increasingly Muslims were given positions in the local bureaucracy formerly dominated by Christians. This was accompanied by a growing importance of religion and the decreasing influence of *adat* (tradition and customary law) in Maluku.

9. If not stated otherwise, the following account is based on participant observation and interviews with journalists and other people actively or passively involved in the multilayered media scene conducted in Maluku from 2002 to 2007 and on my intensive online research in Moluccan cyberspace from 1999 to 2003.

10. For a policy-oriented analysis, see Institute for the Studies on Free Flow of Information (2004). For an overview of the press in Maluku from 1908 to

1969, see Ely (1987). On the role of the internet, see various publications by Bräuchler, and Hill and Sen (2002). The Institute for the Studies on Free Flow of Information in Indonesia dedicated one issue of *Pantau* magazine to the Moluccan tragedy, analysing coverage in the national daily newspapers *Kompas, Suara Pembaruan* and *Republika* (Institute for the Studies on Free Flow of Information 2000). None of the dailies had made any effort to foster investigative journalism in the Moluccan case or tried to contribute to its solution; they either sharpened the conflict, ignored or hid it (Eriyanto and Qodari 2000). For further analysis of newspapers' reporting of the Moluccan case, see Rahabeat (2004).

11. Although I will restrict my analysis here to local or localised media, the media split went far beyond that to the national and international levels.
12. *AE* was the only Ambon newspaper with colour printing and a large print run (approximately 5,000) during the conflict (Tunny 2007).
13. For a detailed analysis of *SM, AE* and *SL,* see Eriyanto (2003). In the following years, some other dailies emerged. *Metro Maluku* was founded by *Suara Maluku* journalist Max Apono in 2000, *Koran Info* and *Info Baru* in 2002 and 2003 by (Muslim) businessmen, and *Dewa* and *Marinyo* in 2004 and 2005/2006 by former (Christian) *Siwalima* partners. Several other newspapers appeared irregularly, such as *Seram Pos* or *Tragedi Maluku*. Some, such as *Suisma* (Suara Umat Islam Maluku, The Voice of the Islamic Community in Maluku; 2000–2), did not survive long.
14. See also note 7 above.
15. They maintained a well-visited website and a mailing list: http://www.laskarjihad.co.id and http://groups.yahoo.com/group/laskarjihad. On the Laskar Jihad's online presence, see Bräuchler (2004).
16. The tabloid was produced on Java, appeared biweekly and had a print run of 70,000–100,000, about 5,000 of which were sent to Ambon for distribution during the crisis.
17. *Nusroh,* for instance, was a Laskar Jihad bulletin covering *dakwah* (proselytising), social, educational and health issues in Maluku as well as the Muslims' struggle. *Bel@* (Berita Laskar, Laskar News) was one example of a Laskar Jihad leaflet that covered news from Ambon and Poso. These pamphlets had a print run of several thousand and were distributed in busy areas in Ambon City (such as the harbour and in front of the mosque), in villages and on the neighbouring islands, and were posted on walls.
18. Syafruddin and Prasetyo are on the executive committee of the FKAWJ (Public Relations and Information Department). Information on the FKAWJ's media is based on my interviews with the FKAWJ's media people and its public relations and information department, with Moluccans reached by these media, and my own observations. When the FKAWJ was dissolved in October 2002, all its media disappeared. The mailing list's activities were halted before that, in late 2001, because too many advertisements were attached to the mails by Yahoo showing bikini-clad women. The list's archives are still available online.
19. As Spyer (2002a: 34) argues, while VCD traffic was relatively small-scale and closely controlled among Christians in Ambon, Muslim VCDs, by contrast, were 'not only mass-produced, sold in the markets and streets of much of Indonesia, but transnationally popular and quite homogeneous: Ambon's

VCDs look much like Kashmir's, Bosnia's, and video representations of Palestine shown in Malaysia and elsewhere'.
20. http://www.geocities.com/ambon67. The GeoCities service was shut down in 2009, but some snapshots are still available via the WayBackMachine. See e.g. https://web.archive.org/web/20010801161216/http://www.geocities.com/naulu67/index.htm (last retrieved 23 October 2019).
21. The authority of the governor had been strengthened to deal with the crisis by the allocation of extensive civil emergency powers from the central government in June 2000.
22. Suing and beating up journalists or blocking the media's access to conflict areas is still common in Indonesia and, as Woodier (2006) argues, is a means by which politicians, local strongmen, religious groups and sections within the police and armed forces try to reassert control of the media and the flow of news and information. For cases in Maluku, see Maluku Media Centre (2007b).
23. However, my own in-depth studies show that the internet played an important role. It was used by local actors (the Protestant Masariku Network, the Catholic Crisis Centre and the Laskar Jihad) as a strategic part of their information politics. These actors expanded the Moluccan conflict into cyberspace, where the fighting continued with other means and where influence on an international audience was exerted (Bräuchler 2003, 2013).
24. The AJI was formed in 1994 by a group of Indonesian journalists who were no longer willing to submit to 'the state-engineered obstruction of information' and rejected the concept of a single press organisation controlled by the state, the Union of Indonesian Journalists (PWI) (see Luwarso 1998: 85). In setting up the MMC, the AJI had received funding from the Asia Foundation (TAF). In 2004, after a meeting in Makassar supported by the AJI, the Media Development Loan and Fund (MDLF) and Tifa, MMC became an independent forum, which meant that from 2005 onwards, it had to seek its own funding. This resulted in the closure of MMC's webpage. From 2007 onwards, MMC was supported by FreeVoice, Dutch Support for Media in Development. For a good insight into MMC's direction and activities, see the centre's journal *Tabaos* that was launched in 2007. For a short history of the MMC, see Tunny and Passal (2007). I would like to thank Rudy Fofid, the director of the MMC (in 2007), and other MMC staff and journalists for providing me with insights into Moluccan media policies and transformations.
25. See http://www.mdlf.org (last retrieved 27 October 2019).
26. Internews is an international media development organisation whose mission is to empower local media worldwide (see http://www.internews.org).
27. I thank Rudy Fofid, Dien and Yayat from the MMC and *Ambon Ekspres* journalist Yani for sharing their analyses with me.
28. http://ambon.provokatordamai.org (last retrieved 27 October 2019).

References

Aditjondro, G.J. 2001. 'Guns, Pamphlets and Handie-Talkies: How the Military Exploited Local Ethno-religious Tensions in Maluku to Preserve Their Political and Economic Privileges', in I. Wessel and G. Wimhöfer (eds), *Violence in Indonesia*. Hamburg: Abera-Verlag, pp. 100–28.

Allen, T., and J. Seaton (eds). 1999. *The Media of Conflict: War Reporting and Representations of Ethnic Violence*. London: Zed Books.

Anderson, B. 1983. *Imagined Communities: Reflections on the Origin and Spread of Nationalism*. London: Verso.

Bräuchler, B. 2003. 'Cyberidentities at War: Religion, Identity, and the Internet in the Moluccan Conflict', *Indonesia* 75: 123–51.

———. 2004. 'Islamic Radicalism Online: The Moluccan Mission of the Laskar Jihad in Cyberspace', *Australian Journal of Anthropology* 15(3): 267–85.

———. 2013. *Cyberidentities at War: The Moluccan Conflict on the Internet*. New York: Berghahn Books.

———. 2015. *The Cultural Dimension of Peace: Decentralization and Reconciliation in Indonesia*. Basingstoke: Palgrave Macmillan.

Bräuchler, B., and J. Postill (eds). 2010. *Theorising Media and Practice*. New York: Berghahn Books.

Cole, B. 2006a. 'Conclusion', in B. Cole (ed.), *Conflict, Terrorism and the Media in Asia*. New York: Routledge, pp. 117–24.

———. (ed.). 2006b. *Conflict, Terrorism and the Media in Asia*. New York: Routledge.

Cottle, S. 2006. *Mediatized Conflict: Developments in Media and Conflict Studies*. Maidenhead: Open University Press.

Couldry, N. 2004. 'Theorising Media as Practice', *Social Semiotics* 14(2): 115–32.

Eickelman, D.F., and J.W. Anderson. 1999. 'Redefining Muslim Publics', in D.F. Eickelman and J.W. Anderson (eds), *New Media in the Muslim World: The Emerging Public Sphere*. Bloomington: Indiana University Press, pp. 1–18.

Ellis, D.G. 2006. *Transforming Conflict: Communication and Ethnopolitical Conflict*. Lanham: Rowman & Littlefield.

Ely, M.A. 1987. *Pers nasional di Maluku*. Jakarta: Pustaka Baca.

Eriyanto, O. 2003. *Media dan Konflik Ambon*. Jakarta: Kantor Berita Radio 68H, Majalah Pantau dan Media Development Loan Fund.

Eriyanto, O., and M. Qodari. 2000. 'Mempertimbangkan Jurnalisme Damai', *Pantau* 9 (Petaka Maluku): 41–48.

Frey, S. 1999. *Die Macht des Bildes: Der Einfluß der nonverbalen Kommunikation auf Kultur und Politik*. Göttingen: Hans Huber Verlag.

Galtung, J. 1964. 'An Editorial', *Journal of Peace Research* 1(1): 1–4.

———. 1985. 'Twenty-Five Years of Peace Research: Ten Challenges and Some Responses', *Journal of Peace Research* 22(2): 141–58.

———. 1998. 'High Road, Low Road', *Track Two* 7(4), December. Retrieved 15 January 2002 from http://ccrweb.ccr.uct.ac.za/two/7_4/p07_highroad_lowroad.html.

Giesen, B. 2004. 'Noncontemporaneity, Asynchronicity and Divided Memories', *Time & Society* 13(1): 27–40.

Ginsburg, F.D., L. Abu-Lughod and B. Larkin. 2002. 'Introduction', in F.D. Ginsburg, L. Abu-Lughod and B. Larkin (eds), *Media Worlds: Anthropology on New Terrain*. Berkeley: University of California Press, pp. 1–36.

Hill, D.T., and K. Sen. 2002. 'Netizens in Combat: Conflict on the Internet in Indonesia', *Asian Studies Review* 26(2): 165–87.

Howard, R. 2005. 'Media and Peacebuilding: An Operational Framework', in R. Howard, F. Rolt, H. van de Veen and J. Verhoeven (eds), *The Power of the Media: A Handbook for Peacebuilders*. Utrecht: European Centre for Conflict Prevention, pp. 21–48.

Howard, R., F. Rolt, H. van de Veen and J. Verhoeven (eds). 2005. *The Power of the Media: A Handbook for Peacebuilders*. Utrecht: European Centre for Conflict Prevention.

Hudson, M., and J. Stanier. 1998. *War and the Media*. New York: New York University Press.

Husain, R., and A.M. Salay. 2013. *Provokator Damai*. Documentary. Ambon, Indonesia.

Hussain, S. 2016. 'Analyzing the War: Media Nexus in the Conflict-Ridden, Semi-democratic Milieu of Pakistan', *Media, War & Conflict*, 1–20. doi: 10.1177/1750635216682179

Institute for the Studies on Free Flow of Information. 2000. 'Petaka Maluku'. *Pantau* 9: Institut Studi Arus Informasi (ISAI).

———. 2004. *The Role of Media in Peace-Building and Reconciliation: Central Sulawesi, Maluku and North Maluku*. Jakarta: Institut Studi Arus Informasi (ISAI).

International Crisis Group. 2000. *Indonesia: Overcoming Murder and Chaos in Maluku*. Asia Report 10. Jakarta.

Joseph, V. 2000. 'De Media en de Molukken: Geruchten, Feiten en Evenwichtige Berichtgeving', in V. Joseph, W. Manuhutu and H. Smeets (eds), *De Molukken in Crisis*. Lelystad: Actuele Onderwerpen, pp. 13–17.

Kavoori, A.P., and T. Fraley (eds). 2006. *Media, Terrorism, and Theory: A Reader*. Lanham: Rowman & Littlefield.

Knightley, P. 1975. *The First Casualty: The War Correspondent as Hero, Propagandist, and Myth Maker from the Crimea to Vietnam*. London: André Deutsch.

Knorr Cetina, K. 2005. 'Complex Global Microstructures: The New Terrorist Societies', *Theory, Culture & Society* 22(5): 213–34.

Latham, R. (ed.). 2003. *Bombs and Bandwidth: The Emerging Relationship between Information Technology and Security*. New York: New Press.

Luckmann, T. 1988. 'Kommunikative Gattungen im kommunikativen Haushalt einer Gesellschaft', in G. Smolka-Kordt, P. Spangenberg and D. Tillmann-Bartylla (eds), *Der Ursprung der Literatur*. Munich: Fink, pp. 279–88.

Luwarso, L. 1998. 'The Liberation of the Indonesian Press', *Development Dialogue 2: The Southeast Asian Media in a Time of Crisis* 85–95.
Lynch, J., and A. McGoldrick. 2001. 'Peace Journalism in Poso: When Reporting Ethnic Conflict, Journalists Can Make a Difference', *Inside Indonesia* 66: 24–25.
Maluku Media Centre. 2007a. *Tabaos: Ironi Tanpa Koma – Potret Sosial Ekonomi Jurnalis Maluku*. Edisi April.
———. 2007b. *Tabaos: Eksekutif Represif, Pers Beraksi*. Edisi Mei.
———. 2007c. *Tabaos: Pers di Zona Perang*. Edisi Agustus.
———. 2007d. *Tabaos: Lintasan Siaran Radio Di Angkasa Maluku*. Edisi Juli.
Manuputty, J. et al. (eds). 2014. *Carita Orang Basudara: Kisah-kisah Perdamaian dari Maluku*. Ambon: Lembaga Antar Iman Maluku.
———. (eds). 2017. *Basudara Stories of Peace from Maluku: Working Together for Reconciliation*. Clayton, Victoria: Monash University Publishing.
Marks, J. 2005. 'Preface', in R. Howard, F. Rolt, H. van de Veen and J. Verhoeven (eds), *The Power of the Media: A Handbook for Peacebuilders*. Utrecht: European Centre for Conflict Prevention, pp. 13–17.
Nanere, J. 2000. *Kerusuhan Maluku: Halmahera Berdarah*. Ambon: BIMASPELA (Yayasan Bina Masyarakat Sejahtera dan Pelestarian Alam).
Ortner, S.B. 2006. *Anthropology and Social Theory: Culture, Power, and the Acting Subject*. Durham, NC: Duke University Press.
Passal, I. 2007. 'Harian Suara Maluku: Si Tua Yang Tak Renta', *Tabaos (Journal of the Maluku Media Centre)* Edisi April: 14–16, 23.
Pemerintah Republik Indonesia. 1999. Undang-Undang Republik Indonesia, Nomor 40 Tahun 1999, Tentang Pers (Press Law No. 40, 1999). Jakarta.
Peteet, J. 1996. 'The Writing on the Walls: The Graffiti of the Intifada', *Cultural Anthropology* 11(2): 139–59.
Pottier, J. 2003. 'Modern Information Warfare versus Empirical Knowledge: Framing "The Crisis" in Eastern Zaire, 1996', in J. Pottier, A. Bicker and P. Sillitoe (eds), *Negotiating Local Knowledge: Power and Identity in Development*. London: Pluto Press, pp. 215–40.
Rahabeat, R. 2004. *Politik Persaudaraan: Membedah Peran Pers*. Yogyakarta: Buku Baik.
Salampessy, Z., and T. Husain (eds). 2001. *Ketika Semerbak Cengkih Tergusur Asap Mesiu: Tragedi Kemanusiaan Maluku di Balik Konspirasi Militer, Kapitalis Birokrat, dan Kepentingan Elit Politik*. Jakarta: TAPAK Ambon.
Saya, I. (ed.). 2003. *Bunga Rampai: Surat Perdamaian*. Ambon: Pemerintah Ambon, Perpustakaan Nasional Provinsi Maluku, UNICEF.
Schatzki, T.R., K. Knorr Cetina and E. von Savigny. 2001. *The Practice Turn in Contemporary Theory*. London: Routledge.
Sen, K., and D.T. Hill. 2000. *Media, Culture and Politics in Indonesia*. Oxford: Oxford University Press.
Southeast Asian Press Alliance. 2002. 'Firery Reporters: Ambon & Aceh Special', *ALERT Magazine* 3(1).

Spyer, P. 2002a. 'Fire without Smoke and Other Phantoms of Ambon's Violence: Media Effects, Agency, and the Work of Imagination', *Indonesia* 74: 21–36.

———. 2002b. 'One Slip of the Pen: Some Notes on Writing Violence in Maluku', *'Indonesia in Transition' Workshop*, August. Retrieved 17 July 2004 from http://www.knaw.nl/indonesia/transition/workshop/work_in_progress09.pdf.

Syafruddin, A., and E. Prasetyo. 2001. *Tragedi Kebun Cengkeh: Fakta Pembantaian Paramedis, Pasien & Warga Sipil Ambon*. Jakarta: Jihad Press (LJ Media).

Thalib, J.U. 2000. *Buku Petunjuk dan Latar Belakang Pengirim Laskar Jihad ke Maluku*. Malang: Forum Komunikasi Ahlus Sunnah Wal Jama'ah.

———. 2001. *Laskar Jihad Ahlus Sunnah Wal Jamaah Mempelopori Perlawanan Terhadap Kedurjanaan Hegemoni Salibis-Zionis Internasional di Indonesia*. Jakarta: Jihad Press (LJ Media).

Thrall, A.T. 2000. *War in the Media Age*. Cresskill, NJ: Hampton Press.

Tunny, M.A. 2007. 'Dari Bilik Kamar Kos, Menjadi Koran Terbesar di Maluku', *Tabaos (Journal of the Maluku Media Centre)* Edisi Agustus: 22–24.

Tunny, M.A., and I. Passal. 2007. 'Maluku Media Centre: Rumahnya Jurnalis Maluku', *Tabaos (Journal of the Maluku Media Centre)* Edisi Maret: 11–12.

Vladisavljević, N. 2015. 'Media Framing of Political Conflict: A Review of the Literature', *Media, Conflict and Democratisation*, May. Retrieved 23 October 2019 from http://www.mecodem.eu/wp-content/uploads/2015/05/Vladisavljevi%C4%87-2015_Media-framing-of-political-conflict_-a-review-of-the-literature.pdf.

Warde, A. 2005. 'Consumption and Theories of Practice', *Journal of Consumer Culture* 5(2): 131–53.

Woodier, J. 2006. 'Perning in the Gyre: Indonesia, the Globalised Media and the "War on Terror"', in B. Cole (ed.), *Conflict, Terrorism and the Media in Asia*. New York: Routledge, pp. 41–60.

Afterword

John Postill

This volume lays the foundations of a theory of conflict mediation in the contemporary age. Not mediation in the usual sense of the term, but rather in that favoured by anthropologists who study media: the multiple – and multidirectional – ways in which media forms and practices are implicated in people's lives. As the editors note in the Introduction, the concept of mediation does not lend itself to the diffusionist idea that a universal 'media logic' has colonised practically all spheres of modern life – an idea carried by the sociological notion of 'mediatisation' (*Mediatisierung*). Instead, the term 'mediation' provides ethnographers, and other qualitative researchers, with a powerful lens through which to observe the messy tangles of people, practices, actions and technologies invariably found in all contemporary conflicts.

As always with ethnography, the risk here is to get so caught up in fieldwork events that the theory becomes ahistorical – a story told in the present continuous, as it were (Postill 2017a). The editors and other contributors wisely avert this risk by stressing the need for longitudinal and other diachronic studies of conflict mediation (see e.g. the chapters by Bräuchler, Kummels and Pype, this volume; and Bräuchler 2015). Because these studies are still a rarity, the book should inspire a new wave of conflict research that takes this temporal dimension seriously rather than as a mere afterthought. Like all other social life forms, conflicts are finite processes with a beginning, a middle and an end. In other words, all conflicts have a collective life course – a curriculum vitae – amenable to detailed biographical reconstruction and analysis. In this spirit, the book explores 'how humans in different times and places use media to create, escalate, de-escalate, manage, and end conflicts'. Throughout its pages, the unfolding, 'lived reality' of conflict mediation is foregrounded via case studies that explore the phenomenological, sensory experience of living through a conflict, including the sounds and sights of being 'digital witnesses' to a violent event (see Sumiala, Tikka and Valaskivi, this volume). Conflicts also have an afterlife; this may come in a range of cultural forms and (re)framings, including that of 'peace and reconciliation', as explored in Part VII of this book.

Where there is mediation, there are mediators. Contributors to the volume pay careful attention to the key agents and sites – both human and nonhuman, online and offline – of conflict mediation, with the emphasis being on human agency. Decades ago, the Manchester School of Anthropology demonstrated that the dynamic 'political fields' formed around a conflict – for instance, the Hidalgo uprising in colonial Mexico (Turner 1974) – can dramatically expand and contract as the action spills over time and space. A more apposite term to our present discussion would be *conflict fields*. Future field-theoretical (Fligstein and McAdam 2011, 2015) and time-geographical (Giddens 1984; Hägerstrand 1967) analyses of the unruly dynamics of conflict fields as they evolve over time could yield powerful insights.

The inherently mercurial nature of conflict fields is enhanced today by new media actors such as social media celebrities, political 'hacktivists', movement entrepreneurs and other specialists interacting in contingent ways with both new and old agents (Postill 2018). Chadwick and Collister (2014) have shown that those political agents who are able to conjoin the 'hybrid logic' of new and old media – e.g. the team formed in 2013 by Edward Snowden and *The Guardian* – often enjoy a competitive advantage over their rivals.

As anthropologists of religion have found in various cultural contexts, there is a paradoxical side to new forms of mediation. This is the promise of mediation as *disintermediation*; a certain holy book, website or smartphone app will grant its users direct access to a supernatural being or some other highly prized entity. Thus, Eisenlohr (2006: 278) argues that religious practitioners tend to have unmet 'desires for immediacy', i.e. they wish they could help their followers connect directly with the transcendental. These efforts have deep historical roots, but some new religious mediators see digital forms as offering 'technical solutions' to the conundrum (2006: 278). Similarly, radical transparency advocates like Julian Assange or Edward Snowden have precipitated new forms of mediated conflict by means of hacks, leaks and other digital 'solutions' to the old problem of gaining access to political truths concealed behind a veil of elite secrecy. The technical affordances of today's networked devices enhance this sense of immediacy by making it possible for people almost everywhere to participate in conflicts remotely as they unfold (see e.g. the chapters by Meis and Mollerup in this volume; Gray 2016; Postill 2017b).

It follows that each key site of an evolving conflict has unique sociotechnical qualities and 'media ensembles' (Bausinger 1984). These sites increasingly entail smartphones and other mobile devices; that is, media ensembles are becoming *mobile* ensembles (Monterde and Postill 2014). Today, of course, the devil is in the digital, and ethnographers are ideally placed to track the distinctive mediations and (im)mobilities of a conflict site and draw up conflict site typologies from the ground up. This will often include describing precisely through which technologies and human agents a conflict transforms a site of everyday conviviality into a 'site of contention' (Sell 2013). Sometimes this transformation will happen overnight, surprising regulars of a given locale; at other times, it will be a more gradual process of change over time. For instance, in my anthropological research on local activism in a middle-class suburb of Kuala Lumpur, in Malaysia (Postill 2011), I found that a local web forum normally used for light-hearted banter and information exchange would on occasions morph into an 'arena' of contention (Turner 1974) among the more vocal residents, before reverting to its habitual state of conviviality.

This brings us to the question of social practices. The volume's practice-theoretical approach to conflict mediation inaugurates a new line of investigation both for practice theorists and for the comparative study of media and conflict. Conflict(-related) practices come in many different forms and they take place at all stages of a conflict's life and afterlife. As the editors suggest, such practices 'must be tracked in both their continuities and changes over time in specific sites and [at specific] scales of conflict'. Combined with the notions of *conflict sites* and *mobile ensembles*, the term 'conflict practices' is bound to reap rich empirical rewards for scholars working in this area. However, here I would urge us all not to overlook the logical companion to practices, the other side of the praxis coin, namely *actions*. While practices are the sets of activities that all humans (including those caught up in a conflict) conduct on a regular basis, actions are irregular, one-off interventions in the flux of life (Postill 2018: 178). In order to understand conflicts and their multiple mediations, then, we must examine how they are shaped both by regular practices and irregular actions – some of them collective, others individual. For instance, no account of the digital mediation of the Occupy movement in North America would be complete without considering the day-to-day, largely hidden 'connective labour' of volunteers managing Occupy's social media accounts, many of them women (Boler et al. 2014), or indeed more conflictual, media-friendly actions like the use of physical violence by the New York riot police (Juris 2012).

The volume also wrestles with the *bête noire* of media and communication scholars since the 1950s: media effects. In keeping with current thinking in the field, most chapter contributors avoid this notion, refraining from positing (digital) media as having a unidirectional effect, or impact, on contemporary conflicts. Instead of worrying about effects, argue the editors, it is better to think of media and conflict as ceaselessly reconstituting one another. Alas, the trouble with 'ignoring' media effects is that, like a pack of rabid dogs you pretended not to see, they might come back and bite you on the cheek. For instance, the editors approvingly cite Igreja's (2015) ethnographic work on violent films in conflict zones of Mozambique. Rejecting simplistic notions about the negative effects of such films on young viewers, Igreja goes on to say that they can 'enhance ongoing processes of self-assertion among young people in unpredictable ways' (2015: 678). But isn't this enhancing precisely a media effect, albeit a complex and open-ended one? Similarly, they quote Straus (2007: 631) in order to argue that radio did not trigger ethnic violence in 1990s Rwanda. Instead, it 'emboldened hard-liners … and reinforced face-to-face mobilization, which helped those who advocated violence … assert dominance and carry out the genocide'. Again, what are emboldening, reinforcing, helping and so on if not complex *effects* in need of careful ethnographic unpacking?

This book therefore invites us to theorise conflict mediation as a finite, multi-sited, dynamic process in which old and new mediators shape the lived reality of a conflict field both on-site and from afar – a mercurial field where specific media practices, actions and ensembles will have unpredictable effects on its life and afterlife course. In order to illustrate how this sketch of a theory of conflict mediation may work in practice, let me turn briefly to a recent political conflict, that surrounding Spain's indignados (15M) movement.

On 15 May 2011, tens of thousands of people marched through the streets of more than 60 Spanish cities demanding 'real democracy now!' ('*¡democracia real ya!*') against a backdrop of economic crisis and a loss of faith in the country's political elites. That night, inspired by the recent Arab uprisings, some forty of them decided to set up camp in Madrid's central square, Puerta del Sol. When the police tried to evict them, hundreds more joined the camp. Soon, thousands of other protesters around Spain replicated this *mediated action*, which they learned about mostly through social media. The indignados (15M) movement was officially born. Over the next four weeks, the occupied squares turned into huge encampments (*acampadas*), 'cities within cities' with their own *transient practices* (debating, deliberating, cooking, cleaning, tweeting, reporting, etc.), practices that would cease to exist or become recontextualised once the squares were vacated. While some people participated in the conflict on-site, others did so remotely, through digital devices.

For a short while, the movement became a global transmedia phenomenon, with both old and new mediators – e.g. legacy journalists, bloggers, hackers, citizen journalists and Twitter influencers – shaping the news agenda, including via widely shared contents. These virals typically featured footage of violent police actions against peaceful demonstrators (Postill 2014). Smartphones played a crucial role as 'new articulators of online spaces and occupied physical spaces, especially via Twitter and live streaming' (Monterde and Postill 2014: 429). These mobile ensembles evolved with the movement, especially as the focus shifted away from the squares. In the first weeks of the movement, the conflict between the occupiers and the authorities evolved very quickly. Yet, after the occupiers decided to vacate the squares in June 2011, it slowed down as the movement relocated to local neighbourhoods and to online sites of contention. Over the following months, it lost energy and eventually died out, gaining a new lease of life in 2014 and 2015 when movement offshoots like 15MPaRato, Podemos and Barcelona en Comú scored a series of political successes at the local, national and EU levels.

Put differently, at each stage in the evolution of the 15M conflict field, a new sociopolitical 'game' was played. Prior to the square encampments, the collective name of the game was 'marching the streets'. This was replaced by the game of 'occupying the squares', followed by a protracted period of dispersal until another big game was found in early 2014: 'taking the institutions', i.e. electoral politics (see Postill 2017c). Each of these games, or phases of the unresolved conflict between a large section of Spain's civil society and its political elites, had its own key sites and configurations of technopolitical mediation. First the streets, then the squares, and finally the town halls and parliaments became the main mediated arenas of the struggle.

John Postill holds a Ph.D. in anthropology from University College London. He currently teaches communication at RMIT University in Melbourne. His publications include *The Rise of Nerd Politics* (Pluto Press, 2018), *Digital Ethnography* (Sage, 2016, with Sarah Pink, Heather Horst, Larissa Hjorth, Tania Lewis and Jo Tacchi), *Localizing the Internet*

(Berghahn Books, 2011), *Theorising Media and Practice* (Berghahn Books, 2010, with Birgit Bräuchler) and *Media and Nation Building* (Berghahn Books, 2006). He is now working on his first novel, *Life of Pinas*.

References

Bausinger, H. 1984. 'Media, Technology and Daily Life', *Media Culture & Society* 6(4): 343–51.

Boler, M. et al. 2014. 'Connective Labor and Social Media: Women's Roles in the "Leaderless" Occupy Movement', *Convergence* 20(4): 438–60.

Bräuchler, B. 2015. *The Cultural Dimension of Peace: Decentralization and Reconciliation in Indonesia*. Basingstoke: Palgrave Macmillan.

Chadwick, A., and S. Collister. 2014. 'Boundary-Drawing Power and the Renewal of Professional News Organizations', *International Journal of Communication* 8: 2420–41.

Eisenlohr P. 2006. 'As Makkah Is Sweet and Beloved, So Is Madina: Islam, Devotional Genres and Electronic Mediation in Mauritius', *American Ethnologist* 33(2): 230–45.

Fligstein, N., and D. McAdam. 2011. 'Toward a General Theory of Strategic Action Fields', *Sociological Theory* 29(1): 1–26.

———. 2015. *A Theory of Fields*. Oxford: Oxford University Press.

Giddens, A. 1984. *The Constitution of Society*. Cambridge: Polity Press.

Gray, P.A. 2016. 'Memory, Body, and the Online Researcher: Following Russian Street Demonstrations via Social Media', *American Ethnologist* 43(3): 500–10.

Hägerstrand, T. 1967. *Innovation Diffusion as a Spatial Process*. Chicago: University of Chicago Press.

Igreja V. 2015. 'Legacies of War, Healing, Justice and Social Transformation in Mozambique', in B. Hamber and E. Gallagher (eds), *Psychosocial Perspectives on Peacebuilding*. Berlin: Springer, pp. 223–54.

Juris, J.S. 2012. 'Reflections on #Occupy Everywhere: Social Media, Public Space, and Emerging Logics of Aggregation', *American Ethnologist* 39(2): 259–79.

Monterde, A., and J. Postill. 2014. 'Mobile Ensembles: The Uses of Mobile Phones for Social Protest by Spain's Indignados', in G. Goggin and L. Hjorth (eds), *Routledge Companion to Mobile Media*. London: Routledge, pp. 429–38.

Postill, J. 2011. *Localizing the Internet: An Anthropological Account*. Oxford: Berghahn Books.

———. 2014. 'Democracy in an Age of Viral Reality: A Media Epidemiography of Spain's Indignados Movement', *Ethnography* 15(1): 51–69.

———. 2017a. 'The Diachronic Ethnography of Media: From Social Changing to Actual Social Changes', *Moment: Journal of Cultural Studies* 4(1): 19–43.

———. 2017b. 'Doing Remote Ethnography', in L. Hjorth et al. (eds), *The Routledge Companion to Digital Ethnography*. London: Routledge, pp. 61–69.

———. 2017c. 'Field Theory, Media Change and the New Citizen Movements: Spain's "Real Democracy" Turn as a Series of Fields and Spaces', *Recerca* 21: 15–36.

———. 2018. *The Rise of Nerd Politics: Digital Activism and Political Change*. London: Pluto Press.

Sell, S.K. 2013. 'Revenge of the "Nerds": Collective Action against Intellectual Property Maximalism in the Global Information Age', *International Studies Review* 15(1): 67–85.

Straus, S. 2007. 'What Is the Relationship between Hate Radio and Violence? Rethinking Rwanda's "Radio Machete"', *Politics & Society* 35(4): 609–37.

Turner, V.W. 1974. *Dramas, Fields and Metaphors: Symbolic Action in Human Society*. Ithaca: Cornell University Press.

Index

4chan, 141, 177

abuse, 37, 104, 140–44, 148, 219–21, 233, 312
access, 11, 47, 59, 71, 186, 202, 300, 320
    knowledge, 279
    water, 210, 289
    See also media, internet
accusation, 166, 197, 243–46, 248–49, 285, 302, 312
    politics of, 246
activism, 21, 41, 109, 113, 140, 184, 225, 231, 321
    cultural, 197–98
    diaspora, 218–33
    digital, 19–20, 141, 159, 161–63, 169–71, 198
    local, 321
    nonviolent, 21
    political, 13–14, 82, 104–5
    See also campaign: activist, grassroots, media, movement: activist, peace
aesthetics, 124–25, 127–28, 241, 243–44, 261–62
    audiovisual, 125–26, 246
    protest, 13, 239
affective, 101–2, 106–9, 112, 116, 122, 127, 172, 211, 220, 247, 262, 264
    resonance, 231–33
affordances, 104, 113, 169–70, 172, 184, 239, 320

agency, 7, 14, 58, 63, 144, 212, 266, 272, 281, 284, 297–99, 320
    local, 4
    -oriented, 19, 295
    political, 104
aggression, 11–12, 141–43, 147, 163, 166, 207, 240, 248–49, 251
agrarian dispute. *See* conflict: agrarian
amateur digital witnessing, 58, 60, 62–63, 69–70, 197
ambivalence, 20–21, 84, 88–90, 106, 109–10, 112–13, 244, 279
antagonism, 142, 250, 269, 291
anthropology, 10, 238–39
    legal, 11, 44
    Manchester School of, 320
    See also conflict, media, religion, sound, trauma
appropriation, 201, 268, 297–98, 309–10
Arab Spring, 20, 76, 91n1, 102
Armenia, 218–19, 221, 229
Armenian
    diaspora, 15–16, 220, 222, 224–25, 228, 232–33
    Genocide (1915), 217, 219–21, 226, 264–65
Armenia Fund Telethon, 218–19, 222–24, 228–29, 231. *See also* telethon
army, 122, 126–28, 131, 132, 140, 182, 183, 202, 289. *See also* military
art, 77, 139, 205, 207, 247, 265

atrocities, 82, 258–59, 261, 264, 269, 271–72, 280–81
attacks, 81, 87, 118–19, 121, 141, 145–148, 163, 183, 185, 230, 249–52, 281
    distanced, 118–19, 121–22, 124, 129
    sonic, 117–18, 130n4 (*see also* sound: weaponisation of)
    terrorist, 7, 18, 34, 57–58, 69–70, 122, 312
audience, 6–7, 14, 20, 39, 59–62, 67–68, 99–102, 106, 109–12, 121, 151, 166, 198–99, 208, 261, 264–65, 288–89, 304
    global, 200
    nonindigenous, 202, 211
audiovisual, 84, 124–25, 189, 204–5, 229, 246–47
Australia, 15, 138, 145–46
authenticity, 77, 82, 86, 88–90, 125, 127, 139, 142, 149, 169, 171, 206, 262, 269
authoritarian, 19, 82, 278–79, 282, 295–96
authority, 42–45, 48, 107, 182, 198–99, 202, 206–7, 209–10, 269, 296, 305
    local, 42, 48
avoidance, practices of, 11, 19, 277–291
Ayutla (Mexico), 196–98, 201–4
Ayuujk ja'ay (ethnic group), 196–201. *See also* Mixe
Azerbaijan, 217–18, 220–21, 224, 231, 234

Beirut, 14, 101, 106
Belgium, 241, 244–246
belonging, 3, 139–40, 246, 249, 283
    senses of, 199–201, 211–12
blogging, 145–46, 149, 198, 226, 311, 323
body, 13, 18, 69–70, 122–24, 128–29, 145, 184–86, 251, 281, 303
    mind and, 188–90
boundary
    maintenance, 170–72
    markers, 140, 167, 201–3
    construction, 10, 164, 169, 250–52

Brussels, 241, 244, 251
bullying, 145–49. *See also* cyberbulling

Cairo, 101, 104–6, 183, 190
camera, 4, 86, 184, 191
    handheld, 80–81
    mobile phone, 60–64, 82
    video, 87, 197
campaign
    activist, 221, 303–4
    boycott, 226, 228, 231, 233
    disinformation, 80
    political, 137, 308–9
    media, 138, 145–48, 151
    social media, 218–19
    See also internet
celebrity, 15, 138, 145–46, 149–51
    media, 15
    social media, 320
censorship, 158, 281, 283–84, 290, 295
Charlie Hebdo attacks, 18, 22, 57–70
chronotope, 18, 116–17, 119–21, 125, 128–29
cinema, 257–58, 266–67
    global, 258, 264
    and memory, 263–64, 270–71 (*see also* memory)
    and trauma, 22, 258, 260–65, 271–72 (*see also* trauma)
circulation, 225, 230–31, 310
    arenas of, 9
    digital, 69–70, 251
    global, 224
    media, 9, 57, 62–67, 122, 303–5
civic initiative, 225–26, 227, 230
civil
    protest, 76
    society, 6, 41, 76, 89, 206–7, 230, 282–83, 323
    war, 7, 12, 76, 80–81, 89–90, 106, 261, 277 (*see also* Syrian Civil War, war)
co-constitutiveness
    of media and conflict, 4, 6, 10, 12, 17–19, 22, 77–78, 90, 118, 138, 192, 272, 288, 295–97, 300
colonisation, 33, 45, 196, 202, 208, 237, 240, 247, 267–69, 320

Combattants movement, 238–46, 250–52
commemoration, 260, 264, 266, 269, 271
communal land tenure, 200–2, 208, 212
communication, 12, 138–40, 144, 149–52, 158, 185–86, 199, 239, 285, 297–99
    channel, 19
    computer-mediated, 170
    culture, 11, 20
    digital means of, 197
    disorder of, 137–40
    indirect, 247–48
    infrastructure, 22, 36–40, 44, 46
    political, 239
    ritualisation of, 141 (*see also* media: rituals)
    routines of, 139
    sphere, 247
    technology, 12, 35, 45, 59–60, 137, 159, 182–83
    transnational, 242
communicative
    breakdown, 137,
    environment, 35, 140, 143
    network, 69
    phenomenon, 20
    practice, 166, 250
    process, 17, 186, 309–10
    repertoire, 298–99
community, 164, 197–98, 212, 241, 303
    diaspora, 201
    governance, 199, 202, 204, 206–7
    imagined, 171–72, 295
    local, 160
    media, 22, 36, 202
    mediated, 58, 67
    migrant, 237–39, 242–43
    transnational, 204, 272
compassion fatigue, 99
conflict
    -affected, 33–39, 43, 77, 88–89, 302–3
    agents, 63, 321
    agrarian, 20, 196–97, 199–201, 205–6, 210–12
    anthropology of, 4, 6, 11–12, 21, 199, 211
    culture of, 250
    de-escalation, 21, 77, 87–90
    discursive, 239
    dynamics, 3, 5, 8, 16, 204, 209, 297, 300, 305, 309, 320
    escalation, 3, 21, 77, 87–90, 160, 228, 231
    ethnic, 10, 198, 283, 291n1
    experience, 17, 46–47, 69, 76, 79, 83, 89, 101–2, 108–12, 310, 320
    expression, 14
    framing of, 15–16, 219, 320
    genre, 20, 238, 240, 247–50
    intra-ethnic, 220, 233
    intra-indigenous, 208
    journalism, 22, 61, 101–3, 104–6, 183, 191, 196, 282–89, 300–1
    language, 22, 162, 166, 238, 249
    lived experience, 5, 58, 69
    lived realities of, 4–6, 9–11, 20, 137
    local, 13, 16, 296
    logic, 44
    mediation of, 4, 8, 60, 69–70, 102, 112, 319–22
    mediatisation of, 10, 197, 198, 204, 219, 239, 296
    phenomenology of, 10, 101–2, 109–10, 319–20 (*see also* phenomenology)
    -related, 10, 15, 22, 257, 261–62, 265, 269–71
    religious, 9, 159, 250, 299
    ritualisation of, 15
    setting, 7, 13, 16, 76, 82, 89, 188, 200, 309
    stages, 83, 321
    transformation, 4–6, 10, 272, 321
    violent, 4, 34, 59, 76, 158–59, 164, 170, 181, 186, 192, 251, 270, 295, 299 (*see also* violence)
    See also water conflict
Congo, Democratic Republic of the (DRC), 37, 237–40, 246, 251
Congolese diaspora, 20, 22, 241–44
connecting the unconnected, 4, 33, 35–36, 40, 47

contextualisation, 5–6, 8, 10, 19–21, 36, 42, 77–78, 84–85, 89, 92, 158, 278, 283, 295
conviviality, 105–6, 166, 321
creativity, 11, 14, 15, 113, 200, 205, 226, 298, 309, 311
culture
    digital, 13–14, 163–64
    discursive, 279–80, 282
    local, 16, 170–71, 200
    popular, 121, 239, 280–81
        See also communication, conflict, internet, media, protest, violent texts
customary law, 44
cyberbullying, 145, 148. *See also* bullying
cyberwar, 8–9, 204–5, 208, 210–11. *See also* war

Dawson, Charlotte, 138, 141, 144, 146, 152–57
decolonisation, 47, 267
democratisation, 40, 43, 62, 82, 158, 295–96
deritualisation, 15, 224, 226, 230, 232–33. *See also* ritualisation
dialogue, 22, 34, 41, 123, 127, 167, 171–72, 250, 269, 290, 297, 307, 310
    computer-mediated, 160, 170
    cross-cultural, 160, 170
    cross-national, 159, 161
diaspora. *See* activism, Armenian, Congolese diaspora, global, media, politics, protest: diasporic, Somali
diatribe, 237–38, 247. *See also* rant
digital
    invectives, 239, 250
    militarism, 160
    natives, 199, 206
    platforms, 9, 63, 87
    suspicion, 169
    witnessing (*see* amateur digital witnessing)
        dynamics of, 58
    See also activism, culture, ethnography, media, protest, video
digitality, 239, 251
discursive
    act, 247, 250
    field, 78, 88
    hegemony, 85, 170
    networks, 263
    practices, 20–21, 77–78, 249
    relations, 85
    significance, 85
    space, 107, 249
    strategies, 163
    variability, 90
    visibility, 84–85
disinformation, 4, 80, 211
    society, 15, 137–38, 151 (*see also* information society)
distance, 100, 199, 219–20, 239–40, 250–51
    safe, 190, 252
doubling of place, 181, 188, 190–91
drama, 100, 121, 265
    social, 250
drones, 4, 19, 33

effects, 146, 170, 199
    aesthetic, 85
    authenticating, 86
    discursive, 85
    perceptive, 83
    traumatic, 259
    See also media, mobile phone: (de)escalating effects of, social media, sound, trolling
Egypt, 106, 182
Egyptian uprising (2011), 17, 182–84, 191–92
elections, 241
    media and, 13, 34, 38–40, 48, 308–9
    violence and, 221–22
email, 79, 117, 143, 305
emotions, 15, 100, 108, 110–11, 127–28, 141–43, 184, 257, 264, 300, 303
Estonia, 8
Ethiopia, 35, 38–39, 42
ethnic influencers, 16, 198–99, 203–9, 211. *See also* influencer, social media: influencer
ethnicity, 280, 293

ethnographic
    fieldwork, 5, 13, 17, 60, 63–64, 102, 117, 182, 218–19, 292n1, 319
    methods, 5–6, 10, 21
    perspective, 77, 277–78
    thinking, 77–80
    turn, 6–7
ethnography, 3, 7, 10, 12–13, 40–41, 47–48, 79, 161, 319–22
    digital, 60, 63–64
    multi-sited, 11, 16
    multi-temporal, 11
    diachronic, 11, 320
everyday life, 11–12, 14, 90, 101–4, 106–8, 137, 147, 170, 199, 211, 268, 310
eyewitnessing, 29, 57, 61, 68–70, 197, 304. *See also* amateur digital witnessing

Facebook, 4, 33–35, 38, 57, 64–65, 76, 81, 107, 141–43, 145, 161, 183–84, 197–200, 204–8, 222, 241, 243, 310. *See also* social media
fake
    account, 169
    news, 34–35, 37–38
    profile, 206
feelings, 125–26, 142, 149, 265–68, 283, 288, 303, 307, 311
film, 7, 19, 121, 127, 168, 203, 260–63, 310, 322
    imagery, 124
    industry infrastructure, 264
    -makers, 261–62, 265, 270–72
    violence, 7
    See also trauma: and film
filming, 64, 70, 79, 86, 184, 190, 242
flaming, 140, 172, 206
framing, 100–1, 109, 139–40, 143–44, 150–51. *See also* conflict
France, 65, 67, 242
freedom
    of expression, 40–41, 46, 139, 280–83
    of speech, 67, 82, 245, 284
    See also media, press freedom
fundraising, 218, 221–23, 232

Gaza War (2014), 20, 22, 159–63, 170
gender
    -based aggression, 207
    construction, 139
    discourses, 206, 211
    hierarchies, 141
    relations, 7
    rights, 198–99, 206
genocide, 100, 259, 261, 263, 265
    ideology, 284–86, 292n8
    See also Armenian, Rwandan Genocide
Germany, 21, 37–38, 77, 79
global, 16, 21, 182–83, 263
    diaspora, 232
    See also audience, cinema, circulation, journalism, media, spectacle
Google, 4, 33, 35, 37
graffiti, 3, 296, 298, 300, 302–5, 308
grammar nazis, 164–66, 170
grassroots
    activism, 19, 224
    democracy, 199, 207
    journalism, 219
    media, 231
    reconciliation, 310

hacktivism, 8, 320, 323
Hamas, 20, 22, 158–59, 161–72
haptics, 117–18, 123, 127–29
hashtags, 47, 67, 72n3, 140–41, 146, 172–73n2, 184, 222
hate
    media, 279–80, 312n4
    radio, 7, 19, 280–81
    speech, 16, 36, 37–38, 281, 286, 290
Hollywood, 122, 127, 261, 265, 269
Holocaust, the, 261, 264, 266–67
homeland, 219–20, 226–27. *See also* violence
Horn of Africa, 8, 35
hostility, 139, 143–44, 151, 233
human rights, 104, 106, 199, 206, 208, 256, 312n7
    violation, 13, 81, 101
    See also media

humanitarianism, 16, 103, 198, 218–20, 222, 224, 231–33
humour, 105, 163–64, 166–68, 170
    as defence mechanism, 168–69

identity, 15, 105, 108, 144, 246, 271
    collective, 19, 171, 258, 260, 279, 282, 284, 288, 310
    cultural, 258
    deception, 143
    diasporic, 219
    management, 107
    national, 259, 277–78, 295
    political, 238
    politics, 200
ideology, 36, 91n6, 130n2, 170–71, 258, 301
    political, 8, 42–43, 48
    See also genocide
images, 14–15, 18, 62, 68, 78, 81, 84–86, 112, 148–49, 183–84, 188–89, 198, 242–43, 245, 303. *See also* photos, pictures
    power of, 305
    shocking, 140–41
immediacy, 17, 83–84, 320
impunity, 182, 238–40, 250–51
indigenous, 211
    group, 196
    intra-, 198, 208
    rights, 198, 207–10
Indignados movement, 13, 322–23
Indonesia, 3, 19, 250, 263, 270–71, 295–314
influencer, 37, 198. *See also* ethnic influencers, social media
information and communications technology (ICT), 35, 46, 137
information society, 137. *See also* disinformation society
infrastructure, 218, 220–22, 224, 232, 257. *See also* communication, film: industry infrastructure, internet, media
insult, 237–39, 243, 246, 248–49, 251, 303
    politics of, 20, 237–40
internet, 3, 8–9, 14, 34–35, 47–48, 63, 76, 90, 139, 164, 197, 237, 241–43

    access, 33–34, 37, 41–44, 46, 145, 211, 238–39, 296, 303–4
    campaigns, 41–43
    conflict and, 158, 171, 200, 296, 300, 303, 306, 309, 313n10, 314n23
    connectivity, 33, 35–37, 220, 225
    culture, 142, 163, 166, 168
    disorder, 137–38
    infrastructure, 33, 36
    platforms, 7, 158, 241
    shutdowns, 38, 41, 43, 48n4
    users, 147, 231
Iraq, 118–20, 267
irony, 91n8, 107–8, 112, 118, 165–67, 170, 171, 173n2
Islamic State (IS), 83, 148
Israel, 159–63, 168, 170, 303
Israeli-Palestinian conflict, 19, 22, 158–72

journalism, 14, 17–18, 19, 37, 44, 61–62, 65, 76, 82, 225, 249, 278, 290–91
    citizen, 4, 80–81, 323
    embedded, 4, 17–18
    global, 102
    online, 232
    routines of, 101–8
    war, 306–7
    See also conflict, grassroots, peace

Kabila, Joseph, 237, 240–41, 246–47, 251, 252n1
Kinshasa, 237, 240, 244, 251–52
krètch, 248–251

land dispute, 196–212
Laskar Jihad, 299, 301–305, 307
leaflet, 296, 302, 305
Lebanon, 104, 106
legal, 197, 201
    evidence, 82
    framework, 37, 285
    power, 148
    processes, 36
linguistic
    displacement, 239
    patterns, 20, 238
    proficiency, 165

strategy, 246–47, 251
lived experience, 5, 8, 58, 69, 101
local, 16, 21, 35–36, 48n2, 78, 102, 199, 323
    context, 286, 290, 298
    governance, 45–46
    society, 11
    See also activism, agency, authority, community, conflict, culture, media
Los Angeles, 204–5, 217–22, 224–26, 228–33

Malaysia, 321
Maluku (Indonesia), 3, 19, 299–314. *See also* Moluccan conflict
Maluku Media Centre (MMC), 306–7, 314
manipulation, 8, 10, 15, 18, 38, 171, 283, 300
    political, 284
    See also media
map, 16–17, 187, 198–99, 206, 208, 211, 213n7
mbwakela, 237, 239–40, 243, 247–252
media
    access, 9, 14, 21, 39, 209, 283, 298, 309, 314
    activism, 4, 80–81, 107, 221, 224, 226–32, 298
    aesthetics, 10, 77–80, 84–86, 90, 240
    anthropology of, 4, 6, 8, 12, 21, 23, 63, 185–86, 200, 211, 258, 262, 298, 309
    apparatus, 77–78, 86
    broadcast, 19, 37, 57–59, 81, 218–24, 226, 228, 230, 285, 292, 301
    -centrism, 8
    convergence, 19–20, 159
    communication studies and, 5
    -conflict relations, 3, 6, 13, 137, 296
    consumption, 110–111, 117
    control and, 80–81, 85, 87, 119, 129, 149, 161, 221, 290, 295, 305, 314n22

coverage, 7, 9, 87, 91n2, 99, 160, 162–63, 296, 305, 313n10
culture, 19, 101, 104–9
diasporic, 15–16, 219, 221, 226, 229, 240
effects, 4–8, 12, 21, 40, 281, 301, 322
ensembles, 321
environment, 16, 20, 46, 57, 59, 197, 277–78, 288, 291, 297–98
events, 15, 59–60, 142, 200, 218, 222–24, 229, 232
    violent, 18, 58, 60–65, 68–70
freedom, 41, 278, 281, 286, 290
global, 58–60, 65, 222, 323
human rights, 228
inflammatory, 4, 40, 47, 281
infrastructure, 15
landscape, 3, 11, 23, 80, 159, 278–79, 283, 290–91
law, 44, 284, 290–91, 292n4
literacy, 38, 200
local, 296–98, 300, 303–5, 309, 313n11
logic, 13, 23n3, 223, 264, 319–20
mainstream, 39, 80, 82, 86, 138, 143, 147, 150, 163, 296, 298
-makers, 197, 200, 202–3, 206
manipulation, 10, 34, 37–38
mass, 10, 45, 162, 172, 257–60, 266
materiality of, 18, 184
mobile, 181, 192
narration, 59, 66–67
national, 22, 36, 42, 197, 278, 296, 298, 310
-oriented practices, 13, 18, 58, 60, 63–65, 67–70, 185, 298
outlets, 36, 45, 65, 80, 85, 92n11, 182, 207, 212, 225
participatory, 17, 218, 225, 229, 233
personality, 138, 145, 148 (*see also* celebrity)
place-making and/as, 17, 22, 61, 181, 183, 185–88, 191–92
platforms, 8, 46, 59–60, 63, 66, 70
power, 9, 220, 224, 226–27, 232–33

practices, 5, 11, 13, 21, 122, 200, 204, 223, 258, 309, 322 (*see also* social media)
    activist, 219, 221, 226, 229, 232 (*see also* media: activism)
    digital, 62, 212
  production, 13, 110–11, 117
  regulation, 37, 145, 148, 279, 283, 290, 292n4 (*see also* self-regulation)
  -related practices, 4, 6, 13, 58, 185, 191, 223
  representation, 61, 63, 100, 205, 228, 251, 258 (*see also* representation)
  rituals, 9, 16, 22, 219–20, 222–24, 232–33 (*see also* communication: ritualisation of, rituals: communicative)
  routines, 59, 170
  small, 296, 302, 306
  sonic, 117, 121
  sound of, 116
  strategy, 90, 198–99
  studies, 4–6, 10, 41, 47, 183–86, 295
  technologies, 7, 9, 12, 14, 20, 58, 152, 158, 209, 296, 298
  transformation, 299, 307
  usage, 21, 77, 87, 231, 311
  war, 8, 16–17, 197, 200, 205–6, 209–12 (*see also* cyberwar, visual: warfare)
  witnessing, 60–62, 70 (*see also* amateur digital witnessing, eyewitnessing)
mediascape, 20, 130n3, 309
mediation, 4, 12–13, 21, 22, 23n3, 69–70, 99–100, 109–12, 259, 263, 319–20, 323
  as disintermediation, 320
  See also conflict, remediation
mediatisation, 10, 23n3, 199–200, 212, 220, 319. *See also* conflict
mediators, 320, 322–23
memory, 257–272, 310
  collective, 258–60, 262, 298
  divided, 305

  prosthetic, 266
  wars, 263–65
  See also cinema: and memory, remembrance
Merabet, Ahmed, 57, 60, 63–70
metaphor, 3, 239–40, 247–48
Mexico, 20, 22, 198–99, 201–2, 207–8, 320
migration, 199, 201, 204, 220, 226, 231, 237, 239–40, 243, 251, 272
military, 19, 37, 76, 80–82, 90, 118, 120, 122, 126–29, 160–163, 172, 182, 188, 191, 231, 299, 304. *See also* army
Mir, Jordi, 57, 60, 63–65, 68–70
Mixe (ethnic group), 196–97, 199–201. *See also* Ayuujk ja'ay
mobile
  camera, 57, 62, 64
  digital devices, 17, 321
  ensembles, 321, 323
  money, 44
  technology, 126
  See also media
mobile phone, 80–82, 87, 89, 91n2, 165, 183–84, 190–91, 226
  videos (MPVs), 21, 57, 60, 62, 64–65, 76–90, 197, 203
    (de)escalating effects of, 22, 77, 87–90, 92n13 (*see also* media: effects)
    perception of, 77, 80, 82, 84, 87–90 (*see also* perception)
mobilisation, 14–15, 82, 159, 161, 170, 199, 202, 204, 206, 242, 282, 291n1, 298–99
Moluccan conflict (1999–2003), 3, 171–72, 299–306. *See also* Maluku
moral engagement, 65, 68–69
Morsi, Mohammed, 182
movement, 183–84, 187–89, 191–92, 233, 238–43, 320
  activist, 13
  Combattants (*see* Combattants movement)
  decolonisation, 47
  Indignados (*see* Indignados movement)
  Occupy (*see* Occupy movement)

protest, 20–21, 91n2, 163, 244
    (*see also* protest)
    social, 23n3, 207, 311
    student, 42
Mozambique, 7, 322
multisensoriality, 183, 188, 190–91
music, 22, 39, 105, 118–20, 126–28,
    241–243, 247–50, 252n2, 311
    as torture, 120–21, 125, 130n5
    (*see also* torture: sonic)
    protest, 247
    See also politics: music and
Myanmar, 34–35

Nagorno-Karabakh conflict, 15–16,
    217–19, 221–24, 232–33
narrative, 19, 21, 41, 70, 81, 100, 112,
    160–61, 198, 263–64, 266–67, 269,
    271, 296
    dialogue, 79
    filmic, 125, 260, 272
    framework, 65, 67, 70
    historical, 280
    traumatic, 261, 264
    visual, 22, 70, 198
    See also media: narration
news media, 4, 9, 60, 63–67, 69, 81, 89,
    295, 297–98
newspaper, 3, 38, 65–66, 101, 138, 146,
    148, 197, 210, 279–80, 286, 288, 296,
    298, 300, 302, 305–6, 309, 313n10,
    313n12, 313n13
New Zealand, 145–46
non-media-centric
    media studies, 183–86
    research approach, 6, 8–9, 58,
        113, 223
nonviolence, 12, 21, 41, 311

Oaxaca (Mexico), 16, 196–198, 201,
    207, 210, 212n4
Occupy movement, 13, 21, 321–22
off-the-record, 16, 278–79, 286, 290–91
othering, 199–200, 205, 211

Palestine, 158–59, 160–63, 314n19
pamphlet, 247–48, 250–51, 300, 313n17
Paris, 18, 65–66, 241–43

peace, 3, 12, 14–17, 19–20, 33–34, 37,
    48n2, 160–61, 205, 218–19, 270, 286,
    295–301, 306–10, 311n1, 312n2, 320
    activism, 172, 310–11
    dynamics, 8, 306, 309
    images of, 297
    journalism, 297, 299, 306, 311n1
    -making, 34, 45, 297–98
    provocateurs, 310
    road, 224–25, 231
peacebuilding, 18–19, 45, 310
perception, 15, 17, 21, 39, 76–78, 89,
    127, 166–67, 182, 186–87, 189–90,
    201, 206, 269, 291
    mis-, 40, 270
    multisensoriality of, 183
    place and, 190
    sensory, 9
    See also mobile phone videos
phenomenology, 14, 22, 101–3, 181,
    183–86, 191, 287. *See also* conflict
photography, 37, 80, 84, 184, 311. *See
    also* war: photography
photos, 81, 84, 100, 217, 224, 305, 309.
    See also images, pictures
pictures, 4, 18, 60, 69, 82, 191, 222,
    230, 245, 300, 303–4. *See also* images,
    photos
place, 17, 21, 102, 110, 123, 139,
    181–83, 188–92, 246
    as event, 187
    -making (*see* media: place-making
        and/as)
poetry, 3, 45, 238–39, 310–11
polémique, 239, 248–250
politics, 108, 137–38, 170, 219, 279,
    289, 308–9
    cultural, 205
    diaspora, 220–22, 232
    music and, 250
    national, 40–43
    right-wing, 141
    ritualised, 201, 209 (*see also*
        ritualisation)
    See also identity: politics
post-conflict, 5, 7, 19, 23, 36, 257–58,
    264, 266, 269–71, 278, 290
post-genocide, 19, 225, 277, 279, 291
posters, 298, 308

power relations, 138, 166, 171–72, 201, 287
practice theory approach, 13, 58, 113, 185, 258, 279, 287, 289–90, 291, 321
presence, 17, 59, 61, 86, 117, 183, 187–88, 190, 192, 198, 206, 220–21, 231
press freedom, 80, 82, 91n5, 278, 280, 305–6. *See also* freedom, media: freedom
propaganda, 4, 5, 80–82, 140, 158, 160, 165, 205, 206, 297, 303
protest, 34, 47, 76, 80–81, 91n1, 170, 182–84, 188, 190, 192, 237, 241, 322
    culture, 20, 106, 163
        digital, 20, 238–39, 244, 246, 250–52
        diasporic, 241, 243
        nonviolent, 13, 40–41 (*see also* nonviolence)
        social, 5
        songs, 238
        violent, 40–41 (*see also* conflict: violent)
    See also aesthetics, movement
provocations, 239, 242–43, 245, 250, 302, 310

qualitative research, 5, 10, 319
quantitative data, 5, 161

radio, 3, 7, 37–40, 44, 148, 188, 196, 248, 277, 289, 291n1, 296, 298, 300–2, 304–5, 307–8, 322
Radio Machete (Radio Télévision Libre des Mille Collines, Rwanda), 279–282
rant, 238–39, 243–46, 248, 250. *See also* diatribe
recognition, 22, 100–3, 107–113, 138–39, 148, 150, 159, 169, 184, 221, 270–71
reconciliation, 15, 19, 34, 160, 172, 201–2, 209–12, 221–22, 269–72, 278, 281, 286, 288, 291, 295, 297, 301, 306–8, 320
    in cinema, 257, 263
        grassroots, 310

    meetings, 201, 204, 209, 212
    post-traumatic, 268
refugees, 21, 101, 103, 104, 225, 262
religion, 3, 5, 9, 10, 15, 58, 66, 201, 203, 220, 243, 260, 299, 300–10, 312n7, 8
    anthropology of, 320
religious
    rituals, 15
    symbolism, 15, 299, 305
    terror, 58, 70
    See also war
remediation, 18, 60, 67–68, 70, 243, 263. *See also* mediation
remembrance, 16, 19, 260, 262–64, 269–72
    collective, 168–69, 257–58, 266
    See also memory
representation, 15, 21, 62, 99, 112–13, 121–22, 129, 200
    filmic, 19, 258
    logic, 84
    visual, 63
    witnessing, 64, 69
    See also media, sound, trauma
resistance, 11, 13, 81, 112, 139, 160–61, 163–64, 170, 226, 243
rituals, 11, 13, 15, 67, 138, 264, 307–8
    communicative, 16, 171 (*see also* media: rituals)
ritualisation, 16, 68, 232–33. *See also* communication, conflict, deritualisation
rivalry, 237–38, 247–50, 320
    female, 247–48
routines, 108, 110, 167, 209
    affective, 106
    See also communication, journalism, media, self-censorship, self-regulation
rumours, 41–42, 143, 248, 251, 286, 299, 302, 310
Rwanda, 19, 22–23, 42–43, 246, 282–83
Rwandan Genocide (1994), 7, 264–65, 277–82, 289–91, 291n1, 322

satellite, 33, 184
    video conferencing, 43

screens, 100, 111, 184, 187–91, 260–63
TV, 62
self-censorship, 80, 284, 286–88, 290
routines of, 286–89
self-regulation, 284–85, 286–89, 290
routines of, 286–89
sensory apparatus, 189
silencing, 137, 139–142, 149, 151
situated knowledge, 77–80
smartphone, 17, 87, 225, 229, 320–21, 323
SMS, 40, 310
snipers, 80, 88, 184, 191–92, 203, 205
Snowden, Eduard, 320
social capital, 108
social media, 13–14, 17–18, 20–21, 38, 42, 59–60, 67, 69, 76, 79, 82, 104, 109, 197–98, 210–12, 230, 249, 296–97, 310–11, 320–22
    effects, 34–35, 48n3 (*see also* media)
    events, 208 (*see also* media)
    influencer, 149, 323 (*see also* ethnic influencers, influencer)
    logic, 64, 70 (*see also* media)
    platforms, 16, 35, 65, 81, 84, 89–90, 92n10, 161, 163, 166, 238
    practices, 159–60, 163, 170–72 (*see also* media)
    See also campaign, celebrity, Facebook, Twitter, YouTube
society
    transformation of, 3, 200, 237, 277–78, 279, 291, 299, 309–10
solidarity, 67–68, 102–3, 108, 110–11, 113, 205–7, 230, 240–43, 307
    cross-cultural, 272
    in-group, 170–72
    national, 162
Somalia, 35, 37, 44–46
Somali diaspora, 45
sonic materiality, 119, 121–23, 125, 128–29. *See also* torture: sonic
sound, 18, 20, 22, 82, 83, 116–18, 129, 187, 189, 244, 320
    anthropology of, 116, 129
    design, 123, 127–28

    effects of, 123, 127 (*see also* media)
    events, 119, 121–22, 128–29 (*see also* media)
    representation of, 117
    studies of, 129
    weaponisation of, 117–20, 130n4
Spain, 13, 322
spectacle, 14, 100, 102, 218, 265–66
    global, 296
    trauma as, 265
speech genre, 238
subjectivity, 14, 103–4, 106, 108–9, 111–12, 238, 263
suffering, 12, 14, 62, 68, 108, 112, 150, 160–61, 163, 173n1, 232, 265, 268, 270, 272, 304
    distant, 99–102, 110
    mediated, 99, 101
suicide, 147–48, 150
surveillance, 13, 17, 158, 242, 280
symbols, 15, 68, 185–186, 200, 202, 211, 225–26, 299, 303, 307, 309
Syria, 76, 79, 87
Syrian Civil War (from 2011), 18, 20–22, 30, 76–77, 80–87, 89–90, 101, 234

Tahrir Square (Cairo, Egypt), 102, 182–185, 188
Tamazulapam (Mexico), 196–98, 200–205, 208, 210–12
technology companies, 4, 34, 38, 48
telethon, 15–16, 218–19, 224–29, 231–33
    counter-, 219, 224–29, 231–33
    See also Armenia Fund Telethon
television, 38–39, 57–58, 61–62, 68, 86, 89, 122, 138, 142, 145, 147, 149, 150, 188, 218, 231, 248
    cable, 225, 228
    channel, 217, 224
    diasporic, 225, 231 (*see also* media)
    satellite, 44
    station, 44, 242–43, 296, 298, 300–2, 305, 308
theatre, 3, 311
third place, 181, 183, 188, 191

torture, 80, 100
    sonic, 118, 120–21, 125, 130n5 (*see also* sonic materiality)
transnational, 16, 35, 45, 59, 196–97, 198–99, 212, 217–20, 222, 224, 227, 230–33, 242, 257–58, 263, 265–66. *See also* communication, community
trauma, 16, 19, 120, 257–72
    anthropology of, 268
    collective, 257–60
    conflict-related, 22, 257, 261–62, 265, 269–71
    and film, 257–58, 268–72
    historical, 259–60, 262, 264, 268
    national, 260
    post-conflict, 262
    representation of, 100, 258–62, 263–66, 269–72
    theory, 258–60, 266–68, 271
    See also cinema: and trauma, effects: traumatic, narrative: traumatic, spectacle: trauma as, violence: traumatic
trolling, 15, 16, 22, 137–38, 140–44, 150–52, 166, 169, 170
    effects of, 143–44 (*see also* social media)
Twitter, 19–20, 41, 47, 60, 65, 67, 102, 107, 140–43, 145–46, 149–50, 159, 161–165, 167, 169–71, 183, 184, 200, 205, 207, 210, 211, 242, 310, 323. *See also* social media

United Nations (UN), 34, 37, 44, 46, 48n2, 206, 210
United States, 8, 15–16, 34, 35, 47, 117, 199, 204, 220–21, 261, 269

video, 67–68
    amateur, 57, 76, 81, 122
    analogue, 202
    CDs, 296, 298, 307
    digital, 18, 69–70, 85
    footage, 65, 80–82, 84, 87, 227, 242, 244, 323
    games, 4, 18, 83, 121–22, 126–29
    -making, 5, 21, 227, 303
    music, 245, 252n2
    online, 17, 57, 64–65, 76, 80, 82–83, 89–90, 92n10, 203–5, 242 (*see also* YouTube)
    as technology of witnessing, 64, 227–28
    See also camera, mobile phone, violence
violence, 3–5, 7, 11–17, 34–36, 38, 44, 47, 57, 68, 70, 103, 110, 144, 172, 181, 183, 203, 220, 233, 281, 288, 302–4, 310–11, 322
    absence of, 14, 311n1
    collective, 116
    and communication, 138
    discursive, 240
    homeland, 229–32
    images of, 18, 88, 192, 196–97
    language and, 238
    mass, 296
    mediated, 108–9
    place and, 188, 190–92
    as social performance, 238
    structural, 14
    traumatic, 268
    videos of, 187–88, 190–92, 196–97
    See also elections: violence and, film
violent texts
    culture of, 20, 237–40, 248
virality, 14, 17, 65, 82, 197, 323
visual
    evidence, 62, 65–67, 69–70, 202
    warfare, 198, 202, 208, 211
    See also audiovisual, narrative, representation
visuality, 14, 17–18, 60–61, 110, 201, 303

war, 10–12, 18, 20, 299
    -affected, 44
    films, 18, 117, 122–25, 129
    information, 7
    materiality of, 18
    music, 122
    photography, 19
    propaganda, 4, 206
    religious, 299–303
    video games, 126–29 (*see also* video: games)

wounds of, 257–58, 271–72
See also civil: war, cyberwar, Gaza War, journalism, media, memory, Nagorno-Karabakh conflict, Syrian Civil War, visual: warfare

water conflict, 196–97, 202–204, 208–10

website, 8, 33, 63, 65, 145, 197, 207, 238, 241–42, 304–5, 310

witnessing. *See* amateur digital witnessing, eyewitnessing, media

xeer law, 44–46

YouTube, 57, 63, 65, 76, 81, 83, 91n8, 92n10, 184, 187, 203, 226, 229, 241–244. *See also* social media

Zuckerberg, Mark, 34, 40

www.ingramcontent.com/pod-product-compliance
Lightning Source LLC
Chambersburg PA
CBHW070905030426
42336CB00014BA/2309